Liberalization and Foreign Policy

Sponsored by the Foreign Policy Studies Committee
of the Social Science Research Council

Liberalization and Foreign Policy

Edited by Miles Kahler

COLUMBIA UNIVERSITY PRESS

NEW YORK

Columbia University Press
Publishers Since 1893
New York   Chichester, West Sussex
Copyright © 1997 Columbia University Press

Library of Congress Cataloging-in-Publication Data

Liberalization and foreign policy / edited by Miles Kahler.
        p.   cm.
    "Sponsored by the Foreign Policy Studies Committee of the
    Social Science Research Council "—P.
    Includes bibliographical references and index.
    ISBN 0–231–10942–3 (cloth : alk. paper). —
    ISBN 0–231–10943–1 (pbk.)
    1. World politics—1945– 2. Economix history—1945–
I. Kahler, Miles, 1949– . II. Social Science Research Council
(U.S.). Committee on Foreign Policy Studies.
    D843.L456 1997
    327—dc21   97–10996
                                                          CIP

Casebound editions of Columbia University Press books are printed
on permanent and durable acid-free paper.

Printed in the United States of America
c 10 9 8 7 6 5 4 3 2 1
p 10 9 8 7 6 5 4 3 2 1

Contents

Contributors

Lisa Anderson School of International and Public Affairs, Columbia University

Jeffry A. Frieden Department of Government, Harvard University

Kurt Taylor Gaubatz Department of Political Science, Stanford University

Joanne Gowa Department of Politics, Princeton University

Jeffrey Herbst Woodrow Wilson School, Princeton University

Miles Kahler Graduate School of International Relations and Pacific Studies, University of California, San Diego

Lisa Martin Department of Government, Harvard University

Sylvia Maxfield Department of Political Science, Yale University

Victor Pérez-Díaz Analistas Socio-Políticos, Research Center and Complutense University, Madrid

Juan Carlos Rodríguez Analistas Socio-Políticos, Research Center and Complutense University, Madrid

Acknowledgments

The editor and authors gratefully acknowledge the support of the Foreign Policy Studies Committee of the Social Science Research Council, under whose auspices this volume was planned and completed. We wish to thank the Ford Foundation and the Pew Charitable Trusts for their financial support of this project. Robert Huber and Eric Hershberg mobilized key staff support at the Social Science Research Council and served as helpful advisers and critics at different stages of the project. The volume has benefited from the comments and criticisms of many individuals mentioned in the individual chapters. Here, we wish to thank collectively the participants in the March 1991 workshop in La Jolla and the July 1992 conference in Ballyvaughn, Ireland.

Liberalization and Foreign Policy

Liberalization and Foreign Policy

Miles Kahler

The global wave of political liberalization that has gained force since the mid-1970s and the even wider movement toward liberal economic policies that accelerated in the 1980s provide the subjects for a new agenda in international relations. Because these changes have marked so many societies, determining whether liberal states and economies conduct distinctive foreign policies is central to both interpretation of contemporary international politics and prediction of future patterns. With the end of the decades-old Cold War system, the consequences of domestic change for foreign policies and international politics are likely to grow in importance. Those arguing for and against particular images of future order and disorder often base their prognoses on the importance of regime change and the likelihood that liberal politics and economics will be consolidated.[1] Such arguments are often difficult to evaluate, however, since they are seldom based on an explicit model of the links between liberalizing political and economic change and foreign policy.

The end of the Cold War has also accelerated the erosion of neorealist theoretical pretensions in international relations. Neorealist hostility toward "reductionist" arguments based on the domestic determinants of foreign policy has been an important barrier to serious, systematic investigation of such relationships. The inability of neorealist theory to explain many of the important international changes of the last decade—particularly the dissolution of the Soviet Union and the end of the Cold War—from a purely structural or systemic perspective has opened intellectual space for theorizing at the level of national policy. Although a coherent alternative to neorealism has not been devised at the level of either the system or the national unit, investigation of the consequences of liberalization for foreign policy may produce constituents for such a theoretical construction and permit a test of key assumptions of liberal theories of international relations.[2]

Finally, an assessment of the foreign policy consequences of the newest wave of liberalization holds important implications for the foreign policy stance of the major industrialized democracies. The Western democracies have attached great rhetorical weight to encouraging democratization and market reforms, but the resources devoted to those goals remain slender when compared to the military forces deployed to contest the Cold War. In an intensifying struggle between domestic and external demands, those resources are unlikely to grow without a compelling argument that liberalizing changes are beneficial, not only for the societies involved but for existing liberal democracies as well. The emerging conventional wisdom, summarized by Howard Wiarda in the case of Latin America, deserves more careful scrutiny:

> In Latin America, we have discovered, democratic regimes seldom get involved in stupid wars (the Falkland/Malvinas conflict between Argentina and Great Britain comes to mind), seldom seek to subvert and destabilize their neighbors, do not invite Soviet missiles and brigades, do not systematically violate the rights of their citizens—all actions that cause endless grief for U.S. foreign policy and policymakers.[3]

An estimate of both the efficacy of influence and the benefits of liberalization must figure in policy prescriptions that urge support for political and economic liberalization. Changes in the foreign policies of liberalizing regimes may provide a large share of any projected benefits.

The essays in this volume contribute to the understanding of the foreign policy consequences of political and economic liberalization in three important ways. First, they reexamine the significant finding that liberal democracies pursue foreign policies toward one another that are significantly different from the foreign policies of other regimes. Second, they explain the foreign policies of liberalizing or transitional regimes and compare them with the foreign policies of established democracies. Finally, they describe the foreign policy consequences of economic liberalization and explain one important consequence of such liberalization—strategies of international collaboration within international institutions. Before turning to those three dimensions of liberalization and foreign policy, however, we must define liberalization itself.

Although some students of democratic transition have defined liberalization and democratization as distinct processes that are theoretically separable, here the term "political liberalization" will designate a halfway house to democratization, an incomplete or partial variant of democratic institutions.[4] Borrowing from existing definitions of liberal democracy or polyarchy, I will define political liberalization as the introduction of greater *competition* in the political system, wider *participation* (larger numbers of actors are enfranchised), and greater *transparency* in the conduct of politics and governance. In institutional terms, these three processes imply the introduction or growing importance of electoral competition and political parties, a larger role for legislative institutions, and the emergence of more independent sources of information in the form of the media being less subject to government control.[5] Although a regime demonstrating such characteristics can be labeled liberalizing, no assumption should be made that liberalization inevitably leads to full democratization. Huntington argues that for the most recent wave of democracies, liberalized authoritarianism is not a "stable equilibrium," but his sample is limited to states that democratized successfully. A larger set of countries that includes those in East and Southeast Asia suggests that liberalization may advance and retreat; partially liberalized regimes may advance to full democratization very slowly, if at all. Singapore, Indonesia, and China are only three examples of this pattern.

Defining economic liberalization is less problematic than setting the boundaries of political liberalization. Like its political counterpart, economic liberalization has as one of its central features the introduction of additional competition through reduction in state regulation or control of market transactions. Such a program of enhanced competition has both a domestic and an international face. The latter typically includes lowering tariff and nontariff barriers to imports, reducing restrictions on foreign investment, and removing or reducing foreign exchange restrictions and controls.[6]

These definitions emphasize institutional dimensions of liberalization; a complementary definition employs the shifting boundary between state and society. Political liberalization implies an expansion in the sphere of political action by civil society and, correspondingly, an elimination or reduction of state monopolies in the political sphere. Economic liberalization also implies a rolling back of the boundaries of state action, whether through the reform or privatization of state enterprises, the elimination of state-administered pricing, or the relaxation of state controls over economic transactions at national borders.

Choosing liberalization or liberalizing regimes as the object for investigation rather than established liberal democracies alone both enriches and complicates the search for clearly defined foreign policy outcomes. Liberalization permits an examination of the effects of analogous changes in both economic and political regimes. Treating liberalization as a possible continuum of political and economic change also permits investigation of a wider array of regime types than does the dichotomous examination of democratic and nondemocratic regimes. As Lisa Martin describes in her essay, even among established liberal, capitalist democracies considerable institutional variation persists. Outside the accepted liberal democracies, the dimensions of liberalization suggest that certain features of regimes normally classified as "authoritarian" or "nondemocratic" might be arrayed on a common institutional continuum with liberal regimes. To view regimes in such a way, however, implies that certain "liberal" dimensions extend beyond regimes characterized as liberal democracies. Whether liberalization is a smooth continuum raises the related issue of transitional regimes, in which the levels of competition, participation, and transparency displayed go beyond those of established authoritarian regimes but stop short of those of liberal democracies. Such a mixed regime may be stable over time. On the other hand, in some of the cases considered in this volume, transitional status combines both intermediate values on the dimensions of liberalization and an *absence* of a stable institutional equilibrium.

A final issue bedevils the study of democratization or liberalization, however defined: the divergence between formal regime characteristics and the informal mechanisms of control and veto. Although the empirical task of determining whether power lies in new democratic political institutions or with elements of the old regime (the military, for example) may be difficult, it is not impossible. Drawing on new institutionalist analysis of American politics, Lisa Martin offers one strategy for determining the influence of "silent" institutions in the making of foreign policy in democratic regimes; that same methodology could be transferred to semidemocratic or liberalizing settings.[7]

POLITICAL LIBERALIZATION, DEMOCRATIC DYADS, AND FOREIGN POLICY

Two long-standing traditions in political philosophy have produced contradictory predictions concerning the effects of political liberalization on foreign policy. The skeptical or realist tradition views the external policies of liberal regimes as war-prone and volatile, because of a fickle and irrational public opinion. In this view, liberal states are ill-suited to statecraft or the long-term pursuit of national interests. Alexis de Tocqueville is representative of this position, arguing that democracies fight well but are not suited for the patient pursuit of their goals through diplomatic means.[8] This tradition has also found voice in the writings of Walter Lippmann and George Kennan and was even reflected in the American Constitution, which strengthened executive powers in foreign policy in reaction to perceived weaknesses under the Articles of Confederation.[9] This skeptical view of the competence of liberal regimes endorses what Robert Dahl has labeled "guardianship," particularly in the sphere of foreign policy: the complexity of foreign affairs and the slight attention paid to external events by the citizens of liberal democracies argue for placing responsibility in the hands of an expert minority.[10] A second, explicitly liberal, tradition, represented by theorists such as Immanuel Kant and Joseph Schumpeter, holds that a world composed of liberal states would be more pacific and predictable, because of the institutional constraints imposed by liberal politics and the reflection of liberal norms—such as respect for law—in the international sphere.[11]

Both traditions, with their different readings of the implications of political liberalization, are difficult to employ in a more systematic, empirical investigation of liberal politics and foreign policy. In both instances, normative judgments are central: evaluation of liberal regimes and their foreign policies is at issue. Shifting normative standards introduce confusion: earlier theorists, such as Machiavelli, who do not share later liberal predispositions against war, were not alarmed by the warlike and imperialist character of republican regimes. As warfare itself came to be viewed as an international ill and was assigned an increasingly negative place in liberal theorizing, the alleged pacifism of liberal regimes became one of their principal merits. The specific characteristics of liberal regimes that produce these outcomes are often obscure, and little attempt is made to differentiate among such regimes in ways that would illuminate particular institutional or ideological explanations.

Since contemporary social science began the exploration of relationships between regime and foreign policy, by far the greatest attention has centered on the conflict and war involvement of liberal democratic and nondemocratic political systems. Here, clear-cut evidence has been found for a narrow version of the Kantian thesis: liberal democracies rarely, if ever, make war on one another.[12] Tests of the finding on a wider historical and cultural sample that goes beyond the modern Western states system have found limited support as well. Democracies did occasionally make war on one another in ancient Greece (most notably the Athenian expedition against Syracuse), and evidence from ethnographic data indicates that political units with wider participation conduct less warfare with one another than do those societies with less-participatory politics.[13]

Both the apparent narrowness and the increasing scope of this finding add to its interest. On the one hand, although disputes among democracies demonstrate a lower tendency to escalate to the display or use of force (short of war), democracies are no less likely than other types of states to engage in war with nondemocracies.[14] In other words, it is democratic dyads that are distinctive, not the foreign policies or conflict propensities of liberal democracies themselves.[15] A less systematic survey of the oldest liberal democracies—the United States, Great Britain, and France—indicates repeated willingness to initiate military conflict with nondemocratic regimes.[16]

The claim that war is absent or very rare between democratic dyads has been challenged on a number of grounds. Some have argued that the coding in certain key cases, such as pre-1914 Germany, is wrong; others have advanced alternative explanations, such as geographical distance between democracies, the Cold War and American hegemony after 1945, or advanced industrialized states' learning about the cost of modern warfare. A final line of criticism concerns the statistical significance of the finding when war and democracies have both been rare events.[17] One other alternative—that the dyadic relationship reflects homogeneous regimes rather than liberal democratic characteristics—is given limited support by Maoz and Abdolali, who find between autocracies a reduced predisposition toward war, although not an absolute aversion.[18] Perhaps the most compelling criticism—one that is considered more carefully below—is that the distinctiveness of democratic dyads is limited in time, strengthening as the number of democracies increases and achieving statistical significance only after 1945.[19]

The distinctiveness of democratic dyads is a narrow, although apparently robust finding concerning regime type and foreign policy. At the same time, the *scope* of that distinctiveness continues to expand as investigators discover other characteristics of the foreign policies of liberal democracies that demonstrate the same pattern. Democratic states appear to be more likely to form alliances with other democracies, although there is some variation in the affinity over time.[20] Liberal states also behave differently in the legal and other means with which they manage disputes with one another.[21] Kurt Taylor Gaubatz extends the scope of intraliberal foreign policies in this volume by examining the duration of alliances among liberal democratic states.

Gaubatz and two other authors of essays in this collection, Lisa Martin and Joanne Gowa, also address the knottiest aspect of the "3D" (distinctiveness of democratic dyads) finding: developing an acceptable model to explain the foreign policies that mark democratic dyads. Since confirmed patterns in the foreign policies of liberal democratic states apply only to dyads in which *both* states are liberal democracies, explanations must include a "reflective" or strategic component as well. Three broad explanations have been advanced for the distinctiveness of democratic dyads: interests, institutions, and ideology or norms.

An argument from interests holds that the preferences of civil society may be more clearly reflected in the foreign policy of a liberal democratic state than in other types of regimes. Such an interest-based model of foreign policy in liberal democracies may predict specific policy outcomes. For example, a neo-Schumpeterian might argue that liberal democracies will award less influence to the traditional bureaucratic institutions that dominate external policy in authoritarian regimes, particularly the military. A more familiar link to interests, one that is related to economic liberalization, is an association between economic interdependence (economic openness) and domestic interests that serve to moderate conflicts. Gowa points out the difficulties with models based on economic interests, and other studies in this volume suggest that the interests and preferences reflected in liberal democracies are likely to be diverse and highly specific to each society.[22] Broader empirical studies have produced mixed results when measures of economic interdependence are related to levels of international conflict.[23] Few noneconomic domestic interests in liberal democracies could explain the near-absolute quality of the link between liberal democratic dyads and avoidance of war.

Liberal democratic institutions seem to offer a more convincing explanation for the characteristic foreign policies of democratic regimes. Those institutions embody wider participation, greater competition, and intensified transparency when compared with other regimes. Typically, liberal institutions are portrayed as imposing additional *constraints* on elites; the constraints, in turn, produce a more prudent foreign policy. These constraints are particularly important in dealings with other democracies, whose regimes are viewed as similarly configured. As Bruce Russett outlines the institutional model for the absence of war among democracies, "The constraints of checks and balances, division of power, and need for public debate to enlist widespread support will slow decisions to use large-scale violence and reduce the likelihood that such decisions will be made," other states will be aware of these constraints, and leaders of other democracies in particular will not fear preemptive attack, thus permitting peaceful resolution of conflicts.[24]

Bruce Bueno de Mesquita and David Lalman present the most elaborated model of democratic institutional constraints that are likely to produce the 3D results.[25] Their case for an institutional explanation has two bases: the information that is reliably conveyed to other regimes about "hawkish" or "dovish" preferences by democratic institutions and the likelihood that democratic politicians will be punished more reliably than authoritarian rulers for unsuccessful military conflicts. More recent work by Randolph M. Siverson and Bueno de Mesquita appears to confirm the latter assumption.[26] David Lake's argument for the reduced propensity of liberal democracies for rent-seeking and aggressive foreign policies is also based on institutional differences that ensure greater transparency in decision making and lower costs in controlling the state.[27]

The institutional explanation for the distinctiveness of democratic dyads depends on a reliable relationship between a set of institutions and constraints on national leaders. The structure of liberal democracies varies considerably, however, and the institutions that appear to impose constraints in one setting may have very different effects in another. For any measurable type of behavior, democratic institutions may also have different effects that, taken together, cancel each other. For example, in crisis behavior, some institutions may induce riskier behavior and others encourage more prudent behavior.[28] Even the same institutions may elicit different foreign policy responses by rational politicians in different circumstances: a Congress that checks one president and renders him more prudent may induce another, in Theodore Lowi's phrase, to oversell the threat and commit to more risky actions.

Electoral cycles, a central feature of any democratic regime, have received considerable scrutiny, and, within the set of liberal democracies, might be expected to constrain foreign policy behavior in a consistent fashion. Gaubatz has found that democratic states are more likely to enter wars early in their electoral cycles (soon after elections) rather than later, at a time when, arguably, the ability of the electorate to sanction the political leadership is lowest.[29] Gaubatz's findings could lend support to the general view that liberal political institutions check military action by elites. Miroslav Nincic, however, has discovered support for a somewhat different cycle of hostility and cooperativeness in American policy toward the Soviet Union: hostility peaked in election years and carried over to the first year of a new administration; cooperation increased in the second term of a two-term president when electoral constraints were weaker.[30]

Finally, liberal democratic institutions may play only a weak independent role, reflecting the preferences of the electorate or a dominant political coalition, and, as described above, those preferences may be indeterminate.[31] Whether the electorates or elites of liberal democracies will endorse foreign policies that reflect a particular method of conflict resolution, whether they will be consistently more dovish and less conflict-prone, at least toward other democracies, draws attention to liberal democratic norms, a third explanation for the 3D findings.

The distinctiveness of democratic dyads—particularly the aversion of liberal democracies toward war with other democracies—may lie not in institutions or interests but in the shared ideology or norms of liberal democratic regimes. The operative norms have been described as a domestic attachment to peaceful means of conflict resolution, such as law and constitutional government. These dispute settlement norms are extended to the international realm by democratic regimes. Such normative or ideological constraints are only (or most powerfully) operative when reflected in other liberal democratic states, hence the dyadic character of democratic war aversion.[32]

This model of "dyad-only" normative constraint has proved difficult to specify and to investigate empirically. The precise means by which norms regulating domestic conflict are externalized remain obscure. Domestic "peace" must also be demonstrated, and liberal democracies have had their share of domestic violence and civil wars. Proxies used for the existence of domestic democratic norms, such as incidence of civil wars or political violence, may reflect not norms of conflict resolution but the deterrent police and military power of particular regimes. A second key indicator of norms employed by Bruce Russett is political stability (measured by regime persistence).[33] Although regime duration is arguably related to the development of strong norms, more-established regimes could independently produce predictability for others in the international system, a feature that is not limited to democratic regimes.

Joanne Gowa argues in her essay here that norms must be clearly separated from alternative explanations: what appears to be normatively driven behavior may be reflective of interests that are not domestically derived. State interests, reflected in alliance memberships, may provide the most parsimonious explanation of the distinctiveness of democratic dyads, particularly after 1945. As Russett argues, however, there is no reason to believe that "interests" (defined as threat perception or in some other way) do not include political regime as one of their components.[34]

Disentangling the alternative explanations for the distinctive qualities of foreign policies among democratic states has led to closer examination of those relations in specific historical cases. John M. Owen asserts that both liberal ideas and liberal institutions interact to produce the democratic peace.[35] His distinction between the bearers of liberal ideology and liberal institutions permits the separation of normative explanations from institutional ones. Owen's definition of the irreducible content of liberal ideology and the sources of liberal political influence remains unclear, however. Owen's emphasis on *perceptions* of liberal attributes resembles Thomas Risse-Kappen's (and

even the critic David Spero's) explanations for distinctive liberal foreign policies toward other liberal states.[36] Risse-Kappen offers a constructivist elaboration of the normative explanation for the liberal
democratic peace, arguing that democracies infer potentially threatening external behavior from the internal violence of repressive
regimes. Since there is little evidence that repressive regimes are necessarily more violent in their foreign policies, Risse-Kappen (and
some other proponents of the normative explanation) must explain
this mistaken learning trajectory.

FOREIGN POLICY AND TRANSITIONAL REGIMES

The distinctive character of international relations among liberal
democracies appears to strengthen over time, whether between specific pairs of states or among the cluster of all democracies. The level
of militarized disputes and crises between the United States and the
other liberal great powers declined from the nineteenth century to
the twentieth: well before the onset of the Cold War a de facto security community existed among the small number of democratic great
powers.[37] A strengthening of the democratic peace after 1945 is conceded by both supporters and skeptics of its earlier reality. The normative explanation for the democratic peace is based explicitly on
stable democratic polities over time. All of these observations could
be attributed to the consolidation of democratic regimes, of movement from purely formal or institutionally defined liberal regimes to
regimes in which the democratic rules of the game are virtually
unquestioned.

What is to one observer a newly democratized or liberalized state is
to another a fragile, transitional regime. Students of democratic transition disagree sharply over the hallmarks of regime consolidation and
the possibility for an indefinite transitional state of weak or incomplete democracy. For Giuseppe Di Palma and others, too stringent a
definition of consolidation would consign even established regimes
such as Italy to transitional limbo; for others, such as Guillermo
O'Donnell and Philippe Schmitter, hybrid or incomplete forms of
transition are possible and may be stable over a period of years.

This controversy would not be critical to an analysis of foreign policy effects of liberalization if one could assume a strictly additive character to the process: increments of wider participation, greater com-

petition, or enhanced transparency would produce measurable increments in a particular foreign policy outcome associated with liberal
democracies.[38] Such an assumption is undermined, however, if a liberal democratic foreign policy requires a certain lower threshold of
such characteristics or if it is institutionalization (or institutional stability) that is captured in many of the characteristic definitions of liberal democracy. Gaubatz's essay here defines liberal democracies to
include regularized leadership changes, institutional stability, and
stability of preferences, none of which would apply to many liberalizing regimes.[39] Russett employs the longevity of a democratic regime
as one of the principal proxies for the influence of democratic
norms.[40] It is this dimension of institutionalization, the presence or
absence of an agreed institutional equilibrium within a given polity,
that separates liberal democracies from transitional regimes.

Even a modest degree of political liberalization may influence foreign policy, but foreign policy outcomes may not be those expected
of established democratic regimes. As Lisa Martin notes, England and
the Dutch Republic fought three wars in the seventeenth century,
when they were the only states in Europe with representative institutions. She suggests that institutional instability in the relations
between Crown and Parliament both affected the conduct of these
wars and restrained British policy in some instances. As would be the
case in many other transitional regimes, foreign policy became an
instrument in the struggle for internal institutional predominance,
ultimately handicapping England in international competition.[41]

Models of foreign policy in transitional, liberalizing but not yet
established democratic regimes often parallel the diversionary theory of war.[42] Such explanations for conflict posit a scapegoat effect, in
which domestic conflict is managed through externalization: leaders
shore up their internal position through aggressive foreign policies.
One of the difficulties with such theories, as Jack Levy notes, is their
failure to specify the level and type of conflict that results in such
scapegoating behavior. One hypothesis is that diversionary foreign
policy actions are most likely when the level of domestic conflict is
neither very low nor very high: if political transition is nearly consensual with little threat of violence, then the payoff to externalization is low, given the risks; if a near-revolutionary situation exists
internally, foreign policy paralysis and quiescence are more likely
than belligerence.

The pre-1914 case of a liberalizing autocracy—Russia—offers some support for this generalization. Following the 1905–1906 revolution in Russia, the political elite adopted a widely shared lesson from the recent domestic conflict: another war would mean another, probably fatal, revolution. By 1913–1914, however, as recovery and renovation were widely perceived to be complete and domestic conflict to be lower, this lesson was inverted: public opinion was seen as demanding action; capitulation to Russia's adversaries abroad was believed to endanger the tsarist regime at home.[43]

Conditions of struggle over the institutional rules of the game—producing a lack of clarity internally and a lack of predictability externally—seem most likely to encourage an instrumental use of foreign policy for domestic purposes. The cases of pre–World War I liberalizing monarchies once again offer some support. Russia, Austria-Hungary, and Germany were clearly transitional regimes, regimes in institutional flux, in which the internal rules of the game were being challenged and control of foreign policy was a contentious issue. In a recent study of Russian foreign policy during this period, David McDonald describes the profound effects on foreign policy of liberal reforms enacted following the revolution of 1905–1906. Even though foreign policy was explicitly reserved to the tsar and excluded from the oversight of the new (and weak) Duma, ministers felt that they had to work with the legislature, cultivate the press, and also respond to an often inchoate public opinion.[44] A similar pattern could be observed in the other autocracies as popular demands for greater participation collided with entrenched military and bureaucratic interests. Neither the institutional nor the normative bases for liberal democratic foreign policy were in place, as the militarization of disputes among the three, their weak alignment with the liberal democracies, and, ultimately, their decisions for war in 1914 demonstrated.

Conclusions based solely on the liberalizing yet conflict-prone regimes of the early twentieth century are as questionable as the automatic attribution of liberal democratic foreign policies to new and fragile democracies, however. Although transitional regimes may have foreign policies that do not resemble the relations among democratic dyads, claims that they are uniquely conflict-prone are also overdrawn.[45] Coding of these regimes often fails to capture the common understanding of "transitional" in comparative politics. In particular, the portmanteau category of "anocracy" includes societies engulfed in civil war (Angola 1975–1986, Zaire 1960–1966), stable authoritarian regimes (Singapore 1965–1986), and other polities that are transitional as defined here (Portugal 1974–1975).[46] Models constructed to explain the foreign policies of liberalizing or transitional regimes are often plagued by a severe sampling problem: only democratizing states that engage in international conflict are examined; the large number of such states that may not have engaged in conflict are ignored. Models are also skewed to imply that democratization is the sole stimulus for external conflict; in the cases described above, the limited character of democracy and the lingering power of military and bureaucratic elites could be assigned equal or greater importance. The foreign policy behavior of regimes in the absence of political liberalization—a crucial counterfactual—is not considered.

One compelling (perhaps overwhelming) source of evidence is completely omitted in alarmist accounts of the foreign policies of liberalizing or transitional regimes: the latest wave of democratization, which has resulted in more transitional or democratizing regimes than at any other time in this century. Nevertheless, with the exception of a few cases in the former Soviet Union and the former Yugoslavia, instances of an upsurge in interstate violence connected to this wave of democratization are virtually absent. In some regions of widespread democratization, such as Latin America, many previous territorial disputes have subsided in importance and important measures of disarmament—negotiated and unilateral—have occurred.

Transitional regimes—defined as liberalizing states in which a new political equilibrium remains elusive—may display foreign policies that do not match the strong findings of the "3D" specialists. Several transitional dynamics may overturn the characteristic behavior of more established or institutionalized democratic regimes. Nevertheless, the category of transitional regimes requires careful definition and disaggregation; not all transitional regimes display the same foreign policies across regions or across time.

ECONOMIC LIBERALIZATION AND ITS FOREIGN POLICY EFFECTS

In classic descriptions of the pacific union of liberal states, economic exchange among those states played a prominent role. The wide-

spread adoption of programs of economic liberalization, only occasionally coupled with political opening, calls into question the easy
assumption that economically open states will characteristically possess liberal democratic regimes and that the foreign policy effects of
economic liberalization will necessarily reinforce those of liberal
institutions and norms. The posited linkages, both positive and negative, between economic and political liberalization remain controversial.[47]

Economic liberalization was defined to include dimensions of foreign economic policy—trade liberalization and reducing foreign
investment controls, for example. Taking those foreign policy consequences as given, economic liberalization may also produce second-
order foreign policy effects. One cluster of such effects may influence
the involvement of states in international conflict through increasing
or decreasing available resources. Here, the consequences of economic liberalization may change over time, offering different incentives and disincentives for conflictual behavior. The resource effects
of economic liberalization can be portrayed as a J-curve: declining
resources available for external (particularly military) demands as
the fiscal effects (typically a decline in government revenues) of economic liberalization take hold and then increasing resources when
(and if) the growth effects of policy reforms are felt. Examples of
both effects can be cited from current liberalization episodes: a sharp
decline in military budgets throughout Latin America and in the former Soviet Union (unless specifically protected by transitional pacts)
and increasing military budgets in Southeast Asia and China as
rapidly growing economies devote a stable or even declining share of
their national income to external purposes. Liberalization may also
imply a permanent downward shift in the ability of societies to extract
resources for external purposes because of the reduced role of the
state, but that effect, if it exists, must be separated from independent
shifts in preferences that could also produce reduced spending for
military or foreign policy ends.

Economic liberalization also implies an increase in external economic transactions and heightened interdependence with other
economies. These effects have attracted the most attention from liberal theorists. Interdependence may increase the vulnerability of a
state to the policies of other states. This vulnerability may create
potential issue linkage or leverage: economic vulnerability in one
issue area is employed in bargaining to obtain offsetting gains in

other areas of foreign policy. Through state-to-state bargaining linkages, whether explicitly or implicitly employed, economic interdependence may serve to constrain foreign policy more broadly and to induce a more prudent, less volatile, and less belligerent external posture. These positive results, often assumed by liberal theorists, are more likely in symmetric relations of interdependence; asymmetries of influence may mobilize into politics perceptions of international vulnerability, thus creating more conflict rather than less.

Economic interdependence induced by economic liberalization may also create interests—governmental and nongovernmental—that are affected favorably or unfavorably by international economic exchange. Those groups will in turn have a differential influence on policy, constraining or encouraging foreign policies in directions that will benefit them. For example, Etel Solingen argues that participation in nuclear regimes is closely related to economic liberalization and its supporting coalitions. In part the liberalizers are concerned about the possible economic sanctions that might be deployed against nuclear proliferators (anticipated linkage); the liberalizing coalition's goal of reducing state power also fits with denuclearization, since the nuclear-industrial complex is typically state-dominated.[48]

A final and more profound change in foreign policy has also been attributed to economic liberalization: transformation in underlying foreign policy preferences. This transformation can be defined as an elevation at the national level of goals of economic welfare (and a concurrent devaluation of the old values of military status and territorial acquisition).[49] An alternative view emphasizes a decline in ideologically driven or "passionate" foreign policies under the onslaught of the market. Ideology is replaced by a careful reckoning of economic costs and benefits, regardless of regime type. In many respects this transformation (if demonstrated) runs counter to the ideological effects of political liberalization, which predicts international alignment and support on the basis of regime type.

Constructing causal links between economic liberalization and changes in conflict behavior and foreign policy orientation is difficult, particularly in those cases when internal political and international changes move states in the same direction. One additional and widespread foreign policy consequence of economic liberalization is central to the essays in this volume: the adoption of external cooperative strategies and engagement with international institutions to manage the effects of growing external economic ties.

International collaboration and institutional engagement follow from four internal dynamics induced by economic liberalization. First, political elites may discover that programs of economic liberalization benefit from (or require) additional credibility supplied by international institutions; part of that added credibility is provided by the resources of those institutions.[50] International engagement may also serve to bind succeeding governments to a liberal economic program in the face of shifting political incentives or elite preferences. The credibility rationale for international institutional ties is likely to be strongest at the beginning of a program of economic liberalization, when institutional and group beneficiaries of the program are likely to be weak, and in regimes that have little past record of carrying out liberal economic programs.

Economic liberalization also impels states toward cooperative strategies through reshuffling the influence of domestic economic institutions. Those institutions representing the old, closed economic order may enter a cumulative decline that magnifies the impact of interests pressing for more liberalization. Coincident with the decline or transformation of institutions designed for a less liberal economic order, new domestic institutions are created or elevated. New foreign trade and export promotion agencies may assume prominent roles in foreign economic policy, edging out more traditional bureaucracies, such as foreign ministries. Central banks have also assumed prominent roles under economic liberalization, as Sylvia Maxfield's account of Mexican liberalization documents, since central banks are often assigned the role of gatekeeper between international and domestic financial markets. Domestic institutions favored by liberalization will often seek collaborative transgovernmental arrangements with their counterparts in order to strengthen their policy position internally and reassert their position vis-á-vis private actors internationally.

New economic interests, created by programs of economic liberalization, may make their weight felt in the foreign policy process; on the other side of foreign policy battles will be those interests that are threatened by the increase in international competition and seek to roll back or limit the extent of such programs. Those groups supporting the liberalization program may align themselves with international institutions in order to strengthen their credibility as reformers and increase the deterrent threat against those advocating a rollback of reform. At the same time, opponents of economic opening can use the intervention of international actors, whether other governments, foreign investors, or international institutions, as a weapon in a nationalist campaign against economic liberalization.

Finally, spillover effects from the consequences of economic liberalization in other issue areas will often result in a ratcheting up of international institution building in order to deal with cross-issue disturbances. The connections between national macroeconomic management and exchange rates or between trade and financial reforms may push states toward reinforcing existing multilateral arrangements or constructing new ones.

THE FOREIGN POLICY CONSEQUENCES OF POLITICAL AND ECONOMIC LIBERALIZATION

Although research on regime change and foreign policy is in its infancy, one island of investigation has attracted intensive scholarly attention: the distinctive foreign policies of democratic dyads. That distinctiveness expands in scope yet remains subject to challenge by skeptics. Competing models contend as explanations for both aggregate and case study data. The first three essays of this volume scrutinize the 3D findings and assess existing and alternative explanations for those results. Kurt Taylor Gaubatz, Lisa Martin, and Joanne Gowa suggest additions to the scope of those findings, delineate an institutional path toward constructing a model for democratic constraints, and suggest flaws in the existing explanatory alternatives.

The uncertain politics of the former Soviet Union and the violence in what was once Yugoslavia has heightened attention to the differences between established liberal democracies and liberalizing or transitional regimes. The latter risk definition by tautology (i.e., by distinctive foreign policies that diverge from recognized democratic regimes). Boundaries are difficult to set: when is consolidation completed and a democratic (or market-oriented) transition ended? Both historical cases and contemporary evidence suggest that considerable variation characterizes such regimes and their foreign policies. Here, as in the analysis of authoritarian and democratic regimes, more refined institutional analysis is required.

Five of the essays discuss the implications of political liberalization and democratic consolidation for foreign policy. Their cases are dispersed in time and across regions. Lisa Martin reaches back in time to consider the first liberalizing regimes and the ways in which foreign policy became part of a struggle over a new institutional equilibrium. Lisa Anderson and Jeffrey Herbst explore the likely foreign policy consequences of political opening in two regions—the Middle East and sub-Saharan Africa—that have little previous experience of democracy, regimes whose elites resist and obstruct the construction of new democratic rules of the game. Victor Pérez-Díaz and Juan Carlos Rodríguez explain the rapid transition of Spanish foreign policy to that of an established European democracy. Ronald Linden conducts a similar survey of the foreign policy consequences of political liberalization in East Europe, a more recent and perhaps more fragile development. These investigations outline distinctions among transitional regimes and explain their characteristic foreign policies.

Economic liberalization is more widespread than political liberalization, and its foreign policy effects may be more systematic, although they have attracted less attention from investigators. Economic integration, spurred by programs of economic liberalization, has encouraged new cooperative strategies (or the reinforcement of old ones) and deepened engagement with international institutions.

Three of the essays trace the relations between economic liberalization, foreign economic policies of international collaboration, and institutional choices at the international level. Pérez-Díaz and Rodríguez document the importance of international institutional anchors for political and economic liberalization in Spain. Jeffry Frieden models European economic and monetary integration, offering an interest-based model for the pattern of European institution building across time. Sylvia Maxfield examines a key liberalizer in the developing world, Mexico, and suggests the avenues by which economic liberalization changes the policy preferences of key groups and the government.

The foreign policies of liberal and liberalizing states have become an important question of foreign policy priority in established liberal democracies like the United States. If there are benign effects in a world of democratic states, then policies to promote democratization should be reinforced. If transitional regimes exhibit conflict-prone foreign policies or if economic liberalization is deepened by institutional engagement, additional policy prescriptions may follow. The concluding essay summarizes the findings of the contributors, situates those findings in the existing debate over liberal regimes and their external behavior, and draws policy conclusions for programs of democratic support.

Notes

The author wishes to thank the University of California Pacific Rim Research Program for its support of this project and also Barton Fisher and Timothy Johnson for their research assistance. Judith Goldstein, Robert O. Keohane, Bruce Russett, Lisa Martin, Jeffrey Herbst, and other members of the Social Science Research Council Liberalization and Foreign Policy project provided helpful comments on earlier versions of this introduction.

1. See, for example, Stephen Van Evera, "Primed for Peace: Europe After the Cold War," and F. Stephen Larrabee, "Long Memories and Short Fuses: Change and Instability in the Balkans," *International Security* 15, 3 (Winter 1990/91): 26–28, 43–44, 60–65.

2. The debates over the theoretical implications of the end of the Cold War include Richard Ned Lebow and Janice Stein, *We All Lost the Cold War* (Princeton: Princeton University Press, 1994), and William C. Wohlforth, "Realism and the End of the Cold War," *International Security* 19, 3 (Winter 1994/95): 91–129. For one effort to redefine liberalism as a plausible contender with neorealism, see Andrew Moravscik, "Liberalism and International Relations Theory" (unpublished paper, September 1991).

3. Howard J. Wiarda, *The Democratic Revolution in Latin America* (New York: Holmes and Meier, 1990), p. 270.

4. O'Donnell and Schmitter, for example, have defined liberalization and democratization as two distinct processes—the former a "micro" extension of rights to individuals and groups, the latter a "macro" process of broadened political participation. Limitations on either liberalization or democratization lead to the categories of "liberalized authoritarianism" (*dictablandas*) and "limited democracies" (*democraduras*); see Guillermo O'Donnell and Philippe Schmitter, *Transitions from Authoritarian Rule* (Baltimore: Johns Hopkins University Press, 1986), pp. 7–11.

5. For a widely accepted definition of liberal democracy, see Robert A. Dahl, *Democracy and Its Critics* (New Haven: Yale University Press, 1989), pp. 220–221.

6. Although the two faces have been joined in many economic reform programs of the 1980s, historically they have not always been closely connected. The inner face of nineteenth-century American capitalism was liberal; its outer face was highly protectionist. Japan and the East Asian newly industrializing nations in the 1970s also demonstrated an inner face of economic policy that was far more liberal than their external economic policies.

7. Lisa L. Martin, "Legislative Influence and International Engagement," ch. 2 in this volume.

8. Josef Joffe, "Tocqueville Revisited: Are Good Democracies Bad Players in the Game of Nations?" *Washington Quarterly* (Winter 1988): 161–189.

9. James Ceaser, *Liberal Democracy and Political Science* (Baltimore: Johns Hopkins University Press, 1990), p. 191.

10. For a critique of this view, see Robert Dahl, *Controlling Nuclear Weapons: Democracy Versus Guardianship* (Syracuse: Syracuse University Press, 1985).

11. Michael W. Doyle, "Liberalism and World Politics," *American Political Science Review* 80, 4 (December 1986): 1151–1163.

12. Studies supporting this robust finding include Steve Chan, "Mirror, Mirror on the Wall . . . Are the Freer Countries More Pacific?" *Journal of Conflict Resolution* 28, 4

(December 1984): 617–648; Michael Doyle, "Kant, Liberal Legacies, and Foreign Affairs: Parts I and II," *Philosophy and Public Affairs* 12 (1983): 205–235, 323–353; Jack Levy, "The Causes of War: A Review of Theories and Evidence," in *Behavior, Society, and Nuclear War* (Oxford: Oxford University Press, 1989), pp. 267–271; Bruce Russett, *Controlling the Sword* (Cambridge: Harvard University Press, 1990), ch. 5; Zeev Maoz and Nasrin Abdolali, "Regime Types and International Conflict, 1816–1976," *Journal of Conflict Resolution* 33, 1 (March 1989): 3–35; Zeev Maoz and Bruce Russett, "Alliance, Contiguity, Wealth, and Political Stability: Is the Lack of Conflict Among Democracies a Statistical Artifact?" *International Interactions* 17, 3 (1992): 245–269; Bruce M. Russett, *Grasping the Democratic Peace: Principles for a Post–Cold War World* (Princeton: Princeton University Press, 1993).

13. Russett, *Grasping the Democratic Peace*, pp. 43–71, 99–118; Neta C. Crawford, "A Security Regime Among Democracies: Cooperation Among the Iroquois Nation," *International Organization* 48, 3 (Summer 1994): 345–386.

14. For an exhaustive examination of such conflict relations, see Maoz and Abdolali, "Regime Types and International Conflict"; also Erich Weede, "Democracy and War Involvement," *Journal of Conflict Resolution* 28, 4 (December 1984): 649–664.

15. A persistent dissenter from this restrictive view of liberal democratic foreign policies is R. J. Rummel; see "Democracies ARE Less Warlike than Other Regimes," *European Journal of International Relations* 1, 4 (December 1995): 457–479.

16. Randall Schweller argues that a second clear pattern emerges in the waging of preventive wars: democracies do not initiate such conflicts against either democratic or nondemocratic regimes. His coding of preventive wars and power transitions casts considerable doubt on this finding, however; see "Domestic Structure and Preventive War: Are Democracies More Pacific?" *World Politics* 44, 2 (January 1992): 235–269.

17. John J. Mearsheimer, "Back to the Future: Instability in Europe After the Cold War," *International Security* 15, 1 (Summer 1990): 5–56; Christopher Layne, "Kant or Cant: The Myth of the Democratic Peace," *International Security* 19, 2 (Fall 1994): 5–49; David E. Spiro, "The Insignificance of the Liberal Peace," *International Security* 19, 2 (Fall 1994): 50–86.

18. Maoz and Abdolali, "Regime Types and International Conflict," p. 23.

19. Henry S. Farber and Joanne Gowa, "Polities and Peace," *International Security* 20, 2 (Fall 1995): 123–146.

20. In particular, immediately before World War II, democracies appear to have formed fewer alliances with one another than would have been expected; Randolph M. Siverson and Juliann Emmons, "Democratic Political Systems and Alliance Choices," *Journal of Conflict Resolution* 35, 2 (June 1991): 285–306.

21. Anne-Marie Slaughter Burley, "Law Among Liberal States: Liberal Internationalism and the Act of State Doctrine," *Columbia Law Review* 92, 8 (1992): 1907–1996; William J. Dixon, "Democracy and the Peaceful Settlement of International Conflict," *American Political Science Review* 88, 1 (March 1994): 14–32.

22. Joanne Gowa, "Democratic States and International Disputes," ch. 3 in this volume.

23. Nils Petter Gleditsch, "Democracy and the Future of European Peace," *European Journal of International Relations* 1, 4 (December 1995): 546–548.

24. Russett, *Grasping the Democratic Peace*, p. 40.

25. Bruce Bueno de Mesquita and David Lalman, *War and Reason*, pp. 145–177.

26. Randolph M. Siverson, "Democracies and War Participation: In Defense of the

Institutional Constraints Argument," *European Journal of International Relations* 1, 4 (December 1995): 481–489; Bruce Bueno de Mesquita, "War and the Survival of Political Leaders: A Comparative Study of Regime Types and Political Accountability," *American Political Science Review* 89, 4 (December 1995): 844–855.

27. David A. Lake, "Powerful Pacifists: Democratic States and War," *American Political Science Review* 86, 1 (March 1992): 24–37.

28. On this point, see D. Marc Kilgour, "Domestic Political Structure and War Behavior," *Journal of Conflict Resolution* 35, 2 (June 1991): 266–283.

29. Kurt Taylor Gaubatz, "Election Cycles and War," *Journal of Conflict Resolution* 35, 2 (June 1991): 212–244.

30. Miroslav Nincic, "U.S. Soviet Policy and the Electoral Connection," *World Politics* 42, 3 (April 1990): 370–396.

31. This is one interpretation of the findings of T. Clifton Morgan and Sally Howard Campbell, "Domestic Structure, Decisional Constraints, and War," *Journal of Conflict Resolution* 35, 2 (June 1991): 187–211.

32. See Doyle, "Kant, Liberal Legacies, and Foreign Affairs," p. 230; Doyle, "Liberalism and World Politics," pp. 1160–1161; Russett, *Grasping the Democratic Peace*, pp. 30–38.

33. Russett, *Grasping the Democratic Peace*, p. 81.

34. Ibid., p. 27.

35. John M. Owen, "How Liberalism Produces Democratic Peace," *International Security* 19, 2 (Fall 1994): 87–125.

36. Spiro, "The Insignificance of the Liberal Peace," p. 80; Thomas Risse-Kappen, "Democratic Peace—Warlike Democracies? A Social Constructivist Interpretation of the Liberal Argument," *European Journal of International Relations* 1, 4 (December 1995): 491–517.

37. For an account of the diminishing level of militarization in disputes between Britain and the United States, see Owen, "How Liberalism Produces Democratic Peace."

38. Russett and Maoz find such a relationship between democracy and conflict behavior (Russett, *Grasping the Democratic Peace*, p. 86).

39. Gaubatz, "Democratic States and Commitment in International Relations," chapter 1 in this volume.

40. Russett, *Grasping the Democratic Peace*, p. 27.

41. Lisa Martin, "Legislative Delegation and International Engagement" chapter 2 in this volume.

42. For a description and critique of this theory, see Jack Levy, "The Diversionary Theory of War: A Critique," in Manus I. Midlarsky, ed., *Handbook of War Studies* (Boston: Unwin Hyman, 1989), pp. 259–288.

43. David MacLaren McDonald, *United Government and Foreign Policy in Russia, 1900–1914* (Cambridge: Harvard University Press, 1992), pp. 196–197, 205–206.

44. Ibid., pp. 99, 121–124.

45. For claims of this kind, see Edward D. Mansfield and Jack Snyder, "Democratization and the Danger of War," *International Security* 20, 1 (Summer 1995): 5–38.

46. An example of such coding, based on Ted Robert Gurr's Polity II data, is given in Russett, *Grasping the Democratic Peace*, pp. 94–97.

47. On this question, see "Capitalism, Socialism, and Democracy," special issue of *Journal of Democracy* 3, 3 (July 1992); Adam Przeworski, *Democracy and the Market*

(Cambridge: Cambridge University Press, 1991); and Stephan Haggard and Robert R. Kaufman, *The Political Economy of Democratic Transitions* (Princeton: Princeton University Press, 1995).

48. Etel Solingen, "The Political Economy of Nuclear Restraint," *International Security* 19, 2 (Fall 1994): 126–169.

49. This transformation resembles Kant's "cosmopolitan law" and the arguments of such liberals as Richard Cobden in the nineteenth century.

50. Whether international institutions provide policy credibility or national governments offer credibility to international institutions is a knotty issue; see John T. Woolley, "Policy Credibility and European Monetary Institutions," in Alberta M. Sbragia, ed., *Euro-politics* (Washington, D.C.: Brookings Institution, 1991), pp. 157–190.

I

Liberal Democracies and Their Foreign Policies

ONE

Democratic States and Commitment in International Relations

Kurt Taylor Gaubatz

> *The Four Hundred . . . departed widely from the democratic system of govern-ment. . . . They also sent to Agis, the Lacedæmonian king, at Decelea, to say that they desired to make peace, and that he might reasonably be more disposed to treat now that he had them to deal with instead of the inconstant commons.*
> —Thucydides[1]

> *Confederations are dissolved for the sake of some advantage, and in this republics abide by their agreements far better than do princes. Instances might be cited of treaties broken by princes for a very small advantage, and of treaties which have not been broken by a republic for a very great advantage.*
> —Machiavelli[2]

The traditional view of popular government as shifting and unreli-able, which Thucydides attributes to the Athenian oligarchs, has a long and distinguished history. Machiavelli, who takes issue with this view, attributes it to "all writers" and "all historians."[3] The significant, if still somewhat tenuous, worldwide trend toward democratization of the past decade has renewed interest in the implications of democra-tic governance for the international behavior of states.[4] Most of that interest has focused on the relationship between democracy and con-flict. But, as is made clear in the work of both Thucydides and Machiavelli, there are long-standing debates about other important dimensions of the international behavior of popular governments. I return here to the basic question suggested by Thucydides and Machiavelli as to the ability of democratic states to make commitments in their international relations. I argue that there is both a theoretical and an empirical basis for rejecting the traditional view of the "inconstant commons."

The ability of states to make commitments is a critical dimension of the international system. Between two states, commitments run the gamut from formal defense treaties to casual assurances between diplomats. For liberal institutionalists, the ability to make commitments is central to the process of international institutionalization.[5] But commitments do not have to reflect only cooperative behavior. Even for realists, the ability to make commitments is critical to international interactions. The efficacy of deterrence threats and the functioning of alliance politics clearly hinge on the ability of actors to make credible commitments.[6]

The dominant assumption in the study of international relations has been that the ability, or the lack of ability, to make commitments is a function of the anarchic international system.[7] Recent work in conflict studies, combined with the apparent trend of democratization, has raised anew the question of whether there are theoretically worthwhile distinctions to be made in analyzing the international behavior of different regime types.[8] Given the importance of commitment and the traditional concern about the inconstancy of popular rule, the possibility that liberal and democratic domestic political and economic arrangements may have distinct effects on the ability of states to make credible international commitments would seem well worth investigating.

On the face of it, the challenge of signaling and maintaining commitment in political systems that require public deliberation and approval for major international actions would seem formidable. But the relationship between international commitments and domestic politics is more complex than might be assumed from a narrow focus on the idea of "the inconstant commons." In this essay I set out a working definition of liberal democracy and draw out of that definition several implications for the ability of states to make international commitments. As against the common perspective of democratic inconstancy, I argue that there are both normative and structural characteristics of liberal democratic states that can significantly enhance the strength of their international commitments. I then

turn to a consideration of democratic alliance behavior as a preliminary empirical indicator for the distinctive nature of democratic commitments in the international system. In particular, I bring forward
strong empirical evidence to show that alliances between liberal
democratic states have proven more durable than either alliances
between nondemocratic states or alliances between democratic and
nondemocratic states.

Democracy and commitment are both complex phenomena.
Many books have been written on both subjects. For the purpose of
this analysis, I offer working definitions that, while inadequate as
complete philosophical statements, can serve as the basis for a discussion of these phenomena within the context of international
affairs.

A state makes a commitment to a course of action when it creates
a subjective belief on the part of others that it will carry through with
that course of action. There are trivial commitments that involve
doing things that are clearly in one's interest to do. The more interesting commitments are those that bind the state to take some set of
actions that do not look to be in its narrow self-interest as an international actor.[9] Thus, the commitment problem for the United States in
using nuclear deterrence to defend Europe against a Soviet attack
was how to make it clear to both the Europeans and the Soviets that
in the event of a war American leaders would be prepared to sacrifice
New York in order to save Berlin or Paris.[10] In this essay I will deal in
particular with alliance commitments. Alliances, at their core, are a
reaction to the problem of nontrivial commitment.[11] If the narrow
self-interest of one alliance partner would be served by defending the
other, the two would not need to formalize their commitment on
paper, beyond some minimal efforts to coordinate defense policies
and practices. The creation of a formal alliance is an attempt to signal both to the alliance partners and to other states that a genuine
commitment to some level of mutual defense exists.

The definition of democracy is even more problematic. I focus in
this paper on the notion of "liberal democracy." Scholars, of course,
continue to debate the relationship between these two terms, but my
argument proceeds analytically from both concepts. "Liberalism"
refers to a conception of the state that faces juridical limits on its powers and functions.[12] "Democracy" refers to a form of government in
which power rests with the majority. Democracy requires governments to be able to garner majority approval of their performance in

order to stay in power. At the same time, liberalism will require that minority opinions can be expressed and that rivals for power will be able to exercise their rights to try to form alternative majorities. The demands that power be limited and that it rest with the majority can be in tension.[13] In the modern world, however, liberalism and democracy have become strongly, though not perfectly, interconnected. Indeed, a number of scholars argue that modern democracy in its juridical or institutional sense is a natural extension of liberalism.[14] For the purposes of this analysis, then, liberal democracies are states that are limited in their conduct of international affairs by constitutionally defined institutions of popular will and of juridical constraint.[15]

At the domestic level, the survival of liberal democracy and the ability of governments to make credible commitments are inherently intertwined. The existence of liberal democracy ultimately rests on the ability of the majority to convince minorities that it will not remake institutions when its narrow self-interests might be better served by abandoning the notion of limited government. A central question of liberal democratic theory, then, is how it is that the majority commits to accept limits on its power.[16]

Similarly, scholars have long debated the implications of limited government and majority rule for external commitments. Before moving to the analytic portion of this inquiry, it is worth a brief detour to summarize some of these existing perspectives on the ability of liberal democratic states to make commitments in their international relations.

THREE PERSPECTIVES ON DEMOCRATIC COMMITMENTS

The traditional views on the ability of democratic states to make international commitments can be grouped into three perspectives. The first perspective emerges from the dictate of structural realism that internal organization will be irrelevant to the external behavior of states.[17] In this view the ability of states to make commitments will be based on the demands of the distribution of power in the anarchic international system. There is little room, then, for different behaviors to arise systematically from variations in domestic regimes. In the words of Kenneth Waltz, "International politics consists of like units duplicating one another's activities."[18] All states will have trouble making commitments because the system is anarchic, and the incentives for keeping or breaking commitments will be no different for democratic or nondemocratic regimes. To date, the vast majority of the literature on the nature of commitments in international relations has treated regime type as irrelevant.

Those who have addressed domestic dynamics and the impact of regime type have tended to take a second perspective, which views democratic states as distinctively less capable of making strong commitments. As Machiavelli asserts, there is a long tradition of skepticism regarding the efficacy of internal democracy for external relations in general, and regarding the ability of democratic states to make external commitments in particular. Democratic foreign policy, in this view, is dependent on the vagaries and passions of public opinion. Thucydides' reference to the possibility that other states might be more willing to enter into agreements with the oligarchy of the Four Hundred than with the "inconstant commons" expresses this basic concern. Tocqueville's oft-quoted observation that "in the control of society's foreign affairs democratic governments do appear decidedly inferior to others" is bolstered by his claim that a democratic government tends "to obey its feelings rather than its calculations and to abandon a long-matured plan to satisfy a momentary passion."[19] The nineteenth-century British prime minister Lord Salisbury points to the regular changes of leadership demanded by democratic publics as a significant limitation on the ability of any given leader to commit the state to a course of action. "For this reason, if no other," he argues, "Britain could not make military alliances on the continental pattern."[20]

The third perspective sees democracies as well able to enter into long-term commitments. Some who hold this view make a positive argument about the characteristics of democracy that will enhance the strength of international commitments, while others attribute the strength of democratic commitments to an inability to change course rapidly. Machiavelli typifies the more negative view that the cumbersome machinery of democratic foreign policy making will increase democratic reliability even after objective interests have changed. Immanuel Kant exemplifies the positive view, holding that states with "republican" forms of government will be united by bonds of trade and shared norms. In Kant's regime of "asocial sociability," the democratic norms of nonviolent problem solving will be operative between as well as within democratic states.[21] It is for this third perspective that I will argue here: distinctive institutions and preferences should enhance the ability of democratic states to make credible international commitments.

THE THEORETICAL BASES FOR DEMOCRATIC DISTINCTIVENESS

I make the argument for a distinctive democratic capability to make lasting international commitments in three parts. First, I look at several arguments about the basic stability of democratic foreign policy. I then argue that there are particular and distinctive values and foreign policy preferences in democratic states that can contribute to stable international commitments. Finally, I suggest that some characteristics of the internal institutions of democratic states are critical in enhancing the credibility of external commitments.

The Stability of Foreign Policy in Liberal Democratic States

The central argument of those who question the ability of democratic states to make credible commitments in the international system focuses on the putative instability of democratic policy choices. I will therefore begin at that point in setting out the case for strong democratic commitments. The stability of policy making in liberal democratic states is, of course, an enormous and significant subject. I briefly assess foreign policy stability here in terms of the stability of public preferences, the stability of democratic leadership, and the stability of foreign policy institutions. In each case I begin with a look at the traditional view of democratic instability and then turn to a positive argument for the stability of the international commitments of democratic states.

The Stability of Public Preferences Gabriel Almond sets the tone for the view of fickle democratic foreign policy making in his classic analysis of the American public and foreign policy:

> An overtly interventionist and "responsible" United States hides a covertly isolationist longing, . . . an overtly tolerant America is at the same time barely stifling intolerance reactions, . . . an idealistic America is muttering

soto voce cynicisms, . . . a surface optimism in America conceals a dread of the future.[22]

This image has been further bolstered by the public opinion work that emphasizes the weakness of political conceptions in the general public.[23] If democratic publics are fickle, and if democratic foreign policies are especially sensitive to public preferences,[24] then we might expect democratic foreign policies to be highly unpredictable.

While the image of changeability is a strong one, it is not one we should accept too hastily. The most significant of the recent work in this area has argued that democratic states are actually quite stable in their domestic preference orderings.[25] In assessing the stability of democratic policy, it is well to remember Waltz's warning that when evaluating the abilities of democratic states in the foreign policy arena it is important to consider those abilities relative to the abilities of nondemocratic states.[26] That democratic states flip and flop between isolationism and interventionism may be true, but this does not mean that other states have stable preferences simply because they are headed by a single despot.[27] Machiavelli makes such a comparative argument in rejecting the view of the masses as fickle—a view that he ascribes to Titus Livy and "all other historians":

> I claim, then, that for the failing for which writers blame the masses, any body of men one cares to select may be blamed, and especially princes. . . . The nature of the masses, then, is no more reprehensible than is the nature of princes, for all do wrong and to the same extent when there is nothing to prevent them doing wrong. Of this there are plenty of examples besides those given, both among the Roman emperors and among other tyrants and princes; and in them we find a degree of inconstancy and changeability in behaviour such as is never found in the masses.[28]

In the more contemporary setting, we can consider the frequent criticisms of the response of democratic states to the rise of Nazi Germany.[29] If analysts wish to draw strong lessons from the vacillation of the democracies in the interwar years, then it is only fair to point to the dramatic shifts in Soviet-German relations in that period as well. The democratic states were uncertain about how to interpret their obligations to Czechoslovakia. They did, however, finally pursue their treaty obligations with Poland in quite certain terms. Meanwhile, the Germans and Soviets were experimenting with dramatic shifts in their positions toward one another. Ultimately, of course, the Nazi-Soviet Pact proved worthless. The democratic states, on the other hand, maintained the basic shape of their commitments to one another despite very high international and domestic costs.

Contrary to the pessimism of many analysts, foreign policy issues do seem to have played an important role in American electoral politics.[30] This role has not led to the extremes of either chaos or paralysis, as the critics of democratic foreign policy have predicted. The policy views of the public in aggregate have been reasonably stable and well connected to the exigencies of external events.[31] When we look at the issue of policy stability from an empirical angle, the reality seems to be that democracies can maintain stable equilibrium policies.[32]

Social Choice Problems in Democratic States A final point of concern about the stability of democratic foreign policy preferences needs to be addressed. A recent set of arguments posits that the limitation of government power by institutions of popular will may bring daunting problems of social choice mechanisms into the foreign policy arena.[33] When more than two decision makers have a voice in a decision that involves more than one dimension, there is a high probability that there will be cycling between different social choices. The social choice mechanisms of democracy should be particularly prone to this problem.[34] To the degree that cycling is a problem, democratic states will find that without robust equilibrium choices it will be difficult to sustain commitments. Today's policy could shift tomorrow if the agenda is rephrased or if coalitions shift even very slightly.

While important, the problem of cycling should not be overstated. Indeed, one of the preeminent analysts of this phenomenon, William Riker, argues that the danger of shifting majorities can actually enhance policy stability in liberal democracies. In his definition of liberalism, voting is viewed as a tool for restraining officials and limiting government rather than a tool for revealing some "true" construct of the general will. He suggests that the prospect of electoral accountability will force leaders to choose policies with sufficient appeal to avoid offending a variety of potential majorities.[35]

Even if we had doubts about Riker's defense of liberal democracy, we could return to the comparative perspective. Nondemocracies should also face cycling to the degree that there are multiple dimensions to a given foreign policy problem.[36] As was evident in the twists and turns of policy in the disintegrating Soviet Union, factionalism can undermine the consistency of policy making in a wide variety of political regimes. The more concentrated the decision making, the less likely that this will be a problem, but even a single decision maker could succumb to incoherence and cycling when making judgments about issues that involve multiple dimensions of value that are difficult to compare.[37]

The Stability of Democratic Leadership A central fact of the constraints on government power in the modern liberal democracies has been limitations on the tenure of government leaders, in the form of either formal limits on the length of public office or informal limitations imposed by the application of changeable public preferences in the process of assessing and ratifying government leaders. The fact of regular leadership change is an important element in thinking about the relationship between democracy and commitment. Henry Bienen and Nicholas Van de Walle have shown that the leaders of democratic states do tend to have shorter tenures than the leaders of nondemocratic states.[38] Those who would enter into commitments with democratic states must face the possibility that a new leader will be less inclined to honor previous commitments. The United States faces the prospect of major leadership change every four years. In parliamentary systems, the government could fall at any time. Some kinds of agreements surely will survive across governments, but it is plausible that the myriad small understandings that condition relations between states might be threatened by a new administration with its new team of top foreign policy makers and ambassadors. In the late nineteenth century, Otto von Bismarck had strong preferences for the Conservative Party in England, headed by Salisbury, over the Liberal Party, headed by William Gladstone. Bismarck's desire to avoid dealing with Gladstone spilled over into the Anglo-German relationship even when Salisbury was in power. C. J. Lowe describes this dynamic as important to several issues, including Anglo-German cooperation to guarantee the integrity of Persia:

> Although Bismarck had considerable regard for Salisbury personally there was no guarantee that Gladstone would not return to office (as in fact happened in January 1886). Though Salisbury had thought there would be "continuity of policy in this matter" Bismarck did not, and, to his mind, dealing with Gladstone was an impossibility.[39]

The simple fact that leadership change is more frequent is not, however, necessarily a negative factor for commitment. Again, a comparative perspective is important. Democratic leadership changes are *regularized* as well as being regular. The ability of democratic states to make smooth leadership transitions can help improve the stability of commitments. Indeed, Riker argues that rapid elite circulation can itself stabilize policies.[40] Nondemocratic states that do not have effective means for making leadership transitions may have fewer leadership changes, but those changes may be accompanied by greater shifts in preferences and policies. Thus, such states may present an even greater risk for other states that demand a reasonable probability of continuity for entering into a commitment. The transition from President Carter to President Reagan pales in comparison to the change from the Shah of Iran to Ayatollah Khomeini, from Mao Tsetung to Deng Xiaoping, from Joseph Stalin to Nikita Khrushchev, or from Leonid Brezhnev to Mikhail Gorbachev.

Finally, it is important to remember that the juridical nature of liberal democracy gives current leaders the power to commit future leaders. Political power in liberal democracies rests abstractly with the office and is limited by juridical principles, rather than resting with specific individuals or being unlimited. Thus, future leaders are bound by the domestic legal environment to honor the treaty commitments of their predecessors. In this way international commitments are strengthened by the ability of the liberal democracies to make internal commitments.

The Stability of Democratic Institutions While the political life of individual leaders may be relatively short and unpredictable in liberal democracies, domestic political institutions themselves are considerably more stable. As I have argued above, liberal democracy requires that majorities be able to commit to stable institutional arrangements that codify minority rights and constrain majority powers. To the degree that democratic states possess institutional stability despite regular and regularized leadership change, it should be easier for them to enter into commitments. Stable civil service bureaucracies that handle foreign affairs, for example, help ensure some degree of policy continuity and thus make democratic states more likely to maintain commitments. The measurement of the stability of institutional structures is more difficult than the simple observation of leadership turnover or political violence. The United Kingdom and the United States have had very stable political institutions. Whether there has been stability in the foreign policy institutions or personnel of countries such as France or India is an empirical question that warrants future consideration.

The Distinctive Preferences of Liberal Democracies

A demonstration that democratic foreign policy preferences do not exhibit the extremes of changeability that some have predicted is important but is not itself a sufficient answer to the basic question about the ability of democratic states to make international commitments. In responding to the traditional critique of democratic foreign policy making, we also need to look at the kinds of values democratic states bring to bear in thinking about international commitments. It is common for analysts of the liberal democratic states to focus on their political culture. In this line of argument there is something distinctive about the ideas and values that are held by democratic publics. Whether such distinctive ideas are a result of democratization or a cause of it is an important question, but it does not need to concern us here. For my purposes it is sufficient to ask whether there are distinctive preferences that would make democratic states either more or less able to make commitments than are other kinds of states.

Tocqueville made a number of assertions about the distinctive preferences that would emerge in democratic political culture. It should come as no surprise to those familiar with his generally pessimistic assessment of the foreign policy prowess of democratic states that he viewed these preferences as largely inimical to effective foreign policy commitments and sustained international involvement in general.[41] Isolationism is a characteristic frequently attributed to democratic states. To the degree that democratic states turn inward, they will pay less attention to their international obligations and may thus prove less reliable. But this logic is not definitive. There are at least two other possible connections between isolationism and international commitments. First, following Machiavelli's argument, an isolationist turn may make states take less account of the need to abandon a commitment that begins to conflict with their interests.[42] Second, the isolationist state may be inclined to make only those commitments that involve truly vital national interests and thus are more likely to be honored.[43]

The Role of Law in Liberal Democracy Tocqueville also suggests that respect for law is a critical component of democratic political culture.[44] As I suggested above, the internal practice of liberal democracy requires a basic respect for legal commitments. More recently, some have argued that these *internal* norms are also reflected in preferences over *external* policies.[45] While it is arguable whether law is an overwhelming force in democratic foreign policy making, there is some evidence for a connection between international commitments and domestic legal commitments. For example, international law has long been expressly incorporated into the domestic legal order in the Anglo-American legal tradition and has spread to most of the other major liberal democracies as well.[46] In relations between states, legalism and the reputation of a state for reliability do seem to have at least significant rhetorical appeal in democratic polities. Whether the respect for law emerges from practice, from ideology, or from some other fundamental inclination, if democratic peoples hold legal norms to be of some overarching legitimacy, then this will increase their sense of the binding nature of international commitments.[47]

Democratic Interdependence Tocqueville identifies a third source of distinctive preferences in liberal democratic states pointing to the effects of "interdependence." The combination of openness and wider political participation that characterizes democratic states may allow for more of what Robert Keohane and Joseph Nye call "multiple channels of communication" than we would expect to see in relationships between relatively more closed nondemocratic societies. Liberal economic orders that lead to increased trade and other associations between their citizens will naturally make them more interdependent. This logic follows closely Kant's argument about the "pacific union" of democratic states, based on the free flow of people and goods.[48] Tocqueville suggests interdependence as a basis for the lack of war between democratic states:

> As the spread of equality, taking place in several countries at once, simultaneously draws the inhabitants into trade and industry, not only do their tastes come to be alike, but their interests become so mixed and entangled that no nation can inflict on others ills which will not fall back on its own head. So that in the end all come to think of war as a calamity almost as severe for the conqueror as for the conquered.[49]

Tocqueville focuses on conflicts between two interdependent liberal states. But suppose that there are two interdependent liberal democracies and another state that chooses to attack one of them. We might paraphrase Tocqueville to suggest that a third-party attack on an ally might be almost as severe for the interdependent ally as it is for the attacked state. Thus, interdependence can increase the credibility of commitments between states faced with an outside threat.

More recently, an important line of research in international relations theory argues that in an interdependent world, repeated interactions increase the likelihood that states will be able to make commitments because of the iterative nature of their relationships.[50] The importance of interdependence remains a contentious issue,[51] but to the degree that we hold it to be important, it seems likely that democratic states will be particularly prone to its dynamics. Interdependence will generate groups within each state that have a vested interest in the commitment relationship between the states.

The Institutional Resources for Democratic Commitments

Liberal democracy makes it more likely that interdependent interest groups will be able to push the larger society to take their interests into consideration. The role of interest groups with vested interests in international commitments not only reflects on the distinctive preferences of liberal states but also points to the role of their internal institutions in strengthening commitments.

The Multiple Levels of Democratic Domestic Politics The notion of liberal democracy as a system of majoritarian and juridical limits on government action is suggestive of Robert Putnam's argument that two-level games are a useful analogue for many aspects of international politics.[52] In his model, state leaders must negotiate in the international arena and then return home to sell commitments in the domestic arena. Wide participation in the political process makes this a particularly acute issue for democratic leaders. If foreign policy is dependent on public approval, and if public preferences are either distinct from leader preferences or are constantly and dramatically changing, then the state will have difficulty making the credible commitments it would otherwise choose. In this regard, Putnam makes a particularly interesting distinction between voluntary and involuntary defection from cooperative schemes. As with Woodrow Wilson and the League of Nations, or Jimmy Carter and the SALT II Treaty, democratic leaders can enter into international agreements in good faith but then find themselves unable to implement the agreement because of democratic constraints on their power at home.

This, however, is not a sufficient consideration of the role of domestic constraints. Walter Lippmann worried in *Essays in the Public Philosophy* that democratic states would be frozen into undesirable policies by the inability to mobilize public support for change.[53] This is also the basis of Machiavelli's assertion that democratic states are less likely to break treaties, even when they have strong incentives to do so.[54] By this logic, the same factors that make it difficult for democratic states to enter into commitments also make it harder to get out of them. For example, the stronger role of domestic actors makes it more difficult to break or renegotiate commitments once the difficult barrier of ratification has been passed.

Domestic politics will be particularly effective at increasing the ability of democratic leaders to make commitments that accord with the interests of a strong domestic constituency. In this regard, the "liberal" component of liberal democracy is particularly important. The assurance that minority opinions will not be suppressed creates a plethora of interest groups that may have a concentrated interest in a particular international commitment. The United States can make effective commitments to Israel even without a formal alliance because it has a substantial domestic audience that will monitor and enforce that commitment in the domestic arena. Leaders with differing perspectives on the Middle East may come and go (though there are some obvious constraints on that process as well), but Israel and the Arab states can reasonably predict that there will be strong incentives for a pro-Israeli policy in the American domestic political process. The United States is a particularly dramatic set of these kinds of incentives because of its diverse ethnic makeup. But similar dynamics can certainly be at work in other states as well. One example here would be Germany's somewhat reticent acquiescence to the 1994 round of the Basel Convention banning all exports of hazardous wastes. Germany's compliance with the agreement will be closely monitored, not only by the other parties but also by Germany's own environmental activists. Thus the combination of interdependence and a strong voice for domestic actors has the potential to substantially increase the ability of democratic states to make commitments when the interests of other states are shared by significant domestic groups.

The Transparency of Democratic Domestic Politics The multiple levels of democratic policy making take on particular significance because democratic political systems are relatively transparent. Without the ability to observe what the government is doing and the freedom to express and organize alternative political views, the liberal notions of limited government and political competition would be meaningless. It is very difficult, however, to discriminate against external actors in providing transparency to internal actors. Outsiders will be able to observe with relative ease what is going on inside democratic states. Any embassy can subscribe to the major newspapers that provide day-to-day investigative services on the policy-making activities of the democratic state. Of course, foreign analysts may have just as much trouble making sense of the wealth of information that is available as do the legions of confused analysts within democratic states. Nevertheless, the difference between this and the process of discerning the policy process in closed societies with small and tight-knit leadership groups is vast. This transparency has an important implication for the ability of democratic states to make international commitments, because outsiders can observe linkages between commitments made to them and commitments made to the domestic audience. When a democratic leader makes a public commitment to a specific course of action, deviation from that course might bring domestic as well as international repercussions. When President Bush vowed to remove Iraqi troops from Kuwait, the Iraqis should have known that that vow would bear on the ensuing election as well as on the international situation.

Recent work at the interstices of economics and political science has shed new light on the relationship between social organization and the ability of states to make commitments to domestic audiences. Two particularly interesting examples of this literature are Douglas North and Barry Weingast's interpretation of the Glorious Revolution as an exercise in recasting a constitution in order to increase the ability of the state to make commitments, and François Velde and Thomas Sargent's similar interpretation of the French Revolution.[55] In these pieces the respective authors argue that democratic institutions can increase the ability of the state to make commitments to large numbers of domestic actors. This literature does not reflect directly on the ability of the state to make commitments in the international arena, where the number of actors is small and repeated interaction already is likely. My argument here is that in the international arena, the ability to link external commitments transparently with internal commitments will allow democratic states to draw on domestic audiences to aid their international credibility.

Thomas Schelling points to the importance of political costs for enhancing the credibility of international commitments.[56] He focuses on incurring political costs within the international system itself. But similar benefits can be derived from incurring these costs at home if they can be adequately observed from outside. The linkage between external commitments and internal political costs is represented formally in James Fearon's work on the role of audience costs in international interactions.[57] When democratic leaders send signals in the international arena that bear domestic costs at home, those signals will have more credibility than would similar signals that bore no significant domestic costs. All states face some domestic costs for their international actions, but democratic states may be distinctive in the degree of domestic accountability. The critical aspects of democracies in this regard are (1) that there are a number of institutions that can be easily used for linking internal and external commitments—such as elections—and (2) that internal commitments and domestic costs can be more easily observed from the outside because of the nature of information institutions within democratic states.

Domestic costs can enhance commitments in two distinct ways. First, taking actions that bear immediate domestic costs can send a signal about the genuine importance of an issue to an actor.[58] Second, some actions can create domestic costs for a failure to maintain a commitment in the future. A trade agreement, for example, may lead to the development of a domestic constituency with a vested financial interest in maintaining the trade relationship. To renege on such an agreement would incur domestic costs proportional to the strength of that constituency. More generally, statements and actions may create domestic expectations that will lead to later audience costs or electoral punishment if a leader fails to carry out an international commitment.

Making credible international commitments is difficult at best for all states. I have argued here that, contrary to the traditional image of unreliability, democratic states should be relatively effective at making international commitments. The task now is to turn to some empirical attempts to assess the overall ability of democratic states to make commitments and to abide by them.

Empirical Soundings: Democratic Alliance Behavior

Alliances are the most salient form of commitment behavior in the current international system. States join formal alliances in order to indicate both to their alliance partners and to other states that there is a level of commitment that is greater than the level of commitment that would be expected based simply on observed international interests. My research focus here is on the duration of alliance commitments. If democratic states are unreliable because of shifting majority preferences, we would expect to see this reflected in the length of time that they are able to maintain alliances.

Alliance duration is not a perfect indicator of the ability of democratic states to make effective international commitments. Conceptually, there are many reasons why alliance relationships might endure or be cut short. But in the aggregate, if those other reasons are independent of the democratic status of a state, we should still be able to pick up some meaningful variation in looking at alliance duration. Similarly, we might prefer to measure more directly the effectiveness of alliance commitments under stress. When states are attacked, do their allies back them up? Do allies help out in wars? We know from other studies that allies rarely join in when wars break out.[59] But this indicator is almost surely biased by the deterrence effect of allies who are expected to be reliable. Unreliable alliances are more likely to be challenged than reliable alliances. Thus, while future work could well benefit from attempts to carefully measure, code, and analyze these more direct concepts, for this analysis I have started with the more straightforward consideration of alliance durability as an appropriate first cut at this issue.

The analysis of alliance commitments is also appropriate to the degree that they are an indicator of international community. Drawing on Kant's essay "On Perpetual Peace," Michael Doyle's explanation for the liberal peace turns on a natural community of liberal states:

> Since morally autonomous citizens hold rights to liberty, the states that democratically represent them have the right to exercise political independence. Mutual respect for these rights then becomes the touchstone of international liberal theory. When states respect each other's rights, individuals are free to establish private international ties without state inter-

ference. Profitable exchanges between merchants and educational exchanges among scholars then create a web of mutual advantages and commitments that bolsters sentiments of public respect. These conventions of mutual respect have formed a cooperative foundation for relations among liberal democracies of a remarkably effective kind.[60]

Ultimately, it would also be useful to examine other indicators of "the web of commitments" between liberal states. Alliance behavior is a good starting point, since it is a manifestation of the commitments between states for which some data are readily available.[61] Alliances have been used as indicators of a number of important international phenomena, including the basic interests of states, their attitudes toward risk, and the effectiveness of international norms.[62] Military alliances are also a good starting point for this line of research in that this is an area in which we would expect to find the least distinctiveness to democratic behavior. As outlined in the liberal logic, it is in the economic sphere that we would more expect to see the effects of interdependence.[63] It would be a strong result, then, to find evidence of a distinctive character to democratic commitments in this area.

There has been some empirical work on the question of democratic alliance behavior. Ole Holsti, Terrence Hopmann, and John Sullivan included a polity variable in their 1973 analysis of alliance politics.[64] Their conclusions about democratic alliance behavior are mixed. In their survey of all alliances between 1815 and 1939, they find that ideological similarity disposes states to ally with each other and to effect some increase in the length of alliances,[65] though their bottom line is that after alliances are formed, the impact of ideological differences is minimal.[66] They also find some areas of democratic distinctiveness in their case study work. For example, looking at the differences between Chinese and French defection from their respective alliance systems in the 1950s, they argue that in pluralistic polities intra-alliance disputes tend to stay confined to a narrow range of issues, while in nonpluralistic polities intra-alliance disputes tend to spill over into all issue areas.[67] In an argument that echoes the Kantian hypothesis, they posit that the source for this effect is the complex interdependence that creates a large number of nongovernmental ties between pluralistic states.

Randolph Siverson and Juliann Emmons, in an analysis that focuses specifically on democratic states, confirm with more rigorous statistics the observation of Holsti, Hopmann, and Sullivan that ideologically similar states are more likely to form high-commitment alliances.[68] They show that at the dyadic level there is a strong tendency for democratic states to form alliances with each other at a greater rate than would be expected from the null model assumption that alliance formation should be independent of ideological orientation.

My goal here is to expand on these existing results with an attempt to assess the relative durability of democratic and nondemocratic alliances. The statistical analysis of Holsti, Hopmann, and Sullivan is largely limited to contingency table analysis. I focus on the case of democratic states to confirm the rather tentative relationship they describe for the relationship between alliance duration and ideological affinity. By using more sophisticated techniques for analyzing duration data, I am able to provide a more nuanced assessment of the effect of shared democratic norms on alliance duration.

The Data: Measuring Democracy and Measuring Alliances

Two kinds of data are required for this analysis: data about polities and data about alliances. Both of these present difficulties and require certain judgment calls. The danger in this kind of endeavor is that the specific research objectives can unduly influence the making of these judgments. For this reason, and not incidentally as a matter of efficiency, I have relied on the data collection efforts of others. I have used Michael Doyle's coding of liberal regimes[69] and the coding of alliances from the Correlates of War Project.[70] In so doing, of course, I have inherited the controversies that surround both of these efforts.

For my purposes, the democracy measure is reasonably straightforward. It is not necessary to resolve the significant debates about the meaning of these terms in political philosophy and comparative politics in order to advance propositions about the implications of liberal democracy for foreign policy and international relations. Even the problematic distinction between "liberal" and "democratic" retreats in importance in the face of the empirical reality that the two phenomena have been highly coincident in modern history. There is a relatively clear set of states that have been regularly labeled "democratic" or "liberal." While one might disagree about some cases on the edges, the results I report here are relatively insensitive to small definitional changes. Still, it should be acknowledged that by adopting a binary measure of democracy that aggregates across a number of important features of democracy, we lose the ability to assess the relative importance of different aspects of democratic governance. I will not be able to evaluate here the degree to which differences in the ability to enter into durable alliances result from regular elections, constitutionalism, or the distinctive preferences of democratic citizens. Even more serious is the possibility that the causality may flow from other factors that this class of states largely have in common. This becomes a problem to the degree that these factors, though historically correlated with democracy, are not an essential part of it. Of course, all analytic categories are constructs of lesser and correlated concepts. Democracy, too, could be broken down into its constituent parts and correlates. But such a move would come at the expense of the ability to do any kind of aggregate analysis. In the end, then, the analysis that follows is a description of the behavior of a specific group of states, and it remains to be shown that it is democracy, and not something else, that is the determinative characteristic of this group.

The conceptual problems surrounding the measurement of alliances are more immediately serious. In thinking about these problems it is important to start by emphasizing that the things that we can easily observe about alliances are not necessarily the phenomena in which we are most interested.[71] Theoretically, we are most interested in the *quality* of international interactions. Is some set of countries more or less amicable in its relations? Would its component states defend one another if attacked?[72] Will the states refrain from action that might be injurious to an alliance partner? Consider, for example, the fact that there is no formal defense pact between the United States and Israel. Israel, the United States, and most other interested states know that there is a substantial defense commitment between the United States and Israel (though the question of its exact extent may be a matter of considerable consequence and concern for Israel and its enemies). In using alliances as an indicator of defense relationships we will be limited to the degree either that good relationships are not formalized or that bad relationships are. The case of Israel and the United States is fairly clear-cut, but states will often have difficulty assessing the quality of relationships. Indeed, alliances can be seen as a mechanism for trying to deal with these uncertainties in the international environment. Nonetheless, there are some particu-

lar kinds of uncertainties that are probably more severe for the analyst trying to consider a large number of alliances than for the state
trying to assess the quality of a given relationship at a given point in
time.

One particularly vexing conceptual issue is whether alliance behavior should be analyzed with the alliance as the unit of measurement
or with the dyad as the unit. The Correlates of War data are organized
by dyads. Holsti, Hopmann, and Sullivan, as well as Bruce Russett,
have worked with alliances as the unit of observation.[73] Siverson and
Emmons base their study on dyadic relationships.[74] There are conceptual arguments in both directions. A focus on the formal treaties
would lead us to concentrate on the alliance as the observation: how
long treaties are in force would be the most relevant question. If, however, we are interested conceptually in the underlying relations
between individual countries, we will need to turn to the analysis of
dyads. A focus on the alliance as the unit of observation also runs into
problems when multiple treaties reflect the same relationship. For
example, while a single treaty unites the NATO countries, the Warsaw
Pact countries cemented their relationship with a large number of
bilateral treaties. The use of treaties as the unit of observation would
bias the data toward this kind of multilateral relationship. The use of
dyads as the unit of observation would give extra weight to multilateral treaties. Both biases present serious problems. In both cases multilateral alliances lead to problems in assessing the relationship
between individual states when formal relationships end because of a
falling-out between other alliance members. Future work might benefit from trying to assess more subjectively the true extent of multilateral relationships. In this analysis, my approach is to run the statistical tests with both kinds of data. The fact that the findings are reasonably robust with both kinds of data increases our confidence in
the results.

Alliance dyads are coded from the Singer-Small set, and then a
democracy score is added from Doyle's listing. Again, the central
drawback to this coding scheme is that some multilateral alliance
relationships get very high weight because of the large number of
individual countries involved. The worst offender in this regard is the
Organization of African Unity, which is coded as an entente and
counts for 362 of the 1,321 dyad observations.

Translating the Singer-Small data to the alliance level, rather than to the dyadic level, is more complex than it might appear at first blush.[75] The decisions I have made in this regard are not always transparent, and thus they bear some discussion. Should we count the West European Union as a different treaty than NATO? Is the Rio Pact with Cuba a different alliance than the Rio Pact without Cuba? I have used two different kinds of decision rules, and the results seem reasonably insensitive to these coding variations. First, I tried to identify the individual treaties and gave them their longest life, regardless of new members coming and going (Reduced Model I). Second, I identified starting and ending dates in the dyadic data set and collapsed the data around these values (Reduced Model II). The first method tends to overcount multilateral alliances that use bilateral treaties, such as the Warsaw Pact. The second method overcounts multilateral alliances that have more changes over time, such as NATO or the Arab League.

Multilateral treaties are also problematic for coding the democracy variable when they include states with different political systems. My focus is on relationships between democratic states, so I have chosen in both of these reduced data sets to decompose treaties that have mixed democratic and nondemocratic members. Thus, for example, I code NATO as three observations: a relationship between democracies, a relationship between democracies and nondemocracies, and a relationship between nondemocracies. Interestingly, this affected only six alliances, including three nineteenth-century alliances involving Britain, France, or Italy in their democratic periods, NATO, the Rio Pact, and the Arab League (which included Lebanon when it was coded as liberal).

International Alliance Behavior and Democratic States

Figure 1.1 tracks the average number of alliance relationships for democratic and nondemocratic states for each decade between 1816 and 1965. Several salient points are noteworthy in this plot. Before 1870 there are very few democratic states, and those that there are have decidedly fewer alliance relationships of any kind than do the nondemocratic states. After 1870, the curves for the democratic and nondemocratic states track each other very closely. From 1870 until 1920 alliance relationships are at a fairly low level for both democratic and nondemocratic states. Finally, in 1920 a strong trend began toward an increasing number of alliance relationships. One small but noteworthy point that I do not show on this

FIGURE 1.1

Average Alliance Density per Decade

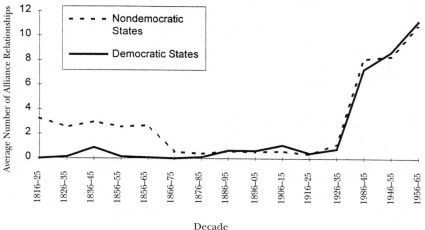

Sources: See sources for table 1.2.

chart is that from 1930 on, the democratic states have tended to be in more defense pact relationships—the highest form of defense commitment in the Correlates of War coding—than the nondemocratic states have.[76]

Figure 1.1 is, of course, a simple presentation of the relationship between alliances and democracy with no controls for confounding factors. On its face, this pattern would give the most support to the expectation that domestic regime type should not make much difference in international behavior in general and in the ability to make commitments in particular.[77] These results do not support the idea that democratic states should be more alliance-prone, but neither do they support the more often expressed concern that democratic states cannot make credible commitments. Democratic states find just as many alliance partners as nondemocratic states do. More recently they have been able to find more partners willing to enter into high-level defense pacts. Either Salisbury was wrong or something has changed since he suggested that democratic states cannot keep their promises and thus will have trouble entering into alliances. At a minimum, democratic states are finding other states that are at least willing to sign the papers.

The broad review of international alliance behavior represented in figure 1.1 does not suggest significant differences between democratic and nondemocratic states in terms of their propensity to form alliance relationships.[78] But the question in which we are most interested is not simply how many alliance relationships democratic states enter but what level of commitment those relationships represent. We can move one analytic step closer to this more fundamental issue by considering the length of time that democratic and nondemocratic alliances tend to last.

The Duration of Alliances

Statistical analysis of duration data is made treacherous by several factors. Briefly, the two primary problems are nonlinear relationships and the censoring of data.[79] Duration data are said to be right censored when some of the events are still ongoing at the end of the observation period. For example, a seemingly robust alliance that starts just two years before the end of the observation period should not be coded as having ended after just two years. If we did not take censoring into account, we would bias our analysis for all the cases of alliances that were still in effect at the end of the period of observation. This bias is nontrivial because it would tend to be the longest-lasting alliances that would be censored. This is of particular importance in the study of alliances because a large number of alliances are still ongoing.

The most common method for examining survival data, given these problems, is the use of Kaplan-Meier or product-limit estimates of the survival function. This is a nonparametric technique for estimating, in our case, the probability that an alliance will survive a given number of years. The Kaplan-Meier estimate of the probability that an alliance will last k years is the product of the estimate of the probability that the alliance will last $k-1$ years and the observed survival rate in year k. Thus, censored observations will provide information as to the number of alliances that last $k-1$ years, while the uncensored observations will provide the observed survival rate in any given year.[80] Figure 1.2 displays the Kaplan-Meier estimates of survival times for the first reduced data set based on treaties. The three lines show the estimated survival function for democratic alliances, nondemocratic alliances, and mixed alliances. The distinctiveness of democratic alliances is clearly visible in this figure. Reading across the chart at the 50 percent survival mark, we can see that the median survival time for both mixed and nondemocratic alliances is about seven

FIGURE 1.2
Alliance Survival Functions (Kaplan-Meier Estimates)
Alliances by Treaty (Reduced Set 1)

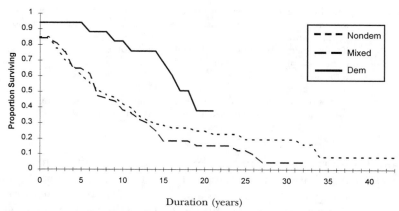

Sources: See sources for table 1.2.

years, while democratic alliances have a median survival time of about seventeen years.[81]

The central limitation of the Kaplan-Meier estimates is that they are nonparametric. While they provide an effective visual indicator of survival patterns, it is difficult to control for important covariates and to specify more exactly the independent effect of democracy on alliance duration. A next step, then, is to turn to a parametric survival model. The model I use here to assess the effects of democracy on alliance duration is an accelerated failure time model.[82] In this procedure the following model is estimated:

$$\text{Duration} = e^{x'B} T_0^{\sigma}$$

Where T_0 is a time value from a baseline Weibull distribution with σ as a scale term.[83] X is a vector of covariates and B is a vector of coefficients, so that $\exp(x'B)$ is a proportional scale on the baseline distribution. The nature of the model is more easily seen with the natural log transformation of each side:

$$\ln(\text{Duration}) = x'B + T_0^{\sigma}$$

TABLE 1.1

Specification of Independent Variables

Variable	Value
Dem2	1 if the observation is a relationship between two democracies and 0 otherwise.
Dem1	1 if the observation is a relationship between a democracy and a nondemocracy and 0 otherwise.
Major2	1 if there are two major powers in the dyad and 0 otherwise.
Major1	1 if there is only 1 major power in the dyad and 0 otherwise.
Type1	1 if the alliance is a defense pact and 0 otherwise.
Type 2	1 if the alliance is a neutrality pact and 0 otherwise.
Number	Number of states in the alliance in the first reduced dataset model and the number of dyads in the alliance in the second reduced dataset model.
Year	Year in which the alliance started.

In this transformation it can be seen that a specific coefficient B_k will represent the change in the natural log of the duration for a given change in a covariate x_k. There is also a more straightforward interpretation of the coefficients in this model since the coefficient B_k will approximate the percentage change in duration for a unit change in x_k.

We deal with censoring in these estimations by calculating the maximum likelihood estimators of the parameters with the probability density function for the uncensored durations and the survivor function for the censored durations. In other words, the estimating procedure maximizes the likelihood for the parameter estimates using the known survival times of the uncensored durations and the predicted survival times based on the predicated underlying distribution for the censored observations.[84]

The Covariates The dependent variable in this model is the duration of the alliance. The independent variables are the year of entry, the type of alliance, the major power status of the states, the number of states in the alliance, and whether the alliance members are democratic. Discrete variables are transformed into dummy variables for each of their values. In order for the model to be full rank, coefficients can only be provided for *n-1* of *n* discrete levels. The specification and definitions of the independent variables are shown in table 1.1.

There are no variables *DEM0, MAJOR0,* or *TYPE3* because of the rank requirement. If both *DEM2* and *DEM1* are equal to zero, then

TABLE 1.2

Alliance Dyads

	All Alliances	Defense Pacts Only
Uncensored Observations	285	188
Censored Observations	999	377
Scale Parameter (Ω)	0.660	0.70
Intercept	-26.65***	-25.06***
Dem1	-0.09	0.43**
Dem2	0.47**	1.3**
Type1	.86***	NA
Type2	-0.29*	NA
Major1	-0.27**	0.99***
Major2	-0.47**	0.73***
Year	.015***	0.014***

Sources: Regimes data from Doyle, ``Kant, Liberal Legacies, and Foreign Affairs,'' 1983a. Alliance data from Singer and Small, *Annual Alliance Membership Data*, 1966. Major power status from Singer and Small, *Wages of War*, 1984. Treaties data from Grenville and Wasserstein, *The Major International Treaties*, 1987; Degenhardt, *Treaties and Alliances of the World*, 1986; Grenville, *The Major International Treaties*, 1974; Hurst, *Key Treaties for the Great Powers*, 1972.

Notes: *** $p<0.0001$

** $p<0.01$

* $p<0.05$

the equation is being estimated for the case of no democracies. When *MAJOR2* and *MAJOR1* are both zero, then the model is estimated for the case of no major powers. The expected duration for an entente will be estimated when both *TYPE1* and *TYPE2* are zero.

Tables 1.2, 1.3, and 1.4 show the results of fitting the model to six different subsets of the data. Table 1.2 examines dyads. Table 1.3 examines the data set with the dyadic observations collapsed around treaties as the unit of observation. Table 1.4 collapses the data set around alliance starting and ending dates, as described above. For each of the tables, the analysis is run with all three kinds of alliance relationships and with just defense pacts. Seven extreme cases, in which the alliance lasted longer than thirty years, have been removed from the data set.[85]

As should be apparent from each table, this model does show a significant effect for the duration of alliances between liberal democracies. These effects are consistent in direction across all of the aggregations of the data and are statistically significant for the dual democracy coefficient in all of the models that use all alliances and for one of the dual democracy coefficients in the defense pact models. The

TABLE 1.3

Reduced Model I
Alliances by Treaty and Democratic Status

	All Alliances	Defense Pacts Only
Uncensored Observations	134	70
Censored Observations	43	28
Scale Parameter (Ω)	0.86	0.94
Intercept	-19.93***	-25.87***
Dem1	-0.22	0.01
Dem2	0.74*	0.51
Type1	0.30	NA
Type2	-0.11	NA
Major1	0.30	0.71**
Major2	0.03	0.07
Number of States	0.09*	0.09
Year	0.011***	0.015***

Sources: See sources for table 1.2.

Notes: *** $p<0.0001$
** $p<0.01$
* $p<0.05$

TABLE 1.4

Reduced Model II
Alliances by Date and Democratic Status

	All Alliances	Defense Pacts Only
Uncensored Observations	127	70
Censored Observations	57	28
Scale Parameter (Ω)	0.71	0.92
Intercept	-11.64**	-25.87***
Dem1	0.01	0.01
Dem2	0.64**	0.51
Type1	0.23	NA
Type2	0.02	NA
Major1	0.02	0.71
Major2	-0.15	0.07
Number of States	0.12**	0.09
Year	0.007**	0.015***

Sources: See sources for table 1.2.

Notes: *** $p<0.0001$
** $p<0.01$
* $p<0.05$

TABLE 1.5

Predicted Alliance Durations
(Expected duration in years of a defense pact starting in 1925 between two major powers)

	Democratic Alliances	Mixed Alliances	Nondemocratic Alliances
All Alliances			
Dyads	17.1	9.8	10.7
Model I	8.8	3.4	4.2
Model II	12.6	6.7	6.6
Defense Pacts			
Dyads	39.0	16.3	10.6
Model I	30.6	18.5	18.4
Model II	30.8	18.7	18.5

Sources: See sources for table 1.2.

magnitude of the democracy effect varies from 0.47 to 1.3, though all but one of the coefficients fall between 0.47 and 0.74. The impact of these coefficients can be seen more concretely in the examples given in table 1.5, in which I have presented the expected durations of a defense pact between two major powers that starts in 1925.[86] With all of the other independent variables held constant, the effect of the democracy variables is clearly visible in each row of the table. Most of the models predict fairly similar results.

As in the Siverson and Emmons work and in the work on democracies and wars, it is again the dyadic effects of democracy that are the most notable. We can make a distinction between the case of two democracies and that of either one or no democracies. But there is no statistically significant separation between the cases of one democracy and no democracies. Democracies are no different from nondemocracies when it comes to relationships with nondemocracies. It is only alliances between democracies that appear to be more durable. If alliance duration is an indicator of the ability to make commitments, then democracy by itself does not appear either to increase or to decrease the ability of a state to make commitments to nondemocracies.

That democracies would be no worse at making commitments

than nondemocracies are is itself interesting in light of the frequent concerns about the instability of democratic decision making. The dyadic finding, however, suggests that the most important explanations do not lie within the stability of democratic institutions themselves. Rather, the most promising source of explanation for these findings is likely to be either in the distinctive preferences that democratic states may hold for maintaining their relationships with each other or in the institutional elements that develop in the relationships between democratic states.

Technical Limitations of the Analysis As so often, there are a number of limitations in the data that should temper our confidence in the results I have reported here. There is some multicollinearity between the covariates. Democratic dyads tend more often to involve major powers and are more often related by defense pacts. More important, until very recently, the number of democracies in the world has been small. Though there are 1,322 dyads, only 121 of them are coded as involving two democracies. In the reduced set, of the 185 alliances, there are only 17 that are coded as democratic. Equally problematic for the analysis is the fact that many of these democratic alliances are of more recent vintage. Most of them are still in effect and are thus censored (only 15 of the 121 democratic dyads and 8 of the 17 democratic alliances are uncensored). Of course, it is not theoretically trivial in a study of alliance durability that most democratic relationships are still in effect. The coefficients for the democracy variables are reasonably consistent between a pre-1945 and a post-1945 partition of the data, though they tend to get both smaller and less statistically significant.[87]

The other major factor that tempers these results is the problem of unobserved heterogeneity. There are, no doubt, all manner of difficult-to-measure factors that may be driving these results. We may be comfortable with leaving some of them under the umbrella label of "liberal democratic states." If, for example, alliance durability is a function of intense trading relationships, and if we believe that democracy and trading relationships tend to go together, then it is interesting, but not problematic, for the model to leave out trade. Trade, in this situation, would just be one of the component characteristics of democratic states that drive the relationships between them. If, however, we believe that levels of trade are independent of democratic status, then this is a more serious omission.

Conclusions

The central characteristic of liberal democracies is juridically limited majority rule. For foreign policy decision making, this has meant that decision makers are limited in their ability to commit the state both because of the limits in their power at any given time—for example, the requirement that the president of the United States submit treaties to the Senate for ratification—and because of the possibility that public preferences will change. Drawing on these characteristics, the most traditional argument about the relationship between democratic states and commitment in the international system focuses on the "inconstant commons" and the expectation that democratic governance will be particularly ill-suited to long-lasting commitments. The relationship between polity type and the ability to make commitments is more complex than this traditional argument would allow. As Riker has argued, there is a theoretical basis for policy stability in liberal democratic regimes, and this position has been supported in several studies of foreign policy stability. Moreover, at the theoretical level the creation of links between external commitments and internal commitments and the development of shared preferences through interdependence should also enhance the ability of liberal democracies to forge effective international commitments.

Ultimately, these factors will have to be disentangled and their individual importance assessed empirically to discern the net effect of the factors that push for and against democratic commitments. I have offered here a start on that empirical task with a broad analysis of the duration of democratic alliances. Consistent with the conjectures of Doyle and Kant, there are distinctive elements in the alliance behavior of democratic states. As Siverson and Emmons have shown, democracies tend to ally with other democracies. I have shown here that there is also a tendency for these alliances to last longer than either the relationships between nondemocracies or the relationships that mix democracies and nondemocracies. Democratic alliances do appear to be distinctively durable when measured against the background of the constantly shifting international environment. Considerably more work will be required before we will want to endorse a robust version of the "pacific union" of democratic states. We can be more emphatic in the assertion that contrary to the pessimistic views of the likes of Tocqueville or Salisbury, democratic states have not demonstrated an inability to make lasting commitments.

Notes

I have benefited greatly in this project from the comments of the other participants in the Social Science Research Council Liberalization and Foreign Policy project and from the comments of three anonymous reviewers. John Ferejohn, Jeffry Frieden, Joanne Gowa, Miles Kahler, Lisa Martin, and Barry Weingast have been particularly helpful. I am indebted to Kenneth Schultz and Marissa Myers for their able research assistance. Funding was generously provided by the Center for International Security and Arms Control and by the Institute for International Studies, both at Stanford University. Doug Rivers was of considerable help in thinking about the statistical dimensions of this paper. For much of the data used in this project I am grateful to the Correlates of War Project and the Inter-university Consortium for Political and Social Research (ICPSR).

This chapter was published previously as "Democratic States and Commitment in International Relations," *International Organization* 50 (1) (Winter 1996):109–139. © 1996 by the IO Foundation and the Massachusetts Institute of Technology.

1. Thucydides, *The Peloponnesian War*, book VIII, ch. 25, para. 70, p. 491.

2. Machiavelli, *The Discourses*, book I, discourse 59, p. 259.

3. Ibid., book I, discourse 58, p. 252.

4. See Huntington, *The Third Wave*.

5. Keohane, *After Hegemony*.

6. Schelling, *The Strategy of Conflict; Arms and Influence*.

7. Grieco, "Anarchy and the Limits of Cooperation."

8. Babst, "A Force for Peace"; Small and Singer, "The War Proneness of Democratic Regimes"; Doyle, "Kant, Liberal Legacies, and Foreign Affairs," parts 1 and 2; Chan, "Mirror, Mirror on the Wall . . ."; Weede, "Democracy and War Involvement"; Doyle, "Liberalism and World Politics"; Maoz and Abdolali, "Regime Types and International Conflict"; Russett, *Grasping the Democratic Peace*.

9. The way in which international commitments bind states to future actions is a matter of considerable interest but is beyond the scope of this analysis. Snyder and Diesing (*Conflict Among Nations*) argue that explicit commitments engage important values such as honor, resolve, and reputation. Fearon ("Domestic Political Audiences and the Escalation of International Disputes") makes a similar argument pointing to the role of "audience costs" in the calculus of state actions.

10. See Schelling, *Arms and Influence*, ch. 3.

11. This theme underlies the discussion of Kegley and Raymond (*When Trust Breaks Down*) in which they examine the evolution of alliance norms over time.

12. Manning, *Liberalism*, p. 15; Bobbio, *Liberalism and Democracy*, p. 1. One might also stress liberalism's focus on the standing of individuals, but for the purposes of this analysis the notion of legal limits on government power is sufficient.

13. Bobbio, *Liberalism and Democracy*, p. 2.

14. Ibid., p. 31. The strong connection between liberalism and democracy also can be seen clearly in Rawls's *Political Liberalism*. On the other hand, the recent trend toward democratization has brought about some weakening of the connection between liberalism and democracy. See Anderson, "Democratization and Foreign Policy in the Arab World," ch. 4 in this volume. Karl and Schmitter capture a part of this phenomenon in their distinction between "consolidated" and "unconsolidated" democracy; see "Democratization Around the Globe," pp. 54–55.

DEMOCRATIC STATES AND COMMITMENT   59

15. This definition accords well with the notion of democracy that has been used implicitly by a number of authors who have recently written in this area. See, for example, Bueno de Mesquita and Lalman, *War and Reason.*

16. Mill and Tocqueville are exemplars of the importance of this tension in the rise of nineteenth-century liberalism. For some recent treatments of this vexing issue, see Hochschild, *What's Fair*, and Riker, *Liberalism Against Populism.*

17. On some of the limitations of the realist approach in this area, see Barnett and Levy, "Domestic Sources of Alliances."

18. Waltz, *Theory of International Politics*, p. 97. Interestingly, in the 1960s Waltz wrote a book on the impact of democratic politics on foreign policy (*Foreign Policy and Democratic Politics*). An important conclusion in that book, however, is that democracies were probably no worse than other states in their foreign policy endeavors. This conclusion stands against the prevailing wisdom of that time that democracy could be a serious barrier to effective and timely foreign policy decision making.

19. Tocqueville, *Democracy in America*, vol. I, part II, ch. 5, sec. 13, pp. 228–229.

20. Lowe, *The Reluctant Imperialists*, p. 10.

21. Kant, "Perpetual Peace." A more recent proponent of this position is Dixon, "Democracy and the Management of International Conflict." See also Maoz and Russett, "Normative and Structural Causes of Democratic Peace."

22. Almond, *The American People and Foreign Policy*, p. 67.

23. Converse, "The Nature of Belief Systems in Mass Publics."

24. See Monroe, "Consistency Between Public Preferences and National Policy Decisions," and Page and Shapiro, "Effects of Public Opinion on Policy."

25. Shapiro and Page, "Foreign Policy and the Rational Public"; Russett, *Controlling the Sword*, pp. 92–95.

26. Waltz, *Foreign Policy and Democratic Politics*, p. 17.

27. Hartz, *The Liberal Tradition in America*; Klingberg, "The Historical Alternation of Moods in American Foreign Policy."

28. Machiavelli, *The Discourses*, book I, discourse 58, p. 254.

29. See, for example, Taylor, *The Origins of the Second World War*, p. xi.

30. Aldrich, Sullivan, and Borgida, "Foreign Affairs and Issue Voting."

31. Page and Shapiro, *The Rational Public*; Holsti, "Public Opinion and Foreign Policy"; Nincic, *Democracy and Foreign Policy.*

32. Russett, *Controlling the Sword*; Page and Shapiro, *The Rational Public.*

33. For a useful introduction to this issue, see McLean, *Public Choice.* For an application to the role of public opinion in foreign policy making, see Gaubatz, "Intervention and Intransitivity."

34. Riker, *Liberalism Against Populism*; Jervis, "Rational Deterrence," p. 205.

35. Riker, *Liberalism Against Populism.*

36. Waltz, *Foreign Policy and Democratic Politics*, p. 309.

37. Jervis, "Rational Deterrence," p. 206.

38. Bienen and Van de Walle, *Of Time and Power.*

39. Lowe, *The Reluctant Imperialists*, p. 90.

40. Riker, *Liberalism Against Populism.*

41. Tocqueville, *Democracy in America*, vol. I, part II, ch. 5, sec. 13, p. 223.

42. Machiavelli, *The Discourses*, book I, discourse 59, p. 259.

43. I am indebted to an anonymous reviewer for this second point.

44. Tocqueville, *Democracy in America*, vol. I, part II, ch. 6, sec. 4, p. 240.

45. Doyle, "Kant, Liberal Legacies, and Foreign Affairs," p. 230. See also Dixon, "Democracy and the Peaceful Settlement of International Conflict," and Maoz and Russett, "Normative and Structural Causes of Democratic Peace."

46. von Glahn, *Law Among Nations*, ch. 3.

47. Burley ("International Law and International Relations Theory") argues that liberal states operate within a "zone of law" in which transnational legal arrangements strengthen ties between the liberal democratic states. Dixon ("Democracy and the Management of International Conflict") argues that domestic dispute resolution procedures within democracies carry over to their international relations.

48. Kant, "Idea for a Universal History," p. 50. For a recent review of the notion of a cosmopolitan international economic order, see Neff, *Friends But No Allies*.

49. Tocqueville, *Democracy in America*, vol. II, part III, ch. 26, p. 660.

50. Keohane and Nye, *Power and Interdependence*; Axelrod, *The Evolution of Cooperation*. These two works suggest two mechanisms for this dynamic. In Axelrod, the potential for repeated interactions increases the shadow of the future that makes cooperative behavior more likely. For Keohane and Nye, the growth of intertwined interests increases the mutual vulnerability and sensitivity of state policies.

51. Grieco, "Anarchy and the Limits of Cooperation."

52. Putnam, "Diplomacy and Domestic Politics."

53. Lippmann, *Essays in the Public Philosophy*, pp. 18–19.

54. Machiavelli, *The Discourses*, book I, discourse 59, p. 259.

55. North and Weingast, "Constitutions and Commitment"; Velde and Sargent, "The Macro-economic Causes and Consequences of the French Revolution."

56. Schelling, *Arms and Influence*, p. 49.

57. Fearon, "Domestic Political Audiences and the Escalation of International Disputes."

58. The foundational work in this area is Spence, *Market Signaling*.

59. Sabrosky estimates that states joined a war on the side of an ally in only 27 percent of the cases in which there was an opportunity to do so. If, however, we include the act of abstaining or remaining neutral, which is all that many alliances call for, then alliances were "honored" in 88 percent of the cases (Sabrosky, "Interstate Alliances," p. 177).

60. Doyle, "Kant, Liberal Legacies, and Foreign Affairs," p. 213.

61. The use of alliances as an indicator of community is, of course, a nontrivial assumption. Bueno de Mesquita (*The War Trap*) has argued, for example, that allies are more likely to fight than non-allies. But in Bueno de Mesquita's formulation this is because of the *closeness* rather than the *conflict* of their interests. Furthermore, this dynamic has not proved to be operative for democratic alliance dyads. See Siverson and Emmons, "Birds of a Feather."

62. See, for example, Bueno de Mesquita, *The War Trap*; Lalman, "Conflict Resolution and Peace"; Kegley and Raymond, *When Trust Breaks Down*.

63. Keohane and Nye, *Power and Interdependence*.

64. Holsti, Hopmann, and Sullivan, *Unity and Disintegration in International Alliances*.

65. Ibid., pp. 62–68.

66. Ibid., pp. 61–64.

67. Ibid., pp. 160–161.

68. By "high-commitment alliance" Siverson and Emmons mean defense pacts in

the Correlates of War coding, as opposed to the lower commitment level of ententes and neutrality pacts; see Siverson and Emmons, "Birds of a Feather."

69. Doyle, "Kant, Liberal Legacies, and Foreign Affairs."

70. Singer and Small, *Annual Alliance Membership Data.*

71. The formal definition of alliances used by Singer and Small, while more tractable for empirical work with a large number of observations, is particularly limited in this way. See Walt, *The Origin of Alliances.*

72. Sabrosky ("Interstate Alliances") notes that in roughly two-thirds of the cases states fail to act when there is an opportunity to join an alliance partner in a military conflict. My initial review of these data comparing democracies and nondemocracies suggests that the two kinds of states are roughly similar on this dimension. These data are, however, very sensitive to case selection. If we include the Korean War (in which a number of democracies made at least token contributions to the U.S. effort), we find democracies to be much more likely to participate in the disputes of their democratic allies. If we leave Korea out, the two classes of regimes are roughly similar, with a slight advantage to the democracies. One of Sabrosky's measures involves the propensity of allies to attack each other. Here, following the literature on the lack of wars between democratic states, there is a significant advantage for the democracies.

73. Holsti, Hopmann, and Sullivan, *Unity and Disintegration in International Alliances;* Russett, "An Empirical Typology of International Military Alliances."

74. Siverson and Emmons, "Birds of a Feather."

75. Two errors in the distributed Correlates of War alliance data have been corrected. Yugoslavia, Greece, and Turkey entered into an alliance in 1953, rather than Yugoslavia, Greece, and Libya as the Correlates of War codes it. China and Russia entered into an alliance with *North* (rather than South) Korea in 1961.

76. There were an average of eight defense pact relationships for the democratic states as against five for the nondemocratic states. Using a t-test with Satterthwaite's adjustment for unequal variances, this difference is significant at the .01 level.

77. This picture of systemwide trends would support Kegley and Raymond's contention that alliance norms have evolved over time (*When Trust Breaks Down*).

78. If we had a theory of alliance formation sufficiently robust to suggest a set of measurable independent variables for which we could control, we might yet find an underlying difference in the alliance propensities of democratic and nondemocratic states.

79. See Kiefer, "Economic Duration Data and Hazard Functions," for an extensive review. For a discussion that is more oriented to political science, see Bienen and van de Walle, *Of Time and Power,* ch. 3. Other basic sources would include Kalbfleisch and Prentice, *The Statistical Analysis of Failure Time Data;* Lawless, *Statistical Models and Methods for Lifetime Data;* Allison, *Event History Analysis;* Lancaster, *The Econometric Analysis of Transition Data;* and Lee, *Statistical Methods for Survival Data Analysis.*

80. See Lee, *Statistical Methods for Survival Data Analysis,* chs. 4 and 5.

81. A generalized Wilcoxon rank test shows the difference between the survival functions for democratic alliances and for nondemocratic and mixed alliances to be significant at above the .005 level.

82. The accelerated failure time model is equivalent to the more common proportional hazards model for the special case of the Weibull distribution, as I use here. The estimation is done using the LIFEREG procedure in SAS.

83. The data were also run with exponential, gamma, lognormal, and loglogistic

models. For all of the data sets, either the Weibull provided the best fit or it provided a fit that was statistically indistinguishable from the gamma. I have used the Weibull throughout because it is one parameter more straightforward than the gamma and because of the benefits of consistency in having to display and explain the results from only one distribution.

84. See Kalbfleisch and Prentice, *The Statistical Analysis of Failure Time Data*, ch. 3.

85. These seven cases involve 38 dyads. The inclusion of these dyads weakens the fit of the model but does not substantively or significantly change the results.

86. These values are chosen simply for illustration. Durations are predicted to get longer by between 0.7 and 1.5 percent per year. The effects of differences in power between alliance partners are not particularly stable across the models, so there is no simple description of the difference between two major powers and the other configurations.

87. Partitioning the data set too finely is difficult because of the small number of democratic cases. The results change very little if we drop the nineteenth-century cases. The direction of the coefficients is the same if we restrict the cases to those alliances starting before 1930 (thus eliminating the NATO partners from the analysis), but the significance and stability of the coefficients are greatly limited.

Bibliography

Aldrich, John, John Sullivan, and Eugene Borgida. 1989. "Foreign Affairs and Issue Voting." *American Political Science Review* 83(1): 123–141.

Allison, Paul D. 1984. *Event History Analysis: Regression for Longitudinal Event Data.* Beverly Hills: Sage.

Almond, Gabriel. 1950. *The American People and Foreign Policy.* New York: Praeger.

Anderson, Lisa. 1997. "Politics Unleashed: Liberalization and Radical Politics in the Arab World," ch. 4 in this volume.

Axelrod, Robert. 1984. *The Evolution of Cooperation.* New York: Basic Books.

Babst, Dean. 1972. "A Force for Peace." *Industrial Research* (April): 55–58.

Barnett, Michael N., and Jack S. Levy. 1991. "Domestic Sources of Alliances and Alignments: The Case of Egypt, 1962–73." *International Organization* 45(3): 369–395.

Bienen, Henry, and Nicholas Van de Walle. 1991. *Of Time and Power.* Stanford: Stanford University Press.

Bobbio, Norberto. 1990. *Liberalism and Democracy.* Translated by Martin Ryle and Kate Soper. London: Verso.

Bueno de Mesquita, Bruce. 1981. *The War Trap.* New Haven: Yale University Press.

Bueno de Mesquita, Bruce, and David Lalman. 1986. "Reason and War." *American Political Science Review* 80(4): 1113–1130.

———. 1992. *War and Reason: Domestic and International Imperatives.* New Haven: Yale University Press.

Burley, Anne-Marie. 1993. "International Law and International Relations Theory: A Dual Agenda." *American Journal of International Law* 87:205–238.

Chan, Steve. 1984. "Mirror, Mirror on the Wall . . . Are the Freer Countries More Pacific?" *Journal of Conflict Resolution* 28:617–648.

Converse, Philip. 1964. "The Nature of Belief Systems in Mass Publics." In David Apter, ed., *Ideology and Discontent,* pp. 206–261. New York: Free Press.

Degenhardt, Henry. 1986. *Treaties and Alliances of the World.* 4th ed. Essex: Longman Group.

Dixon, William. 1993. "Democracy and the Management of International Conflict." *Journal of Conflict Resolution* 37(1): 42–68.

——. 1994. "Democracy and the Peaceful Settlement of International Conflict." *American Political Science Review* 88(1): 14–32.

Doyle, Michael. 1983a. "Kant, Liberal Legacies, and Foreign Affairs," part 1. *Philosophy and Public Affairs* 12(3): 205–235.

——. 1983b. "Kant, Liberal Legacies, and Foreign Affairs," part 2. *Philosophy and Public Affairs* 12(4): 323–353.

——. 1986. "Liberalism and World Politics." *American Political Science Review* 80(4): 1151–1169.

Fearon, James. 1994. "Domestic Political Audiences and the Escalation of International Disputes." *American Political Science Review* 88(3): 577–592.

Gaubatz, Kurt Taylor. 1995. "Intervention and Intransitivity: Public Opinion, Social Choice, and the Use of Military Force Abroad." *World Politics* 47(4): 534–554.

Grenville, J. A. S. 1974. *The Major International Treaties: 1914–1973.* New York: Stein and Day.

Grenville, J. A. S., and Bernard Wasserstein. 1987. *The Major International Treaties Since 1945.* London: Methuen.

Grieco, Joseph. 1988. "Anarchy and the Limits of Cooperation: A Realist Critique of the Newest Liberal Institutionalism." *International Organization* 42(3): 485–507.

Hartz, Louis. 1955. *The Liberal Tradition in America.* New York: Harcourt, Brace, Jovanovich.

Hochschild, Jennifer. 1981. *What's Fair.* Princeton: Princeton University Press.

Holsti, Ole. 1992. "Public Opinion and Foreign Policy: Challenges to the Almond-Lippmann Consensus." *International Studies Quarterly* 36(4): 439–466.

Holsti, Ole, Terrence Hopmann, and John Sullivan. 1973. *Unity and Disintegration in International Alliances: Comparative Studies.* New York: Wiley.

Huntington, Samuel P. 1991. *The Third Wave: Democratization in the Late Twentieth Century.* Norman: University of Oklahoma Press.

Hurst, Michael. 1972. *Key Treaties for the Great Powers: 1814–1914.* 2 vols. New York: St. Martin's.

Jervis, Robert. 1989. "Rational Deterrence: Theory and Evidence." *World Politics* 41(2): 183–207.

Kalbfleisch, John D., and Ross L. Prentice. 1980. *The Statistical Analysis of Failure Time Data.* New York: Wiley.

Kant, Immanuel. [1794, 1970] 1991. "Idea for a Universal History with a Cosmopolitan Purpose." In *Kant: Political Writings.* Edited by Hans Reiss. Translated by H. B. Nisbet. 2d ed., pp. 41–53. Cambridge: Cambridge University Press.

——. [1795, 1970] 1991. "Perpetual Peace: A Philosophical Sketch." In *Kant: Political Writings.* Edited by Hans Reiss. Translated by H. B. Nisbet. 2d ed., pp. 93–130. Cambridge: Cambridge University Press.

Karl, Terry, and Philippe Schmitter. 1994. "Democratization Around the Globe:

Opportunities and Risks." In Michael T. Klare and Daniel C. Thomas, eds., *World Security: Challenges for a New Century*, pp. 43–62. New York: St. Martin's.

Kegley, Charles, and Gregory Raymond. 1990. *When Trust Breaks Down: Alliance Norms and World Politics*. Columbia: University of South Carolina Press.

Keohane, Robert. 1984. *After Hegemony: Cooperation and Discord in the World Political Economy*. Princeton: Princeton University Press.

Keohane, Robert, and Joseph Nye. 1977. *Power and Interdependence: World Politics in Transition*. Boston: Little, Brown.

Kiefer, Nicholas. 1988. "Economic Duration Data and Hazard Functions." *Journal of Economic Literature* 26: 646–679.

Klingberg, Frank. 1952. "The Historical Alternation of Moods in American Foreign Policy." *World Politics* 4(2): 239–273.

Lalman, David. 1988. "Conflict Resolution and Peace." *American Journal of Political Science* 32(3): 590–615.

Lancaster, Tony. 1990. *The Econometric Analysis of Transition Data*. Cambridge: Cambridge University Press.

Lawless, Jerald. 1982. *Statistical Models and Methods for Lifetime Data*. New York: Wiley.

Lee, Elisa. 1992. *Statistical Methods for Survival Data Analysis*. 2d ed. New York: Wiley.

Lippmann, Walter. 1955. *Essays in the Public Philosophy*. Boston: Little, Brown.

Lowe, C. J. 1967. *The Reluctant Imperialists: British Foreign Policy, 1878–1902*. Vol. 1. London: Routledge and Kegan Paul.

Machiavelli, Niccolò. 1970 (1530). *The Discourses*. Translated by Leslie Walker. Edited by Bernard Crick. Middlesex, Eng.: Penguin.

McLean, Iain. 1987. *Public Choice: An Introduction*. Oxford: Basil Blackwell.

Manning, D. J. 1976. *Liberalism*. New York: St. Martin's.

Maoz, Zeev, and Nasrin Abdolali. 1989. "Regime Types and International Conflict, 1816–1976." *Journal of Conflict Resolution* 33(1): 3–35.

Maoz, Zeev, and Bruce Russett. 1993. "Normative and Structural Causes of Democratic Peace, 1946–1986." *American Political Science Review* 87(3): 624–638.

Monroe, Alan. 1979. "Consistency Between Public Preferences and National Policy Decisions." *American Politics Quarterly* 7(1): 3–19.

Neff, Stephen C. 1990. *Friends But No Allies: Economic Liberalism and the Law of Nations*. New York: Columbia University Press.

Nincic, Miroslav. 1992. *Democracy and Foreign Policy: The Fallacy of Political Realism*. New York: Columbia University Press.

North, Douglas, and Barry Weingast. 1989. "Constitutions and Commitment: The Evolution of Institutions Governing Public Choice in Seventeenth-Century England." *Journal of Economic History* 49(4): 803–832.

Page, Benjamin, and Robert Shapiro. 1983. "Effects of Public Opinion on Policy." *American Political Science Review* 77(1): 175–190.

———. 1991. *The Rational Public: Fifty Years of Trends in Americans' Policy Preferences*. Chicago: University of Chicago Press.

Putnam, Robert. 1988. "Diplomacy and Domestic Politics: The Logic of Two-Level Games." *International Organization* 42(3): 427–460.

Rawls, John. 1993. *Political Liberalism*. New York: Columbia University Press.

Riker, William. 1982. *Liberalism Against Populism*. San Francisco: W. H. Freeman.

Russett, Bruce. 1971. "An Empirical Typology of International Military Alliances." *Midwest Journal of Political Science* 15(2): 262–289.

————. 1990. *Controlling the Sword: The Democratic Governance of National Security.* Cambridge: Harvard University Press.

————. 1993. *Grasping the Democratic Peace: Principles for a Post–Cold War World.* Princeton: Princeton University Press.

Sabrosky, Alan. 1980. "Interstate Alliances: Their Reliability and the Expansion of War." In J. David Singer, ed., *The Correlates of War II.* New York: Free Press.

Schelling, Thomas. 1960. *The Strategy of Conflict.* Cambridge: Harvard University Press.

————. 1966. *Arms and Influence.* New Haven: Yale University Press.

Shapiro, Robert, and Benjamin Page. 1988. "Foreign Policy and the Rational Public." *Journal of Conflict Resolution* 32(2): 211–247.

Singer, J. David, and Melvin Small. 1966. *Annual Alliance Membership Data: 1815–1965.* ICPSR #5602. Ann Arbor: ICPSR.

————. 1984. *Wages of War, 1816–1980: Augmented with Disputes and Civil War Data.* ICPSR #9044. Ann Arbor: ICPSR.

Siverson, Randolph, and Juliann Emmons. 1991. "Birds of a Feather: Democratic Political Systems and Alliance Choices." *Journal of Conflict Resolution* 35(2): 285–306.

Small, Melvin, and David J. Singer. 1976. "The War-proneness of Democratic Regimes, 1816–1965." *Jerusalem Journal of International Relations* 1(4): 50–69.

Snyder, Glenn, and Paul Diesing. 1977. *Conflict Among Nations: Bargaining, Decision Making, and System Structure in International Crises.* Princeton: Princeton University Press.

Spence, Michael. 1974. *Market Signaling: Informational Transfer in Hiring and Related Screening Processes.* Cambridge: Harvard University Press.

Taylor, A. J. P. 1961. *The Origins of the Second World War.* 2d ed. New York: Fawcett.

Thucydides. 1951 (400 B.C.). *The Peloponnesian War.* Translated by Richard Crawley. New York: Random House.

Tocqueville, Alexis de. 1969 (1835). *Democracy in America.* Translated by George Lawrence. Garden City, N.Y.: Doubleday.

Velde, François, and Thomas Sargent. 1995. "The Macro-economic Causes and Consequences of the French Revolution." *Journal of Political Economy* 103:474–518.

von Glahn, Gerhard. [1965] 1992. *Law Among Nations: An Introduction to Public International Law.* 4th ed. New York: Collier.

Weede, Erich. 1984. "Democracy and War Involvement." *Journal of Conflict Resolution* 28(4): 649–664.

Walt, Stephen. 1987. *The Origin of Alliances.* Ithaca: Cornell University Press.

Waltz, Kenneth. 1967. *Foreign Policy and Democratic Politics: The American and British Experience.* Boston: Little, Brown.

————. 1979. *Theory of International Politics.* Reading, Mass.: Addison-Wesley.

Legislative Influence and International Engagement

Lisa L. Martin

The process of political liberalization involves establishing a legislature with some degree of control over policy, including foreign policy. In spite of this observation, however, theories of international relations have tended to slight the study of legislatures, either by assuming that the state is a unitary actor or by concentrating on the activities of the executive branch, such as the president, prime minister, secretary of state, or bureaucracy.[1] In contrast, students of American politics have developed numerous models of legislative-executive interaction and its impact on policy. This essay argues that such models are applicable to foreign as well as domestic policy settings and presents a case for extending the analytical framework to democracies other than the United States.

Work in comparative foreign policy has been hampered by lack of an overarching analytical framework. This lack has led to one of two pathologies. Sometimes scholars have treated each country as unique, asserting that processes found in one cannot be generalized, so that research has not actually been comparative in nature. At other times attempts to generalize without adopting an explicit analytical framework have led to the generation of lists of variables that may or may not have significance in some unspecified direction under some unspecified conditions. I argue that spatial models of policy making and consideration of the problem of delegation and principal-agent relationships provide a structure on which to hang more specific, comparative theories of the role of legislatures. This is not to argue that politics in Britain or Argentina, for example, is "the same as" politics in the United States but that models of delegation provide us with a unifying language with which to assess and measure the differences among established legislative systems.

Most models of legislative delegation focus on the U.S. House of Representatives. The applicability of such models to other countries remains an open question. I focus on Britain as a contemporary case because the conventional wisdom about British politics suggests that transporting American models to this setting should be especially difficult. The British system, unlike that of the United States, includes a parliamentary government with strong party discipline (although both countries have single-member districts, which creates a certain similarity in electoral and party incentives).[2] The separation of powers and district-level sources of support for legislators in the United States combine to give Congress an influential role in the American policy-making process. In contrast, the development of the British party system since the mid-nineteenth century has contributed to a situation in which most analysts find that the House of Commons plays a passive role in policy making, having abdicated its powers to the government chosen by the majority party. Given these difficulties, it would be a promising start on building a general approach to legislatures and foreign policy if the framework developed in the U.S. case can be shown to have explanatory leverage in Britain as well.

Spatial models are a class of equilibrium models, which identify outcomes from which no actor has an incentive to deviate unilaterally. As used here, they assume a fixed constitutional setting with well-defined and respected roles for various bodies of government. These assumptions do not hold for regimes in transition, those undergoing a process of liberalization. In fact, much of the political debate surrounding transitional regimes has to do with precisely the question of defining institutional roles, such as that of the legislature. In nonliberal regimes, foreign policy is, almost without exception, the prerogative of the head of state. The story of liberalization is in large part the story of the assertion of popular control over policy, typically through a legislative body. To provide a comparison for contemporary cases of liberalization, in the first section I briefly examine the struggle for control of foreign policy in a historical case of liberalization. England in the seventeenth century illuminates the ways in which legislatures enhance their authority over foreign policy. Paradoxically, it appears that legislatures are most insistent on asserting their right to influence foreign policy early in the process of liberalization. Because this process is about establishing property rights to policy making, legislators are reluctant to concede in the institutional power struggle by allowing the executive much discretion. In contrast, in established democracies we typically see extensive delegation (but rarely abdication) to the executive branch.

Turning to such established democracies, the second section discusses the common understanding of the key differences between the House of Commons and Congress in terms of their impact on policy. After mentioning models of delegation that may be most useful for U.S. foreign policy analysis, I argue that the observation of legislative behavior in the House of Commons is not sufficient, in and of itself, to prove that members of Parliament (MPs) have no influence on policy. The third section develops the general case for considering the influence of MPs on policy and offers simple spatial models that allow us to identify key differences between the U.S. and British patterns of legislative-executive interaction. The fourth section turns to empirical evidence on the British decision to join the European Community (EC) to bolster the case that the House of Commons is an important source of direction and constraint in contemporary British foreign policy. This essay highlights three types of arguments: the struggle for legislative influence in liberalizing states; the use of spatial models to assess the conditions for influence and contrasts between democratic systems; and the evidence for overlooked legislative influence on important foreign policy decisions.

TRANSITIONAL REGIMES AND CONTROL OVER FOREIGN POLICY

Processes of political liberalization are characterized by—perhaps defined by—debate about the authority of representative institutions in various policy areas. This debate extends to the realm of foreign policy, where it is often particularly intense, since the demands of international politics penalize states with ill-defined responsibilities for making foreign policy.[3] During transitions, constraints established by international interactions, especially the threat of or actual engagement in war, interact with changes in domestic institutions. In established democracies, as discussed below, legislatures often have more influence on foreign policy than a casual observer would infer.

In this first section, I ask how legislative involvement in foreign policy in transitional regimes responds to the simultaneous demands of international engagement and domestic liberalization.

To provide some historical context for current transitions, I turn to the example of England in the seventeenth century. England presents an interesting case for a number of reasons. First, the restructuring of English political institutions allowed the state to extract significant resources from the population and otherwise raise funds, while at the same time limiting the scope for arbitrary exercise of power. It thus set the groundwork that allowed Britain to become a major force in European politics during the eighteenth century. Second, shifting and dispersing responsibility for decisions had clear and immediate effects on foreign policy. Third, the pressures of international competition and engagement fed directly into the ongoing domestic political struggle, sometimes significantly changing the incentives facing key actors.

During the seventeenth century, English politics charted a difficult course from monarchy to representative government, with many retrenchments along the way.[4] In 1660, following a failed experiment with new institutions after a civil war, the monarchy was restored. Over the next twenty-five years, the Crown responded to political and financial struggles by encroaching on the powers of other actors. By the late 1680s an organized opposition to the Crown arose and removed James II in the Glorious Revolution of 1688. During the revolution Parliament restructured political institutions, guaranteeing itself a say in policy matters and creating a structure that allowed the government as a whole to make credible commitments to others, including financial markets.[5]

During the transition to parliamentary ascendance, England was involved in three wars with the Dutch: in 1652–1654, 1665–1667, and 1672–1674. This observation should raise red flags for a simplistic expectation that democratizing processes will reduce the probability that states will go to war with one another, since England and the United Provinces were the only two major European states of this era with even partially representative institutions.[6] In England the authority of Parliament was not firmly established until after the revolution, since the king could dissolve Parliament. Yet even during the transition, historians have noted, Parliament constrained the ability of the Crown to pursue foreign adventures. Usually, historians find that parliamentary influence was detrimental to English conduct of these wars.[7] While formal authority for foreign policy decisions remained in the Crown's grasp, Parliament nevertheless found leverage through its control of financial resources. The source of parliamentary influence is quite straightforward: the monarch had to convene Parliament in order to raise funds to fight wars, and Parliament used its power of the purse as an opportunity to force the monarch to conduct war as it preferred.[8]

The first Dutch war, fought during a time of great domestic political turbulence in England with the intent of eliminating Dutch commercial competition, showed the complex ways in which domestic and international political struggles interacted with one another. This war was launched by one regime in England, continued by a second that took office after a coup in April 1653, and ended by a third. One study concludes that "these unexpected changes largely determined the outcome of the war, playing a more important part than actual operations at sea."[9] The war was begun by a government (the Rump) attuned to mercantilist commercial interests. From the government's perspective, the war was the logical continuation of a policy of intense commercial competition and unwillingness to compromise, especially with an opponent that appeared to be vulnerable because of internal divisions. The second government (the Nominated Parliament) took a more strategic approach to foreign affairs and saw the Dutch war as one that could benefit the Catholic powers of Europe by disrupting the existing balance of power. The Nominated Parliament was thus less committed to total victory than was the previous government. The third government (under Oliver Cromwell) was also interested in maintaining a European balance of power and so was unwilling to demand punitive concessions from the defeated Dutch, anticipating that such demands would destabilize the already weak Dutch government. Critics called the resulting peace treaty unnecessarily lenient. In sum, the extent to which the English government represented commercial interests had a direct impact on the conduct of this first Anglo-Dutch war. As Mark Brawley argues, the more responsive to mercantilist interests the government was, the more it chose vigorously to pursue war with the Dutch.[10]

In the 1660s, mercantile interests still interested in ridding themselves of Continental competition took advantage of a lack of centralized control over policy to engage the Dutch in a second war. Although the monarch (Charles II) was not enthusiastic about war, he found himself unable to stop the slide to aggression once it had begun. During this second war, the government realized the importance of maintaining a show of unity in order to negotiate successfully with the Dutch. Maintaining harmony between the king and Parliament became a high priority and thus provided Parliament with a say in the conduct of negotiations and the war itself.[11] However, lack of a consistent strategy and parliamentary reluctance to appropriate sufficient funds meant that the second war, like the first, did not achieve its commercial objectives.

From 1667 to 1688, the turbulence of domestic politics meant that no voice within the government carried any authority in foreign affairs:

> Instability, factional divisions within ministries as well as in Parliament and the country, universal distrust and cynicism were to be the permanent characteristics of English politics up to the final crisis of 1688, while foreign policy was to be so tortuous and so governed by mercenary considerations that after a time neither Charles, James, their ministers nor their parliamentary opponents carried any independent influence or reputation.[12]

During this period, a struggle for power was waged with financial weapons. Parliament was concerned that providing the king with forces to fight European wars would allow him to turn these same on them, establishing absolutism at home. Parliament was therefore reluctant to provide long-term military financing, instead keeping the king on a short leash.[13] The Crown turned to other sources of funding, within Europe and at home, but an inability to guarantee repayment meant that these sources were limited and costly.[14] Levels of taxes and national debt were high, but not as high as they would later grow after the ability to make credible commitments to repay was established.[15]

Nevertheless, England did engage the Dutch in a third war during 1670–1671. In preparation, Parliament approved additional taxes to pay off old debts and prepare the navy for combat. The lack of established patterns of accountability allowed the Crown to achieve approval of this money through deception. Ministers assured Parliament that these preparations for war were intended to balance against France; instead, they planned to ally with France, the strongest Continental power, to guarantee defeat of the Dutch. This deception quickly became obvious, and coming on top of a pattern of deception and intense distrust between the branches, it meant that the king could not return immediately to Parliament after the war started to request more funds. In fact, the king had sufficient resources to finance only a single campaign.

The king's gamble on a quick victory did not pay off. In February 1673 he was forced to convene Parliament in order to raise funds to send the fleet back out to sea, since he was unwilling to concede defeat to the Dutch. MPs took advantage of this opportunity to attack the methods with which the war was carried out, and they linked any new financing to dismantling of the king's government. Dissolution of Parliament was considered, but the only alternative source of funding was Louis XIV, and he opposed dissolution. So, ironically, Parliament succeeded in dismantling the ministry in order to allow its members to pursue their goal of continuing the war. As one historian concludes, "The Civil War, Commonwealth and Protectorate, together with the autocratic follies of James II, showed just how difficult it was for the monarch—or any head of the executive—to dispense with parliament."[16]

Lack of funds severely limited the ability to fight wars. In the 1680s, Britain remained aloof from most European conflicts for this reason. In fact, Charles II and his successor, James, promised France that they would remain inactive in exchange for remarkably small, irregular subsidies from Louis XIV, further tying their own hands in the foreign policy realm. James's dependence on Louis contributed to hostility toward James during the exclusion crisis of 1678–1683 and to loss of support during the 1688 revolution.

After the revolution, a division of authority similar to that developed during the transition was institutionalized, but the tide turned toward those who favored involvement in European wars. The Crown remained formally responsible for all foreign policy decisions, including those about alliances, treaties, and the conduct of war.[17] Parliament retained a say in the exercise of these powers through its powers of the purse. During the Nine Years' War, beginning in 1689, William personally made many war decisions. However, he periodically had to return to Parliament to explain his actions in order to receive necessary funds to continue fighting. The Commons, with the power to reject funding proposals for the army and navy, took advantage of this power to propose deep cuts in military spending and in subsidies to Continental allies, both subjects of regular parliamentary debates. William's arguments about the importance of preventing the collapse of the alliance against France were convincing, and he managed to receive most of what he asked for. In exchange for financing the war, MPs gained an unusually high degree of oversight regarding its operations.[18] Parliament forced William to maintain a smaller army and a larger navy than he would have preferred.[19] And he paid another price for his success, in that immediately when the war ended Parliament forced most of the standing army to disband and impeached his ministers.

John Brewer argues that, paradoxically, the involvement of Parliament in decision making, which was necessitated by financial considerations created by international engagement, led to the development of a strong and legitimate central state capable of extracting high levels of resources from society. This transformation provided the necessary conditions for Britain to take its place as a great power in Europe and allowed it to become an active player in the Continental political struggles of the eighteenth and nineteenth centuries, consistent with the logic of delegation in established democracies.[20] This picture of the state stands in stark contrast to that of the transitional period, when even the pursuit of diplomacy was severely hindered by monetary constraints. Ambassadors were left largely to their own devices to support themselves during the 1660s through the 1680s, and those who were unfortunate enough to be of modest means were dependent on their hosts for financial support, making any centralized direction of British diplomacy nearly impossible.[21]

Overall, the story of British domestic politics and foreign policy in the seventeenth century suggests a number of insights into the relationship between domestic liberalization and international engagement. Brawley argues that the triumph of Parliament led to a definitive turn away from the mercantilist motives of the Anglo-Dutch wars to forging a strong anti-French alliance, tracing this shift to the economic interests of Parliament versus the Crown.[22] Although formal authority for foreign policy remained in the Crown's hands, through control of the state's purse strings Parliament gained a say in the conduct of war and diplomacy. Because this intrusion of the legislative voice was not yet institutionalized or accepted by the Crown, it was haphazard. The legislature, distrusting the monarch, was unwilling to delegate authority through the mechanism of long-term financing. These domestic struggles directly affected the way in which Britain fought the three Anglo-Dutch wars; they also served to keep Britain out of some European conflicts. Only after the pattern of authority had been regularized could the British state efficiently extract resources and make authoritative decisions that allowed it to become a major player in international politics.

The similarities between this historical case and contemporary examples of political liberalization, such as in Russia, are striking. Because control of foreign policy becomes part of a larger struggle for influence during transitions, newly powerful legislators refuse to allow the executive much discretion to pursue foreign policy. During this period the control of legislators over policy making appears extensive but also self-defeating. Lack of institutionalized patterns of authority means that the state cannot act as a unified actor on the international stage, a situation that the strategic interaction of international politics penalizes. As democracies become established, the need to make credible commitments and otherwise interact effectively with other states leads to delegation of authority. As the following sections argue, delegation can meet the demands of strategic interaction without depriving the legislature of the ability to influence foreign policy. Formal, regularized patterns of accountability allow simultaneous legislative influence and effective state action.

AMERICAN LEGISLATIVE ASSERTIVENESS AND BRITISH PASSIVITY

Political scientists have conflicting opinions about the role of Congress in the foreign policy process. Some studies argue that lack of public knowledge about foreign affairs, a need for secrecy, and a need to respond quickly to crises have contributed to the dominance of the executive branch in international politics. In the decades after World War II, the concept of the "imperial presidency" described the great discretion allowed the executive branch.[23] On the other hand, other studies—and often even the same ones—note that in certain circumstances Congress can and has played a significant role, either constructive or destructive, in the policy process. Most textbooks on U.S. foreign policy devote a significant amount of space to the study of Congress and legislative-executive interactions.[24] Formally, Congress plays a number of roles—appropriating funds (for military spending and foreign aid, for example), declaring war, ratifying treaties. The analytical question addressed in this section is whether these formal powers endow Congress with actual influence over policy. How do we make sense of those occasions on which Congress asserts itself in the foreign policy realm, such as the debate over assistance to the contras in Nicaragua, sanctions against South Africa in the 1980s, or the failure to ratify SALT II? How do we weigh them against the executive's discretionary powers embodied in approval of the Gulf War, the Gulf of Tonkin Resolution, or fast-track procedures for trade negotiations?

Those studying domestic policies in the United States have confronted similar issues in analyzing the relations between Congress and executive agencies. The use of principal-agent models and consideration of the logic of delegation has demonstrated that the observation of little congressional oversight activity does not always imply a lack of congressional influence.[25] Lack of overt legislative activity is not necessarily equivalent to abdication to the executive branch.[26] The logic underlying such models is that of anticipated reactions. Legislators, if rational and motivated by electoral considerations, want to achieve particular outcomes, such as low rates of inflation, public works projects in their districts, or tariffs for industries they represent. Sometimes these outcomes are best achieved, given limitations on organization, information, and other resources, by delegation under particular rules and conditions to executive branch actors.

Thus, in equilibrium, we should not expect to see Congress expending vast resources on oversight or micromanagement of particular activities. Instead, legislators achieve their objectives through careful manipulation of delegation regimes and the incentives facing their agents, such as the bureaucracy.[27] Extensive legislative activity, like that on aid to the contras in Nicaragua, implies a failure of delegation, not an isolated instance of congressional influence. Delegation is a proxy for congressional policy making, and those interested in foreign policy should therefore pay as much attention to the reasons that underlie congressional decisions to delegate as to the decisions about actual policies.

Such a perspective on legislative influence has been characterized inaccurately as one of "congressional dominance."[28] Particularly in the uncertain and complex world of international relations, we need to be aware of the agency losses that accompany legislative delegation to the executive branch. Once Congress surrenders its right to amend tariff levels, for example, the president gains leverage over the outcomes of international negotiations on trade. Sometimes, however, this is the best outcome Congress can hope for, and it does not imply the disappearance of legislative influence on tariffs. Legislators are aware of agency losses and typically do not decide to delegate authority without good reason, such as the need to encourage investment in specialized information or to engage in tough negotiations with other countries. Spatial models tell us that fast-track procedures, which are analogous to a closed rule in consideration of legislation, give rise to different outcomes than we would find under an open rule, where Congress could adopt any policy it chose through the amendment process.[29] The same models, however, allow us to specify conditions under which a majority of congressmen prefer closed-rule procedures and concomitant agency losses to the result they would achieve without delegation, under micromanagement; they also specify how outcomes diverge from those that an unconstrained president might choose.[30]

In foreign affairs, models of delegation have been most extensively explored in trade policy, although even this work is at a preliminary stage.[31] Because the microeconomic foundations of incentives facing legislators on trade issues are well understood, at least relative to those on other foreign policy issues, we have a good understanding of preferences in this area, and work has proceeded relatively quickly. Authors have offered a number of rationales to explain the variation we observe in the level of control Congress exerts over trade policy and the resulting levels of protection. Congress may delegate to solve its own collective action problems,[32] to gain information about the economic effects of the policies it adopts,[33] to enable successful negotiation with other countries,[34] or to bind succeeding Congresses. These models allow us to develop expectations about the degree of delegation that will take place, given structural conditions and preferences, and about the effects of delegation on the policies chosen. For example, consideration of the collective action problem faced by Congress in adopting product-specific tariffs leads to the expectation that delegation will increase and tariff levels decrease when Congress and the presidency are controlled by the same party.[35]

Delegation, in the context considered here, though often a second-best solution, may be the best available to Congress. Delegation is not equivalent to abdication, meaning that it does not allow the agent complete control over the policy adopted. Frequently, procedural or substantive constraints are placed on the agent—such as a requirement to negotiate only reciprocal trade reductions, or to keep them within specified limits—or the policies proposed by the executive are subject to an up-or-down vote by Congress, as in fast-track legislation. At the same time, deciding to delegate pulls outcomes away from those that Congress would adopt on its own. Thus Congress confronts a trade-off between the benefits of delegation, such as increased information or strategic advantages vis-à-vis other countries, and maintaining tight control over policy. Models of delegation allow us to be more precise in specifying how legislators will evaluate this trade-off in different issue areas and under different political and economic conditions.

Overall, both theoretical work and empirical investigations now suggest that Congress is an influential foreign policy actor in the United States. Empirically, this seems particularly true since 1970, when disillusionment with the results of wide executive discretion catalyzed by the failures of Vietnam and Watergate led to an activist Congress reclaiming authority from the president. Models of delegation suggest why authority would have been reclaimed under these circumstances, while reminding us that the threat of such action served to constrain the executive's actions even during the period of the so-called imperial presidency.

The image of an assertive Congress is in direct contrast to the prevailing view of the role of Parliament in British foreign policy. The House of Commons, most observers find, has little influence in any issue area and is particularly weak in foreign policy. As evidence, authors point to the lack of amendment of government legislation by MPs and the overwhelming rate of passage of government legislation. Since 1945, on average, 97% of government legislation has passed into law; during at least eight parliamentary sessions, 100% of government bills passed.[36] This pattern has led one British observer to conclude that "the present achievement of the evolution of our constitution has been to replace a despotic monarch with an autocratic government."[37] Another refers to the British system as an "elective dictatorship" or "modern monarchy," concluding that "the office of the prime minister by the late twentieth century resembled nothing so much as the Continental absolute monarchies which the English had once prided themselves on rejecting."[38] Even a more balanced accounting of the powers of Parliament finds that "there is little dispute, however, that in the normal run of British politics Parliament is a relatively weak influence in the foreign policy process."[39]

In contrast to studies of U.S. foreign policy, books on British foreign policy frequently bypass the House of Commons altogether.[40]

Formally, the Commons does not have to ratify treaties (although any necessary changes in domestic law require parliamentary assent), nor does it have the power to declare war. One author concludes that "the monopoly which is accorded the Executive in the sphere of foreign affairs *de jure* is consistent to a remarkable degree with the general supremacy of the contemporary Executive over Parliament *de facto*," leaving the executive unfettered, for all practical purposes.[41] Although a fair amount of debate and questioning of ministers about foreign policy issues takes place on the floor of the Commons, authors do not find that this leads to any real influence. As a recent survey concluded, "The most obvious unchanging reality which persists over the years is the fact of executive dominance in the foreign policy process. . . . Foreign policy was always, and remains, in the hands of the executive."[42]

While some analyses credit the passivity of Parliament to British political culture or a tradition of bipartisanship, others find the source in the incentives created for MPs and party leaders by the electoral system. In the mid-nineteenth century, during the "golden age" of Parliament, MPs responded to small, easily defined constituencies, since the franchise was severely restricted. This responsiveness led to significant independence on the part of individual MPs and to a political process that seems to resemble U.S. politics today.

As the franchise expanded, however, MPs found that they had to rely more heavily on party labels to gain widespread recognition.[43] As the number and complexity of issues on which government had to act increased, Parliament delegated more authority to the cabinet in order to solve its own collective action problems. Due to this delegation, a ministerial position was now sought-after and valuable, so that party leaders could use the promise of these positions as a reward to enforce party discipline. MPs found it in their own interest, as long as they cared about career advancement, to obey the dictates of party discipline and approve any legislation the government proposed, usually without amendment. Thus independence of MPs declined, and governments, with guaranteed majorities to support their agendas, gained a monopoly over policy. The "iron cage" of party discipline meant that Parliament became, and remains, minimally effective,[44] and "modern British government is government by party leaders in Cabinet."[45]

If we were to take these statements at face value, there would seem to be little reason to pursue a study of the role of the legislature in

British foreign policy. But just as discussions of the imperial presidency often contain qualifications noting the occasional act by Congress, most authors who accept that the cabinet is dominant nevertheless note that Parliament on occasion constrains or indirectly influences policy. Gary Cox finds that the Commons has retained veto power and some amendment power.[46] David Vital notes that "while the ability of the Executive to ram through any policy of its choosing is hardly in doubt . . . the fact remains that it does not invariably do so."[47] William Wallace finds that Parliament acts as a constraint on foreign policy.[48] These qualifications suggest that the conventional wisdom on parliamentary impotence may rely on the same kind of equilibrium fallacy as the abdication hypothesis in U.S. politics, leading to the same kinds of inconsistencies in analysis. Simply put, the fact that the government rarely loses important votes or accepts amendments offered on the floor by MPs does not imply that MPs have no influence over policy. An alternative interpretation, one relying on anticipated reactions, is that the government skillfully anticipates what the Commons will and will not accept and accommodates these constraints while maintaining a public image of party solidarity and cabinet control, important for electoral reasons.

Consideration of rational, farsighted decisions to delegate authority and of equilibrium behavior of the legislature leads us to speculate that observation of sporadic legislative activity is not sufficient to prove that legislative influence on foreign policy is equally sporadic. Instead, those instances in which Congress or the Commons asserts itself may be best understood as unusual events, where the delegation process has gone awry and the legislature finds it necessary to assert its authority publicly. In normal practice, the executive will understand the conditions of legislative delegation and work within the constraints established by those conditions. As one author explains, "However much they [MPs] may blame governments for dominating their lives, in principle they have it in their power to change things. . . . That things are done as they are suggests that present arrangements suit many people."[49] To use Kenneth Waltz's phrase, "the effectiveness of the cause may account for the invisibility of the result."[50] Spatial models provide us with one mechanism to explore the variation in conditions and resulting policy outcomes in different political systems and under different patterns of interests. The next section discusses what implications such models have for legislative control over foreign policy in the United States and Britain.

The House of Commons and Foreign Policy

In order to understand the nature and degree of influence the Commons has on foreign policy, we need to understand the dynamics of legislative-executive interactions in Britain. This section discusses the rules and processes that govern policy making to put some flesh on the bones of the equilibrium argument outlined above. After further examining the plausibility of the notion that the Commons constrains foreign policy in a regular manner, I use a simple, one-dimensional spatial model to consider how processes in the Commons and the U.S. Congress lead to different patterns of delegation and policy outcomes in the two systems. This discussion allows us to begin resolving some of the inconsistencies in studies of legislative influence by specifying the necessary conditions for the legislature to pull policies in its preferred direction.

Opportunities for Influence

Formally speaking, the powers of the Commons in many ways exceed those of the U.S. Congress. The Commons is unconstrained by any supermajority requirements, such as the two-thirds vote needed for ratification of treaties by the Senate. Instead, the doctrine of parliamentary sovereignty means that, technically speaking, the Commons can do anything it likes by a majority vote.[51] Thus it is just as easy for a standing Parliament to overturn existing legislation as to implement wholly new proposals. In contrast to the separation of powers and emphasis on checks and balances embodied in the U.S. Constitution, the unwritten British constitution provides for concentration of power in the hands of Parliament.[52] As described above, Parliament has chosen to delegate much of this power to the cabinet, which is composed of ministers drawn from the majority party. A majority vote of no confidence can bring down the government and force a new general election. Thus, a key contrast between the United States and Britain is the fact that the executive is responsible to and dependent on Parliament in the British system.[53] Paradoxically, the development of party government is claimed to have weakened parliamentary influence on policy in precisely the political system that concentrates power in the hands of Parliament.

While rarely exercised on the floor, the amendment powers of the Commons are formally similar to those of the U.S. Congress. Bills, which are introduced by the government, have three readings in the

Commons. After the Third Reading, the bill is sent to the House of Lords. In the twentieth century, the House of Lords has lost power to do much except minimally delay legislation. A bill becomes law once it is passed in the same form by both Houses, or after a specified deadline in the form passed by the Commons even if the House of Lords does not pass identical legislation. The legislative process offers opportunities for MPs or ministers to make changes in legislation from the initial form proposed by the government, in committee or on the floor at the report stage, before the Third Reading.[54]

MPs rarely offer significant amendments to government legislation on the floor, in spite of these opportunities, and even more rarely succeed in gaining approval of them. For example, in one thirteen-year period the government moved 1,772 amendments, of which all but 2 were approved, while MPs moved 4,198 amendments without government support, of which only 210 were approved.[55] However, the procedures for consideration of government bills closely resemble those for legislation considered under an open rule by Congress. We therefore need to seek an explanation for the lack of explicit amendment activity by MPs, in contrast to the behavior of members of Congress (MCs).

The traditional answer is that party discipline prevents MPs from offering amendments, since they anticipate retaliation from party leaders. In contrast, I argue that the explanation lies in the importance of the party label for electoral purposes and the highly developed information-sharing capacity and responsiveness of the cabinet. In my proposed framework, MPs are assumed to have significant potential influence. The importance of maintaining an appearance of party unity in the British electoral system, however, means that MPs exercise this influence outside the public spotlight, in party committees and other forums, rather than on the floor of the Commons. Government ministers do, indeed, offer nearly all of the amendments that are eventually incorporated into legislation, but the official source of amendments is irrelevant. Ministers offer these amendments as they acquire more precise information about the preferences of MPs, designing legislation that is as close as possible to the government's desires while still being acceptable to a majority of the party.

The authority to initiate the legislative process presents a starker contrast between the American and British systems. In the United States, legislation can be initiated by any of a number of sources within Congress, although gatekeeping power is often exercised by functionally defined committees. In the Commons, in contrast, the executive has acquired almost exclusive control over the legislative agenda.[56] This means that gatekeeping power for significant policy issues lies with the government rather than with individual MPs or parliamentary committees. If the government anticipates that the legislative process, once started, will lead to an outcome it finds unacceptable relative to the status quo, it will keep the gates closed. The U.S. president, unless such authority has been specifically delegated, has no analogous power. Although procedures exist for Private Members' Bills, and a few such bills pass each year, the executive's control over the Commons' agenda means that the government can prevent consideration of such bills or otherwise obstruct their passage. Private Members' Bills thus deal with only minor, district-specific issues, or controversial issues such as abortion for which the government wishes to avoid responsibility and does not want to impose party discipline.[57] Later in this section I consider the effect of gatekeeping power on the executive's influence over policy outcomes.

Not all legislation is considered by the Commons under the open-rule procedures just described. An alternative procedure exists: "delegated legislation" or "statutory instruments," by which government bills are considered under a closed rule, no amendments allowed. The existence of this alternative procedure itself should cast doubt on the claim that normal procedures give the cabinet a monopoly of decision-making power. If this were true, the use of statutory instruments would be irrelevant and superfluous, since the procedure would have no impact on the outcome of legislation. Instead, the use of statutory instruments has grown over time and remains the subject of significant controversy within Parliament. One MP claims that "in very many areas . . . Members find it extremely limiting that they do not have at their disposal the power to introduce amendments in the way they could do to the original Bill. . . . Clearly such a procedure delivers too many weapons into the hands of the government."[58] Approximately two thousand statutory instruments go into effect each year.[59] Interaction with the European Community has led to extensive use of statutory instruments for implementation of EC agreements.

Overall, unless the Commons has approved the use of statutory instruments, the amendment process provides MPs with opportunities to influence legislation, even if this influence is exercised out of public view. If MPs are unsuccessful in gaining approval of desired changes to bills, however, what recourse do they have? In the United States the answer is simple: refuse to vote for the legislation if its final form is unacceptable. Most analyses of the House of Commons suggest that party discipline has made this option unavailable to MPs. Unless they wish to sacrifice their careers, members of the majority party will follow the government's advice and vote in favor of the government's legislation. This guarantees the government a majority for its proposals. The government makes sure that backbenchers know its wishes through use of the "whip." By underlining parts of legislation up to three times, the government signals the importance it attaches to specific legislation. A "three-line whip" indicates that the government considers this legislation vital and demands party loyalty on the issue, with party-line voting in the divisions. The decision to dispense with the whip, allowing members to vote as they please, is known as allowing a "free vote."

Recent works have begun to call into serious question the proposition that MPs are unwilling to dissent. Philip Norton has collected data on the incidence of dissent.[60] In the 1950s, the level of dissent was very low. During this decade, consistently less than 3% of divisions saw any dissenting votes from MPs of the majority party. However, the level of party voting has declined significantly since then. From 1970 to 1974, 20% of all divisions had dissents; in 1974–1979, 28% did.[61] Dissent did occasionally lead to government defeats —six times in 1970–1974, and forty-two times in 1974–1979.[62] Initially, observers believed that the breakdown of party discipline expressed in dissenting votes was an issue only for the Labour Party.[63] But the pattern begun during the Labour government of the late 1960s continued and intensified in the Conservative government of the early 1970s,[64] then persisted into the 1980s and 1990s. As Norton finds, "What was remarkable—and unprecedented—during this period [the 1980s] was that there were occasions when a large overall majority was not sufficient to stave off defeat or the threat of defeat."[65]

It seems clear that a new equilibrium pattern of behavior has been established. Previously, open dissent was extremely rare and not tolerated by the government. Now, dissent is relatively common— although still far below the levels seen in the United States—and there is not much the government can do about it. Once widespread dissent, or voting on the basis of constituency interests in addition to party affiliation, is the norm among MPs, government threats of retaliation, refusing to promote dissenters, and making every vote a vote of confidence lose credibility.[66] The single-member electoral districts that characterize both the British and the American political systems create incentives for representatives to pay attention to constituent demands if they care about reelection.[67] While procedures in the Commons put more pressure on MPs to vote with the party majority than their counterparts in Congress feel, constituency characteristics explain a significant amount of variation in the willingness of MPs to dissent.[68]

As this evidence indicates, MPs do have a choice, and they sometimes exercise it by refusing to vote in favor of the legislation proposed by their party leaders. Party leaders are aware of this and anticipate it by doing their best to make sure their legislation will be acceptable to a majority. This consultation gives backbenchers a means through which to influence government policy even if they are reluctant to confront the government with hostile amendments on the floor.[69] Norton concludes that the willingness to dissent forces the cabinet to anticipate parliamentary reaction and makes the prime minister responsive to MPs' opinions.[70] Dennis Kavanagh argues that "the predictability of the division lists . . . failed to do justice to the ability of many back-benchers to force concessions from the party leaders."[71]

Parliamentary committees and caucuses provide forums for the discussion of disagreements on policy issues and proposed legislation. Some observers have noted that party whips are present at committee meetings, of both the party itself and the Commons as a whole, and infer that their presence inhibits the expression of dissenting opinions by MPs. Such an inference depends on the assumption that the major function of whips is to enforce party discipline through threats of disciplinary action. Studies suggest, however, that the actual level of disciplinary power wielded by whips is quite low. Ian Budge and David McKay, for example, find that "various Whips have publicly admitted their limited disciplinary powers and dissenters have boasted that they ignore them at will."[72] In practice, threats to withdraw party affiliation or prevent promotion are rarely carried out.[73] Instead, whips act as channels of information, sending reliable signals from MPs to ministers and vice versa.[74] In order for the kind of "behind-the-scenes" influence that I posit here to operate, the cabinet must have good information about backbencher preferences so as to avoid costly floor fights. The party whips provide such information in a timely manner.

Consistent with the argument that solid party-line voting does not reflect lack of policy influence, Kavanagh concludes that "what is now clear is that back-bench MPs traditionally lacked not so much the means as the political will to defeat the party whips."[75] Norton also argues that a new equilibrium that allows for backbench influence has emerged: "Once triggered, there was no returning to earlier practices of unthinking loyalty; and, indeed, as the incidence of dissent increased, so it encouraged a change of attitude on the part of many MPs, discarding their old deferential attitude toward government."[76] A comprehensive study of dissent and whips in the 1950s and 1960s concluded that both rebels and whips

> expect backbenchers to be able to influence party policy even though a high degree of solidarity is also required, and they agree that there are very few devices for punishing dissidents which can be effective in practice. Rebels and Whips both think that a private and subtle process of accommodation takes place in the Labour and Conservative parties and that rebellion and discipline are only public symptoms that this process has failed to operate.[77]

This description is remarkably similar to anticipated-reaction analyses of congressional influence in the United States. The process of acquiring detailed information about MPs' preferences and accommodating them in legislation is constant. In an electoral system that places a high value on party solidarity, revelation of deep internal differences provides the Opposition with golden opportunities and could be devastating in elections. Thus, a system has evolved whereby the whip is a liaison, allowing ministers to estimate precisely what they can get away with without causing outright dissent within the party and allowing backbenchers to exercise influence over policy without having to vote against the party leadership.

Contrasting the American and British Systems

Careful consideration of the process of legislation and incentives facing legislators in the House of Commons suggests that the image of government supremacy is misleading. As one study concluded, "Any Prime Minister who thought he could dispense with consideration for the views of his party in Parliament would wholly misunderstand his position."[78] Yet it would also be misleading to assume that the legislative process in Britain therefore leads to the same outcomes as in the United States. As discussed above, a fundamental difference in the

FIGURE 2.1

A Spatial Model with the Status Quo Close to the Head of Government's Preferred Outcome

SQ	P		MP	MC

FIGURE 2.2

A Spatial Model with the Status Quo Far from the Head of Government's Preferred Outcome

P	x		MP	y	MC	SQ

two systems is that the government in Britain exercises gatekeeping power.

To consider how the two different systems may give rise to different outcomes, consider the one-dimensional spatial models illustrated in figures 2.1 and 2.2. In these figures, executive and legislative preferences over ideal outcomes are not identical. If they were, institutional features would have no impact on outcomes in a complete-information setting, since all actors would choose the same policies. Conflicting interests are easily generated in the United States, where the executive and legislative branches are independently elected. We also observe such conflicts in Britain. Factions exist within the parties, so there is no guarantee that a minister will agree with the preferences of the median party MP on every issue. Other than the issue of devolution, policy toward the EC has reflected the deepest split within parties.[79] Without some conflict of interest between governing-party backbenchers and the cabinet, the question of "parliamentary power" would become meaningless. Thus, a necessary condition for the arguments I make here is the existence of some intraparty divisions. In the two figures here, "SQ" represents the status quo policy; "P" represents the ideal point (most-preferred policy) of the president or prime minister; "MP," the ideal point of the swing voter in the majority party in Parliament; and "MC," the ideal point of the median member of Congress.[80]

In these figures, the horizontal line represents a single policy issue, such as the preferred level of tariffs or foreign assistance to some other country.[81] In the configuration of figure 2.1, the status quo could be, for example, a very low tariff. The president or prime minister prefers a slightly higher tariff, while the swing voter in the legislature prefers a significantly higher tariff. Assuming majority-rule voting, we can find the structure-induced equilibrium that is the predicted outcome under different rules, given this configuration of preferences.[82] Consider first open-rule voting. In the United States, an open rule would lead to a tariff level of MC, since any bill would be amended on the floor to the ideal point of the median member of Congress.[83]

In the British system, however, the gatekeeping power of the government leads to a dramatically different outcome. Ministers anticipate that once the legislative process is set in motion, the need to accommodate members' preferences will lead to an outcome near MP. As drawn in figure 2.1, the status quo is closer to the prime minister's ideal point than is MP. Thus, the prime minister (or, if a specific ministry is exercising gatekeeping power, the relevant minister) will refuse to introduce a new tariff bill.[84] Thus the predicted outcome in Britain is no change, for the policy to remain at SQ.

Under these conditions—open-rule voting and a status quo that is far from the swing member's ideal point but close to the president's or prime minister's—gatekeeping power leads to a large difference in outcomes in the United States and Britain. In the British system, gatekeeping power in the hands of the executive creates, in this situation, a status quo bias. It allows the executive to achieve outcomes closer to his ideal point than the president can achieve in the U.S. system. However, this result changes when we amend the rules to allow a closed-rule procedure. Now the executive is allowed to make any proposal he likes, and the House simply subjects this proposal to an up-or-down vote. If the proposal fails, the status quo remains in place. For example, on trade policy a closed rule is something like a fast-track procedure, where the president presents a completed deal to Congress with no possibility of amendment. Under these rules, the predicted outcome in both the U.S. and the British cases is P. The executive can present a proposal at his ideal point, and because the swing voter in the legislature prefers P to SQ, he will approve it.

As this example illustrates, the influence implicit in gatekeeping power is contingent on specific rules and patterns of preferences. In some cases it allows the British prime minister to achieve outcomes more to his liking than the U.S. president could achieve. On the other hand, exercising this influence under an open rule requires accepting the status quo even though Pareto-superior outcomes, which are preferred to the status quo by both the prime minister and the swing MP, exist. A solution to this problem of suboptimal outcomes resulting from gatekeeping power is to grant the prime minister a closed rule.

When we treat procedural rules as exogenous, as in the previous example, we find that they have a significant impact on the outcome and that the difference between the U.S. and British systems vanishes under closed-rule procedures. This simple example also suggests, however, a difference in the rules we should expect to see used in the two systems. Paradoxically, in the British case the swing voter in the Commons prefers the result under a closed rule to the result under an open rule, as does the executive: P is closer to MP than is SQ. Thus we should expect the swing voter to be willing to implement closed-rule procedures, such as those embodied in the use of statutory instruments or other delegated legislation. This is not true in the U.S. case, where the median member of Congress prefers the outcome under an open rule.[85] Thus, when the status quo is strongly disliked by the swing voter in the legislature, as in figure 2.1, we should anticipate greater delegation of authority to the executive through closed-rule procedures in Britain than in the United States. This result can be seen as an attempt to avoid Pareto-inferior outcomes under conditions where the prime minister has gatekeeping power and may account for the observation of greater executive discretion in Britain than in the United States.

Figure 2.2 represents, for contrast, a different configuration of preferences. In this example, the status quo is very unsatisfactory from the executive's perspective but closer to the median legislator's ideal point. In this case, open-rule procedures give rise to the MC outcome in the United States and to MP in Britain. The prime minister will not exercise gatekeeping power, since the status quo is worse for him than is MP, and he is thus willing to accept the outcome of the accommodation process. A closed rule leads the executive to make a proposal that makes the swing voter indifferent between the proposal and the status quo. The executive will not propose P in this example, since it is farther from the median legislator's ideal point than is SQ and will therefore be defeated. The executive thus compromises by offering a proposal that will just barely beat the status quo while remaining as close to the executive's ideal point as possible. The predicted outcomes under a closed rule are therefore something like the point marked "x" in Britain and "y" in the United States.

In this example, gatekeeping power does the prime minister no good. When he intensely dislikes the status quo, he has no incentive to exercise gatekeeping power. Any difference in outcomes between the United States and Britain under these conditions results solely from different positions preferred by the swing voter in the legislature. In Britain, he prefers the outcome under an open rule (MP, his ideal point) to that under a closed rule (x). The same pattern holds in the United States. Thus, the configuration of preferences shown in figure 2.2 does not lead us to anticipate any systematic difference in delegation regimes across the two countries. Because different structures of rules give rise to different policy outcomes, the choice of a rule can be quite significant, as studies of congressional organization have found.[86] In addition, we observe that legislators argue fiercely about choices of rules and complain when they are subject to rules of which they don't approve, suggesting the importance of procedure.

These simple examples illustrate how spatial models and consideration of delegation regimes can be used to analyze differences in the role of the legislature on foreign policy issues in established democracies. Examination of policy-making procedures and incentives in the United States and Britain suggests that a key difference lies in the gatekeeping power acquired by the executive in Britain. Under specifiable conditions, this constitutes a source of influence over policy outcomes; under others, it has no significant impact. If we are able to order the preferred outcomes of key players relative to the status quo, spatial models provide a tool for developing expectations about outcomes, choices of delegation regimes, and the role of the legislature.

The image of the House of Commons as an insignificant actor in policy making is misleading. Instead, the right to offer amendments, the willingness to dissent under some conditions, and the process of communication and accommodation with party leadership provide MPs with leverage over policy not wholly unlike that exercised by members of Congress, although it is exercised in private rather than in public. Spatial models allow us to begin sorting out the conditions under which the executive cannot act in an unconstrained manner and suggest conditions under which we will see increased delegation, as in the use of statutory instruments, to the executive. For example, they suggest that the gatekeeping power of the cabinet leads to decreased parliamentary influence when the executive is happier with the status quo than are most backbenchers. Because of the importance of party, it also appears that the potential for backbench influence is highest when there are deep internal differences on policy issues, such as Europe, and when the government's majority in Parliament is slim. While the argument thus far seems plausible in the abstract world of rules and models, further research must turn to studies of actual legislation to assess parliamentary influence. As a step in this direction, the next section examines the role of the legislature in the British decision to join the European Community.

Britain and EC Membership

As mentioned earlier, most analyses of British politics claim that Parliament is particularly ineffective when it comes to foreign policy issues. The lack of constituent interest and knowledge, monopoly over information by the executive, and tradition of bipartisanship are reasons offered to explain the low level of attention and influence exercised by MPs. Reflection on the impact of bipartisan traditions calls this assertion into question, however. Precisely because most voters usually make their choices in elections on issues other than foreign policy, international affairs may not clearly differentiate the two major parties from one another. When foreign policy issues do assume importance, as in the area of relations with the EC, cleavages as often run through parties as between them. Intraparty factions and governing party ministers often deeply disagree with one another on policy toward Europe. Thus, party discipline is especially difficult to enforce, or even to define.

If party discipline is the putative cause of minimal legislative influence, we should expect greatest influence precisely on those issues, such as the EC, where the parties are not clearly differentiated from one another and internal divisions exist. The conclusion that MPs cannot influence foreign policy does not follow from a pattern of bipartisanship—in fact, just its opposite does, since party discipline is less effective. Studies of dissent have found that rebellion sufficient to lead to government defeats often occurs on issues usually understood to involve relations with other countries.[87] Recently, governments have lost on issues including immigration and policy toward the Middle East. The assertion that MPs do not engage in active opposition on foreign policy issues is often nothing more than a tautology, in that once political activism begins, analysts tend to redefine an issue as "domestic."

Perhaps the most significant foreign policy decision Britain has made since World War II was to join the European Community in 1973. Because negotiation of treaties is a Crown prerogative exercised by the prime minister and not subject to parliamentary control, the treaty of accession itself did not have to be ratified by the Commons. However, the treaty was meaningless until its provisions were enacted into British domestic law, which required an explicit majority vote. Thus the European Communities Bill of 1972 became the mechanism by which Britain officially joined the EC. Throughout the process of engagement, and ever since joining, the Commons has constrained British policy toward the EC. The *Economist* expressed the hope in April 1992 that "for the first time since Britain joined the EC in 1973, its role in Europe can be framed without regard to the minutiae of domestic politics."[88] But the necessity of ratifying the Maastricht Treaty led other analysts to note that the House of Commons continues to involve itself in EC issues.[89]

When the European Coal and Steel Community (ECSC) was created in 1951, Britain chose not to join, preferring to emphasize its Commonwealth ties and not believing that the ECSC would ever amount to much. As relative economic decline set in during the 1960s and the EC seemed to lead to economic growth for its members, however, interest in joining grew. Britain had attempted to gain similar benefits without the obligations of the EC by creating the European Free Trade Association (EFTA) in 1959. But EFTA did not include any of the EC countries, which were the economic powerhouses of the Continent, and so did not provide the benefits available through the EC. Two attempts were made to join the EC in the 1960s, both of which met with a veto from French president Charles de Gaulle.

De Gaulle's vetoes were not entirely exogenous, in that the conditions the British government was demanding, often under constraints set by the Commons, contributed to his actions. His veto allowed politicians retrospectively to exaggerate the chances that negotiations could have succeeded on terms acceptable to Parliament.[90] Kenneth Waltz writes:

> If there had been a change in the publicly and politically accepted definition of what British interests require, the government would have been able to enter negotiations with its hands free. Had the government in the absence of such change been able to maneuver freely in international negotiation, both its courage and its power would have been impressive.

Neither of these conditional statements describes what actually took place.[91]

British analyses of de Gaulle's vetoes from the 1960s show a keen appreciation of the ways in which the domestic political situation in Britain contributed to the vetoes, and perhaps saved the Conservative government from the immensely embarrassing situation of not being able to sell at home an important international agreement. One analysis suggests that de Gaulle saw Macmillan's weakness at home, along with political difficulties on other foreign policy issues, as "ample ground for the august and calculating bride [i.e., de Gaulle] to turn back from the altar."[92] Another argues that the task of selling any agreement at home would have been so difficult that "the French decision to break off the negotiations may well have saved it [Britain] from one of the most agonizing decisions a British government has ever had to face."[93] A Conservative MP, L. P. S. Orr, used much the same language, saying "he was 'saved from making the agonizing decision of voting against my own government at that time by the actions of President de Gaulle.'"[94] It was widely accepted in the government that any deal possibly agreed upon in Brussels could not be approved in Westminster.[95]

Both the Labour and the Conservative parties were deeply split on the principle of EC entry and the terms under which it should take place.[96] This has meant that in many cases the discipline of party politics has not applied to policy toward the EC.[97] These divisions had devastating effects on negotiations with the EC, since member states did not believe the British government to be able to make credible commitments.[98] Prime Minister Harold Macmillan could not find a deal that simultaneously satisfied domestic interests and his negotiating partners in 1961.[99] Even those, such as Bruce Lenman, who argue that Parliament nearly always lacks influence, concede that the terms negotiated in Brussels were strongly motivated by "unavoidable" political constraints back home and that Macmillan could not declare a commitment to entry without also committing political suicide.[100] Pressure from backbenchers forced the British government to make unreasonably high demands on the original six EC members.[101]

Harold Wilson, although leading a Labour rather than a Conservative government, faced similar constraints in 1966–1967. He was aware that de Gaulle's veto was in part attributable to the British domestic situation,[102] believed that Macmillan had made a mistake by avoiding debate in the Commons, and so called for votes on the principle of application. Although the Commons did approve the application, the negative votes of thirty-six Labour MPs and the abstention of approximately fifty others in spite of a three-line whip again created questions about the government's ability to commit credibly to ratification of international agreements.[103] Wilson continued to face severe disciplinary problems within his party, forcing him to hold a series of party meetings.[104]

After the failure of Wilson's attempt to negotiate, many in the Labour Party turned against the idea of entry. Concern about the neoliberal economics and Christian Democratic politics of major EC partners made many in the Labour Party skeptical, while opponents to entry in the Conservative Party emphasized the importance of maintaining ties to the Commonwealth and the United States in preference to ties with the Continent. Wilson nevertheless decided to push for negotiations when Georges Pompidou replaced de Gaulle in June 1969. By the time of British general elections on 18 June 1970, preparations for negotiations were far advanced. The Conservative Party won the election and began negotiations twelve days later on the terms set in place by the outgoing government.

Edward Heath, who had been deeply involved in the previous Conservative attempt to negotiate EC entry, took over the position of prime minister. He was committed to entry and appointed a cabinet that was pro-entry, for the most part. Heath was, however, concerned about the prospects for success. One possibility was that terms acceptable to the cabinet "would be so distasteful to a sufficient number of Conservative anti-Marketeers and Labour MPs that the cabinet would lose heart and jib at presenting them to Parliament."[105] An even more frightening possibility was that "Parliament might actually throw the Accession Treaty out, with or without the government to boot."[106] These prospects led Heath to bargain for good terms of entry, gaining Britain special exemptions for Commonwealth countries on tariff and quota treatment, and to engage in a campaign to persuade the public and sufficient numbers of MPs to approve of entry. For example, a White Paper on the terms of entry played up the tangible economic benefits of EC membership. But, "it was to the vote in the House that all energies had in the last resort to be directed."[107]

The first key vote, on the principle of accession, was timed strategically by Heath for October 1971. Party whips had warned in the spring against an early vote, since they estimated that the government stood a good chance of losing. The Conservatives' majority in the

Commons was narrow, so defections had to be kept under a dozen unless support from other parties was forthcoming. Delay over the summer allowed MPs to talk to their local party associations to gain a better sense of their constituency interests, which Heath believed would tend to favor entry. A longer delay, however, would have jeopardized the negotiations themselves as the government's credibility was questioned.

Given the narrow government majority, party whips were constantly engaged in efforts to estimate as precisely as possible the number of likely defections. Over the summer, they guessed that between twenty and thirty votes were dependent on achieving a change in the EC's fisheries policy.[108] One study found that the fisheries

> issue was a politically dangerous one for the Government, not simply because of the inherent strength and attractiveness of the fishermen's case, but also because constituencies containing areas heavily dependent on inshore fishing included some whose Members would normally belong to the parliamentary majority favouring entry.[109]

The basic problem was that the EC's common fisheries policy allowed free access to all territorial waters, and British inshore fishermen vociferously opposed allowing other EC members access to their waters, ports, and markets. In this instance, political constraints succeeded in gaining concessions from the EC, so that nearly all British waters within a twelve-mile limit of shore, including 95% of British territorial fishing grounds, were granted protection. The British government forced additional substantial changes in a fisheries policy that had just been renegotiated within the EC, due to domestic-parliamentary constraints.

As a result of Heath's efforts and progress on the fisheries issue, by the October Conservative Party conference only about thirty members were believed to be willing to defy a whip and vote against the principle of entry. This number, however, would be sufficient to lead to a government defeat unless some members of the Labour and Liberal Parties could be enticed to vote for the government. Thus, Heath decided to allow a free vote, which encouraged pro-entry members of the Opposition to defy their party leaders and support the government. This decision shows the hollowness of the assumption that party discipline overrides all dissent. On 28 October, the Commons approved the principle of accession by a vote of 356 to 244. Thirty-nine Conservative MPs voted against the government, and two abstained.[110] The free vote encouraged 69 Labour MPs to vote yes and 20 to abstain, significantly contributing to the government's majority.

In the summer of 1972, as the treaty of accession was completed and a vote to implement it into domestic law approached, the government maneuvered to overcome opposition. In addition to the fisheries issue, MPs demanded concessions on the EC budget, imports of Commonwealth sugar, and imports of dairy products from New Zealand. The government succeeded in getting such concessions. Without them, approval of the accession treaty was unlikely. The government attempted to avoid some parliamentary constraints by having the European Communities Bill considered in standing committee rather than on the floor. Since it had partial control over the makeup of the committee, the government could stack it with pro-Market MPs. Sending the bill "upstairs," however, required majority approval, which was not forthcoming, so the government was forced to deal with the entire bill on the floor. In the end, the EC Act passed by a vote of 301 to 284, and support from Labour in defiance of a party whip was essential to the legislation's passage.

Parliamentary influence on engagement with the EC did not end with the EC Act. Because the process of accession had split the Labour Party deeply, when it came into office in October 1974 it made continued membership contingent on a popular referendum. Again, domestic pressure led to concessions in the process of renegotiation.[111] These concessions were enough to allow the Labour Party to recommend that MPs vote in favor of membership, although the cabinet itself voted only 16 to 7 in favor. In an unusual move, ministers were allowed to dissent from the party's position and lobby against continued membership in the run-up to the referendum.

Consideration of the logic of legislative action on foreign policy suggested that the conventional wisdom about the House of Commons' lack of influence contained logical flaws. Formally, MPs can block and amend government initiatives, and they have at times done so. Their influence may be even greater, however, when they do not have to vote against the government, since this can indicate successful government accommodation of members' preferences. If these statements are correct, the same methods used to study legislative-executive interactions in the United States should be applicable to Britain and provide a means to develop propositions about differences in delegation and policy outcomes in the two countries. Establishing the conditions and extent of Commons' influence will require further research, but an overview of the British decision to join the EC suggests that the Commons significantly constrained British policy and had an impact on the nature of the deals struck with the EC. Without the veto and amendment power of the Commons, Britain would not have joined the EC on the terms that it did.

This essay addresses one of the key institutional changes that emerge during political liberalization: the creation of a legislature with influence over policy. It considers three issues: the legislative role in foreign policy during the transition to liberalization; the use of spatial models and theories of delegation to specify the conditions for legislative influence in different types of democratic systems; and the case of British entry to the EC as an instance of underappreciated legislative influence on a major foreign policy decision. Systematic analysis of the role of legislatures in foreign policy requires that we adopt a set of tools and models that can be applied across countries and issues. Spatial models and models of delegation have the potential to provide the necessary analytical leverage to avoid some of the pitfalls of earlier forays into comparative foreign policy. Such models allow us to assess the impact of different configurations of preferences and procedures on policy outcomes and to develop hypotheses about the choice of delegation regimes by legislatures. However, these tools have been developed primarily by those studying domestic policy in the American context.[112] Because most students of British politics assume that the House of Commons has little impact on policy because of the dictates of party discipline and that it is particularly handicapped in the area of foreign policy, Britain provides a difficult case for the development of delegation models in a non-U.S. setting.

Spatial models assume a fixed constitutional specification of powers, so that applications to transitional periods, when property rights over decision making are in flux, are probably misleading. The example of Britain in the seventeenth century suggests that during transitions, legislative bodies can exercise control over foreign policy through their power of the purse. In fact, until patterns of authority are firmly established, these legislative constraints can hamper a state's ability to develop foreign policy, as political actors fear that international struggles will be used to influence the outcome of domestic ones. Legislative "interference" in foreign policy appears to be particularly intense and disruptive during transitions, when policy making is consumed by a struggle to establish property rights over policies. This pattern appears to hold in seventeenth-century England as well as twentieth-century Russia.

In established democracies, the demands of international interaction lead to significant delegation of authority to the executive. However, the notion that the contemporary legislature in Britain has abdicated its influence to the executive suffers from the same logical weaknesses as similar assertions about the U.S. Congress. Consideration of the rules and incentives facing legislators and executives suggests that inactivity is not equivalent to impotence and allows us to specify the conditions for legislative influence. With conflicting policy preferences and good information about them, anticipated reactions can be expected to operate so that executives are constrained by the reactions they expect from the legislature. In Britain, the importance of party and the gatekeeping power of the executive lead to outcomes not generally consistent with what we would expect under similar conditions in the United States. This difference does not mean that the executive is unconstrained, nor does it invalidate the use of spatial models. Instead, these models provide a means by which to assess systematically similarities and differences across the two systems. Even in the "high politics" world of international negotiations, executives in Britain and the United States cannot act without considering the constraints on policy emanating from the legislature. In established democracies we observe a great deal of delegation to the executive and apparent passivity in the legislature, but this pattern of activity masks deeper patterns of institutionalized influence.

Notes

My thanks for valuable comments and suggestions go to Jim Alt, John Ferejohn, Jeff Frieden, Judy Goldstein, Joanne Gowa, Miles Kahler, Bob Keohane, Bob Putnam, and participants in the Social Science Research Council Liberalization and Foreign Policy project. I gratefully acknowledge the support of the SSRC's Advanced Foreign Policy Fellowship Program and the Hoover Institution's National Fellows Program.

1. Robert D. Putnam, in "Diplomacy and Domestic Politics: The Logic of Two-Level Games," *International Organization* 42, no. 3 (Summer 1988): 427–460, represents an exception to this pattern by suggesting an approach that integrates a role for the legislature or other ratifying bodies.

2. Malcolm Walles, *British and American Systems of Government* (Oxford: Philip Allan, 1988).

3. David Kaiser, *Politics and War: European Conflict from Philip II to Hitler* (Cambridge: Harvard University Press, 1990).

4. Mark R. Brawley, *Liberal Leadership: Great Powers and Their Challengers in Peace and War* (Ithaca: Cornell University Press, 1993), pp. 41–55. For a rational-choice interpretation of electoral incentives in the early seventeenth century, see John Ferejohn, "Rationality and Interpretation: Parliamentary Elections in Early Stuart England," in Kristen Renwick Monroe, ed., *The Economic Approach to Politics: A Critical Reassessment of the Theory of Rational Action* (New York: HarperCollins, 1991), pp. 279–305.

5. Douglass C. North and Barry R. Weingast, "Constitutions and Commitment: The Evolution of Institutions Governing Public Choice in Seventeenth-Century England," *Journal of Economic History* 49, no. 4 (December 1989): 803–832; Derek McKay and H. M. Scott, *The Rise of the Great Powers, 1648–1815* (London: Longman, 1983): 46.

6. J. R. Jones, *Britain and the World, 1659–1815* (Atlantic Highlands, N.J.: Humanities Press, 1980), p. 52. While these states were hardly representative by today's standards, they were the most representative in Europe at the time. See Charles Wilson, *Profit and Power: A Study of England and the Dutch Wars* (The Hague: Martinus Nijhoff, 1978), p. 146. On transitional states and war, see Edward D. Mansfield and Jack T. Snyder, "Democratization and the Danger of War," *International Security* 20, no. 1 (Summer 1995): 5–38.

7. See, for example, Keith Feiling, *British Foreign Policy, 1660–1672* (London: Frank Cass, 1968), p. 3.

8. Charles Wilson, *England's Apprenticeship, 1603–1763*, 2d ed. (London: Longman, 1984), p. 93.

9. Jones, pp. 68–69.

10. Brawley, p. 55.

11. Jones, p. 76.

12. Ibid., p. 97.

13. John Brewer, *The Sinews of Power: War, Money, and the English State, 1688–1783* (Cambridge: Harvard University Press, 1990), p. 9.

14. North and Weingast, p. 822.

15. Brewer, p. vii.

16. Ibid., p. 21.

17. Jones, p. 136.

18. Brewer, p. 139.

19. Christopher Hill, *The Century of Revolution, 1603–1714* (New York: Norton, 1980), p. 237.

20. Brewer, p. 137. A similar story can be told about early twentieth-century Russian reforms; see David MacLaren McDonald, *United Government and Foreign Policy in Russia, 1900–1914* (Cambridge: Harvard University Press, 1992).

21. Keith Feiling, *British Foreign Policy, 1660–1672* (London: Frank Cass, 1968), p. 13.

22. Brawley, p. 55. See also Hill, p. 226; McKay and Scott, p. 46.

23. Aaron L. Friedberg, "Is the United States Capable of Acting Strategically? Congress and the President," *Washington Quarterly* 14 (Winter 1991): 5–23.

24. For example, see Thomas L. Brewer, *American Foreign Policy: A Contemporary Introduction*, 3d ed. (Englewood Cliffs, N.J.: Prentice-Hall, 1992); Cecil V. Crabb Jr. and Pat M. Holt, *Invitation to Struggle: Congress, the President, and Foreign Policy*, 4th ed. (Washington, D.C.: Congressional Quarterly Press, 1992).

25. Mathew D. McCubbins and Thomas Schwartz, "Congressional Oversight Overlooked: Police Patrols Versus Fire Alarms," *American Journal of Political Science* 28, no. 1 (February 1984): 165–179; Barry R. Weingast and Mark J. Moran, "Bureaucratic

Discretion or Congressional Control? Regulatory Policymaking by the Federal Trade Commission," *Journal of Political Economy* 91 (1983): 765–800; Mathew D. McCubbins, Roger G. Noll, and Barry R. Weingast, "Structure and Process, Politics and Policy: Administrative Arrangements and the Political Control of Agencies," *Virginia Law Review* 75 (1989): 431–482.

26. D. Roderick Kiewiet and Mathew D. McCubbins, *The Logic of Delegation* (Chicago: University of Chicago Press, 1991).

27. Arthur Lupia and Mathew D. McCubbins, in "Can Democracy Work? Persuasion, Enlightenment, and Democratic Institutions" (unpublished manuscript, University of California, San Diego, 1995), explore the informational conditions for effective delegation, finding that they are not terribly stringent.

28. Terry M. Moe, "Political Institutions: The Neglected Side of the Story," *Journal of Law, Economics, and Organization* 6, special issue (1990): 213–253.

29. Elizabeth M. Martin, "Free Trade and Fast Track: Why Does Congress Delegate?" (Stanford University, November 1991, mimeographed).

30. Susanne Lohmann and Sharyn O'Halloran, "Divided Government and U.S. Trade Policy: Theory and Evidence," *International Organization* 48, no. 4 (Autumn 1994): 595–632.

31. See, for example, Gene M. Grossman and Elhanan Helpman, "Trade Wars and Trade Talks" (Princeton University, October 1992, unpublished manuscript).

32. Lohmann and O'Halloran.

33. E. M. Martin.

34. Jongryn Mo, "The President and Congress in a Reciprocal Trade Negotiation Game: The Role of Delegated Authority" (University of Texas, Austin, and Hoover Institution, August 1991, mimeographed).

35. Lohmann and O'Halloran. For similar stories about the rationales for delegation, particularly on the Reciprocal Trade Agreements Act of 1934, see Stephan Haggard, "The Institutional Foundations of Hegemony: Explaining the Reciprocal Trade Agreements Act of 1934," in John Ikenberry, David Lake, and Michael Mastanduno, eds., *The State and American Foreign Economic Policy* (Ithaca: Cornell University Press, 1988), and I. M. Destler, *American Trade Politics: System Under Stress* (Washington, D.C.: Institute for International Economics, 1986). The volume edited by Ikenberry, Lake, and Mastanduno adopts an institutional approach similar to that used in this essay, although for the most part it does not concentrate on legislatures.

36. Richard Rose, *Politics in England: Change and Persistence*, 5th ed. (London: Macmillan, 1989), pp. 112–113.

37. John Garrett, *Westminster: Does Parliament Work?* (London: Victor Gollancz, 1992), p. 15.

38. Bruce P. Lenman, *The Eclipse of Parliament: Appearance and Reality in British Politics Since 1914* (London: Edward Arnold, 1992), p. 9.

39. Michael Clarke, *British External Policy-making in the 1990s* (Washington, D.C.: Brookings Institution, 1992), p. 114.

40. For example, see David Vital, *The Making of British Foreign Policy* (New York: Praeger, 1968).

41. Ibid., p. 49.

42. Michael Clarke, "The Policy-Making Process," in Michael Smith, Steve Smith, and Brian White, eds., *British Foreign Policy: Tradition, Change, and Transformation* (London: Unwin Hyman, 1988), pp. 72–73.

43. Gary W. Cox, *The Efficient Secret: The Cabinet and the Development of Political Parties in Victorian England* (Cambridge: Cambridge University Press, 1987).

44. Rose, p. 121.

45. Cox, p. 3.

46. Ibid., p. 3.

47. Vital, p. 79.

48. William Wallace, *The Foreign Policy Process in Britain* (London: Royal Institute of International Affairs, 1975), p. 98.

49. Robert Borthwick, "The Floor of the House," in Michael Ryle and Peter G. Richards, eds., *The Commons Under Scrutiny* (London: Routledge, 1988), p. 74.

50. Kenneth Waltz, *Foreign Policy and Democratic Politics: The American and British Experience* (Boston: Little, Brown, 1967), p. 44.

51. Rose, pp. 19–21; Philip Norton, *The Commons in Perspective* (New York: Longman, 1981), pp. 1–2.

52. See William S. Livingston, "Britain and America: The Institutionalization of Accountability," *Journal of Politics* 38, no. 4 (November 1976): 879–894.

53. R. M. Punnett, *British Government and Politics*, 5th ed. (Aldershot: Gower, 1987), p. 186.

54. Philip Norton, *The British Polity*, 3d ed. (New York: Longman, 1994), p. 274.

55. Rose, p. 122.

56. Norton, *The Commons in Perspective*, pp. 19–20.

57. Rose, p. 112.

58. Alan Beith, "Prayers Unanswered: A Jaundiced View of the Parliamentary Scrutiny of Statutory Instruments," *Parliamentary Affairs* 34, no. 2 (Spring 1981): 167, 169.

59. Gavin Drewry, "Legislation," in Ryle and Richards, p. 139.

60. See Norton, *The Commons in Perspective*; Norton, "Dissent in the British House of Commons: Rejoinder to Franklin, Baxter, Jordan," *Legislative Studies Quarterly* 12, no. 1 (February 1987): 143–156; Norton, "Behavioural Changes: Backbench Independence in the 1980s," in Norton, ed., *Parliament in the 1980s* (New York: Basil Blackwell, 1985), pp. 22–47; Norton, "The Changing Face of the British House of Commons In the 1970s," *Legislative Studies Quarterly* 5, no. 3 (August 1980): 333–357; Norton, *Dissension in the House of Commons 1974–1979* (London: Oxford University Press, 1980); Norton, *Conservative Dissidents: Dissent Within the Parliamentary Conservative Party 1970–74* (London: Temple Smith, 1978); Norton, "Dissent in Committee: Intra-Party Dissent in Commons' Standing Committees 1959–74," *The Parliamentarian* 57, no. 1 (January 1976): 15–25.

61. Norton, *The Commons in Perspective*, p. 227.

62. Ibid., p. 230.

63. J. Richard Piper, "Backbench Rebellion, Party Government and Consensus Politics: The Case of the Parliamentary Labour Party, 1966–1970," *Parliamentary Affairs* 27, no. 4 (Autumn 1974): 384–396; Robert J. Jackson, *Rebels and Whips: An Analysis of Dissension, Discipline and Cohesion in British Political Parties* (London: Macmillan, 1968).

64. Norton, *Conservative Dissidents*.

65. Norton, *The British Polity*, pp. 288–289.

66. Dennis Kavanagh, *British Politics: Continuities and Change* (New York: Oxford University Press, 1985), p. 235.

67. Ibid., p. 236. See also Bruce Cain, John Ferejohn, and Morris Fiorina, *The Personal Vote: Constituency Service and Electoral Responsiveness* (Cambridge: Harvard University Press, 1987).

68. Brian Gaines and Geoffrey Garrett, "The Calculus of Dissent: Party Discipline in the British Labour Government, 1974–1979" (Stanford University, May 1992, mimeographed).

69. James J. Lynskey, "The Role of Government Backbenchers in the Modification of Government Policy," *Western Political Quarterly* 23, no. 2 (June 1970): 333–347.

70. Norton, "Opposition to Government," in Ryle and Richards, p. 113.

71. Kavanagh, p. 235.

72. Ian Budge and David McKay, *The Changing British Political System: Into the 1990s,* 2d ed. (London: Longman, 1988), p. 57.

73. Jackson, p. 292.

74. Punnett, p. 190.

75. Kavanagh, p. 237.

76. Norton, *The British Polity*, p. 289.

77. Jackson, p. 200.

78. Ronald Butt, *The Power of Parliament* (London: Constable, 1967), p. 427.

79. Norton, *Dissension*, p. 429.

80. In Congress, majority-rule voting means that the median member of the House as a whole is the swing voter. The influence of party discipline complicates the identification of the swing voter in the Commons. Many analyses suggest that the government wishes to assure passage of legislation without support from minority parties. Thus, on legislation where the whip is in place, the swing voter should be that party member who guarantees the government a majority. This MP may be quite radical, from the government's perspective, with an ideal point far from P. If, on the other hand, the government chooses to allow a free vote, the median member of the Commons should become the swing voter. The government, as a strategic actor, will choose the voting regime that gives it the outcome closest to its ideal point. These speculations should be explicitly modeled in further work.

81. This assumes that one dimension is a reasonable simplification for this preliminary analysis, since even complicated issues can often be conceived of as leading to bargaining along a contract curve.

82. For the concept of structure-induced equilibrium, see Kenneth A. Shepsle, "Institutional Equilibrium and Equilibrium Institutions," in Herbert Weisberg, ed., *Political Science: The Science of Politics* (New York: Agathon, 1986); Kenneth A. Shepsle and Barry Weingast, "Structure Induced Equilibrium and Legislative Choice," *Public Choice* 37 (1981): 503–519.

83. This story is complicated if we allow for the exercise of veto power by the president. MC is no longer necessarily the unique structure-induced equilibrium if the president is willing to exercise his veto. To facilitate comparison between the British and U.S. cases, I do not consider the possibility of a veto in this discussion.

84. The discussion thus far has assumed that the cabinet is a unitary actor. Factional disputes within parties are common and significant, however, and should be explicitly included in the models. See Michael Laver and Kenneth A. Shepsle, "Government Coalitions and Intraparty Politics," *British Journal of Political Science* 20 (October 1990): 489–507.

85. This is true in the very simple example given here, which has assumed away a number of complications, such as collective action problems in Congress, the need to negotiate with other countries, or the desire to gain information about proposed policies from the executive. These factors are especially important in foreign policy and are necessary to explain the adoption of fast-track procedures, for example.

86. Keith Krehbiel, *Information and Legislative Delegation* (Ann Arbor: University of Michigan Press, 1991).

87. James J. Lynskey, "Backbench Tactics and Parliamentary Party Structure," *Parliamentary Affairs* 27, no. 1 (Winter 1973/74): 31.

88. *The Economist*, 11 April 1992, p. 15.

89. For example, see the *New York Times*, 17 May 1992, p. 8; Lisa L. Martin, "The Influence of National Parliaments on European Integration" (CFIA Working Paper 94–10, Harvard University, 1994).

90. See Waltz, pp. 257–258.

91. Ibid., p. 266.

92. Christopher Layton, "Introduction," *Journal of Common Market Studies* 3, no. 3 (1965): 205.

93. Roy Pryce, "Britain Out of Europe?" *Journal of Common Market Studies* 2, no. 1 (1964): 3.

94. Cynthia W. Frey, "Meaning Business: The British Application to Join the Common Market, November 1966–October 1967," *Journal of Common Market Studies* 6, no. 3 (1968): 212.

95. William Pickles, "The Choice and the Facts," *Journal of Common Market Studies* 4, no. 1 (1966): 27.

96. Roy Jenkins, "The Disappointing Partnership Between British Governments and Europe" (Thirteenth Annual Paul-Henri Spaak Lecture, Center for International Affairs, Harvard University, 13 October 1994), p. 11.

97. Philip Allott, "Britain and Europe: A Political Analysis," *Journal of Common Market Studies* 8, no. 3 (1970): 204.

98. Robert J. Lieber, *British Politics and European Unity: Parties, Elites, and Pressure Groups* (Berkeley: University of California Press, 1970), p. 184; Richard Mayne, "Why Bother with Europe?" *Journal of Common Market Studies* 3, no. 3 (1965): 231–232.

99. Stephen George, *An Awkward Partner: Britain in the European Community* (New York: Oxford University Press, 1990), p. 34.

100. Lenman, pp. 218–229.

101. Pickles, p. 26.

102. Frey, p. 198.

103. George, p. 248.

104. Frey, p. 205.

105. Uwe Kitzinger, *Diplomacy and Persuasion: How Britain Joined the Common Market* (London: Thames and Hudson, 1973), p. 105.

106. Ibid., p. 105.

107. Ibid., p. 159.

108. Ibid., p. 170.

109. Simon Z. Young, *Terms of Entry: Britain's Negotiations with the European Community, 1970–72* (London: Heinemann, 1973), p. 99.

110. Kitzinger, p. 188.

111. Anthony King, *Britain Says Yes: The 1975 Referendum on the Common Market* (Washington, D.C.: American Enterprise Institute for Public Policy Research, 1977).

112. For exceptions, see J. Mark Ramseyer and Frances M. Rosenbluth, *The Politics of Oligarchy: Institutional Choice in Imperial Japan* (New York: Cambridge University Press, 1995); John Huber, "Restrictive Legislative Procedures in France and the United States," *American Political Science Review* 86 (September 1992): 675–687.

THREE

Democratic States and International Disputes

Joanne Gowa

As a replacement for the Cold War strategy of containment, the Clinton administration has adopted a foreign policy strategy of "enlargement." According to Anthony Lake, assistant to the president for national security affairs, the administration's strategy is designed to enlarge the world's "community of market democracies."[1] This strategy serves U.S. interests, President Clinton maintains, because "democracies rarely wage war on one another."[2]

The Clinton administration strategy reflects the findings of the rapidly growing body of literature about the democratic peace. Perhaps the most striking conclusion to emerge from this largely empirical literature is the following: democratic states do not wage war against other democratic states. More generally, studies in this literature conclude that the incidence of serious disputes is much lower between democratic polities than between members of other pairs of polities.[3]

In this essay, I examine the three arguments that contributors to this literature most commonly advance to explain their findings. One argument emphasizes the role of norms; the second focuses upon checks and balances; and the third assigns the principal explanatory role to trade. I conclude that none of the three arguments provides a compelling explanation of the peace that is said to prevail between democratic polities. Recent empirical analyses reinforce this conclusion.[4]

The Existing Literature

There is a rapidly growing body of literature that examines whether the foreign policies of democratic states are unique. There is a strong consensus on two related issues. First, democracies do not engage each other in war. Second, and implied by the first, members of pairs of democratic states are much less likely to engage each other in serious disputes short of war than are members of other pairs of states.

Many contributors to the literature under review here examine whether the incidence of war between democracies differs from that of war between other states.[5] According to William Dixon, the democratic-peace literature has produced "very strong and consistent empirical evidence that wars between democracies are at most very rare events."[6] Indeed, on the basis of their analysis of data spanning 150 years, Zeev Maov and Nasrin Abdolali conclude that "democracies never fight one another."[7]

Students of this issue have been very careful to make it clear that whether a state is democratic does not affect its overall propensity to wage war. They note that democracies are just as likely as are other states to engage in war.[8] In addition, there is no strong evidence that democracies are any less likely than are other polities to initiate war. Thus, the incidence of war between democracies is not an indicator of the war-proneness of democracies in general. Instead, the distinctive effect of democracy on war is limited to cases in which both members of a pair of states are democratic.

Another finding that emerges from this literature relates to the outbreak of "militarized interstate disputes" (MIDs). Several studies find that members of pairs of democratic states engage each other in MIDs at a significantly lower rate than do members of other dyads. A dispute is categorized as a MID if (1) it involves "threats to use military force, displays of military force, or actual uses of force" and (2) the threat or deployment of military forces is "explicit, overt, nonaccidental, and government sanctioned."[9] Examples of MIDs include the 1898 Fashoda crisis, the 1962 Cuban missile crisis, and the 1969 Sino-Soviet border crisis. The finding about MIDs echoes that about wars: militarized disputes are much less likely to occur between democracies than between members of other pairs of states.

Using data in the International Crisis Behavior (ICB) data set, contributors to this literature have also analyzed the relationship between democracies and the incidence of crises. The definition of a crisis, according to Michael Brecher and Jonathan Wilkenfeld, is "a situational change characterized by an increase in the intensity of disruptive interaction between two or more adversaries, with a high probability of military hostilities."[10] As in the case of wars and MIDs, crises are less likely to occur between members of democratic dyads than between members of other dyads.[11]

Thus there seems to be consensus that the behavior of democracies in the international arena is distinctive in some respects. War between democratic polities is nonexistent, and MIDs short of war or crises between these polities are relatively rare events. A series of empirical analyses has replicated these findings.

The issue that has been less intensively examined is why democracies behave differently. As I noted above, it has become conventional in the relevant literature to advance one or more of three explanations of the distinctive behavior of democracies. The first relies on norms, the second on checks and balances, and the third on trade. In the next three sections, I examine each in turn.

NORMS

The findings of the democratic-peace literature imply that "Second Image" or domestic political factors are essential to an understanding of the outcomes of state interactions. That is, the latter cannot be explained exclusively in terms of the interests of abstract states, as defined by the logic of the situations in which these states find themselves. This, in turn, implies that a clear distinction should exist between the explanations that this literature invokes to support its findings and those familiar from "Third Image" or realist theory. Norm-based explanations of the democratic peace fail this test.

Norms are "rules for conduct that provide standards by which behavior is approved or disapproved."[12] Much of the democratic-peace literature assigns primary importance to the norm that defines appropriate methods of resolving conflicts within democratic polities. Proscribing recourse to force, the relevant norm legitimates as "proper" the use of either adjudication or bargaining as a method of conflict resolution.[13]

This norm is adduced to explain peace not only within but also between democratic states. According to Zeev Maoz and Bruce M. Russett, domestic norms influence international outcomes because states "*externalize . . . the norms of behavior that are developed within and characterize their domestic political processes and institutions.*"[14] Thus, if a norm mandates the peaceful resolution of disputes within two states, it will also mandate the peaceful resolution of disputes between them. Hence, the democratic peace.

Despite the nominal distinction between norms and interests, however, it is not at all clear that this explanation differs fundamentally from its conventional realist counterpart. The conclusion that the norm-based and the realist explanations are discrete follows from the interpretation of norms that dominates the democratic-peace literature. In this interpretation, norms have "independent motivating power." As such, they are "ex ante sources of action" rather than "merely ex post rationalizations of self interest."[15]

The apparent distinction between norm-based and interest-based explanations would fade, however, if the democratic-peace literature adopted another interpretation of norms. For example, some contributors to the more general literature on norms believe that norms reflect interests, because it is the expectation of external sanctions rather than internalized values that explains adherence to norms. In this interpretation, as James Finley Scott notes, an individual " 'internalizes' or learns a norm to the extent that . . . he conforms to it at a spatial or temporal remove from sanctions." However, learning is the product of "sanctions applied by . . . the social environment." And, Scott adds,

> the learning of norms is never complete, and always involves expectations that sanctions will be applied. Thus even when norms are thoroughly learned, when moral commitment is strong and a sense of obligation is keenly felt, the maintenance of both conscience and conformity depends on the exercise of sanctions.[16]

In this interpretation, it is interests that drive norms: little, if anything, distinguishes between them. If the democratic-peace literature adopted this interpretation, the prominent role it assigns to the norm of peaceful dispute resolution could be recast in terms of the interests of states and the logic of their situations. Then, the interests of states in a peaceful resolution of disputes, whether at home or abroad, would follow from the relative price of that option: bargaining is less costly than war, whether civil or international.[17] From this perspective, what seems problematic is not the interest of states in settling disputes short of war but their failure to do so.[18]

This argument suggests that the norm-based explanation common in the democratic-peace literature is not distinct from explanations of war and disputes that realist theory advances. In the latter, interests are understood as responses to the logic of situations and as independent of the particular states involved. This implies, in turn, that the outcomes of armed disputes should not vary across states according to their regime types.

That just such a lack of variance obtains is the finding that emerges from recent empirical analyses. Its most powerful support derives from the existence of an inconsistent relationship between polities and peace across time: before World War I, no difference exists between the rates at which members of democratic dyads and members of other dyads engage each other in war; after World War II, democracies have a lower incidence of war between them than do other polities.[19]

Variations in patterns of alliance formation across the two periods help explain this inconsistency: before World War I, democracies are significantly less likely to be allied with each other than are other states; after World War II, they ally at a significantly higher rate than do members of other pairs of polities.[20] Because alliances reflect the common and conflicting interests of states, this finding implies that the inconsistent relationship between democracies and war across time is a function of changing patterns of interests.

CHECKS AND BALANCES

The premise of the checks-and-balances argument is that much more effective domestic political constraints on leaders exist in democratic polities than in other kinds of polities.[21] As such, the argument is the clear intellectual descendant of that which Immanuel Kant advanced long ago. In states that are not republics, Kant maintained, "a declaration of war is the easiest thing in the world to decide upon, because war does not require of the ruler, who is the proprietor and not a member of the state, the least sacrifice of the pleasure of his table, the chase, his country houses, his court functions, and the like." As a result, Kant observed, an autocrat may "resolve on war as on a pleasure party for the most trivial reasons."[22]

Even if this assumption about checks and balances were true, it is important to note that structural constraints will not always bind leaders of democratic polities considering the option of war. Whether they will do so depends upon the net welfare consequences of war. In some cases, aggregate social welfare will be higher if states enter into war than if they decline to do so (e.g., allied and U.S. entry into World War II). In these cases, whether checks and balances exist will not make any difference: assuming that the gains from war are distributed across the population, a majority will favor entry into war.[23]

The potential for checks and balances to bite, then, exists only in situations in which distributional rather than efficiency concerns motivate the prosecution of a war. It is these cases, however, that raise questions about whether it makes sense to assume that checks and balances operate as effectively in practice as in principle: by definition, if distributional issues drive decisions about war, political-market failures have led to the breakdown of a checks-and-balances system.

Incomplete information is a common cause of imperfect political markets. Other sources include asymmetries in the cost-benefit distributions associated with many government policies, as well as variations in the political efficacy of different groups. These political-market failures drive a wedge between the de jure and the de facto operation of checks-and-balances systems.

For example, political-market failures produce tariffs and nontariff barriers to trade (NTBs). These barriers exist in most democracies despite the fact that their effect on aggregate social welfare is negative. They do so, in part, because trade barriers produce concentrated benefits and diffuse costs: producers gain; consumers lose. This distributional asymmetry reinforces a skew in political participation: because of their relatively small number and high geographic concentration, producers tend to be more effective political actors than are consumers. Thus, democratic political processes do not constrain leaders to define trade policy so as to maximize social welfare.[24]

As in the case of tariffs and NTBs, the prosecution of a war can also yield a pattern of concentrated benefits and diffuse costs that creates a political-market failure. Producers (e.g., defense contractors) are likely to be more effective political actors than is the population at large. The composition of the armed forces may create an even more skewed political process than exists in trade: whether under a draft or a volunteer system, evidence from the United States suggests that the costs of military service fall disproportionately on low-income constituents—that is, on those whose rates of political participation are relatively low.[25] The net effect, again, is to create a wedge between the principle and practice of checks and balances.

These patterns of political resource endowments benefit heads of state, as well as special rather than general interests. As Adam Smith observed long ago, the voice that democratic regimes give to special interests can produce foreign policies that are inimical to the nation as a whole. Of imperialism, for example, Smith noted:

> To found a great empire for the sole purpose of raising up a people of customers may at first sight appear a project fit only for a nation of shopkeepers. It is, however, a project altogether unfit for a nation of shopkeepers; but extremely fit for a nation whose government is influenced by shopkeepers.[26]

This discussion is not meant to imply that no differences exist between the policy processes that produce tariffs and those that produce wars. Large wars have the potential to precipitate a markedly different political process than do small wars, because their costs are spread more widely across the population than are those of small wars. Yet, because most wars are small wars, the trade analogue is useful for the argument here. In both cases, concentrated benefits and diffuse costs and variable barriers to collective action impede the effective operation of checks and balances.

Further diluting the power of the conventional checks-and-balances argument is the existence of informal substitutes for structural constraints in nondemocracies. The tenure in office of leaders of these polities depends upon a supporting coalition of interests. As a result, these leaders cannot take actions that jeopardize the cohesion of the coalition of forces that maintains them in office. Indeed, empirical analyses suggest that these coalitions and those that exist in democratic polities do not differ on average with respect to their propensity to engage in war: as noted earlier, there is no difference between the rates at which democracies and nondemocracies engage in war.

Leaders of nondemocracies also confront a constraint on their ability to wage war that is unique to them.[27] The construction of a strong military force can place their incumbencies at risk. If the armed forces are strong enough to defeat foreign adversaries, they may also be sufficiently strong to overthrow their nominal commander in chief. Maintaining only weak armed forces, however, is risky too. While this strategy makes a military coup d'état improbable, it facilitates a takeover by rivals to rule outside the state. Heads of state of nondemocratic polities, therefore, confront a dilemma that does not plague leaders of democracies.

This dilemma may make rulers of these states more interested in reducing the incidence of wars than in waging them. Indeed, this interest was one motivation for the establishment of the Organization of African Unity (OAU). Its potential member states did not have large indigenous military units in place. If each agreed to respect the borders of all others, as Gordon Tullock notes, each would be able "to keep relatively small military units, and what is more important, military units that are weak."[28] As a result, the founding states agreed that a pledge to adhere to preexisting borders would be a prerequisite of membership in the OAU. To the extent that the organization confers excludable benefits, then, the OAU can facilitate collusion among incumbent African leaders to preserve their incumbency.

Thus, there are at least two reasons that the checks-and-balances argument is less compelling than it might at first glance appear: political-market failures decrease the efficacy of de jure constraints, and substitutes for them exist in nondemocratic polities. As in the case of the argument about norms, then, the discussion in this section suggests less variation in dispute rates across regimes than does the democratic-peace literature. Indeed, empirical analyses of the relationship between formal constraints and dispute involvement have not found any statistically significant effects.[29]

TRADE

Trade-based explanations of the relationship between polities and peace are less common than are either norm-based or structural-constraint explanations. Nonetheless, in some contributions to the literature under review here, trade plays an important explanatory role. Michael Doyle, for example, maintains that the "cosmopolitan right to hospitality" that democracies accord to each other allows "the 'spirit of commerce' sooner or later to take hold of every nation."[30]

According to this argument, trade flows between democratic states will be higher than are those between other states. This implies that the trade disruption that would ensue from serious interstate conflict would be more costly for members of pairs of democratic states than for members of other pairs of states. Thus, all else being equal, the incidence of conflict should be lower between democracies than between other states.

There are two problems with this argument. First, it seems clear that the "spirit of commerce" does not infect all members of democratic polities. Import-competing industries that file petitions for protection do not discriminate between the exports of democracies and those of nondemocracies. Nor is there any evidence that elected officials discriminate in this way when they supply tariffs or NTBs in response to these petitions or to other demands for protection.[31] The "spirit of commerce" may exist, but it does not seem to be highly infectious.

Thus it is not surprising that empirical analyses do not find strong and consistent evidence that trade flows are higher between democracies than between other states. Edward D. Mansfield and I examined the impact of political factors on bilateral trade flows between major powers in a series of cross sections between 1905 and 1985. We found that whether the trading partners were both democracies mattered in only one case.[32] Extending the analysis to a larger sample of countries during the post–World War II period, Mansfield and Rachel Bronson found no consistent relationship across time: although trade flows between democracies are higher than are those between other states between 1950 and 1965, no difference exists thereafter. Mansfield and Bronson attribute the positive relationship they observe in the early postwar years to the influence of the Cold War.[33]

Second, even if members of democratic pairs of states did trade consistently more with each other than their nondemocratic counterparts did, the conclusion that trade reduces the probability of conflict between them would not necessarily follow.[34] If competitive markets exist, any disruption of trade between two states will simply lead both to alternative markets. As a result, the costs incurred will be limited to the transaction costs that accompany market shifting. If both states incur roughly comparable costs, however, each would have an incentive to continue to trade with the other as long as it is feasible to do so.

Suppose, for example, that a serious diplomatic dispute breaks out between France and Germany. Suppose, in addition, that France imports its widgets from Germany and that Germany imports its goat cheese from France. Will this exchange of widgets and goat cheese exercise a strong influence on the probability that the Franco-

German dispute will escalate to one that involves the threat or use of armed force?

It will do so if and only if France has no other source of widgets or Germany no other source of goat cheese or if one country cannot find alternative export markets. That is, the threat of a breakdown of bilateral trade can act as a powerful deterrent only if France or Germany possesses monopoly or monopsony power in widget or cheese markets. Otherwise, France can import widgets and Germany cheese from other countries, and each country can find a market for its exports in a third country.

Thus a disruption of trade between two countries incident upon an armed dispute between them can inflict large welfare costs only in cases in which alternative markets do not exist. Unless conflict makes trade infeasible, however, neither belligerent may have an incentive to disrupt trade. If both states have equivalent degrees of market power over the prevailing terms of trade, a decision to disrupt trade in the event of conflict would be self-defeating: it would leave both countries worse off.[35] The existence of asymmetric market power does not affect this decision calculus. Presumably, a state able to improve its terms of trade unilaterally would have done so ex ante. If it had waited to do so until the outbreak of conflict, it would in the interim have inflicted costs upon itself in the form of forgone increases in its real income. Similarly, if its trading partner had a more profitable alternative ex ante, it would have not been subject to the exercise of market power. As in the case of a symmetric distribution of trade, then, disrupting trade in goods and services in which asymmetric market power exists will impose costs on both sides.

The logic of this argument applies as well to cases in which monopoly or monopsony power originates in a relation-specific investment. The latter, as Beth and Robert Yarbrough note, is an investment "undertaken to be used in specific transactions with a specific partner." Because its value in other transactions is either negligible or nonexistent, a relation-specific investment can endow a would-be belligerent with the requisite market power to improve its terms of trade.[36]

For example, Japanese investors might design a plant to build cars specifically to meet the demands of the U.S. market. In doing so, they become vulnerable to a U.S. holdup. Once the plant is built, the U.S. government can seek to renegotiate the terms of the agreement, because it is impossible for the owners of the plant to relocate it profitably. Other examples of relation-specific investments include cross-national upstream or downstream integration of a firm.[37]

As in the case of market power more generally, relation-specific investments need not deter dispute escalation. Investors should be aware ex ante of the danger of reneging. Thus they will attempt to minimize the ex post danger of a holdup via contingent contracts and/or the establishment of a bilateral monopoly. If neither is possible, it will be difficult to deter attempts to renege. It is not clear, however, that the onset of a serious conflict will have any effect on these attempts. Absent an effective deterrent mechanism, holdups will occur as soon as they become feasible.

Suppose, however, that reputational concerns had deterred holdups before the initiation of a conflict. In this case, the actual outbreak of armed conflict may precipitate holdups that would not have otherwise occurred. This is so because a reputation for reneging during armed conflicts is unlikely to be very costly, given the infrequency with which such conflicts occur. Thus, in this case, the escalation of a dispute may inflict trade-related costs on its potential belligerents.

Whether it will do so depends, however, upon the distribution of relation-specific investments. Although no direct evidence is available about this distribution, it seems plausible that if all else is equal, these investments will take place in countries that are unlikely to engage in serious disputes with the home country. This suggests that, as in the case of trade, investments will be skewed toward countries allied with the home country.[38]

Because armed disputes between allied countries are relatively rare, opportunism related to such disputes is also likely to be rare.[39] And, as in the cases discussed above, if each party to a dispute has made comparable relation-specific investments in the other, no holdups should occur in the event of a war or of serious disputes short of war: opportunism would only make both belligerents worse off.

None of the three explanations of the alleged democratic peace is persuasive as it stands. The interest of two potential belligerents in a peaceful resolution of disputes between them is not unique to democratic polities. Political-market failures create a wedge between the de jure and de facto operation of checks and balances, and informal substitutes for the latter exist in nondemocracies. Finally, trade can act as a strong deterrent to armed conflict only under much more restrictive conditions than is usually assumed.

It is not surprising, then, that the findings of recent empirical analyses are inconsistent with those of the democratic-peace literature. Nor is it surprising that these analyses assign a major explanatory role to interests. As reflected in alliance ties, changing patterns of common and conflicting interests seem to play a key role in explaining inconsistent dispute patterns across time (i.e., a lower war rate between members of pairs of democratic states and members of other pairs of states after 1945 but not before 1914).[40]

As a consequence, the importance of Second Image variables to an understanding of serious international conflict remains to be demonstrated, and so also does the wisdom of a strategy designed to enhance prospects for peace by promoting the spread of democracy among members of the former Warsaw Treaty Organization.

It may be more useful to build bridges, rather than democracies, abroad.

Notes

For comments on earlier versions of this paper, I am grateful to Robert J. Art, Benjamin J. Cohen, Henry S. Farber, Robert G. Gilpin Jr., Peter Gourevitch, Miles Kahler, Robert O. Keohane, Lisa Martin, and John S. Odell. I also acknowledge with gratitude the research assistance of Matthias Kaelberer and the financial support of the Center of International Studies at Princeton University.

This chapter was published previously as "Democratic States and International Disputes," *International Organization* 49(3) (Summer 1995): 511–522. © 1995 by the IO Foundation and the Massachusetts Institute of Technology.

1. Anthony Lake, "From Containment to Enlargement," *Foreign Policy Statements* (1993).

2. William Clinton, "Confronting the Challenges of a Broader World," *Foreign Policy Statements* (September 1993).

3. See, e.g., Stuart Bremer, "Dangerous Dyads: Conditions Affecting the Likelihood of Interstate War," *Journal of Conflict Resolution* 36 (June 1992): 309–341; Stuart Bremer, "Democracy and Militarized Interstate Conflict," *International Interactions* 18, no. 3 (1993): 231–249; Steve Chan, "Mirror, Mirror on the Wall . . . Are the Freer Countries More Pacific?" *Journal of Conflict Resolution* 28 (December 1984): 616–648; Steve Chan, "Democracy and War: Some Thoughts on Future Research Agenda," *International Interactions* 18, no. 3 (1993): 205–214; William Dixon, "Democracy and the Peaceful Settlement of International Conflict," *American Political Science Review* 88 (March 1994): 14–32; Michael Doyle, "Liberalism and World Politics," *American Political Science Review* 80 (December 1986): 1151–1169; Zeev Maoz and Nasrin Abdolali, "Regime Types and International Conflict," *Journal of Conflict Resolution* 33 (March 1989): 3–35; Zeev Maoz and Bruce M. Russett, "Normative and Structural Causes of Democratic Peace, 1946–86," *American Political Science Review* 87 (September 1993): 624–638; Bruce M. Russett, *Grasping the Democratic Peace: Principles*

for a Post–Cold War World (Princeton: Princeton University Press, 1993); Melvin Small and J. David Singer, "The War-Proneness of Democratic Regimes," *Jerusalem Journal of International Relations* 1 (Summer 1976): 50–68.

4. Henry S. Farber and Joanne Gowa, "Polities and Peace," *International Security* 20 (Fall 1995): 123–146; Farber and Gowa, "Reinterpreting the Democratic Peace: Common Polities or Common Interests?" *Journal of Politics* (forthcoming).

5. See, e.g., Doyle, "Liberalism and World Politics"; Maoz and Abdolali, "Regime Types and International Conflict"; Maoz and Russett, "Normative and Structural Causes of Democratic Peace"; and Erich Weede, "Democracy and War Involvement," *Journal of Conflict Resolution* 37 (March 1993): 42–68.

6. Dixon, "Democracy and the Peaceful Settlement of International Conflict," p. 14.

7. Maoz and Abdolali, "Regime Types and International Conflict," p. 21.

8. Bruce Bueno de Mesquita and David Lalman, *War and Reason: Domestic and International Imperatives* (New Haven: Yale University Press, 1992); Chan, "Mirror, Mirror on the Wall"; Doyle, "Liberalism and World Politics"; Jack Levy, "Domestic Politics and War," *Journal of Interdisciplinary History* 18 (Spring 1988): 653–673; T. Clifton Morgan and Valerie L. Schwebach, "Take Two Democracies and Call Me in the Morning: A Prescription for Peace?" *International Interactions* 17, no. 4 (1992): 305–320; R. J. Rummel, "The Relationship Between National Attributes and Foreign Conflict Behavior," in J. David Singer, ed., *Quantitative International Politics: Insights and Evidence* (New York: Free Press, 1968).

9. Charles S. Gochman and Zeev Maoz, "Militarized Interstate Disputes, 1816–1976," *Journal of Conflict Resolution* 28 (December 1984): 587.

10. Michael Brecher and Jonathan Wilkenfeld, *Crisis in the Twentieth Century* (New York: Pergamon, 1989), p. 5.

11. Maoz and Russett, "Structural and Normative Causes of the Democratic Peace," p. 632.

12. Michael Hechter, *Principles of Group Solidarity* (Berkeley: University of California Press, 1987), p. 62.

13. T. Clifton Morgan, "Democracy and War: Reflections on the Literature," *International Interactions* 18, no. 3 (1993): 198.

14. Maoz and Russett, "Structural and Normative Causes of the Democratic Peace," p. 625, emphasis in the original.

15. Jon Elster, *The Cement of Society: A Study of Social Order* (Cambridge: Cambridge University Press, 1989), p. 125.

16. John Finley Scott, *Internalization of Norms: A Sociological Theory of Moral Commitment* (Englewood Cliffs, N.J.: Prentice Hall, 1971), p. xiii.

17. James D. Fearon, "Threats to Use Force: Costly Signals and Bargaining in International Crises" (Ph.D. diss., University of California, 1992).

18. James Fearon suggests the imperfect process of signaling resolve as a candidate explanation (ibid.); James Fearon, "Domestic Political Audiences and the Escalation of International Disputes," *American Political Science Review* 88 (September 1994): 577–592.

19. Farber and Gowa, "Polities and Peace."

20. Farber and Gowa, "Reinterpreting the Democratic Peace."

21. See, e.g., David A. Lake, "Powerful Pacifists," *American Political Science Review* 86 (September 1992): 24–37. For an exception, see T. Clifton Morgan and Sally Campbell, "Domestic Structure, Decisional Constraints, and War: So Why Kant Democracies Fight?" *Journal of Conflict Resolution* 35 (June 1991): 187–211.

22. Cited in Michael Doyle, "Kant, Liberal Legacies, and Foreign Affairs: Part I," *Philosophy and Public Affairs* 12 (Summer 1983): 229.

23. I am grateful to an anonymous referee for suggestions on this point.

24. For a more complete analysis of the political processes that lead to the adoption of tariffs, see, e.g., Susanne Lohmann and Sharon O'Halloran, "Divided Government and U.S. Trade Policy: Theory and Evidence," *International Organization* 48, no. 4 (Autumn 1994): 595–632.

25. Richard V. L. Cooper, "Military Manpower Procurement: Equity, Efficiency, and National Security," in Martin Anderson, ed., *Registration and the Draft* (Stanford: Hoover Institution, 1982), pp. 343–376. Indeed, during World War I, the United States conscripted men on the basis of their " 'value to society,' with those of 'least value' drafted first" (363).

26. Cited in Robert B. Ekelund and Robert D. Tollison, *Mercantilism in a Rent-Seeking Society: Economic Regulation in a Historical Perspective* (College Station: Texas A&M University Press, 1981), p. 10.

27. This discussion is based on Gordon Tullock, *Autocracy* (Dordrecht, The Netherlands: Kluwer Academic Publishers, 1987).

28. Ibid., p. 37.

29. Morgan and Campbell, "Domestic Structure, Decisional Constraints, and War."

30. Doyle, "Liberalism and World Politics," p. 1161.

31. See, e.g., Peter Gourevitch, *Politics in Hard Times: Comparative Responses to International Economic Crises* (Ithaca: Cornell University Press, 1986); Stephen P. Magee, William A. Brock, and Leslie Young, *Black Hole Tariffs and Endogenous Policy Theory: Political Economy in General Equilibrium* (New York: Cambridge University Press, 1989); Ronald Rogowski, *Commerce and Coalitions* (Princeton: Princeton University Press, 1989).

32. Joanne Gowa and Edward D. Mansfield, "Power Politics and International Trade," *American Political Science Review* 87 (June 1993): 416.

33. Edward D. Mansfield and Rachel Bronson, "Alliances, Preferential Trading Arrangements, and International Trade," *American Political Science Review* (forthcoming).

34. Although trade-related costs may accrue as a consequence of the reallocation of domestic resources incident on war, this is not unique to democratic states.

35. Harry G. Johnson, "Optimum Tariffs and Retaliation," *Journal of Economic Studies* 21 (1953/54): 142–153.

36. Beth V. Yarbrough and Robert M. Yarbrough, *Cooperation and Governance in International Trade* (Princeton: Princeton University Press, 1992), p. 25.

37. For a good discussion of these and other examples, see ibid.

38. For evidence about the trade case, see Gowa and Mansfield, "Power Politics and International Trade."

39. More precisely, controlling for contiguity, allies are less likely to engage in conflicts with each other than are non-allied states (Bremer, "Dangerous Dyads").

40. Farber and Gowa, "Reinterpreting the Democratic Peace."

II

Political Liberalization and Foreign Policy: Cross-Regional Comparisons

FOUR

Democratization and Foreign Policy in the Arab World:

The Domestic Origins of the Jordanian and Algerian Alliances in the 1991 Gulf War

Lisa Anderson

On August 2, 1990, Iraq invaded Kuwait, sparking a major international diplomatic, and ultimately military, campaign to restore the sovereignty of Kuwait and the status quo ante in the Middle East. Although the United States led the opposition to Iraq, American president George Bush made a concerted and remarkably successful effort to create and sustain an international coalition; the United Nations provided the auspices for the military campaign, and more than a dozen countries contributed military equipment and personnel to the war effort.

For the countries of the Arab world, both the Iraqi invasion and the subsequent efforts to reverse it created profound dilemmas. The Iraqi occupation of Kuwait constituted a challenge to the norms of sovereignty and self-determination with which the countries of the region had operated for decades. American leadership tarnished the effort to liberate Kuwait, however, for not only was the United States unwilling to apply equal pressure on Israel to relinquish control of occupied territory but, as the sole remaining superpower, the United States was suspected of harboring hegemonic ambitions in the region. Seeing themselves threatened from both sides, and under immense pressure from both Iraq and the United States to join their respective camps, the countries of the Arab world divided. Those in the Gulf stood with Kuwait and the United States, providing funds, troops, and staging areas for the war effort. At the southern end of the Arabian Peninsula, however, Yemen opposed the war and supported Iraq. In the Levant,

Syria and Egypt joined the American-led coalition, while Jordan and the PLO opposed it, as did all the countries in North Africa.

This pattern of alliance not only posed very serious real-world political puzzles for policy makers but created equally knotty theoretical questions for political scientists: how can we explain the decisions of the various governments to take up the side that they did? More specifically, how can we account for the fact that the more liberal its domestic political regime, the more likely was an Arab state to support autocratic Iraq against the United States–led coalition? The answer proposed here construes these alliance decisions as foreign policy ramifications of political competition in the early stages of democratization by weakly institutionalized and dependent authoritarian regimes.

Most discussions of alliance behavior begin with the regional and international balance of power or, in Stephen M. Walt's reformulation, balance of threat.[1] From this perspective, the serious danger that Iraq posed to its neighbors, as evidenced not only by its invasion of Kuwait but by the preceding decade's war with Iran, should have provoked those neighbors to ally with the United States. Yet, although Syria and Egypt behaved as predicted in the Gulf War, Jordan and Algeria did not. What factors might have intervened?

Walt suggests that weakness may incline a state to bandwagon— that is, to ally with the threatening state rather than against it—and certainly by most measures Jordan, if not Algeria, is a relatively weak state. Yet weak states look for strength; "only when their decision can affect the outcome is it rational for them to join the weaker alliance."[2] Since from the time the United States first came upon the scene it was by far the strongest combatant, by this standard the Jordanian decision to stand by Iraq can only be considered "irrational."

Before resorting to characterization of policy and policy makers in the Arab world as irrational—a temptation to which American policy analysts succumb surprisingly frequently despite its strong odor of both political ethnocentrism and theoretical sour grapes—we might examine the considerable literature in contemporary political science devoted to the myriad ways in which domestic political characteristics contribute to and account for international outcomes.

Among the more provocative of these examinations of the domestic sources of international politics have been the various explanations proffered for the empirical observation that democracies do not go to war with one another. Ideological convergence, institutional transparency, and mass participation have all been said to discourage mutual hostilities between democracies.[3] Unfortunately, however, the relationship between democracy and peace appears to hold only for stable, consolidated democracies; as Edward D. Mansfield and Jack Snyder have shown, while the *condition* of democracy may be positive for peace, the *process* of democratization augurs far better for belligerence and warlike behavior. This they attribute to political competition among old and new elites for mass support; once mobilized, masses are often difficult to control, and "war can result from nationalist prestige strategies that hard-pressed leaders use to stay astride their unmanageable coalitions."[4]

Does political democratization have discernible foreign policy effects short of the actual outbreak of war, in alliance formation? Certainly there was an ideological convergence in the way the Arab states chose up sides in the Gulf crisis, but it was a virtually perfect refutation of the proposition that ideological similarity contributes to foreign policy consensus. In fact, the more democratic an Arab regime, the more likely it was to support Iraq. Only quasi-democratic Egypt took the predicted stand in supporting the coalition. For the rest, it was the authoritarian Gulf monarchies and Syria that were the stalwarts of the American-led coalition, while the recently liberalized regimes of Jordan, Yemen, Tunisia, and Algeria supported Iraq. These cases, where the rulers faced elected officials (and defeated candidates) prepared to question their policies—foreign and domestic—closely and often in municipal councils, national parliaments, and the press, confound the predictions of the conventional theories of both alliance behavior and the democratic peace.

Like making war, making alliances is profoundly influenced by the particular dynamics of transitional or democratizing regimes. The introduction of democratic political institutions alters not only the procedures of decision making but the substance as well, by expanding the issues available for discussion and broadening the universe of possible participants. Even when the actual outbreak of hostilities is thousands of miles away, as for Algeria, or the military capacity of the state is not in doubt, as for Jordan, foreign policy decisions reflect the often transient enthusiasms and resentments of the newly joined domestic political debates as much as they indicate calculated assessments of national interest.

For both policy makers and international relations theorists, the conclusion that domestic democratization complicates foreign policy making may be discomforting. As Michael Hudson has suggested, "There is some plausibility in the realist view that American interests are better served by undemocratic Arab regimes, on the grounds that authoritarian rulers could pursue regime interests without the distraction of unruly and unfriendly public opinion."[5] Although there are many good reasons to promote political democratization in the Arab world and elsewhere, the expectation that domestic institutional convergence will necessarily produce compatible foreign policies should not be among them.

To explore this argument further, in the following pages I examine the causes and consequences of political democratization in the Arab world generally and then pursue the specific consequences of that process for foreign policy in the Jordanian and Algerian reactions to the Gulf War.

DEMOCRATIZATION IN THE ARAB WORLD: CAUSES AND CONSEQUENCES

By world standards, the Arab world is not a region widely renowned for liberalism in either politics or economics.[6] The occasional and hesitant efforts of the last two decades to privatize centralized economies and to democratize authoritarian politics received what was, by and large, the scant attention they deserved.[7] Nonetheless, by 1990 the region was a far cry from the anti-imperialist era of the 1950s and 1960s, when the nonaligned socialisms of Egypt's Gamal Abdel Nasser and Algeria's Ahmed Ben Bella categorically rejected liberal politics and market economics. From the dramatic (if less than thoroughgoing) reversal of Nasser's foreign and domestic policies by his successor Anwar Sadat in the 1970s to the Algerian government's recognition of dozens of political parties and independent newspapers in the late 1980s, there was ample evidence of the growth of interest in liberal political and economic ideas and institutions during those two decades.

Although the causes for this shift were various—and no doubt included reasons as simple as changes in global intellectual fashions[8]—two important dimensions bear on the policy consequences of political democratization and economic liberalization in the Arab world. First, to the extent that the democratizing countries have had no prior experience with democratic institutions, their introduction is likely to occasion political instability considerably greater than the routinized uncertainty associated with consolidated democracy.[9] Second, to the extent that the political economy in which liberalization takes place is not characterized by competitive market relations, the introduction of democracy will precipitate rather than reflect the organization of societal interests, thus amplifying the instability and ambiguity of domestic political coalitions.

As far as the first dimension is concerned, a crude but useful distinction should be drawn between regimes that have had some prior experience with democratic institutions and those—far more plentiful in the Third World—that have none.[10] To attain comparable degrees of liberality, polities that have already experienced some measure of liberalism or democracy have fewer adjustments to make than their wholly "preliberal" authoritarian counterparts. At least some of the existing interests, institutions, and ideologies will have been formed by and remain compatible with liberal democracy, and its reinstitution may be accomplished by relatively small-scale adjustments.

By contrast, in the transition from authoritarian regimes without liberal or democratic antecedents, the effects of democratization will necessarily be of a greater magnitude. Existing interests, institutions, and ideologies may find themselves competing with entirely new forces, including those created by the democratization itself. The immediate effect of the introduction (as opposed to the reintroduction) of new interests, institutions, and ideologies in the process of democratization is likely to be more rather than less uncertain, unstable, and passionate politics, both at home and abroad.

Moreover, the relative absence of competitive markets in the Arab world heightens the association of democratization and instability. Not only has the Arab world had scant exposure to liberal or democratic politics—the competitive politics of the interwar period in French Algeria and British-dominated Egypt and Iraq having been projections of European debates and requirements far more often than genuine expressions of domestic interests and ideas[11]—but the post–World War II international political economy of the region also discouraged open domestic politics and market economics. The mechanisms by which the new states were inserted into the international economy and political system facilitated imposition of repressive, centralized domestic regimes. As a result, the institutional apparatus of the previous regime is less important than might be the case elsewhere. Whether formally a monarchy, as in the Jordanian case, or a single-party socialist government, as in Algeria, the political regimes are poorly institutionalized, relatively unresponsive to domestic constituencies, and unusually reliant on external financing of the distributive policies and coercion by which they control, rather than respond to, popular opinion.

Since the wane of European imperialism in the region, rulers availed themselves of their pivotal position in the two-level game of simultaneous domestic and foreign policy making to maintain themselves in power.[12] These rulers profited from their control of valuable human and natural resources and of geographical locations of strategic value in the Cold War to obtain revenues from international markets and patrons. These revenues in turn permitted them to act domestically as distributors of externally generated resources rather than as managers of production or extractors of surplus.[13] As such, they could—and did—demand political acquiescence in return for the distributed goods and services.

It is in this context that the quite specific causes and implications of economic liberalization and political democratization in the Arab world must be understood. By and large the trends toward more democratic politics and liberal economies have reflected the exhaustion of external sources of state revenue—thanks to the end of the Cold War foreign aid, decline in oil prices, attainment of international credit limits, et cetera—and the consequent inability of the state elites to sustain existing distributive programs. These difficulties were long in the making, and some of the region's countries, such as non–oil exporting Egypt and Tunisia, were required to begin economic and political liberalization programs in the early 1970s. It was the oil glut and the worldwide recession of the mid-1980s, however, that brought the problems to a head in much of the region. In the cases considered here, for example, the decline in oil prices and the consequent drop in Arab aid and in remittances from workers in Europe and the Persian Gulf wreaked havoc in already troubled economies. Despite Algeria's hydrocarbon exports, for example, the country's debt service as a percentage of exports grew from slightly over 3 percent in 1970 to 25 percent in 1980 to nearly 55 percent in 1986 and 77 percent in 1988. By the beginning of that year, the growth rate of both Algeria and Jordan was negative and Jordan's remaining foreign exchange reserves covered less than two weeks of imports.[14]

Economic reform was unavoidable, and both Algeria and Jordan initiated structural adjustment programs that implied major reorganization of the ownership of productive resources and substantial belt-tightening for consumers. In shrinking the public sector and encouraging the market, economic liberalization was to serve two purposes for the state elites simultaneously. It held out the institutional and ideological possibility of relieving the state of its self-imposed distributive obligation at home, while also positioning those elites to make a case for more external aid in the new, post–Cold War liberal international political economy.

Insofar as the governments abandoned their historic role as providers for the citizenry, however, ideological and institutional space opened for development and expression of alternative interests. Of particular importance in the Arab world was the appearance of a private regional economy based upon the resources of private capital and labor in the major oil-producing countries. The "dependent bourgeoisie" created by the privatization of state enterprises may not initially have had a significant impact on government policy in their own countries, but through regional investment and philanthropy they were instrumental in providing funds for oppositional political movements throughout the region.[15] Similarly, the remittances of laborers working in both the oil-producing states of the Middle East and, to a lesser extent, the industrial economies of Europe have provided resources for nongovernmental, often oppositional, political organizations.

Although the development of these organizations and ideologies was facilitated by the democratization policies of the governments, they are not necessarily liberal or democratic themselves. The domestic, and indeed, foreign constituencies for liberal and democratic political platforms in the Arab world have been strikingly frail. Although there are small political movements espousing democratic (and more often social than liberal democratic) positions, they have received little support abroad, even from erstwhile patrons of democratic causes.[16] In fact, as many observers have remarked, among the most important beneficiaries of democratic institutional reform in the Middle East have been Islamist movements whose political (though not necessarily economic) platforms are avowedly illiberal.[17] Insofar as the state elites espouse liberal economic programs and policies—whether out of conviction or convenience—the political opposition is likely to coalesce around anti-liberal political ideologies, not only for the purposes of "product differentiation" but also because economic liberalization is associated with the end of egalitarian distributive policies and the introduction instead of preferential treatment for relatively well-endowed segments of society at the expense of the "popular sectors." As a result, the short-term consequence of political democratization in conjunction with economic liberalization has been to enhance the position and amplify the voice of those who oppose the very policies from which they are benefiting.

Moreover, in much of the Arab world, Islamist political movements have been the best-organized, most-efficient, and most-scrupulous providers of social services, including health insurance, education, garbage collection, and so forth. In both word and deed, they are articulate critics of government waste and corruption. The Islamist capacity to fill these roles is in large part a legacy of the era when state ownership and management extended to virtually all realms of social and economic life and only the mosque was left outside state control to wither, or so it was then thought, as an anachronism in the modern world. The unintended consequence of this neglect was that devotional life was one of the few areas of human endeavor that remained unsullied by the failures of the regimes, its resources available for mobilization as those failures became increasingly apparent. The Islamist movements therefore constitute one of the very few genuine expressions of civil society in the Arab world, and because of the nature of the states within and over which they contest, they have had little experience of political democracy or liberalism.

Thus, even if in the long run the experience of political freedoms and economic liberties makes democrats of us all—and that remains to be seen—for the foreseeable future the domestic and foreign policies of the states of the Middle East will be profoundly shaped by the dilemma of democratization that evokes an antidemocratic response. This is likely to produce ambivalent and contradictory policy, both at home and abroad, as state elites argue for the necessity of authoritarian interventions in democratic processes in order to "save democracy from itself."[18] Moreover, democratic governments, particularly relatively wealthy and powerful democratic governments, like that of the United States, will be the object of appeals for support from both sides, as the ostensibly liberal governments argue for the need for uncritical support of their regimes to guarantee stability, and apparently nondemocratic oppositions promote pressure on those same regimes to ensure continued adherence to democratic procedures.

The complicated, ambiguous, and often contradictory politics produced by democratic transitions in polities for which both liberal political institutions and market economies are novelties are illustrated in the complex reactions of Jordan and Algeria to the dilemma posed by the Iraqi invasion of Kuwait and the subsequent United States–led efforts to reverse it.

JORDAN: THE "LIBERAL MONARCH" BETRAYS HIS ERSTWHILE PATRONS

The Jordanian experiment with political liberalization and democratization began in April 1989, when countrywide rioting, touched off by cuts in consumer subsidies, brought down the cabinet and led the government to rethink its domestic political arrangements.[19] Barely a year later—but after press censorship had been relaxed, the political role of the security services curtailed, and hotly contested parliamentary elections held—the country faced a major foreign policy dilemma. Iraq's invasion of Kuwait in August 1990 and the subsequent swift deployment of hundreds of thousands of American troops in Saudi Arabia in what proved to be the prelude to a full-scale war to liberate Kuwait pitted the Jordanian regime's traditional foreign backers—the Kuwaitis, Saudis, and Americans—against a regime in Iraq whose political rhetoric and military potential held considerable appeal for the ordinary citizen. That the Jordanian government's early attempts to mediate ultimately gave way to a decided tilt toward Iraq proved very costly economically, as the United States and its coalition partners cut aid to Jordan and enforced economic sanctions on Iraq that further damaged the Jordanian economy. The policy probably saved the crown, however, winning the Hashemite monarch (and, perforce, the monarchy) widespread domestic support in a part of the populace long reluctant to endorse either the dynasty or the king.

The Hashemite Kingdom of Jordan was originally created from political remnants of World War I. Carved by the British from its Palestine Mandate in part to provide a kingdom for Amir Abdallah, the son of an important British ally in World War I and brother of the British-installed ruler in Baghdad, Jordan had little intrinsic political or economic rationale. Accorded independence after World War II, Jordan captured the contiguous areas of Palestine that were not occupied by Israeli forces in the war of 1948—the West Bank, which was promptly annexed by Abdallah—and fell heir to hundreds of thousands of refugees, who were granted citizenship.[20]

Ruled since the early 1950s by Abdallah's grandson, the current King Husayn, Jordan relied on foreign subsidies of its budget from the very outset. Thanks to its crucial geostrategic location, the British, then the Americans, and after the oil booms of the 1970s, the Saudis and Kuwaitis provided subventions that supplemented revenues derived from the country's only other significant resource: the export of skilled labor to the oil-producing countries of the Gulf and elsewhere.

During the mid-1950s, when much of the Arab world was swept by mass mobilizations in the name of anti-imperialism, King Husayn— newly on the throne and still in his early twenties—was challenged by a leftist labor movement and Arab nationalist political parties who contested the legitimacy not only of the monarchy as an institution but of the very existence of an independent Jordanian—as opposed to a greater pan-Arab—state. Having everything to lose in permitting such sentiments to be voiced, heard, or empowered, the king declared martial law and outlawed political parties in 1956. For all intents and purposes, that was the end of legal competitive political life until the 1980s. Although there were carefully managed parliamentary elections in the 1960s, even they ended with the Israeli occupation of the West Bank in 1967.

The relative success of the Jordanian government through the 1960s and particularly the 1970s in obtaining foreign support, and the regime's relatively liberal economic policies, which permitted workers abroad to invest their earnings profitably in Jordan allowed the country's citizens, particularly its elite, to occupy themselves with improving their financial condition. In a situation that would have looked very familiar to the author of the *Eighteenth Brumaire*, the wealthy "accepted the lack of opportunities for political participation in exchange for a political and economic atmosphere ensured by the government that was conducive to making money."[21]

The deal began to break down in the mid-1980s when the government's capacity to renew its externally based revenues appeared to be exhausted. The country's failure to join the Camp David peace process deprived it of American aid; the drop in world oil prices cut into the government's foreign subsidies while also hurting the private-sector recipients of remittances from workers in the Gulf. By the middle of the decade the government had resorted to borrowing abroad, and there were hesitant moves toward the revival of political life—Parliament was recalled in 1984 and elections held for the seats vacated by deaths in the interim. At the same time, however, press censorship remained tight, and government surveillance of political activists was stepped up.

By January 1989 the government defaulted on its foreign debts, and the International Monetary Fund (IMF) intervened to assist in rescheduling; it was as part of the IMF agreement that the consumer subsidy cuts leading to the rioting and subsequent political opening that year were made. In the meantime, the king had also made an important political concession that was to make political liberalization markedly easier. In the summer of 1988, in response to the Palestinian uprising known as the *intifadah,* he had relinquished Jordanian claims to the West Bank, not only setting the stage for the eventual independence of the territory under Palestinian rule but also solidifying his claim to the continued independent existence of a now smaller but more cohesive Jordanian entity under the Hashemite dynasty. With the Palestinian issue and its accompanying evocation of Arab nationalist themes defused, the challenges that might be posed in the ordinary course of open competitive politics were far more likely to center on issues of policy than on questions about the regime and the dynasty or about the boundaries and the composition of the state.

By mid-June 1989, the government had declared its intention to hold parliamentary elections; by August, it was announced that the polling day would be in November. Although martial law was not lifted and political parties remained banned, the regime did suspend many of the regulations censoring the press, and it permitted party activists to run for election. Freedom of expression and assembly was well exercised, as posters festooned the landscape and rallies were held throughout the country. The outcome of the elections came as a surprise to many analysts: the Muslim Brotherhood won about thirty of the eighty seats. The Brotherhood was one of the very few legal political organizations, which greatly enhanced its ability to get out the vote, but subsequent municipal and professional association elections suggested that the Islamist strength was neither overwhelming nor uniform throughout the society. Nonetheless, the Islamists were permitted to take their seats, and the new cabinet included five Islamist members. Thus by the time the Iraqis invaded Kuwait,

Jordanians had begun to experience a fair measure of political freedom. As a result, they felt free to express their opinions of the Gulf crisis, and more important, they expected government policy to reflect those opinions.

There was relatively little disagreement in Jordan about the developments in the Gulf. The general consensus was strong sympathy for the Iraqi position. It derived from several very widespread and long-standing beliefs crossing ethnic Palestinian/Jordanian cleavages as well as left/right ideological divides. In a stance born of older Arab nationalist positions, many people felt that the dispute was an intra-Arab one that should have been resolved by Arab councils, and they were therefore antagonistic toward the side—in this instance the Saudis and Kuwaitis—that called in outside assistance. This aversion to what was perceived as outside intervention was heightened by the perception on the part of leftist nationalists that the United States was merely acting as an imperial power, propping up compliant oil-producing regimes. Islamists also objected, though on different grounds: Saudi responsibility for the holy places of Islam should have precluded the stationing of non-Muslim troops in the kingdom.

In addition to the ideological consensus on this issue, many Jordanian citizens—mostly but not exclusively of Palestinian origin—had had personal experience in the Gulf that discouraged support for Kuwait and its allies, Although hundreds of thousands of Jordanian Palestinians profited handsomely from long work and residence in the Gulf, particularly in Kuwait, they had come to resent the social and political distinction maintained by the ruling families between citizens and noncitizens, as well as the often cavalier lavishness with which Gulf royals spent both privy purses and public funds while others in the Arab world—notably but not exclusively Palestinians—suffered. Finally, among Palestinians particularly, while there was little outright admiration for Saddam Husayn or his Iraq, there was also the widespread conviction that Iraq was Jordan's principal protector against aggression by Israel.

Based as they were in long-standing sentiments—Arab nationalism, leftist anti-imperialism, Islamic pride—these attitudes were not unlike the public opinion that had been ignored by the monarchy for decades. Indeed, had the Jordanian monarch had the financial resources to buy acquiescence in a pro-Kuwait "monarchical solidarity" policy, he might have attempted it. By August 1990, however, it was apparent that he did not have reliable sources of such funds:

Kuwait, Libya, and Algeria had already reneged on their promised support in the mid-1980s, the United States had already halted aid to Jordan for political reasons at least once after Camp David, and the international creditors were unsympathetic to political contingency as a rationale for more debt. More important, in an ironic reversal of the *Brumairian* formula, the king had already decided to trade in his foreign policy freehand for greater access to local wealth. Foreign policy was now at the service of domestic needs rather than the reverse, and the electoral coalition to which the prime minister was accountable after the 1989 parliamentary elections—"a coalition of disparate political groups and individuals, among them the Muslim Brotherhood"[22]—dictated support of Iraq and alienation of the United States.

As a result, at least in the early stages of political liberalization and at least on an emotionally charged issue of war and peace, the foreign policy of Jordan took turns that struck many observers as "irrational"—erratic, unpredictable, inconsistent, even counterproductive. Gone were the relatively stable, compliant foreign policy positions of a rentier state well supplied by the international community and international market with the funds by which the regime might guarantee that there would be, among other things, no popular resistance to those very foreign policies. The Jordanian position in the Gulf War was very much a reflection of popular domestic sentiment freely expressed.

ALGERIA: A "LIBERAL PRESIDENT" DISAPPOINTS POTENTIAL ALLIES

The Algerian government's opposition to the United States–led war against Iraq might have been less unexpected than Jordan's, given Algeria's long history of revolutionary anti-imperialism, but in fact it too reflected domestic political pressure far more than historical government ideology.[23] Indeed, the government's careful, legalist reading—opposed to both the Iraqi invasion of Kuwait and the American resort to arms to reverse it—was consistent with an interest in moving away from its reputation for "tiers-mondiste" solidarity with anti-imperialism and toward a less ideological engagement with international markets and political powers. This careful calibration was derailed by the very widespread popular support for Iraq in Algeria. Like its

Jordanian counterpart, the Algerian government might have been able to ignore that public opinion had it not been for its extremely tight financial circumstances and the challenge from an opposition party—the Islamist Front Islamique du Salut, or FIS—that quickly pressed the government to take a hard-line anti-coalition position. That the FIS itself was required by public sentiment to abandon its initial sympathy for Kuwait and Saudi Arabia, long its principal source of moral and financial support, was one of the reasons for its vociferousness on the subject and contributed to a domestic political competition in which foreign policy became a litmus test of domestic political accountability and popularity.

Although Algeria had been ruled by the very antithesis of a monarchy—an avowedly socialist single party, the Front de liberation nationale, or FLN—since its independence from France in 1962, Algeria's liberalization began much the way Jordan's did, and for many of the same reasons. Like Jordan, the Algerian state and economy of the post-independence era of the 1960s and 1970s depended upon externally generated revenues. For Algeria, however, foreign aid was less important than the revenues from export of hydrocarbons, principally gas, and the independent Algerian government quickly developed a capacity to respond adroitly to the international market while simultaneously controlling nearly every aspect of economic behavior domestically. In part as a response to the exigencies of life after 130 years of French rule and a revolution that took a million lives, the Algerian polity and economy were highly centralized, bureaucratized, and authoritarian. A military coup in 1965 had overthrown the populist Ahmed Ben Bella and installed the technocratic authoritarian rule of the dour Houari Boumedienne. When Boumedienne died in 1978, his successor, Chadli Benjedid, was also selected by and from the army and the ruling party. Although Benjedid's regime was marked by a mildly less repressive atmosphere, structurally it remained a centralized single-party authoritarian regime. In fact, it was not apparent, even then, that there was a genuinely viable alternative.[24]

During the 1970s, the gas revenues financed an ambitious and ultimately only partly successful industrial development program and subsidized egalitarian distributive policies, while very rapid population growth was partly offset by the export of labor to Europe. T h e glut on the world petroleum market in the mid-1980s led to sharply lowered gas revenues, however, and to a European recession that reduced employment opportunities both in Europe and at home. By

1988 the government conceded a negative growth rate, said that unemployment probably exceeded 30 percent of the active labor force, and abandoned its historical commitment to simultaneous, single-minded, and monolithic pursuit of social welfare and economic development. In an effort to stave off IMF intervention, the government undertook its own structural adjustment program, announcing cuts in consumer subsidies in October 1988. Riots broke out throughout the country in response to the announcement, and they were brutally suppressed by the army, called out for the first time since independence.

Within several months, however, President Benjedid declared that a new constitution, providing for freedoms of expression and association (and thus permitting political parties), would be presented for popular vote; it was duly ratified in February 1989. Within the following year more than fifty political parties had registered, including the FIS, the first legally recognized Islamic party in the Arab world. In June 1990, Algerian and foreign observers alike were stunned when municipal and provincial elections widely judged to have been without significant irregularities produced a massive victory for the FIS and a resounding defeat for the ruling FLN.

Sixty-five percent of the eligible voters turned out, and FIS captured 55 percent of that vote, compared to 31 percent for the FLN. Most observers argued that much of the FIS support was a protest vote against thirty years of rule by a single party grown old and corrupt; the FLN's claim to legitimacy as the spearhead of the revolution against France carried little weight among the 75 percent of the population that was under thirty years old. Nonetheless, it was also apparent that FIS did have significant numbers of supporters, for whatever reason, and many in Algeria feared the prospect of FIS in power at the national level. The legislative elections scheduled for June 1991 were therefore anticipated with considerable anxiety on all sides.

It was in this context that Algerians greeted the news of the Iraqi invasion of Kuwait in August 1990 and the subsequent stationing of American troops in Saudi Arabia. As the party of protest, the FIS might have been expected to support Iraq, but its initial reactions to the crisis reflected the political constraints imposed by its financial ties to the Gulf monarchies, and at the beginning of the crisis the party leadership backed Saudi Arabia and attacked Iraq for having invaded Kuwait,[25] a position that proved to be at odds with popular opinion. For most Algerians, as indeed for most North Africans, the Iraqi challenge to the wealthy and powerful of the Gulf and the world mirrored a domestic debate that pitted the numerous disadvantaged against a small wealthy and corrupt elite.

The FIS promptly reversed its position and rallied to the support of Iraq—arguing that the Gulf monarchies had abandoned their responsibilities to Islam by calling upon non-Muslims to aid them against their Muslim opponents—although the political misstep appears to have contributed to the increasingly strident demands voiced by FIS leaders that the presidential elections scheduled for 1993 be moved forward to coincide with the parliamentary elections. The party leaders also challenged the army, backbone of the national government, claiming that the failure to send reinforcements to Iraq was evidence that it was too weak and too corrupt to stand up to the imperialism of the Christian West. The publication in the FIS press of an article titled "The Algerian Army During the Gulf War: A Lion When It Battles Us, an Ostrich in Times of War" could not have been better designed to gall the military backers of the regime and did not contribute to reasoned discussion of foreign policy.[26] In response to widespread FIS-led demonstrations in May and June, President Benjedid declared a state of siege, again called out the army to disperse demonstrators, arrested the principal FIS leaders, replaced his prime minister, and postponed the legislative elections until December 1991.[27]

Although the FIS was said to have lost the financial support of Saudi Arabia as a result of its position during the war, it was believed to continue to receive funds from private Saudi benefactors as well as local business interests who, as it was reported, "out of faith or opportunism are putting their money—or some of it—on an Islamic future."[28] As it turned out, the Gulf crisis had an equally murky impact on the Algerian economy as a whole. A $2.5 billion oil windfall cushioned the badly ailing economy during the early months of the crisis, but the crisis—and the domestic reactions to it—also made international lenders more cautious,[29] and their reluctance to extend credit may in turn have contributed to the sentiment favoring the coup that ended Algeria's democratic experiment in January 1992.

DEMOCRATIZATION AND THE MAKING OF ALLIANCES

The decisions by the governments of Jordan and Algeria to side with Iraq and against the United States in the Gulf War cannot be explained by international factors alone. Neither of these countries behaved in accordance with models of international politics that assume that states are unitary rational actors. In both Jordan and Algeria, foreign policy making was a reflection of very powerful domestic sentiments and constituencies.

That domestic factors play an important role in foreign policy making will surprise only the most die-hard realist theorists of international relations. More intriguing is the suggestion that democratization does not contribute to alliances with other democratic states. On the contrary, in the Gulf War lineup, liberalization was inversely correlated with selection of liberal alliance partners. This, as we have seen, is a consequence of the paradoxical advantage accruing to anti-democratic and illiberal ideologies and movements in the early stages of political liberalization or democratization in rentier states.

Becoming democratic has foreign policy consequences profoundly different from those of being democratic. Consolidated democracies may well "flock together," as may consolidated monarchies or consolidated military regimes. Indeed, measures of consolidation—domestic stability, routinization of policy-making processes—may be better predictors of foreign policy behavior than regime type alone. Interestingly, it was generally the most stable regimes in the Middle East that supported the American-led coalition against Iraq: the oldest democracies—Israel and Turkey—and the original liberalizer among the authoritarian regimes—Egypt—as well as the well-established authoritarian regimes, from Syria to the Gulf monarchies. It was the most recent liberalizers—Jordan and Algeria but also Tunisia, Yemen, and even (to an extent that certainly surprised the king) Morocco—that opposed the anti-Iraq coalition. This suggests that it is partly the instability of transition that accounts for the otherwise anomalous outcome that democratizing regimes do not ally with democracies.

For Jordan and Algeria, as for the other recent liberalizers of the Middle East and North Africa, political democratization produced political competition in an environment in which social cleavages had previously been denied: nationalism and socialism were monolithic ideological formulations that pushed social divisions into limbo.[30] Moreover, the weakness or absence of private-sector industry, labor, or export agriculture in these international rent-based distributive states meant that independent groups of industrialists, labor unions, and agricultural exporters did not appear to argue the pros and cons of foreign policy. Adherence to conceptions of common interest, as distinct from common sentiment, was inhibited by the ideology and political economy of the nationalist, rentier regimes of the region. Liberalization therefore unleashed a politics based on grievance and desire as much as on strategic calculation.

In this context, foreign policy may become an arena on which to project and debate what are often virtually insoluble domestic dilemmas. For both the Algerians and the Jordanians, particularly the Palestinian Jordanians, the Gulf War was a dramatic enactment of their hopes and fears: Saddam Husayn served as Robin Hood; the Kuwaitis filled the role of the wealthy and cowardly nobility; and the United States, as sheriff, upheld the legal prerogatives of the undeserving nobles against the virtuous poor. That the war was far more than theater was apparent in the price Jordan and Algeria paid in foreign aid and investment withheld, but from the perspective of the ordinary citizen, this was a cost borne by the governments rather than by particular groups within the society. The link between foreign policy positions and domestic costs and benefits is intentionally obscured in distributive states, with the result that, at least in the early stages of liberalization, citizens have little basis on which to calculate the relationship.

As domestic interest groups solidify, foreign policy should become less a focus of contending passions and more the target of competing interests. By the time there are industrialists who organize in favor of trade promotion policies or who lobby for tariff protection, tourist industry representatives who want to promote good and stable relations with Europe, or labor unions looking for foreign investment in job creation, foreign policy will reflect the sober calculations of those whose livelihoods depend upon it. The *condition* of democracy, particularly if it is accompanied by competitive market economies, may encourage pacific foreign policy and alliances with other democracies, but at least at the outset, there is nothing about the *process* of democratization itself that does so.

Notes

I would like to thank Judith Goldstein and Miles Kahler for very useful comments on earlier drafts of this essay.

1. Stephen M. Walt, *The Origins of Alliances* (Ithaca: Cornell University Press, 1987).
2. Ibid, p. 29.
3. See, for example, Michael Doyle, "Liberalism and World Politics," *American Political Science Review* 80, no. 4 (1986); Bruce Russett, *Grasping the Democratic Peace:*

Principles for a Post–Cold War World (Princeton: Princeton University Press, 1993); Zeev Maoz and Bruce Russett, "Normative and Structural Causes of Democratic Peace, 1946–1986," *American Political Science Review* 87, no. 3 (1993).

4. Edward D. Mansfield and Jack Snyder, "Democratization and the Danger of War," *International Security* 20, no. 1 (Summer 1995): 2.

5. "Democracy and Foreign Policy in the Arab World," *Beirut Review* 4 (Fall 1992): 23.

6. Neither the conventional nor the technical usage of the terms "liberal," "liberalization," "democracy," and "democratization" is without ambiguities. Liberalization ordinarily denotes two processes that may or may not be associated in practice: the placing of legal constraints on governments to inhibit the arbitrary and capricious exercise of power—the conventional sense of the term in European history—and the withdrawal of government responsibility from what would ordinarily be the realm of civil society or the economy—a sense of the term somewhat more common in postsocialist transitions. Democratization, by contrast, may mean the installation and observance of institutional mechanisms, such as contested elections, associated with established democracies, or it may mean the extension of meaningful political participation to previously disenfranchised or excluded populations.

In much of the Arab world, democratization in the sense of expanding participation has been far less a critical issue than the introduction of and compliance with the liberal rights—freedom of belief, expression, association, and so forth—and institutional mechanisms—regular, free, and fair elections, judicial review, and so on—that will animate and structure egalitarian participation. For that reason, liberalization is usually viewed as a necessary condition of democratization, and I use the terms interchangeably unless a deliberate distinction is clear from the context.

See Aziz Al-Azmeh, "Populism Contra Democracy: Recent Democratist Discourse in the Arab World," in Ghassan Salame, ed., *Democracy Without Democrats: The Renewal of Politics in the Muslim World* (New York: Tauris, 1994); Ahmad S. Moussalli, "Modern Islamic Fundamentalist Discourses on Civil Society, Pluralism, and Democracy," in Augustus Richard Norton, ed., *Civil Society in the Middle East* (Leiden: Brill, 1995).

7. Among the recent notable exceptions are Louis Cantori, ed., "Democratization in the Middle East," *American-Arab Affairs* 36 (Spring 1991); Bernabe Lopez Garcia, ed., *Elecciones, participacion y transiciones politicas en el Norte de Africa* (Madrid: Instituto de Cooperation con el Mundo Arabo, 1991); Muhammad Muslih and Augustus Richard Norton, "The Need for Arab Democracy," *Foreign Policy* 83 (Summer 1991); Ghassan Salame, "Sur la causalité d'un manqué: Pourquoi le monde arabe n'est-il donc pas democratique?" *Revue Francaise de Science Politique* 61, no. 3 (June 1991).

8. One needs only to talk with Ahmed Ben Bella, returned in 1990 to political life as the head of a party in Algeria after twenty-five years of prison and exile, to be struck by the changes in the rhetoric of the intelligentsia of the Third World in the last thirty years. Once one of the principal authors of Algerian revolutionary socialism, the former president returned to lead a party that advocated liberal democracy and contests legislative elections. Personal interview, June 1, 1992, Algiers.

9. See Adam Przeworski, *Democracy and the Market* (Cambridge: Cambridge University Press, 1991).

10. This distinction, too often neglected in the literature on regime transitions, between democratization and redemocratization is treated in Alfred Stepan, "Paths Toward Redemocratization: Theoretical and Comparative Considerations," in Guillermo O'Donnell, Philippe Schmitter, and Laurence Whitehead, eds., *Transitions*

from Authoritarian Rule: Comparative Perspectives (Baltimore: Johns Hopkins University Press, 1986).

11. See Ghassan Salame, *al-Mujtama wa-l-dawla fil mashriq al-arabi* [State and Society in the Arab East] (Beirut, 1987); Roger Owen, "The Practice of Electoral Democracy in the Arab East and North Africa: Some Lessons from Nearly a Century's Experience," in Ellis Goldberg, Resat Kasaba, and Joel S. Migdal, eds., *Rules and Rights in the Middle East* (Seattle: University of Washington Press, 1993).

12. See Robert D. Putnam, "Diplomacy and Domestic Politics: The Logic of Two-Level Games," *International Organization* 42, no. 3 (Summer 1988). The research agenda spawned by Putnam's insight about the nature of the linkages between domestic and foreign policies has been devoted largely to examination of relations among consolidated democracies, but it is nonetheless suggestive in its extension of the realms of foreign policy well beyond issues of war and peace, including international trade and alliance formation.

13. See, within the now considerable literature on rentier, distributive, or allocative states in the Middle East, H. Beblawi and G. Luciani, eds., *The Rentier State* (London: Croom, Helm, 1987). Although the small-population, large-revenue oil producers are the archetypes of this political economy, both through their regional influence and as a result of the superpower rivalry of the Cold War, the region's non–oil producers also mimicked this pattern. In *Privatization and Liberalization in the Middle East* (Bloomington: Indiana University Press, 1992), the editors, Ilya Harik and Denis Sullivan, argue that the continued dependence of what they call the "patron state" in the Middle East on aid from international sources was an inadvertent by-product of the state's self-appointed role as both providing welfare and generating investment in the absence of guaranteed domestic revenues. Whether the initial impetus was the availability of external revenues or the desirability of domestic distributive policies, the outcome was the same.

14. See Karen Pfeifer, "Algeria's Implicit Stabilization Program," and Robert Satloff, "Jordan's Great Gamble: Economic Crisis and Political Reform," both in Henri Barkey, ed., *The Politics of Economic Reform in the Middle East* (New York: St. Martin's Press, 1992); and Laurie Brand, "Economic and Political Liberalization in a Rentier Economy: The Case of the Hashemite Kingdom of Jordan," and Dirk Vandewalle, "Breaking with Socialism: Economic Liberalization and Privatization in Algeria, in Harik and Sullivan, *Privatization and Liberalization.*

15. Relatively little of this activity had been formally studied or even documented, but on banking see the work of Clement Henry Moore, particularly "Les enjeux politiques des reformes bancaires au Maghreb," *Annuaire de l'Afrique du Nord* 26 (1987), and "Islamic Banks and Competitive Politics in the Arab World and Turkey," *Middle East Journal* 44, no. 2 (Spring 1990).

16. It is of note that both Human Rights Watch, the New York–based human rights monitoring organization, and the American government-supported National Endowment for Democracy began their work on the Middle East only after they had established programs virtually everywhere else in the world, viewing the complexities of the region as particularly intractable. As a result of this international posture of skepticism, local human rights organizations and democratic activists have not had the same international moral and material support in the Middle East as their counterparts have enjoyed elsewhere in the world.

17. The economic platforms of most Islamist movements in the Middle East are

vague, but apart from (usually symbolic) measures to accommodate Islamic prohibitions on the taking of interest, they are ordinarily quite compatible with liberal economic policies, including respect for private property and market relations. The economic programs of the Islamist movements reflect their social bases as much as their doctrinal heritage, and in a number of Middle Eastern countries, including Syria and Iran, Islamists found significant support among the middle-class merchants and industrialists.

It should also be noted that although some activists, Muslim and non-Muslim alike, are quick to evoke the age-old battles of the Crusades, the Islamist movements are not in principle anti-American or anti-Western. Most of the Islamist movements oppose the status quo and the international order that upholds it, making them hostile to the United States. As the willingness of the Islamists to cooperate with the United States against the Soviets in Afghanistan should have made apparent, however, they will find friends where they can.

See Moussalli, "Fundamentalist Discourses"; Lisa Anderson, "Obligation and Accountability: Islamic Politics in North Africa," *Daedalus* 120, no. 3 (Summer 1991).

18. This was the rationale for the January 1992 military coup that suspended the legislative elections in Algeria. See below.

19. Much of this section draws upon Laurie A. Brand's excellent discussion in "Liberalization and Changing Political Coalitions: The Bases of Jordan's 1990–1991 Gulf Crisis Policy," *Jerusalem Journal of International Relations* 13, no. 4 (Spring 1991): 1–46. See also Brand, *Jordan's Inter-Arab Relations: The Political Economy of Alliance-Making* (New York: Columbia University Press, 1994).

20. Jordan was the only country in the Arab world to accord the refugees from Palestine citizenship, which led to the accusation against the Hashemites that their policy toward Palestine and the Palestinians has been one of self-aggrandizement at the expense of the Palestinian national movement itself. It has also contributed to the ambiguity about the composition of, and tensions within, Jordan's domestic population, for "native East Bankers," citizens of Palestinian origin—before and after 1948— refugees from the 1967 war and Israeli occupation of the West Bank, and West Bankers themselves all have claims on, and grievances against, the Hashemite monarchy.

21. Brand, "Jordan's Inter-Arab Relations," p. 14.

22. George Hawatmeh, "Jordan: Standing Up to the Right," *Middle East International* 403 (June 28, 1991): 10.

23. For background on Algeria's democratic experiment, see Bradford Dillman, "Transition to Democracy in Algeria," and Robert A. Mortimer, "Algerian Foreign Policy in Transition," in John P. Entelis and Phillip C. Naylor, eds., *State and Society in Algeria* (Boulder: Westview Press, 1992); Dirk Vandewalle, "Breaking with Socialism: Economic Liberalization and Privatization in Algeria," in Harik and Sullivan, *Privatization and Liberalization.*

24. As Michael Hudson has put it, "Some social scientists wondered, and continue to wonder, whether Algeria possessed even the potential for civil society, in light of its long history of French settler colonialism and the further social pulverization that was said to have accompanied the struggle for independence" ("After the Gulf War: Prospects for Democratization in the Arab World," *Middle East Journal* 45, no. 3 [Summer 1991]: 414).

25. Belkacem Iratni and Mohand Salah Tahi, "The Aftermath of Algeria's First Free Elections," *Government and Opposition* 26, no. 4 (Fall 1991): 474.

26. This point was brought home to me by Remy Leveau. See his essay "Algerie: Des adversaires à la recherche de compromis incertains" (prepared for the Western European Union Institute for Security Studies, March 1992).

27. Ultimately, FIS's victories in the first round of balloting on December 26, 1991, raised the possibility that they would have such a commanding majority in Parliament that they would be able to amend the constitution, conceivably to create an Islamic state and end contested elections. Although President Benjedid appeared to feel that his constitutional power to dissolve Parliament was adequate protection against such an effort and that "cohabitation" was a worthwhile experiment on behalf of liberal reform, the army did not agree, and in January he was asked to resign. His erstwhile prime minister and defense minister declared a state of emergency, suspended the elections, and ultimately outlawed the FIS, arresting more than ten thousand FIS supporters and sympathizers and interning them indefinitely without charge. See "Human Rights in Algeria Since the Halt of the Electoral Process," *Middle East Watch* 4, no. 2 (February 1992); "Le drapeau des islamistes flottera-t-il sur l'Algerie?" *Jeune Afrique* 1618, January 9, 1992, and subsequent reports.

28. Tom Porteous, "The Crisis in Algeria: What Chance Democracy?" *Middle East International* 404 (July 12, 1991): 17.

29. Francis Ghilles, "The Impact of the Gulf War on the Maghreb Economies," *Middle East International* 399 (May 3, 1991): 27.

30. One might even say that, to these authoritarian regimes, the model of the "rational unitary actor" is as seductive as it is to the realist theorists of international relations.

Political Liberalization and the African State System

Jeffrey Herbst

Most studies of political liberalization in the Third World rightfully concentrate on the prospects for democratization or a return to the old authoritarianism. These studies assume, either explicitly or implicitly, that political liberalization may bring about wrenching changes but that the nations as currently configured will continue.[1] After the breakup of Czechoslovakia, the Soviet Union, and Yugoslavia into ethnic republics, however, this assumption must be contested. In particular, it is important to examine the prospects that political liberalization will lead to fundamental changes in African boundaries, given the potentially traumatic ramifications of opening political systems. Africa is a particularly interesting arena in which to examine the international consequences of liberalization, because while there is widespread agreement on the continent that many of the boundaries are nonsensical, the countries on the continent have constructed an international regime that has encouraged boundary stability for more than thirty years.

This essay will first examine the origin and maintenance of the boundary regime in Africa. It will then analyze the fundamental changes in Africa and the international system that have radically transformed the incentives for Africans who contemplate altering their national boundaries. Finally, it will examine the microlevel foundations of the relationship between political liberalization and boundary change.

THE SUCCESSFUL BOUNDARY MAINTENANCE REGIME

In the early 1960s, the Organization of African Unity (OAU) recognized that the borders drawn by the colonialists "constitute a grave and permanent factor of dissension." The OAU, and most African governments, believe that cohesive social groups were separated by the boundaries and that groups that had little to do with each other or that were nominally hostile were brought together in the same nation-state. The OAU also recognized, however, that there was no simple way of redrawing the map of Africa. The continent's topography does not provide much in the way of natural frontiers, and many social groupings are actually so fluid that it would be impossible to construct a set of boundaries that would assure ethnic homogeneity. As a result, when the dust settled after massive changes in boundaries, no African leader could be guaranteed that he would still have a country to govern. Since the OAU is fundamentally a leaders' club, it declared that the inherited boundaries were a "tangible reality," and rulers pledged "to respect the frontiers existing on their achievement of national independence."[2]

Several developments at the international level helped the African leaders in their effort to continue the inherited state system. First, the Cold War had the effect of providing African countries with patrons when their boundaries were challenged. The superpowers were concerned with cultivating clients in all parts of the world and were therefore willing to help African nations crush ethnic rebellions or threats from neighbors. Thus, Zaire won crucial aid from the United States in turning back the Shaba rebellions; Chad relied on France to retain its territorial integrity in the face of Libyan aggression; and Ethiopia was given critical military support by the Soviet Union in order to resist Somalia's irredentist claims. The superpowers were also attentive to African sensibilities concerning boundary maintenance. Indeed, not once did either superpower, or any other outside power, support an African effort to overturn an existing boundary.

More generally, the superpowers created a global environment between 1945 and 1989 that made *any* attempt at boundary change appear illegitimate. One of the implicit rules of the Cold War was that supporting efforts to change boundaries was not part of the competition. The superpowers repeatedly expressed their preference for stability—symbolized by a bizarrely divided Berlin—over the potential chaos caused by ethnic self-determination. Thus, between the end of World War II and 1989, the only forcible boundary changes that were not related to the end of colonialism were the creation of Bangladesh, the Israeli annexation of captured territory, and the absorption of South Vietnam.[3] This was a remarkable development in a world where forcible boundary change was once a fairly common event. Indeed, the most stunning aspect of the Iraqi invasion of Kuwait in 1990 was not that it happened but that this sort of armed effort has not occurred more often in a world made up mainly of weak states that cannot defend their boundaries.

Also, the international community in the postwar era had greatly elevated the norm of sovereignty. Especially since the advent of African independence, the world community has allowed any country, no matter how underdeveloped its political and economic institutions, to enjoy the full privileges of sovereignty. In contrast, the norm of self-determination, which Africans relied upon in the struggle against colonialism, was largely ignored. For instance, it was felt that it would be a violation of an African country's sovereignty for the world community to support a dissident ethnic group that was disaffected with the country's government or even to protest too strongly when a government repressed a particular faction. The precedent set by the lack of international support for the Ibo during the Nigerian civil war, despite their suffering and the fact that they could make a credible claim to being a viable national unit, solidified the practice of ignoring claims based on ethnic self-determination. In the postwar era, the norm of self-determination has applied only to people under colonial rule.

Thus the interests of African leaders and those of the great powers were almost identical on the issue of boundary stability. The global community provided not only the arms but also a legal framework in the form of sovereignty to justify African leaders' taking almost any step to crush local rebellions that threatened the African state system. Anthony D. Smith was perhaps exaggerating only slightly when he argued that "given the chance, most ethnic movements in Africa and Asia would opt for outright separatism." Noting the success of the boundary maintenance regime, however, he correctly argued that whether any of these movements achieved independence was dependent on "wider geopolitical factors."[4]

The system also greatly discouraged interstate war. Of course, few African countries even had the ability to invade their neighbors in the

1960s. As African militaries have become more sophisticated, however, the fear of war between nations has not increased dramatically. Rather, most of the weapons that African countries have purchased have been used either to appease the military or to turn against local citizens. The overthrow of Amin in Uganda is the only example of an African leader's being displaced by an invasion by a foreign country, and in that case it was obvious that the Tanzanians did not have any territorial ambitions. Even South Africa, which during the 1980s showed little hesitation in attacking its neighbors and had a near monopoly on military power in its region, has never threatened the territorial integrity of any state in Southern Africa.

As a result, African boundaries did not change until Eritrea voted for independence in 1993. This stability is especially remarkable given the domestic upheavals that have occurred in many nations and the fact that many African countries possess only limited military forces, which they would have trouble deploying to defend their own boundaries. Indeed, boundary maintenance among so many weak countries for such a long period of time is an extraordinary occurrence in the history of international relations.

THE CHANGING INTERNATIONAL CONTEXT

There are now powerful forces at work that will undermine much of the international support previously given to the African state system.[5] First, the end of the Cold War means that African countries no longer have automatic patrons to turn to if they are threatened. The great powers do not have any incentive to aid troubled African countries. Indeed, Gorbachev's pressure on Angola to come to an agreement with South Africa in 1988 heralded a new era in which Moscow and Washington are willing to let old allies that have received significant aid twist in the wind. For instance, U.S. aid policy has switched from supporting countries that were once seen as strategically important (e.g., Zaire, Somalia, Sudan) to aiding those that are relatively successful in adopting political and economic reforms. As a result, in just the last few years, governments in Ethiopia, Liberia, Chad, Rwanda, and Somalia, which had been able to attract significant security and financial resources from their patrons in the past, were abandoned and quickly overthrown. These upheavals were unprecedented because, while African governments were routinely succeeded by their own militaries in the past, only Museveni in Uganda (1986) was able to lead a successful insurgency from the bush in an already independent African country between 1957 and 1989.

The norm of sovereignty has also suffered significant erosion. The first, dramatic symbols of the decline in respect for sovereignty were the conditionality clauses that the International Monetary Fund and the World Bank (and, now, most bilateral aid donors) attached to their loans starting in the early 1980s. While the IMF in particular has always practiced conditionality, the new demands, fueled by a perspective that saw African governments themselves as a substantial part of the economic problem, represented a significant encroachment on areas of public policy that had previously been considered the sole province of national leaders. The now accepted presence of IMF, World Bank, and bilateral aid officials during African government deliberations about the money supply, exchange rate policy, wage policy, subsidy policy, and a host of other issues is a startling indication that African countries have implicitly ceded sovereignty on some economic issues in exchange for being put into international receivership. During the 1980s, nongovernmental organizations, especially in the Horn of Africa, also tested the bounds of sovereignty by conducting cross-border operations without the permission of the governments involved. Thus, the United States/United Nations intervention in Somalia in late 1992 was not a stunning new development; rather, it was simply the logical outcome of the erosion of African sovereignty that began in the early 1980s.

It was probably inevitable that the erosion of sovereignty on economic issues would also have implications for how the international community viewed other aspects of domestic politics in African countries. However, African sovereignty is now especially imperiled because, in the new world order, attention has been directed toward the right of ethnic self-determination, precisely the issue that had been forestalled by the emergence of the norm of sovereignty since the early 1960s. The global community, including the superpowers, has now focused on the need for certain ethnic groups to create their own national arrangements. For instance, German unification was widely perceived to be a question of self-determination, and there was widespread support for the right of the Baltic states to regain their independence. Most important for African countries is the independence achieved by the new ethnic republics in Central Europe and Asia. Baltic independence could at least be rationalized by African leaders as unique because these countries were simply regaining the independence that they enjoyed before World War II. However, the former Central Europe and Soviet republics are the first examples in fifty years of new countries based on ethnic affiliation emerging from existing nations that had once been widely recognized as viable and legitimate. Between 1945 and 1990, global boundary stability reinforced the seeming permanence of African boundaries. Now the world is sending a different message to those who might contemplate upsetting the current state system.

The new emphasis on self-determination at the expense of sovereignty is being expressed in numerous ways. For instance, in 1991, sixty groups who aspire to form new nations created the Unrepresented Nations and Peoples Organization to press their claims for self-determination. This particular grouping would seem quixotic except that four of its founding members (Estonia, Latvia, Armenia, and Georgia) have already become independent states.[6] In the academic literature, several authors are now suggesting that some states in the Third World, including some in Africa, have failed so badly that the possibility of placing them under United Nations trusteeship should be explored.[7] It is not unreasonable to expect that at least some in the international community will soon begin to (correctly) cite the basic characteristics of African states (e.g., the fact that so many are small or landlocked) as a fundamental barrier to development and at least hint that the nature of the states will have to change if growth is to occur. Such developments, which would have been unimaginable a few years ago, suggest just how rapidly sovereignty as an international norm is falling out of favor.

These changes will become more salient to Africans now that Eritrea has voted to become independent of Ethiopia after successfully winning a long war against the Mengistu regime. Thus, Africans now have their own example of a new ethnic state that, ironically, was carved out of the oldest country on the continent.

The prediction that sovereignty will erode in the face of claims of self-determination is controversial. For instance, Robert H. Jackson has argued that "the possibility that the issue of self-determination will be reopened in those ex-colonies where it continues to provoke controversy seems very slim indeed."[8] Jackson argues that self-determination will not reemerge, in part because no group seeking to upset the international order has received backing so far. In and of itself, this means little given the profound changes in international society over the last few years. Critically, Jackson also argues that the international order will not recognize the right of self-determination because "if such claims were allowed in some cases they could very easily encourage demands for the same elsewhere and therefore threaten the territorial integrity of many other states with dissident regions."[9] However, given that international society has now accepted the right of the ethnic groups in Central Europe and the former Soviet Union to create their own states, the tipping point that Jackson so rightly warns of may have been reached.

Also, territorial integrity and international order were especially important to the superpowers because instability created the possibility that one side or another could gain an advantage in a particular territory. Now that the Cold War is over, it is much less clear that mass disorder in large parts of the strategically unimportant Third World will be that important to international society. If Europeans can tolerate the disorder of the former Yugoslavia on their own continent, the world may have developed a higher tolerance to boundary change than Jackson suggests.

Jackson makes a strong case that nonintervention will continue to be a central norm of international relations.[10] It is, in fact, unlikely that the international community will intervene actively to help those who threaten Africa's borders. All that is really needed for the African boundary system to come under stress, however, is for the great powers not to actively aid, as they did in the past, those countries that faced armed threats to their boundaries. As noted above, when African countries have been faced with a sudden loss of patrons, upheaval and change can come surprisingly quickly.

In fact, to some extent intervention is not the right issue. Rather, the real question is if the international community will countenance the kind of repression that African governments and many others across the world have used in the past to retain their territorial integrity. For instance, if Biafra were to happen today, would the world do nothing to the central Nigerian government as it prosecuted a war to defeat the rebels that resulted in the deaths of a million people? Some type of sanctions would almost inevitably be applied. Thus the international community has moved from strongly supporting the rights of states to retain their territorial integrity to a more ambiguous position that may provide rebels, especially those adept at mobilizing international public opinion, with considerable encouragement.

THE DESTABILIZING ASPECTS
OF POLITICAL LIBERALIZATION

Given the erosion of the international underpinnings of the African state system, the question becomes whether Africans themselves will finally end the regime by fundamentally changing their commitment to boundary stability. One possible source of this change in commitment is the wave of political liberalization currently sweeping the continent. Since 1989, dozens of countries have legalized the opposition, national conferences have replaced or neutralized longtime strongmen in Benin, Congo, Mali, Niger, and Togo, national elections have turned out long-standing autocrats such as Kenneth Kaunda of Zambia, and elections that promise an end to years of military rule have occurred in several countries. In the years to come, there will no doubt be many more elections, as well as setbacks, coups, and mass confusion as dozens of countries attempt to create viable political systems. At the very least, it is clear that the old order in many African countries, characterized by one-party authoritarian rulers, is no longer acceptable to many African citizens or international donors.

In addition to the opportunity and chaos that liberalization attempts will cause on the national political scene, there is the strong possibility that political liberalization will place tremendous strain on African boundaries. At the most general level, it is hard to see how so many basic rules of African politics could change while boundaries remain unscathed. Boundary stability came about in part because the leaders, many of whom were in power for decades, were able to establish a cartel of sorts to further institutionalize their rule. Political liberalization will inevitably mean leaders in power for shorter periods of time who may have interests fundamentally different from those of their predecessors. Indeed, the boundary stability regime itself may come under attack by new rulers precisely because it was created by a club of autocrats.

Political liberalization may threaten the boundary maintenance regime in several ways. First, political liberalization inevitably raises the question of what should be the shape of the political community. For instance, in the Soviet Union outside of the Baltics, many informed observers argued that there was a commitment to the idea of the USSR. But as the pace of political liberalization increased, peoples' commitment to the Union, as opposed to their own republic, underwent sudden changes. It emerged that they were committed to the Soviet Union when they could imagine nothing else. The process of political liberalization raised for the first time the possibility of ethnic-based secession, and, almost overnight, commitment to the Soviet Union vanished. Similarly, during Czechoslovakia's "Velvet Revolution," most inside the country said that division of the country into two republics was unimaginable. Physicists might call such episodes phase transitions. That is, changes occur at the system level that are hard to predict by examining microscopic details.[11] In these cases, analysts did not understand that the ability of people to reconsider the nature of their political communities would lead to severe centrifugal pressures on the nation-state through either violent protest or, perhaps even more insidious, a complete lack of interest on the part of citizens in the perpetuity of their nations.

Second, political liberalization may lead to dramatic status reversals among different groups in a country. For instance, since elections have not been consequential in most African countries to date, the transfer of power depended on other factors, notably control of the military. Indeed, Crawford Young referred to coups as the "institutionalized mechanism for succession."[12] Thus one ethnic group could achieve power primarily because of its disproportionate representation in the military. It is now possible, however, for groups that had previously been far from the center of government to achieve real power either by leadership in the democratization movements or through elections themselves. Democratization movements open new routes to power, which may cause significant status reversals because the means of achieving control of the government has changed. For instance, in Benin the removal of President Mathieu Kerekou by the national conference and his replacement by former World Bank official Nicephore Soglo was seen by some in Benin "not as a shift from autocracy to democracy but little more than a shift of power from northern elites (represented by Kerekou) to southern elites (represented by Soglo)."[13] Not surprisingly, in Uganda, when the Uganda People's Democratic Movement returned from exile it demanded that more "northerners" be given more positions in the government.[14] These status reversals, as Young noted, may increase the possibility for ethnic conflict because "social cues carrying cultural symbols are likely to be perceived in communal terms at moments of cultural threat and insecurity" and because "when cultural communities collectively perceive serious threats to communal status in the political environment, group solidarity tends to increase."[15]

The manner in which political liberalization is being implemented in many African countries may aggravate status reversals. In the natural excitement to destroy the old authoritarian system and kick the bums out, little or no attention has been paid in most countries to social pacts or transitional rules that might make the change of political systems and the transfer of power less threatening to groups that had previously benefited from control of the government. For instance, when Frederick Chiluba became the new president of Zambia, he dismissed the commanders of the army, air force, and Zambian National Service almost immediately after taking power, in a housecleaning that will surely be replicated by other leaders eager to remove those who were integral to the ancien régime.[16] It was therefore not that surprising when President Chiluba subsequently declared a state of emergency because of threats from those associated with the Kaunda regime. Except in a few cases, there has been little formal agreement on the liability of soldiers and leaders of old military governments to prosecution for corruption or human rights violations. Subsequent trials of rulers or their subordinates could, as in Argentina, prove to be traumatic and, in particular, serve as a lightning rod for newly felt ethnic grievances.

The third reason why political liberalization may place stress on African boundaries is the dynamics of elections themselves. Especially where elections have not been previously institutionalized, they may aggravate ethnic tensions by placing the question of power very much in an "us versus them" dynamic.[17] For instance, in Rwanda, the advent of multiparty democracy led to the formation of the Coalition for the Defense of the Republic, which demanded even greater Hutu hegemony over the Tutsi and reflected the increasing tensions in the country before the April 1994 genocide began.[18] Also, since sheer numbers matter in elections, it will be necessary for political elites who seek power to mobilize support among the roughly 70 percent of all Africans who live in the countryside.[19] Since the elites are generally not closely associated with the rural populations and since the largely peasant population is itself usually atomistically dispersed over a vast hinterland, it is highly likely that support bases will have to be constructed around a set of shared (albeit recently created) ethnic symbols, icons, and vocabulary. The result, as Anthony D. Smith notes, is potentially disastrous for African states:

> When, therefore, the disaffected intelligentsia turn to a rebellious peasantry, with which they share elements of a common history and culture,

however dimly remembered, their opposition to the regime soon develops towards an open separatism; for the peasantry afford them both the social and regional base they need, to carve out a new bureaucratic unit which can accommodate their career and status aspirations.[20]

In addition, Smith notes that the peasantry, with their " 'primordial' cultural ties and memories" and rituals "lend to a rationalist, urban, parvenu intelligentsia a cultural aura and a depth of sentiment and solidarity, which give force to their claim to a separate political identity."[21]

This dynamic has not appeared yet as vividly elsewhere because most African countries that are liberalizing have yet to experience consequential elections. At the moment, the protests against the old regime are primarily urban[22] and therefore lack the separatist sentiment that could develop later, once consequential elections start to be held and leaders find it necessary to develop links with the countryside. It is quite possible, however, that—especially given the changes in international society—in the future an increase in ethnic tensions may be funneled not only into general protest but, at least in some cases, toward secessionist movements.

If those who felt that they have lost out in the ethnic conflict do decide to challenge their central governments, they may meet with a surprising amount of success. The balance of power between insurgent groups and African states is changing, making the ability of African governments to resist insurgencies much more questionable than before. Whatever their other faults, African states at independence in the early 1960s were in one respect classically Weberian: they held a monopoly on the use of legitimate force. The few weapons in each country were almost inevitably held by the police, and even they did not have an impressive amount of firepower. Now, however, African societies are becoming more militarized. In many countries, it is now relatively easy for almost any group to collect several dozen machine guns in order to start an insurgency. These weapons come from the regional arms markets that have developed from the major conflicts in Angola, Mozambique, Ethiopia, and Chad, as well as from the international arms markets. The enormous surplus of weapons that is being dumped on the international arms market in the wake of the end of the Cold War guarantees that easy access to weapons will continue.

The militarization of African society is particularly important because many states across the continent have atrophied after experiencing fifteen to twenty years of economic decline. Indeed, across sub-Saharan Africa, the gross national product declined at an average rate of 0.8 percent from 1980 to 1993.[23] The continuing fiscal crisis has meant that many governments do not have a significant presence in their countries outside of the major cities. Police, military, and even agricultural extension officers are not present in the country-side because they have not been paid or because the state lacks the transport and fuel to exhibit much of an institutional presence beyond the major urban areas. Of course, the chaos and uncertainty introduced by political liberalization, during which many of the state security structures will suddenly face profound change, may further weaken the ability of the central government to mobilize the repressive apparatus.

Thus, many governments are not capable of even detecting the development of a major insurgency in the rural areas, much less combating it. When they do detect the insurgency they may, as in the case of Doe's Liberia, have to use such blunt instruments of repression because of a lack of institutional contacts that they serve only to further alienate the population and accelerate the revolt. More generally, once a guerrilla movement begins, it can overrun local police stations and armories to collect more weapons. The insurgencies by the Mozambique National Resistance in Mozambique and the Rwandan Patriotic Front indicate just how easily an armed threat to an African government can develop when the local army is underpaid, remains poorly equipped, and has low morale. Thus leaders of potential secessionist movements may feel more emboldened than before to challenge the existing state system and may encourage others by their success. African states may still be able to defeat most of these secessionist threats, but only at a terrific cost in human lives.

The Complications Posed by Economic Reform

The odds of African countries' facing increasing ethnic instability caused by political liberalization are further heightened by the nature of the economic reforms that almost all of these countries are trying to implement simultaneously. Indeed, the policies suggested by the World Bank and the IMF threaten many aspects of the political systems that have evolved over the last thirty years in many African states. For instance, economic reform involves an entirely new way by which leaders are supposed to relate to their constituencies. Under the political systems that were established after independence, most African governments were able to provide a variety of resources—jobs, low prices for basic goods, preferential access to government projects—to favored constituencies. The whole point of economic reform is to eliminate or at least significantly curtail governments' ability to offer these kinds of advantages to their constituencies. As Charles Elliott has noted, "There is a fundamental asymmetry between the way the political system [in African countries] actually operates and the way economic decision making would have to operate if the demanding conditions of equilibrium—i.e., noninflationary balances on internal and external account—were to be achieved."[24]

In particular, economic reform will make it much more difficult for governments to buy ethnic peace through the distribution of patronage and resources. Some governments have established a more or less effective modus vivendi between ethnic groups by distributing resources through parastatals and rigging markets so that the major groups do not feel too alienated. As Richard Sandbrook notes, African leaders will condemn tribalism but resort to "ethnic arithmetic" in order "to suppress divisive tendencies."[25] Economic reform will make this kind of ethnic balancing much more difficult because the opportunities to provide patronage will be more limited. Further, when the ethnic balance is disturbed as a result of factors outside government control (changes in population distribution, natural disasters, fluctuations in the international market), leaders in Africa will find it much more difficult to intervene in economies to restore the old ethnic order or to establish a new one favorable to them.

In addition, economic reform programs themselves have the potential to contribute to status reversals and thereby further raise the potential for ethnic strife in African countries. For instance, many economic reform programs seek to improve the rural-urban terms of trade by raising the prices that farmers receive, abolishing marketing boards, and decontrolling the prices at which foods are sold. These changes have the potential to provide ostentatious benefits to groups based in the rural areas while causing more urban-based groups to feel discriminated against. Devaluation, with its accompanying shifts in income from net importers to net exporters, may also lead to significant status reversals.

Finally, because of a series of profound economic and technological changes, it may no longer seem unrealistic to many Africans that they should create their own state or rearrange national boundaries. Land, as an economic resource, is much less important than it once was because in the last decade of the twentieth century countries become rich by building semiconductors rather than by growing cotton.[26] Also, the current conventional wisdom that economic development will be fueled primarily by export-led growth implies that it is far less important to have a large internal market, defined by population, purchasing power, or land, than was the case under previous orthodoxies. Certainly the calculation of the Baltic states was that they would be better off as small independent countries able to export to Europe and the world than as part of a large market that has been, until now at least, dysfunctional. As a result, African leaders who previously thought (or were told) that the state they wanted to create would not be viable now can look to economic orthodoxy as well as exemplary cases (e.g., Singapore, Hong Kong) to suggest that they might not fare poorly, especially given most African countries' disastrous economic record.

Political liberalization in and of itself is very difficult and has the potential to lead to ethnic strife that could, especially given the changed international environment, spiral quickly and threaten African boundaries. The fact that so many African countries are simultaneously trying to implement economic reform programs eliminates many of the means that leaders previously had to manage ethnic conflict and may further complicate ethnic politics by creating whole new sets of winners and losers. It is certainly true that African countries are more at risk from ethnic-based secessionist movements unleashed by attempts at political liberalization than at any time since the early 1960s.

THE PUTATIVE STABILITY OF AFRICA'S BOUNDARIES

That the question of African boundary stability could be reopened at all is controversial, given the stability of the regime over the last thirty years. It is thus particularly important to examine the arguments of those analysts who believe that Africa's boundaries will not be fundamentally challenged by the profound changes occurring across the continent within the context of a new world order. Crawford Young has been the most persuasive proponent of the view that Africa's boundaries are not threatened. In his now classic study of cultural pluralism, Young argued that Africa, by and large, possessed "culturally neutral states."[27] Because of the artificiality of the states and the obvious multicultural basis of most societies, the ideology of nation building was, almost always, suffused with nonethnic symbols. As a result, "state power has never been placed behind cultural ideology-building, even in the hands of a single group (with the exception of South Africa and Ethiopia)."[28] Young therefore argued that it was "inconceivable" that ethnicity in Africa could develop a political role analogous to Tamil or Sikh nationalism in the Indian subcontinent. Indeed, Young argued that the fact that Europeans termed the Ibo, Yoruba, Kongo, and Ganda "tribes" and not "latent nationalities" (as was the case for the Tamils) buttressed his claim.[29]

In later writings, Young has continued to suggest that there will not be an ethnic challenge to Africa's boundaries. He has in fact argued that "among the major regions where ethnicity is territorially rooted, Africa alone has rendered virtually taboo its articulation as grounds for sovereignty claims."[30] Young argues that the reason for this unique outcome was the effectiveness with which national ideologies asserted the bond between population and territory. As a result, he suggests, "the consolidation of the African state system is an accomplished fact" that will not be challenged even if Eritrea gains its independence in the next few years.[31]

The major assumption underlying this powerful argument is that the OAU has created a public law that has "normative and empirical force" in Africa and that has been absorbed by the broader world order.[32] These laws and norms were nevertheless created under the old world order. Indeed, the assumption that the boundary-maintenance regime will survive given the profound changes occurring at both the international and the domestic levels is at least open to challenge for a few reasons. First, ethnicity did not fuse with separatist political identity in Africa between the early 1960s and the late 1980s, precisely because the international system provided few incentives for leaders to emerge who might threaten the existing boundaries. It is at least open to question whether, now that the incentives provided by the international system have changed so profoundly, ethnicity could not pose much more of a challenge to Africa's boundaries.

Second, there is, in fact, little evidence that the norms of boundary stability have become quite the fait accompli that Young suggests they have. It does not take a very thorough examination of diplomatic history to see that old orders have fallen remarkably quickly once a change has come about in the underlying system of incentives and support. For instance, most analysts in 1985 would have said that the continued existence of the Soviet Union was "an accomplished fact." Similarly, Bismarck's treaty structure, which served to stabilize the Europe of 1871, was rendered moot in the wake of changes fifteen years later. Indeed, Kennan's argument that Bismarck's system fell in part because it did "too much violence" to the "underlying forces for change in European society generally" should be taken as a profound warning to the African state system, given the enormous changes noted above.[33]

At the very least, the African state system has not yet been through a series of traumatic changes that would demonstrate that it has become institutionalized. For instance, the system of state relations that Metternich developed could reasonably be said to have become institutionalized only when Castlereagh, a key figure in the creation of the Concert, had died and the system continued. Then, and only then, was it clear that the moral framework created by Austria had indeed become institutionalized.[34] Given the tremendous changes at the international level, it therefore is legitimate to question whether the processes of political liberalization occurring in dozens of African countries will have a destabilizing effect on the African state system.

Also, there are also at least two reasons to believe that political scientists may be systematically biased toward believing that traumatic changes that upset political orders will not occur. First, most models of predicting revolt are based on the assumption that opposition will be detectable because it will build gradually. As Timur Kuran has observed, however, citizens may falsify their preferences if faced with a political order, such as the current African state system, that is able to wield repressive force.[35] Second, critically, participation in revolt may be based on interdependence of public preferences. That is, people may not join in a revolution until they believe that a critical mass of opponents will revolt. As a result, opposition to an existing order may appear to be at a low level until a relatively small event triggers the widespread consciousness that it is now possible for such a critical mass to develop, with the result that a sudden outpouring of opposition causes a revolution. As Gary Marks notes in his stylized model, either every opponent of the regime protests or nobody does, depending on the information individuals have about the intentions of others. These intentions are extremely sensitive to public cues or demonstration effects. The death of the leader of the ruling elite, reports of a revolution in a neighboring state, the murder of an opposition leader—these are the kinds of cues that transform the possibilities of opposition response to suppression, not by directly altering preferences, but by changing expectations about how others will respond.[36]

Certainly, this model of nonincremental swings in opposition seems plausible both for the Central European revolts of 1989 and for Iran in 1979. More generally, this model provides at least a partial explanation for why a revolution that "seems to be the inevitable outcome of powerful social forces" in fact "surprises so many of its leaders, participants, victims, and observers."[37] Of course, the possibility that revolt will suddenly explode without warning is particularly relevant to studying the stability of the African state system, given the enormous number of changes presently occurring throughout the world and in many individual countries. For instance, the creation of new ethnic states in Europe, Asia, and out of what was once Ethiopia may spark a consciousness in other countries that the old order has fallen and that it is possible to mount fundamental changes to the African state system. Given the artificiality of many boundaries in Africa and the rapid changes occurring in the international system, these challenges to frontiers will, in hindsight, seem inevitable.

Finally, the argument that most ethnic groups in Africa so far have not had territorial aspirations does not mean that they will not do so in the future. Ethnic movements over the last several hundred years have demonstrated a remarkable ability to create, in a short period of time, the necessary social framework to claim nationhood. As Eric Hobsbawm noted, "the nation" and "its associated phenomena: nationalism, the nation-state, national symbols, histories . . . all these rest on exercises in social engineering which are often deliberate and always innovative, if only because historical novelty implies innovation."[38] The history of Africa is replete with examples of entirely new social groupings appearing that had claims or were perceived as having origins in history's ancient mists. For instance, Ranger has documented the emergence of "Shona" and "Ndebele" identities that people are willing to kill over in the latter part of the twentieth century despite the fact that these identities simply did not exist before the nineteenth century.[39] Young has also documented the creation of an

Ibo identity that eventually led to the attempted secession by Biafra in 1967.[40] Indeed, Young notes that, given the malleable nature of most ethnic identities in Africa and elsewhere in the world, it is not inconceivable that political-ethnic movements could not create themselves in the near future to claim their place in the sun. Leroy Vail argues that it may even be easier to create ethnic identities in the future:

> While the backward-looking aspects of future ethnic phenomena—concern for the glories of past history, culture heroes, the central importance of language, and the like—will remain pretty much the same as for examples in the past, the forward-looking aspect of the Janus of ethnicity has the potential of wide variation across the political spectrum. In contemporary Zambia, for example, a main focus of ethnic identity for the Bemba-speaking people who see themselves cut off from state power is the predominantly Bemba miners' union.[41]

That the colonialists did not consider most African groupings to be nations and that they do not currently appear to have the same kind of structure that would lead to secession as movements in Asia are not particularly persuasive points. As Ranger noted, the colonialists themselves invented much of what is now considered traditional African social structure in the early part of the twentieth century. In particular, "small-scale gerontocracies were a defining feature of the twentieth rather than of the nineteenth century. . . . What were called customary law, customary land-rights, customary political structure and so on, were in fact *all* invented by colonial codification."[42] Certainly, Ralph Premdas's warning is relevant to those who believe that ethnic groups in Africa are not of the type to attempt secession:

> In a state of agitation, a nationalist or ethnic group attempts to rediscover its roots. It will need to anoint its language, religious or regional claims with mythical history. . . . This is all a subjective solidarity process. The scholar who seeks to question the legitimacy of the movement on the basis of the objectivity of the primordial and secondary causes will misunderstand what separatist movements are all about. What is significant is the shared belief of a group that its identity and survival are defined by these factors.[43]

In the mid-1960s many were surprised when the Scots, Welsh, French Canadians, Flemish, Basques, and other groups in what were considered well-ordered, stable nations began to demand significant territorial autonomy, if not outright independence.[44] There is no reason to believe that Africa will absolutely escape such pressures, given that the political systems on the continent are undergoing fundamental changes at the same time that the international system is being dramatically altered.

FORMAL AND INFORMAL BOUNDARY CHANGE

It would be a mistake to believe that the only type of boundary change that could occur in Africa would be the formal redrawing of lines. Especially in Africa, where the writ of central governments has never extended throughout the nation, it may be that the lines stay the same but that a region informally secedes. The processes enumerated above do not have to lead only to formal boundary change; many ethnic minorities would be happy to continue to live in the same nation-state if the central government left them alone and they were governed essentially by local leaders. Indeed, informal secession may be easier, since a central government may not fight as hard if the ethnic rebels do not try to embarrass it on the international stage by demanding that the global society recognize the change in boundaries.

The fiction that as long as the lines remain the same the central government is still in charge is very much a Western notion that has little practical application in Africa. Where informal secession does occur in Africa, the local situation may increasingly resemble Europe in the Middle Ages, when there was overlapping sovereignty in many areas. Obviously, a major diplomatic challenge in the future will be how to relate to ethnic rebels who have suzerainty over an area that is still recognized as part of a sovereign state. A central dilemma for foreigners who promote the notion of ethnic self-determination will be the demands by precisely those whose rights are being championed to have some kind of relationship with the outside world beyond the channels provided by the central government. As with Canada, the relations that outside powers create with regions could have a profound effect on domestic politics even if formal secession is not imminent.

Not every experiment in Africa will lead to outright ethnic conflict, nor will every ethnic conflict pose a significant threat to African boundaries. In the context of a fundamentally changed global environment, however, there is the real possibility that some of the attempts at democratization will have the unintended consequence of unleashing forces that threaten once-stable boundaries. As a result, the possibility of secession will soon begin to have an impact on politics across Africa. It may be only a matter of time before other leaders, perceiving the changed international situation and encouraged by the creation of ethnic republics elsewhere, also begin to threaten secession.

If only a few African boundaries are challenged, the whole boundary maintenance regime will be threatened because the international system that the Africans created is predicated on the illegitimacy of any change in frontiers. Unfortunately, it is impossible to forecast in advance whether boundary changes will eventually lead to more viable nations or simply begin a spiral of chaos and destruction that leaves no one better off.

Even if the lines do not formally change, though, it does not mean that there has not been real change in the delimitation of power. Informal boundary change, where the central government simply gives up on ruling an area and the local leaders are content to exist without formal recognition from the outside world, is a possibility. In fact, this sort of change, perhaps prompted by political liberalization, may be more likely than the "normal" type of boundary change associated with the redrawing of lines.

Notes

1. See, for instance, Adam Przeworski, *Democracy and the Market: Political and Economic Reforms in Eastern Europe and Latin America* (Cambridge: Cambridge University Press, 1991); Giuseppe DiPalma, *To Craft Democracies: An Essay on Democratic Transitions* (Berkeley: University of California Press, 1990); and Samuel P. Huntington, *The Third Wave: Democratization in the Late Twentieth Century* (Norman: University of Oklahoma Press, 1991).

2. Organization of African Unity, "OAU Resolution on Border Disputes, 1964," reprinted in Ian Brownlie, ed., *Basic Documents on African Affairs* (Oxford: Clarendon Press, 1971), p. 364.

3. Given the bizarre geography of postindependence Pakistan, even the creation of Bangladesh could arguably be traced to decolonization.

4. Anthony D. Smith, *The Ethnic Revival* (Cambridge: Cambridge University Press, 1981), pp. 138, 147.

5. This argument and the potential policy implications are developed more fully in Jeffrey Herbst, "The Challenges to Africa's Borders in the New World Order," *Journal of International Affairs* 46, no. 1 (Summer 1992): 17–31.

6. Scott Sullivan, "Birthplace of Nations," *Newsweek*, 1 February 1993, p. 28.

7. See Peter Lyon, "The Rise and Fall and Possible Revival of International Trusteeship," *Journal of Commonwealth and Comparative Politics* 31 (March 1993), and Gerald B. Helman and Steven R. Ratner, "Failed States," *Foreign Policy* 89 (Winter 1992/93).

8. Robert H. Jackson, *Quasi-States: Sovereignty, International Relations, and the Third World* (Cambridge: Cambridge University Press, 1990), p. 190.

9. Ibid., p. 190.

10. Ibid., p. 192.

11. James Gleick, *Chaos: Making a New Science* (New York: Viking, 1987), p. 127.

12. Crawford Young, "The African Colonial State and Its Political Legacy," in Donald Rothchild and Naomi Chazan, eds., *The Precarious Balance: State and Society in Africa* (Boulder: Westview Press, 1988), p. 57.

13. Carol Lancaster, "Democracy in Africa," *Foreign Policy*, no. 85 (Winter 1991/92): 154.

14. "Tribalism Said Precluding National Solutions," *Weekly Topic*, 2 November 1990, reprinted in Foreign Broadcast Information Service–Africa (FBIS-AFR), 7 January 1991, p. 15.

15. Crawford Young, *The Politics of Cultural Pluralism* (Wisconsin: University of Wisconsin Press, 1976), p. 161.

16. "New President Dismisses Armed Forces Commander," Johannesburg South African Press Association (SAPA) in English, 27 November 1991, reprinted in FBIS-AFR, 27 November 1991, p. 34.

17. Young, *The Politics of Cultural Pluralism*, p. 156.

18. Jane Perlez, "Violence Roils Rwanda's Embryo Democracy," *New York Times*, 1 June 1992.

19. World Bank, *World Development Report 1995* (Washington, D.C.: World Bank, 1995), p. 223.

20. Smith, *The Ethnic Revival*, p. 143.

21. Ibid.

22. Michael Bratton and Nicolas van de Walle, "Toward Governance in Africa: Popular Demands and State Responses," in Goran Hyden and Michael Bratton, eds., *Governance and Politics in Africa* (Boulder: Lynne Rienner, 1992), esp. p. 49.

23. World Bank, *World Development Report 1995*, p. 163.

24. Charles Elliott, "Structural Adjustment in the Longer Run: Some Uncomfortable Questions," in Stephen K. Commins, ed., *Africa's Development Challenges and the World Bank* (Boulder: Lynne Rienner, 1988), p. 218.

25. Richard Sandbrook with Judith Barker, *The Politics of Africa's Economic Stagnation* (Cambridge: Cambridge University Press, 1985), p. 80.

26. This point is made well by Richard H. Ullman, *Securing Europe* (Princeton: Princeton University Press, 1991), pp. 23–27.

27. Young, *The Politics of Cultural Pluralism*, p. 511.

28. Ibid. A similar argument is made by Patrick Chabal, *Power in Africa: An Essay in Political Interpretation* (London: Macmillan, 1992), p. 134.

29. Young, *The Politics of Cultural Pluralism*, p. 512.

30. Crawford Young, "Self-Determination, Territorial Integrity, and the African State System," in Francis M. Deng and I. William Zartman, eds., *Conflict Resolution in Africa* (Washington, D.C.: Brookings Institution, 1991), p. 341.

31. Ibid., pp. 341–346.

32. Ibid., p. 343.

33. George F. Kennan, *The Decline of Bismarck's European Order* (Princeton: Princeton University Press, 1979), p. 422.

34. See Henry A. Kissinger, *A World Restored* (Boston: Houghton Mifflin), pp. 312–315.

35. Timur Kuran, "Sparks and Prairie Fires: A Theory of Unanticipated Political Revolution," *Public Choice* 61 (1989): 41–74.

36. Gary Marks, "Rational Sources of Chaos in Democratic Transition," *American Behavioral Scientist* 35 (March 1992): 417. See also Kuran, "Sparks and Prairie Fires," p. 70.

37. Kuran, "Sparks and Prairie Fires," pp. 41–42.

38. Eric Hobsbawm, "Introduction: Inventing Tradition," in Eric Hobsbawm and Terence Ranger, eds., *The Invention of Tradition* (Cambridge: Cambridge University Press, 1983), p. 13. See also Benedict Anderson, *Imagined Communities: Reflections of the Origin and Spread of Nationalism* (London: Verso, 1983), esp. p. 123.

39. Terence Ranger, *The Invention of Tribalism in Zimbabwe* (Gweru, Zimbabwe: Mambo Press, 1985), p. 4.

40. Young, *The Politics of Cultural Pluralism*, p. 461.

41. Leroy Vail, "Introduction: Ethnicity in Southern African History," in Leroy Vail, ed., *The Creation of Tribalism in Southern Africa* (Berkeley: University of California Press, 1989), p. 17.

42. Terence Ranger, "The Invention of Tradition in Colonial Africa," in Hobsbawm and Ranger, *The Invention of Tradition*, pp. 249–250. Emphasis in the original.

43. Ralph R. Premdas, "Secessionist Movements in Comparative Perspective," in Ralph R. Premdas, S.W.R. de A. Samarasinghe, and Alan B. Anderson, eds., *Secessionist Movements in Comparative Perspective* (London: Pinter Publications, 1990), p. 23.

44. For a review of this phenomenon, see Robert J. Thompson and Joseph R. Rudolph Jr., "The Ebb and Flow of Ethnoterritorial Politics in the Western World," in Joseph R. Rudolph Jr. and Robert J. Thompson, eds., *Ethnoterritorial Politics, Policy, and the Western World* (Boulder: Lynne Rienner, 1989), p. 3.

SIX

Liberalization and Foreign Policy in East Europe

Ronald H. Linden

A number of intriguing empirical and theoretical questions are raised by the changes in the international organizational structure and behavior of the East European states. East Europe represents an unusual case of an "experimental" situation occurring in the real world. Much has changed domestically and internationally, but much remains the same, e.g., state size, geographic location, recent history. This setting allows us to look in a preliminary way at possible explanations for changes in some forms of state behavior. In the case of foreign policy, we can begin to assess the relative impact of changes in domestic politics and process, the international milieu, and/or international institutions on the East European states' international behavior. Up to this point, relatively little work of this type has been done on East Europe.[1] While not assuming that we will find a neat monocausal chain or that we will be able to settle realist-versus-liberal controversies with so few "data points," we can nevertheless make a contribution by looking at changes in East Europe's international behavior that followed the revolutions of 1989 and the collapse of the Soviet Union.

This essay will offer a brief description of the political and economic changes that have taken place in and around East Europe since 1989. Then we will look for clues in both the domestic policy-making environment and the external milieu that seem to explain movement and differences in East European foreign policies.

POLITICAL AND ECONOMIC LIBERALIZATION IN EAST EUROPE

Since the revolutions of 1989, the "transition" in East Europe has in general meant liberalization of both the political and the economic systems. The process is a differentiated one and is proceeding faster in some places and spheres and more slowly in others. In all cases the revolutions of 1989 swept away one-party rule of communist regimes. Even where reformed or renamed communist parties retained power, such as in Romania and Bulgaria, they did so in conjunction with multiparty parliaments, independent presidencies, and an open print media, and they continue to face the prospect of competitive elections.[2]

In most of East Europe after 1989 political liberalization proceeded more rapidly and broadly than did economic liberalization. In all of the former one-party regimes except Poland, competitive national parliamentary elections were held by mid-1990. Over the next five years parliamentary and local elections were held at various intervals throughout the region, producing coalitions of varying stability and, in some states—Lithuania, Poland, Hungary—an electoral return of communist parties.

Since the transition began, political parties have sprung up by the hundreds, along with a variety of interest groups representing both political and economic positions. Associations of students, farmers, workers, writers, ethnic groups, nationalists, environmentalists, and so on have appeared to press their cases either through or alongside the newly elected governments and competing parties. Media pluralism has emerged, though print media typically reflect much broader viewpoints than electronic media, with the latter in many cases remaining close to or controlled by the government.

While personnel at the very top have changed—all the states had new presidents by the end of 1990—institutions usually were not formally changed. Instead, existing structures began to be infused with genuine political power, to be "authenticated," to use Jan Gross's term.[3] Institutions of public representation, such as national legislatures, as well as executive organs, including the office of prime minister and other ministries, became politically responsible to earned majorities instead of elite proclivities. The most significant institutional change was the elimination of the Communist Party's "leading role" in theory and in practice. This meant that for the first time, other actors have had a legitimate and public role in the policy process.[4] Other dramatic institutional changes in the region involved the elimination of one state entirely, the German Democratic Republic, and the splitting of two others, Czechoslovakia by peaceful partition and Yugoslavia by armed struggle.

Economic change after 1989 was slower in coming, but the region has made substantial progress in most respects.[5] Only Poland embarked on rapid "shock therapy" policies that freed prices, ended government subsidies, and made the Polish *zloty* convertible at a rate that the government was prepared to defend. Hungary, Czechoslovakia, and Romania moved more slowly to free prices, and they accompanied their actions with campaigns to prepare the public. Privatization of small assets—e.g., shops, services, restaurants—proceeded more rapidly than for large state-owned assets, but in the East European states, on average, more than one-half of the gross domestic product had its origins in the private sector by mid-1995.[6] Outside investment has been drawn largely to Poland, Hungary, and the Czech Republic, with smaller amounts flowing to Southeast Europe. But overall investment levels have been lower than expected and still represent tiny shares of global foreign direct investment.[7] The overall performance of the East European economies, already weak before the revolutions, worsened through 1992, but recovery was clearly in evidence throughout the region by the end of 1994.[8]

THE NEW INTERNATIONAL ENVIRONMENT OF THE EAST EUROPEAN STATES

Not only have the revolutions in East Europe produced liberalizing regimes that must formulate their foreign policies under new domestic conditions—e.g., multiple autonomous political actors and pluralistic media—but these policies cannot simply be extensions, or slight modifications, of what had been practiced before, even if the new domestic political scene would allow it. This is because the external environment, to which foreign policy is at least nominally directed, has itself changed. The hovering power of the regional hegemon, the restrictive embrace of the regional alliance systems, the powerful if distorting effects of the Soviet economy, the similarity and familiarity of fellow "fraternal allies," and the usually predictable nature of their interactions and policies all disappeared after 1989, and especially after 1991.

After 1989 the international institutions that the Soviet Union had utilized as one of the instruments for establishing the parameters of acceptable behavior—both domestically and internationally—were quickly dismantled. Both the Warsaw Pact and the Council for Mutual Economic Assistance (CMEA) immediately disappeared and, despite some talk to the contrary, were not replaced by regional military or economic alliances. Some regional initiatives have been pursued, most notably the Visegrad Three—then Four—but the ultimate aim of the group was and is full and rapid integration with the West.[9]

Western alliances, meanwhile, offered only partial acceptance into the most important European communities that all of the new regimes declared to be their new referent group. The European Union offered first the Central European then the Southeast European states "associate membership" but no commitment or timetable to full membership. NATO established an ancillary "North Atlantic Cooperation Council" and in 1994 offered the states of the region a Partnership for Peace. But both NATO and the EU denied these states the alliances' most important benefits of membership: free trade and security guarantees.[10]

The uncertainty engendered by the lack of commonly binding alliance structures has been compounded by a degree of differentiation among the states themselves that was not present during the Soviet period. Historically, East Europe has not been a region where democratic rule has been very robust, and the possibility of a historical replay of the interwar period is not forgotten.[11] As a result of developments during that period, World War II, and then communist rule, the different East European leaders brought different agendas to governance in 1989. For example, the post-communist governments in Budapest consider themselves responsible for the welfare of some three million Hungarians who live in neighboring countries. Romanians now inhabit two states, Romania and Moldova, but neither of these is ethnically pure, while Poland, for the first time in its history, is both free and almost completely Polish. Ethnic dispersal across international borders is less of an issue for Bulgarians, but ethnic diversity within the country is, with a population of approximately one million (out of eight million) Turks and eight hundred thousand Roma (Gypsies). In one case of state fragmentation in the region—Czechoslovakia—ethnicity was less significant than regionalism, while in Yugoslavia, ethnicity and memories of past intercommunal warfare (absent in the Czechoslovak case) offered political entrepreneurs a rich field.[12]

After 1989 the new ruling coalitions in Central Europe were primarily center-right in political orientation. In Hungary, for example, a rapid arrangement between the Hungarian Democratic Forum and the main opposition party, the Free Democrats, allowed the former to gain the government and the latter the presidency. Hungary then moved quickly to open its economy to foreign participation and, compared with Poland, enjoyed remarkable government continuity through 1994. The coalition in Czechoslovakia, by contrast, was weakened by the widening split between the Czech lands and Slovakia and the growing inclination of leaders in both parts of the country to pursue special agendas. By the beginning of 1992 effective national policy on most issues was less the norm than the exception, and by the end of the year two states stood where one had been. In Poland fragmentation of the political landscape among Solidarity's successors and the hovering power of Lech Walesa, elected president in 1990, presented yet another variant of post-communist rule.

In Southeast Europe, communist parties, renamed as Socialists or Social-Democrats, did not have to endure long intervals out of power. In Romania the National Salvation Front won the country's first free elections in 1990 and, despite splitting, won again in 1992. In Bulgaria the Socialists and opposition Union of Democratic Forces traded ineffective years in office until, after a time with a technocratic government, the Socialists won a clear majority in the legislature in 1994. But while Ion Iliescu, a former high official in the Ceausescu era, retained the presidency in Romania, in Bulgaria a former dissident and head of the opposition, Zhelju Zhelev, was elected and reelected president. In these cases the political inclinations and electoral base of the governing parties meant slower progress on liberalizing the workings of the economy. In yet another variant, elections in each of the constituent republics of the former Yugoslavia produced nationalist governments, and by 1991 political diversity gave way to full-scale civil war. This result and the ineffective response of external powers to these consequences represent only one path—the most disastrous one—that the East European movements toward domestic rule could take. But even absent warfare, the new democracies of East Europe, in making foreign policy, cannot be sure how long the new democracy next door will last or what alternative kinds of governments might emerge.

In several other respects as well, the international milieu changed after 1989. The putative military threat from West Germany, so long held up as the raison d'être of the Warsaw Pact and the Soviet security "guarantee," disappeared, replaced by a new kind of German "threat," perceived by some, of economic domination. By mid-1991, for example, 70% of all investment in the Czech Republic—which itself received more than 90% of all foreign investment in Czechoslovakia—was of German origin.[13] In early 1992 the head of the Office for Foreign Contacts and Information of Czechoslovakia wrote to the government warning of an economic "offensive" on the part of Germany against the country. In response, the government called a special meeting to see if there was evidence to back up this claim.[14] In Poland similar concerns were expressed.[15]

At the same time, danger from the East, in the form of Soviet pressure or even intervention, was significantly reduced, but it did not disappear altogether. Concerns of many of the East European governments that history could be reversed were informed by four decades of experience under Soviet hegemony. As Russia exerted pressure on its former republics to join in the Commonwealth of Independent States, to accept Russian troops as peacekeepers, or to blend economies, many in the East European states feared a return to an aggressive foreign policy stance in Moscow. The evident and strident Russian hostility to East European membership in NATO does not ease this fear.

LIBERALIZATION AND FOREIGN POLICY: RESEARCH QUESTIONS FOR EAST EUROPE

East Europe represents as close to a political science laboratory situation as we are likely to find in the real world.[16] The states of the region have all been subject to the same "experiment": the lifting of communist political and economic domination and the removal of Soviet hegemony. All have seen the emergence of multiparty, competitive elections and legislatures, elected chief executives, more or less pluralized media, removal of barriers to foreign influence, and a whittling away of state domination of the economy. In short, to use Miles Kahler's categories, all have seen an increase in political and economic competition, participation, and transparency.

But they bring to the situation quite different characteristics. These include differences in pre-communist history, religious orientation and institutions, level of industrialization of the economy, level of exposure to Western influence during the communist period, and ethnic heterogeneity, as well as differences in size, resources, and population. In this "experimental" situation we do not really have a communist "control" group—the remaining communist states of Cuba, North Korea, and China are too distant and too different to make comparison plausible—so we may want to think of these countries' own communist past as the "control" group.

The question then arises—and is reinforced by a key question that motivates this volume—as to which set of factors has been more important in determining the new foreign policies of the liberalizing states: the changing and liberalizing domestic structures or the dramatically changed international environment?

Activism and Reorientation in Foreign Policy

Let us consider first the overall level of activity and orientation of the East European states' foreign policies after 1989. What effect is liberalization having on these states' patterns of international relations? With the restrictive environment of the Soviet-dominated alliance system removed and economic ties to the East withered, it might be expected that the newly democratic states will display both a more vigorous pattern of foreign policy activism and one that is oriented more toward other democracies. In the literature, the first result is suggested by Hagan[17] and the second by the work of Siverson and Emmons.[18] In the specific case of East Europe, given the stated policy objectives of the new regimes in East Europe, i.e., to return to Europe, we might expect these states not only to become more active but also to seek out other democracies in particular as alliance partners.

Preliminary evidence from East Europe on the question of activism is mixed. Enormous activism characterized the early foreign policies of post-communist Czechoslovakia and Hungary. As expected, most of this was directed toward a "return to Europe." But Czechoslovakia, Romania, and Poland were also active in pursuing ties in Latin America. Are these levels being sustained? Hagan indicates that the degree of foreign policy activism, as measured by specificity, commitment, and independence of activity, is affected in open states by the regime's level of vulnerability and fragmentation.[19] We might expect, then, that open but politically fragmented regimes such as Poland and Bulgaria will not be able to sustain the level of international involvement and commitment seen in the early stages of postrevolutionary activism, while open but less fragmented states such as the

Czech Republic or Slovenia will be able to do so. Zhong offers data suggesting that a constriction of international interactions has occurred for all states of the region, especially with regard to their ties with non-European communist states and less-developed countries.[20]

Other factors affecting activism were tested by Cowhey for the great powers. These results indicate that a state's electoral system, specifically the degree to which collective goods are emphasized as rewards, the division of power, and the transparency of the system, directly affect the ability of a state to sustain multilateral international commitments. States in which power is divided between the executive and the legislature, for example, seem more able to sustain commitments, though these are harder to achieve at first, than those in which a parliament dominates.[21] This would suggest that over time Poland will be more able to sustain its commitment to multilateralism than will Bulgaria, where the president is relatively weak, or even Hungary, where the president is elected by the parliament.

As for seeking other democracies, the evidence is strong that for East Europe, this is indeed the direction of foreign policy movement. The region witnessed a rapid changeover in orientation from East to West, as measured by trade flows, aid and investment orientation, public pronouncements, and organizational membership.[22] Was this primarily a function of domestic liberalization or of shifting forces in the international system? Obviously, the global opportunity structure had changed—i.e., Soviet hegemony had been withdrawn. But given this new milieu, why did all of the states choose to shift their orientations westward? The global distribution of power shifted radically toward the United States—especially in the economic sphere—and thus a certain amount of "bandwagoning" could be expected. But can we learn anything from the fact that some East European states moved in this direction more abruptly or more sharply than others? For example, the Central European states—Poland, Hungary, and Czechoslovakia—were most eager to discard or rapidly transform the CMEA and the system of Soviet–East European economic exchanges. Romania and Bulgaria were less eager but supported some changes. And why did the East European states move so quickly to exit from the shelter of the restrictive but protected world of CMEA? Why did they move to shift Soviet–East European trade to world prices and hard currency at a time when such a move was expected to bring substantial economic disadvantages to them only months into their revolutions?[23]

The answer is that despite the economic "advantage" of staying within the Soviet system a bit longer, politically it was not possible. These new, non-communist governments had come to power promising and determined to return their countries to "normal" and end "distortions" in their foreign relations. Whether the original impetus came from the former ruling parties themselves, as in Hungary and Poland, or from the streets, as in East Germany and Czechoslovakia, the new governments were representations of the national desire to break with the past. At home, this meant relegating the communists to the margins; internationally, it meant "joining Europe."

Unlike the previous ruling (communist) parties, the new governments in East Europe could not afford to ignore this sentiment. The communist parties had sought to maintain a monopoly of political power, which they protected by enforcing a severely restricted political environment, dominating the information environment to the point of monopoly, and excluding the public from involvement in policy making except in the form of mobilized support. Politics existed under the communist regimes, of course, but opposition, when it occurred, was primarily intra-elite, and public opposition activities and organizations were by definition illegitimate and repressed.[24] Foreign policy making and execution represented an even more restricted arena, since it always carried with it the need to be especially attentive to a powerful external constituent, the Soviet Union.

But after 1989 formulation and execution of foreign policy in East Europe became subject to public intervention. Foreign policy, as with other policies, lay within the newly created and newly legitimate realm of public discussion, debate, and criticism. Virtually all aspects of the process, from agenda setting to implementation, were, in principle, open to intervention by actors who were not creatures of the ruling regime. Though a common circumstance for Western democracies, it was a new dynamic for the East European political elites.

Thus all ruling parties, communist or not, faced political competition for the first time, and foreign policy was one of their assets. For the new ruling parties, breaking ties with CMEA and the Warsaw Pact confirmed the new regimes' democratic credentials at home and mirrored internationally their return to "normalcy." The new regimes found themselves in a situation where their legitimacy was high but they faced daunting tasks. In trying to liberalize their economies most were forced, sooner or later, to take several unpopular actions, such as ending price controls and subsidies, allowing for unemployment and bankruptcies. Foreign policy, on the other hand, provided an arena in which these regimes could earn popularity relatively cost-free. This was accomplished partly by aligning the regime most visibly with states popularly perceived to be democracies, i.e., the West. Joining the United States and other European countries in sanctions against Iraq and in the Gulf War, reducing ties with members of the Soviet-approved list of "revolutionary" states (e.g., Cuba, North Korea, and Vietnam), and reestablishing relations with states that had long been on the taboo list (such as Israel, South Korea, and Chile). Of little impact internationally and hardly offering the net gain that a self-help-in-an-anarchic-world perspective might suggest, these actions were important symbolically to the new government's domestic constituencies.[25]

While in general it is the domestic political and economic structure and policies that occupy the central attention of most East European parties, foreign policy issues are not absent and can be useful in competitive elections. In the first free Polish elections (1991), for example, one party, the Confederation for an Independent Poland, long considered a fringe party of the right, achieved significant success (finishing with the third-largest number of seats in parliament), partly because of its reputation as a historic and uncompromising defender of Poland's national independence, a position it steadily contrasted with that of the first post-communist government vis-á-vis external economic powers.[26] In Hungary opposition parties criticized the ruling coalition for "selling out" the country and failing to guard its prerogatives in the face of rapacious Western governments and companies. One such party, the Independent Smallholders and Civic Party, finished fourth in the voting in 1994. Further support for the importance of the battle of domestic forces on this aspect of foreign policy is provided by those cases where the dog did not bark—at least not as loudly. In Romania and Bulgaria, where elections in 1990 kept descendants of formerly ruling communist parties in power, the governments were less eager to break down the old alliances, more willing to settle for reform in the existing system, and more sluggish in shifting their trade.

It is clear, however, that the new democratic governments of East Europe were also being pushed toward increasing Western ties by the external environment. They were, in international relations terms, "regime takers." They needed the loans, trade, and investment of the

Western democracies and their supranational organizations, especially after 1991, when the Eastern option collapsed. Thus, democracies or not, the states of East Europe would have had to look elsewhere for partners. But to understand why they turned west *in the first
place*, one must look to domestic political changes. A domestic perspective is also necessary to understand what Kalypso Nicolaidis calls
the "anticipatory adaptation" of East European economies to the
expected demands of Western economic institutions.[27] Domestic politics also gives us an understanding of why these transition economies
looked to the West instead of, for example, to more forgiving markets
such as those in less-developed countries.

The question of how states respond to international pressure is in
part a question of how the political processes define a country's
future, its preferences, and its identity. According to the construc-
tivists in international relations theory, national preferences are not
given, as structural realists might suggest, but are formed as a product of intersubjective interactions with the outside world.[28] Therefore,
how a state reacts to outside pressure, what views of itself or norms of
behavior elites bring to the interface with the outside world, are for-
mulated and shaped by that interaction and are neither static nor
overdetermined by the external power structure.[29]

For East Europe, a critical aspect of this battle involves economic
choices, as indicated above. Another part of it—and an important
one—involves national ethnic identity. Few of the East European
states are homogeneous; all must in one way or another determine
whether they are both a nation and a state. The return of sovereignty
does not automatically presume a particular choice in the legitimation of that sovereignty.[30] The reemergence of nationalism as a powerful legitimating force in the region derives from several factors,
including its long suppression and delegitimation under communist
rule, the absence of a powerful competing ideology or value system,
the search for identity among national communities now cut loose
from the East but not fully accepted by the West, and the discrediting
of internationalist alternatives by virtue of four decades of the Soviet-
imposed "socialist commonwealth."[31]

The impact of nationalism—as that of other factors—has varied
across the region. But most of the post-communist governments in
the East European states are obliged to respond to charges from
nationalists that other national groups within the state have or seek
too much power, that they seek secession, and that the government

will be betraying the national heritage if it yields to the demands of such groups. In Romania and Bulgaria, for example, a critical issue facing the new governments has been their treatment of minority populations, Hungarians and Turks, respectively. In both of these cases ethnically based political parties act as powerful lobbying groups, pressing for the collective rights of their constituents. The governments in power, but also competing parties, must take positions on whether and when these minorities can achieve full expression of their cultural and civil rights and in what form, e.g., collective or individual. Both government and opposition actions have resonance outside the country, particularly if a referent country is involved—Hungary and Turkey in this case. At the same time, powerful groups in these referent countries push their governments to see to it that co-nationals in neighboring states are fairly treated or even, in some cases, to try to effect border changes. In Romania opposition parties essentially forced onto the agenda the issue of support for the independence of and then possible unification with the new state of Moldova (the former Soviet republic of Moldavia). They wanted the National Salvation Front government and President Ion Iliescu to do more than speak out in favor of the Moldovans. Opposition parties and political umbrella groups forced Iliescu to publicly defend his hesitancy on this issue and ultimately to declare himself opposed to union of the two independent Romanian states. After a referendum and elections in Moldova in 1994 demonstrated a popular rejection of union with Romania, nationalist forces in Romania—some of which were by now in coalition with the governing Social Democratic Party—nevertheless continued their agitation to keep the status of Moldova as an issue in Romanian politics.

The new Hungarian governments have viewed themselves as the protector of co-nationals in all of the neighboring countries. In 1990 Hungarian prime minister Jozsef Antall declared that he saw himself as prime minister of fifteen million Hungarians. As the population of the country at the time was ten million, this statement was widely taken as aggressive interference in neighboring sovereign states' prerogatives at best, as revealing irredentist tendencies at worst. The center-right government tirelessly pressed the issue of Romanian government policy toward its Hungarian minority in various European bodies, with the consequent slowing of that country's ability to "join Europe." The German minority in Poland, residing mostly in the region of Upper Silesia, transferred to Poland after World War II, has directly solicited German aid in improving its situation. During his visit to Poland in July 1992 German foreign minister Klaus Kinkel promised such aid and seemed assured that improvement would be forthcoming, because, as he put it, "Poland wants good relations with Germany."[32]

While nationalism relates most obviously to a state's identity preferences, it also affects its ability to pursue its economic goals internationally. Numerous domestic actors now have an impact on foreign policy in East Europe through their involvement in the debate on the speed, direction, and nature of their country's domestic economic transition. Criticism of government policies, for moving too fast or too slowly, is frequently linked, explicitly or implicitly, to the government's willingness to do the bidding of foreign economic centers.

The most outspoken example of this phenomenon occurred in Hungary, where the vice chairman (at the time) of the ruling Hungarian Democratic Forum, Istvan Csurka, unleashed a vicious broadside against the government of Prime Minister Jozsef Antall. Accusing the government of being under the control of various foreign economic powers, Csurka linked the transformation of Hungary with that which took place after World War II and compared the IMF to the Red Army.[33] Wrapping his criticism in the defense of national sovereignty and seeking as much as possible to link the current transformation with that overseen by the illegitimate communist regime, Csurka said:

> We do not need economic patrons prepared at the desks of the former planning office, but we need a Hungarian national economic policy. Our survival depends on this. There is nothing more sacred than the national interests.[34]

His appeal to Hungarian nationalism was explicit in his rejection of foreign domination in the transition process:

> We must no longer wait for applause from abroad because, prompted by the old banking connections, some foreign countries today applaud precisely helplessness and half-heartedness and regard highway robbery as democratic and market economy orientation.[35]

Csurka himself was not able to mount a successful attack on the ruling HDF policies, but people with similar views were influential in the 1994 elections, largely through the Independent Smallholders and Civic Party. Their leader, Jozsef Torgyan, has been vehement in his denunciations of government attentiveness to Western demands.[36] In late 1995 the Smallholders eclipsed the ruling Socialists as the most popular party in Hungary. In both Hungary and Poland, the communist parties' return to power was facilitated by their charge that the nation's people were paying too high a price in the transition to a market economy.

Throughout the region, other actors have weighed in on the economic transition issue, complicating the ability of East European governments to deal with Western institutions. In most of East Europe trade unions for the first time have begun to act like trade unions. They consider it their obligation to act on behalf of their memberships, or of workers in general, to protect them from the vicissitudes of economic change. Especially during a time of transition, the unions both new and old are faced with a full range of challenges to the welfare of their constituents (or potential constituents, as the unions too must also contest for support). As has happened elsewhere, the unions of East Europe often push their governments not to implement strict IMF guidelines, to move more slowly on ending subsidies to enterprises and allowing bankruptcies, and especially to keep some price controls.[37] No longer the "transmission belts" of economic directives that Lenin envisioned and successive Soviet and East European leaders fashioned, the unions today often form a powerful counterweight to governments eager to comply with international demands for painful economic reforms. In some cases the new governments have tried to co-opt the newly outspoken groups into policy making and thus into implementation of IMF-imposed guidelines. In Romania during 1991–1992 a joint government-union commission and a separate National Consultative Council made up of the three largest unions negotiated a national labor contract covering wage and pension levels. An even broader "social pact" was offered in Poland in 1992 by the government of Prime Minister Hanna Suchochka, after it faced down its own miners in order to try to keep its budget deficit within the IMF's stipulated limits.

Nor are unions the only interest group that the new governments must consider when seeking or making international connections. Farmers have become especially vocal in some East European states. In Poland they object to what they see as a flood of Western imports of foodstuffs that drives their products out of the market while the governments of these very same Western countries keep Polish goods off Western European markets. In August 1991 the National Council of the Polish Peasant Party Solidarity demanded that the Polish government provide "food security" for the country.[38] The next month a new peasant party, called the Feed and Defend Peasant Party, warned that the proposed association of the country with the European Community could cause a "sell-out of Polish land" and said it would oppose "the sale of national assets to foreign hands."[39] After the association agreements with the EU were signed, the Polish government promised its farmers that high import tariffs against foreign agricultural products would be maintained.[40]

If the makers of foreign policy can no longer count on being able to automatically call into line key national interest groups, they must also deal with other actors whose intervention affects foreign policy and who operate at the subnational or even local level. Under communism, the governments of the East European states, with the exception of Yugoslavia, were highly centralized. Since the revolutions, regional—often ethnically based—interests have asserted themselves in several instances, with the most extreme and tragic consequences in Yugoslavia. Before the breakup of Czechoslovakia, one of that country's first foreign policy acts exacerbated a regional split. President Vaclav Havel, eager to regain for the country some of the goodwill it had lost through its enforced alliance with the Soviet Union, executed a number of policy reversals, aimed at reorienting the country's foreign policy along "nonideological" lines. One such action involved trying to reduce or end the country's arms sales, pursued as handmaiden to Soviet interests worldwide. But since the bulk of the arms factories, with thousands of workers, lay in Slovakia, this international issue had direct domestic regional consequences. Objections to halting arms sales were raised, and in fact the sales continued.

The question of Slovakia's role in Czechoslovakia's international policies played an important part in the ultimate breakup of the country. Slovak leaders complained that Prague's eagerness to please Western creditors and its concomitant desire to pursue economic liberalization rapidly hurt the poorer Slovak region more than the Czech lands. Less exposed to Western investment, more tied to Soviet-era state enterprises, such as arms factories, and less able to switch markets nimbly, Slovakia was suffering disproportionately as a result of the country's Westernizing economy.[41] Slovakia needed to develop its own policies and determine its own pace, nationalist leaders like Vladimir Meciar argued. In the end, eager to be rid of what he saw as obstacles to economic change and integration with the West, Czech prime minister Vaclav Klaus not only acceded to Slovakia's separation but encouraged it.

Democracy and Conflict in East Europe

Given the plethora of nationalists and nationalist issues, both "internal" and international, why has the region not seen more conflict? Contrary to the common willingness to generalize from Yugoslavia, in fact East Europe and even the states of the former Soviet Union have seen relatively little interstate conflict. Despite nationalist pressure, conflict has been avoided between Romania and Hungary, for example, and no violent conflict has emerged between Poland and Lithuania, or Hungary and Ukraine, where co-national communities and nationalist pressures exist, nor between Slovakia and Hungary, where this issue is complicated further by the conflict over water resources. Nor have Slovakia and the Czech Republic resorted to threats or armed action, despite differences serious enough to produce a division of their once common country.

Are such conflicts restrained by the international system or is their absence a further illustration of the "liberal peace" that exists between democracies—i.e., the notion that democracies do not fight each other even though they engage in conflict about as often as nondemocracies do? While we can hardly consider the five years or so since the end of communist rule in the region as constituting a full test, we can try to fit these states' behavior—in this case the relative absence of conflict—into the explanatory suggestions offered by the literature as to why the "liberal peace" might hold.

The case for external factors' restraining conflict, especially among small states, would seem to be strong. In Morgan and Campbell's findings, the relationship between political constraints (their operationalization of democracy) and war proneness held for major powers, but it did *not* hold for smaller powers, which the East European states clearly are.[42] Though Morgan and Campbell do not offer conclusions in this direction, one reason why the force of domestic factors did not hold up might be the differing nature of these states' relationship with the external environment, captured in Thucydides' famous dictum "The strong do what they have the power to do and the weak accept what they have to accept." Much other work on small states[43] suggests that whether they are democracies or not, the international environment will exercise a powerful influence

on the direction of their foreign policies. Indeed, work on major powers[44] as well as the author's own investigations of the region itself[45] suggest the important though differentiated impact of international
changes on states' polices, foreign policy not excepted.

In addition, institutionalists would expect that settling into a web
of ties with other democracies would constrain conflictual behavior
among the East European states. Thus a situation with conflict potential might be mediated by "honest brokers" whom the East European
states not only trusted but wanted to please by accepting their solutions. EC mediation in the Gabcikovo-Nagymoros Danube River dam
controversy would be an example of such a situation. This huge bar-
rage and hydroelectric generator project, originally planned in 1977,
has been the subject of controversy since 1989, when Hungary
stopped building its part and then ultimately canceled its participation in the project. Czechoslovakia and then Slovakia pushed ahead
and in October 1992 diverted the river into the canals and reservoirs
of the project. Defusing a potentially dangerous confrontation, EC
intervention did succeed in getting both parties to agree to submit
the main dispute to the International Court of Justice while continuing talks on the amount and consequences of the water diversion.[46] At
the same time, institutionalists would argue that the existing international institutional environment has provided a key arena for the
exercise of international influence and the achievement of national
goals. In this view the existing powerful institutions of West Europe
acted to mitigate the power struggle that might otherwise have
ensued and exerted a powerful influence on the behavior of both the
West and the East European states.[47]

But the utter failure of the West European states or the United
States to prevent conflict among the former Yugoslav states or halt its
spread is a more dramatic example to the contrary. Neither the international power structure nor the international institutions prevented
or mitigated conflict here. If in fact the United States, the European
Community, and/or the United Nations had put into force some
effective constraints on the behavior of Serbia or Croatia, for example, one could argue that the option of resorting to the use of force
elsewhere in East Europe, and hence the presence of conflict, had
been reduced by either the international system or the international
institutions. But the Yugoslav case demonstrates the opposite. The
change in the global power structure away from bipolarity probably
facilitated the conflict in Yugoslavia, as realist thinking would sug-

gest.[48] And the external institutional environment applied only weak constraints. But since these conditions were also operative throughout the region, how do we explain the relative lack of conflict?

The liberal perspective argues that regime type, in this case democracy, is centrally involved in this relative lack of conflict. Despite presumptions that democracies are less warlike, aggregate research suggests that in fact democracies engage in wars about as much as nondemocracies do. As noted, Morgan and Campbell found that the inverse relationship between political constraints and war proneness held for major powers but not for smaller powers. But Maoz and Abdolali, among others, found that democracies tend not to clash with each other and do not fight each other at all.[49] In Bruce Russett's words, "This research result is extremely robust, in that by various criteria of war and militarized diplomatic disputes, and various measures of democracy, the relative rarity of violent conflict between democracies still holds up."[50] Further, Randall Schweller says the evidence is clear that even in situations of global power shift, which realism says predicts conflict, democracies do not engage in preventive wars against democratic challengers and prefer the use of alliances to handle nondemocratic challengers.[51]

Why should this be so? Schweller argues that the inclination to war in democracies is blunted by "liberal complaisance" (concerns about the cost of war), the openness and division of power, and moral values of a democracy that militate against war.[52] But Morgan and Campbell argue that decisional constraints, at least, are very much "context dependent." As they put it, "Political constraints arising from domestic structure may not significantly affect the overall frequency of dispute or war involvement, but they may alternatively raise and lower the probabilities of these behaviors, depending on other conditions."[53] In his comprehensive review of the question of why democracies do not fight other democracies, Russett focuses on two variables: (1) the prevalence of democratic norms, which are externalized and operate to reduce the likelihood of resort to force between democracies (but not necessarily between democracies and autocracies) and (2) institutional constraints—the difficulty and protracted nature of debate and decision in democracies. In studying the data with Zeev Maoz, Russett concludes:

> Normative restraints help prevent both the occurrence of conflict and the occurrence of war. . . . Institutional constraints prevent escalation to war, but they do not by themselves prevent states from becoming involved in lower-level conflicts.[54]

So what can be gleaned from the recent history of East Europe? A rough comparison of the region's nondemocratic period with its democratic phase suggests that conflict and resort to war have been reduced in the brief democratic period. During the period of Soviet and communist dominance, roughly 1945–1989, there were three incidents of military action: suppression of workers' revolts in East Germany in 1953; crushing of the Hungarian revolution in 1956; and the invasion and occupation of Czechoslovakia in 1968. Only the last involved East European states' (as opposed to only Russia) taking action against each other, and only the 1956 Hungary action involved enough deaths to qualify, in the aggregate literature, as a war. Other actions might be added, if the notion of conflict were broadened, to include, for example, Soviet pressure on Poland during 1980–1981 using military maneuvers or border incidents between Yugoslavia and some of its neighbors after its break with Stalin in 1948.

Even given such an expanded notion, and even extending the field to include possible clashes between the Soviet Union/Russia and East European states currently, the present democratic period has not seen such incidents. Of course the democratic period is as yet much shorter than the nondemocratic period, but the range of freedom available to each state (what Maoz and Abdolali call "interaction opportunities") is many times greater, and, as noted, powerful domestic forces, such as nationalist parties, that might tend toward conflict are not restrained, as they were during the autocratic period. Viewed in that light and recognizing that this does not constitute a full empirical test, the recent period in East Europe does seem to conform to the general findings.

But what about the fighting in former Yugoslavia? We could exclude this case from consideration as not involving true interstate war. Fighting there began, after all, as a war of secession between Serbia and first Slovenia, then Croatia, neither of which had been recognized as separate states. The fighting in Bosnia, which did begin after it was recognized, is in large part a civil war between communities struggling to control a piece of, and withdraw from, the new state. But in both the Serb-Croat and the Bosnian fighting there are interstate dimensions; both Croatia and Bosnia were recognized by the international community in 1992 and fighting, of course, continued in both places.

But for purposes of looking at the relationship between democracy and conflict, this is not a true test, in that none of the combatant states had been independent democracies for very long before fighting began. Russett, for example, uses a cutoff point of three years of democratic governance. While highly arbitrary, such a distinction does draw attention to the fact that claiming to be a democracy does not make it so, especially for research purposes. True, elections had occurred in all the Yugoslav republics, but no genuine competitive opposition had emerged (the opposition seceded in Bosnia), nor has an independent press been allowed to function in either Serbia or Croatia.[55] Thus, if one were looking for the institutions of democracy to test in a situation of potential or real conflict, it would have been hard to find them at the time when the conflict began and would be even harder now.

Assuming that the rest of East Europe qualifies as democratic, it seems clear that the institutional constraints Russett refers to have indeed been developing. The most significant change institutionally has been the dilution of the power of the communist party from a dominating body that sanctioned no public competitors to a political party competing for influence and votes. Other changes that have followed involved not so much the creation of new institutions (though some of that has happened) as the instilling of real power into existing institutional shells. Examples of such changes include the presidency in Poland, the constitutional court in Hungary, and legislatures in most of the countries.

With regard to foreign policy, such actors have for the first time demonstrated an ability and willingness to influence foreign relations. While foreign ministries themselves have shown remarkable stability and independence from the domestic political fray, in contrast to most other governing elites,[56] one of the lessons the new democracies are learning is that no matter who runs it, the foreign ministry does not exercise a monopoly over the conduct of foreign affairs. Typically in East Europe there is now a vigorous ministry of international economic relations; a defense ministry eager to build bilateral and multilateral ties; and a ministry of economic reform, which must deal with powerful external economic actors. In some cases, such as Hungary, the prime minister has created his own foreign policy advisory group or council, usually designed to more directly and effectively represent his views and those of his party. Such a proliferation of foreign policy actors led Tamas Katona, a state secretary in Hungary, to complain in May 1991 that there were "too many players" in the foreign policy arena.[57]

Among the other institutions that have taken newly significant roles in foreign relations are the countries' national banks. Responding to the cries of enterprises that they serve, leaders of national banks have often been reluctant to go along with IMF-imposed austerity, especially as it applies to credit restrictions. The central banks in Russia and East Europe, for example, typically report directly to the parliament rather than to the president or the government. This structure has allowed them to pressure politically sensitive leaders who fear the consequences of tight money policies, as happened in Bulgaria and Romania.

At the same time, the very nature of key institutions and their relationships have been in flux. Struggles to formulate and specify arenas of responsibility, rights, and prerogatives have taken place in the foreign policy sphere, along with others, as was evident in the contest between the president and the prime minister of Hungary, for example.[58] Such struggles for institutional influence, both for their own sake and in order to achieve the desired results in the policy area, have occurred before. But they are both more open now and more consequential, partly because the guiding and controlling hand of what had been *the* key institution, the communist party, has disappeared. But, as noted, domestic liberalization has also allowed all struggles, including those over foreign policy, to become part of the competitive political arena. There are now intrusive parliaments, independently elected presidents, vigorous media, and a broad array of social action groups and parties that have demonstrated an ability to slow, halt, or alter key decisions. And now there is a positive incentive for institutional actors to seek support in public politics, an option not previously available.

The picture is further complicated by the fact that the relative independence of institutional actors and the new permeability of the countries' borders mean that interest groups can seek and utilize external actors as allies in domestic policy struggles. Soon after Slovakia's independence in 1993, Hungarian political parties in Slovakia called on the Council of Europe not to admit the country until the new government dealt with the Hungarian minority's economic and political grievances.[59] And governments throughout the region have used the IMF and its rigorous guidelines to justify austerity policies at home.

Finally, both institutional actors and other interests and individuals have the ability to try to influence foreign policy through a pluralized media. Foreign policy, like other policy, is now considered and debated in a much different media environment than that which characterized the communist regimes. All actions are at least potentially subject to criticism and evaluation in the variety of print and, to a lesser extent, electronic media in the states of East Europe. Thus government preferences, whether more aggressive or more passive, are subject to a critical or opposition press and both institutional and public intervention.

As for liberal complaisance and/or the presence of moral values that might restrain resort to war, it is hard to establish a clear connection regionwide. Public opinion surveys in the region show continued evidence of interethnic hostility, and certainly nationalist groups are active and sometimes powerful in the region. In Romania nationalist candidates made a strong showing in the parliamentary elections of 1992, won many local offices precisely in the region of the country inhabited by Hungarians, and in 1994 joined the national government for a time. But there is no evidence that these events translated into a popular willingness to bear the cost of war with Hungary. And in Hungary, which has many nationalist groups of its own, the desire to become part of Europe, which means, inter alia, eschewing the use of force to settle disputes, seems dominant and part of the broad consensus on foreign policy.[60] Both there and in Poland the continuing power of popular sentiment for "joining Europe" was demonstrated by the fact that in these cases the communist and left parties that won elections in 1994 were quick to assert their vigorous interest in continued integration with Europe.

Thus democratic norms would seem also to be operating in the region to reduce the likelihood of violent conflict. Hungary and Romania, despite their clear and serious differences, for example, have been able to sign an "open skies" agreement between them, reducing the likelihood of conflict and even providing for military cooperation. Russett's conclusion that democratic stability and the stability of expectations between such states regarding the continued absence of conflict seem to be supported here and between other adversaries, such as the Czech Republic and Slovakia.

In these cases also, international institutional constraints clearly seem to be operating. Both Hungary and Romania signed on early to the Council of Europe and its strictures, the U.S.-sponsored Partnership for Peace, an EU-brokered multilateral treaty on minority rights, and—most problematical (and still unratified)—a comprehensive bilateral treaty.[61] Both have been eager to maintain a positive image to support their membership in the Western alliances.

Does this mean conflict would never occur among states in East Europe or with states outside the region? No one even vaguely familiar with this region would venture such a prediction. But it does indicate, as the aggregate literature does, that a complex mix of factors is involved in the resort to war by democracies. If the costs of war were at some point to be seen as lower relative to the costs of peace—for example, acquiescence in the loss of territory—then liberal complaisance could be replaced by jingoism. Or if instability in one part of the democratic dyad led the other to expect an escalation of conflict, or if the rewards offered by international institutions were to be significantly devalued or indefinitely put off, the likelihood of violent conflict could increase.

As with other countries, the question of the impact of liberalization on foreign policy in East Europe can only partly be answered in the aggregate and probably not at all satisfactorily by relying only on "internal" or "external" explanations. The likely paths and probable causes can be suggested and valuable guides created. The complex of factors that the literature suggests and the still fresh history of liberalizing East Europe should tell us that an unambiguous answer as to what causes nations to behave the way they do and, most important, what causes them to resort to war, is still probably a few months off.

Notes

I would like to gratefully acknowledge the careful reading and comments by Miles Kahler, Valerie Bunce, and Russell Leng and by the anonymous reviewers of Columbia University Press. I would also like to acknowledge the research assistance of Ben DeDominicis. Portions of this essay appeared in "Domestic Change and International Relations in the New Eastern Europe," in John R. Lampe and Daniel N. Nelson, eds., *East European Security Reconsidered* (Washington, D.C.: Woodrow Wilson Center Press, 1993).

1. Studies with this focus include: Regina Karp, "Postcommunist Europe: Back from the Abyss?" in Daniel Nelson, ed., *After Authoritarianism: Democracy or Disorder?* (Westport, Conn.: Greenwood Press, 1995); Pal Dunay, Gabor Kardos, and Andrew J. Williams, eds., *New Forms of Security: Views from Central, Eastern, and Western Europe* (Aldershot: Dartmouth, 1995); Yang Zhong, "The Fallen Wall and Its Aftermath: Impact of Regime Change Upon Foreign Policy Behavior in Six East European Countries," *East European Quarterly* 28, no. 2 (Summer 1994): 235–257; John Lampe and Daniel Nelson, eds., *East European Security Reconsidered* (Washington, D.C.: Woodrow Wilson Center Press and Sudosteuropa-Gesellschaft, 1993); Joseph C. Kun, *Hungarian Foreign Policy: The Experience of a New Democracy* (London: Praeger Publishers with the Center for Strategic and International Studies, 1993).

2. On the revolutions of 1989, see Gale Stokes, *The Walls Came Tumbling Down: The*

Collapse of Communist Rule in Eastern Europe (New York: Oxford University Press, 1993);
J. F. Brown, *Surge to Freedom: The End of Communist Rule in Eastern Europe* (Durham:
Duke University Press, 1991).

3. Jan T. Gross, "Poland: From Civil Society to Political Nation," in Ivo Banac, ed.,
Eastern Europe in Revolution (Ithaca: Cornell University Press, 1992), pp. 56–71.

4. For a discussion of the party's role in communist states, see T. H. Rigby, "Politics
in the Mono-Organizational Society," and Zygmunt Bauman, "The Party in the
System-Management Phase: Change and Continuity," in Andrew C. Janos, ed., *Authoritarian Politics in Communist Europe* (Berkeley, Calif.: Institute of International Studies,
1976), pp. 31–80, 81–108.

5. *Transition Report 1995* (London: European Bank for Reconstruction and Development, 1995).

6. Ibid., p. 11.

7. "In 1994," writes the European Bank for Reconstruction and Development
(EBRD), "the total FDI into eastern Europe, the Baltics and the CIS, a region with a
population of 400 million, was similar to that into Malaysia with a population of 19
million" (ibid., p. 6).

8. Ben Slay, "East European Economies: Recovery Takes Hold," *Transition* 1, no. 1
(January 30, 1995): 68–72; Kevin Done and Anthony Robinson, "EBRD Praises 'Fast-
Track' Countries," *Financial Times*, November 2, 1995.

9. See, for example, the memorandum from the three Visegrad countries to the
EC in October 1992 (Warsaw PAP, October 22, 1992 [Foreign Broadcast Information
Service, hereafter FBIS], October 23, 1992, p. 3). In 1992 the EC agreed to treat the
Visegrad Three as a unit for customs purposes but declined to grant the group full
membership in the EC. At the same time, partly in response to EC economic pressure,
a free-trade zone was created among the countries. See Karoly Okolicsanyi, "The
Visegrad Triangle's Free-Trade Zone," *RFE/RL Research Report* 2, no. 3 (January 15,
1993): 19–22. In January 1993 Czech prime minister Vaclav Klaus called the grouping
"artificial" (*RFE/RL News Briefs*, January 12, 1993, p. 12).

10. See the discussion in Ronald H. Linden, "The Price of a Bleacher Seat: East
Europe's Entry Into the World Political Economy," in Ronald Liebowitz and Michael
Kraus, eds., *Russia and Eastern Europe After Communism: The Search for New Political,
Economic, and Security Systems* (Boulder: Westview Press, 1996), pp. 315–336.

11. On the interwar period, see Joseph Rothschild, *East Central Europe Between the
Two World Wars* (Seattle: University of Washington Press, 1974).

12. See the discussion in Stokes, *The Walls Came Tumbling Down*, pp. 218–252, and
V. P. Gagnon Jr., "Ethnic Nationalism and International Conflict: The Case of Serbia,"
International Security 19, no. 3 (Winter 1994/95): 130–166.

13. CTSK in English, February 21, 1992 (FBIS, February 26, 1992, p. 2).

14. *Respekt*, no. 7 (February 1992): 17–23 (FBIS, February 1992, pp. 8–10).

15. See *Glos Szczecinski*, June 17–18, 1992 (FBIS, June 30, 1992, pp. 26–28). See also
Jan B. de Weydenthal, "German Plan for Border Region Stirs Interest in Poland,"
RFE/RL Research Report 1, no. 7 (February 14, 1992): 39–47.

16. For a similar point regarding Europe and the end of Cold War, see Robert O.
Keohane, Joseph S. Nye, and Stanley Hoffmann, eds., *After the Cold War: International
Institutions and State Strategies in Europe, 1989–1991* (Cambridge: Harvard University
Press, 1993), p. v.

17. Joe D. Hagan, "Regimes, Political Oppositions, and the Comparative Analysis

of Foreign Policy," in Charles F. Hermann, Charles W. Kegley Jr., and James N. Rosenau, eds., *New Directions in the Study of Foreign Policy* (Boston: Allen and Unwin, 1987), pp. 339–365.

18. Randolph M. Siverson and Juliann Emmons, "Birds of a Feather: Democratic Political Systems and Alliance Choices," *Journal of Conflict Resolution* 35, no. 2 (June 1991): 285–306. The data support this proposition more strongly in the post–World War II period than in the interwar period.

19. Hagan, "Regimes, Political Oppositions, and Comparative Analysis," pp. 356–361.

20. Zhong, "The Fallen Wall and Its Aftermath," pp. 240–248.

21. Peter F. Cowhey, "Domestic Institutions and the Credibility of International Commitments: Japan and the United States," *International Organization* 47, no. 2 (Spring 1993): 299–326.

22. Ronald H. Linden, "The New International Political Economy of East Europe," *Studies in Comparative Communism* 25, no. 1 (March 1992): 3–22; Linden, "The Price of a Bleacher Seat." Zhong, in "The Fallen Wall and Its Aftermath," supports this conclusion with a comparison of international interactions.

23. At the time of the revolutions of 1989 most of the East European states, able to sell overpriced manufactured goods to the USSR for underpriced fuel and raw materials, were running trade surpluses with the USSR. Though artificial because of the lack of a true common convertible currency, these surpluses were expected to turn into sharp and real deficits when trade moved to hard currency and world prices in 1991. Though initially estimated as a likely benefit to the USSR of $12 billion, the virtual collapse in Soviet–East European exports during 1991 in fact led to a small trade surplus for East Europe overall by the end of the year. See John Williamson, *The Economic Opening of Eastern Europe* (Washington, D.C.: Institute for International Economics, 1991), p. 13; *PlanEcon Report* 8, nos. 27–28–29 (July 21, 1992): 4, 7.

24. See the discussion of the "politics of notables" in Ellen Comisso, "State Structures, Political Processes, and Collective Choice in CMEA States," *International Organization* 40, no. 2 (Spring 1986): 195–238.

25. See the discussion "The Uses of Foreign Policy," in Linden, "The New International Political Economy," pp. 11–14.

26. Louisa Vinton, "From the Margins to the Mainstream: The Confederation for an Independent Poland," *Report on Eastern Europe* 2, no. 46 (November 15, 1991): 20–24. See also an interview with Leszek Moczulski, head of the party, in *Kurier* (Vienna), November 3, 1991 (FBIS, November 4, 1991, p. 20).

27. Kalypso Nicolaidis, "East European Trade in the Aftermath of 1989: Did International Institutions Matter?" in Keohane, Nye, and Hoffmann, *After the Cold War*, pp. 196–245.

28. Alexander Wendt, "Anarchy Is What States Make of It," *International Organization* 46, no. 2 (Spring 1992): 391–426.

29. For a constructivist discussion of the end of the Cold War in Europe, see Rey Koslowski and Friedrich V. Kratochwil, "Understanding Change in International Politics: The Soviet Empire's Demise and the International System," *International Organization* 48, no. 2 (Spring 1994): 215–247.

30. For a discussion of the varying bases of legitimation of sovereignty, see J. Samuel Barkin and Bruce Cronin, "The State and the Nation: Changing Norms and

the Rules of Sovereignty in International Relations," *International Organization* 48, no. 1 (Winter 1994): 107–130.

31. Ronald H. Linden, "The Appeal of Nationalism," *Report on Eastern Europe* 2, no. 24 (June 14, 1991): 29–35.

32. *Frankfurter Allgemeine*, August 1, 1992 (FBIS, August 5, 1992, p. 17).

33. *Nepszabadsag*, August 27, 1992 (FBIS, September 3, 1992, p. 9). Csurka's article was originally published in *Magyar Forum* on August 20, 1992; *Nepszabadsag* then published long excerpts.

34. Ibid., p. 11.

35. Ibid., p. 10.

36. See, e.g., *Uj Magyarorszag*, November 13, 1995 (FBIS, November 17, 1995, p. 13).

37. In February 1991 the head of the former government-run trade unions in Poland, Alfred Miodowicz, led protests against the government's economic plan on the grounds that Poland was being run by the IMF, which had "dictated" its economic program (Ben DeDominicis, "Liberals in Poland" [Ph.D. diss., University of Pittsburgh, 1992], p. 271).

38. PAP in English, August 3, 1991 (FBIS, August 3, 1991, p. 30).

39. *Rzeczpospolita*, September 21–22, 1991 (FBIS, September 25, 1991, pp. 22–23).

40. PAP in English, February 24, 1992 (FBIS, February 26, 1992, p. 22).

41. At the end of 1992, unemployment in the Czech republic was 3%, while in Slovakia the figure was nearly 12%.

42. T. Clifton Morgan and Sally H. Campbell, "Domestic Structure, Decisional Constraints, and War," *Journal of Conflict Resolution* 35, no. 2 (June 1991): 187–211.

43. Maria Papadakis and Harvey Starr, "Opportunity, Willingness, and Small States: The Relationship Between Environment and Foreign Policy," in Hermann, Kegley, and Rosenau, *New Directions in the Study of Foreign Policy*, pp. 409–432.

44. Patrick James and John R. Oneal, "The Influence of Domestic and International Politics on the President's Use of Force," *Journal of Conflict Resolution* 35, no. 2 (June 1991): 307–332.

45. Ronald H. Linden, *Communist States and International Change: Romania and Yugoslavia in Comparative Perspective* (Boston: Allen and Unwin, 1987).

46. CTK (Prague) in English, January 20, 1993 (FBIS, January 21, 1993, p. 28); *Nepszabadsag*, November 30, 1992 (FBIS, December 9, 1992, p. 1); for a review of the controversy, see Karoly Okolicsanyi, "Slovak-Hungarian Tension: Bratislava Diverts the Danube," *RFE/RL Research Report* 1, no. 49 (December 11, 1992): 49–54.

47. Stephan Haggard, Marc A. Levy, Andrew Moravcsik, and Kalypso Nicolaidis, "Integrating the Two Halves of Europe: Theories of Interests, Bargaining, and Institutions," in Keohane, Nye, and Hoffmann, *After the Cold War*, pp. 173–195. For a critical view of institutionalist approaches, see John J. Mearsheimer, "The False Promise of International Institutions," *International Security* 19, no. 3 (Winter 1994/95): 5–49.

48. John J. Mearsheimer, "Back to the Future: Instability in Europe After the Cold War," in Sean M. Lynn-Jones and Steven E. Miller, eds., *The Cold War and After: Prospects for Peace*, expanded ed. (Cambridge: MIT Press, 1993), pp. 141–192. For a critique of this view, see Richard N. Lebow, "The Long Peace, the End of the Cold War, and the Failure of Realism," *International Organization* 48, no. 2 (Spring 1994): 249–277. On the end of the Cold War and Yugoslavia, see Susan L. Woodward, *Balkan Tragedy* (Washington, D.C.: The Brookings Institution, 1995), esp. pp. 148–157.

49. Zeev Maoz and Nasrin Abdolali, "Regime Types and International Conflict, 1816–1976," *Journal of Conflict Resolution* 33, no. 1 (March 1989): 3–35.

50. Bruce Russett, *Grasping the Democratic Peace: Principles for a Post–Cold War World* (Princeton: Princeton University Press, 1993), p. 10.

51. Randall L. Schweller, "Domestic Structure and Preventive War: Are Democracies More Pacific?" *World Politics* 44, no. 2 (January 1992): 235–269.

52. Ibid., pp. 240–246.

53. Morgan and Campbell, "Domestic Structure, Decisional Constraints, and War," p. 209.

54. Russett, *Grasping the Democratic Peace*, pp. 88, 90. For a critical view of democratic peace theory, see Christopher Layne, "Kant or Cant: The Myth of the Democratic Peace," *International Security* 19, no. 2 (Fall 1994): 5–49.

55. For a discussion of press control in Croatia and Serbia, see *Christian Science Monitor,* January 26, 1993, pp. 2, 12, 13.

56. See Thomas A. Baylis, "Plus Ca Change? Transformation and Continuity Among East European Elites" (paper presented at national convention of the American Association for the Advancement of Slavic Studies, Phoenix, Arizona, November 19–22, 1992).

57. Kun, *Hungarian Foreign Policy*, p. 119.

58. Judith Pataki and John W. Schiemann, "Constitutional Court Limits Presidential Powers," *Report on Eastern Europe* 2, no. 42 (October 18, 1991): 5–9.

59. *RFE/RL Daily Report*, February 5, 1993.

60. See Alfred A. Reisch, "Hungary Pursues Integration with the West," *RFE/RL Research Report* 2, no. 13 (March 26, 1993): 32–38.

61. *Reuters*, March 19, 1995.

expanding the zone of peace conu—

From Reluctant Choices to Credible Commitments:

Foreign Policy and Economic and Political Liberalization—Spain 1953–1986

Victor Pérez-Díaz and Juan Carlos Rodríguez

The evolution of Spanish foreign policy from the early 1950s to the late 1980s may be explained in a way that suggests some considerations of a more general nature. This evolution holds some puzzles, one of which is the apparent continuity of the objectives of Spanish foreign policy throughout a period extending over two political regimes opposed to one another: the authoritarian state under General Franco and liberal democracy.[1] Clarification of this point requires scrutiny of the institutional and cultural premises of Spanish foreign policy and the interplay between governmental decisions and the civil society.

After explaining the background (sociopolitical coalitions and Franco's mentality) to Franco's foreign policy after the civil war, we focus on the policy choices regarding foreign policy and economic matters of the 1950s and early 1960s. These decisions had an enormous impact, as they marked a significant departure from the earlier years and led Spain along a path of increasing involvement in the economic and defense systems of the West. We argue that these decisions (or options) were "reluctant" insofar as they were made with only partial awareness of their consequences: the domestic conflicts that could arise from them and the subsequent pressures placed on Spain's political institutions and political culture. Francoist leaders were confident that they could control these conflicts and pressures, on the assumption that the conditions of Spanish involvement with the West were such that a tacit pact was established according to which Spain would accept a peripheral position and a reduced status within the Western community in exchange for the latter's allowing her to maintain the *differentia specifica* of her political regime. In a way, the point of quasi-equilibrium for this political exchange was reached around 1962, when the Spanish government asked to open negotiations aimed at achieving the Statute of Associated State of the European Community, and the EC's reply was that, though the Statute of Associate was out of the question because of Spain's political regime, an increasingly close economic relationship between Spain and the EC could be contemplated.

This point of quasi-equilibrium lasted for the next fifteen years. During that time, extraordinary transformations took place in Spanish civil society (Pérez-Díaz 1993), resulting in changes in the basic dispositions of the general public (its informal rules and social conventions), which, in turn, led to the gradual redefinition of Spain's national interests and national identity by underlining that the country did belong within the Western European community.[2] Spain's transition to democracy (or political liberalization) in the mid-1970s did not alter the main objectives of her foreign policy, but it did make the culmination of that trajectory possible: her actual entry into the European Community and into NATO.

First, democracy removed possible objections from other member states to the legitimacy of her application, given that a democratic Spain now fulfilled the criteria set for integration into the European Community and into NATO (allowing here for some inconsistency on the part of the NATO members willing to accept the presence in the alliance of countries with authoritarian governments, such as Portugal, Greece, and Turkey, at least during some period of time). (Still, it should be remarked that acceptance by these foreign countries could not substitute for the will of the Spanish people on the matter. Though the West could impose democracy as a precondition for full membership, Spanish democracy came about not because of such an imposition but as a result of largely endogenous processes. In fact, Western pressure on Spain to change into a democracy was never too strict, and a nondemocratic Spain remained a peripheral, but still significant, member of the geopolitical and economic system of the West for more than three decades.)

Second, democracy allowed for the development of a public sphere (a space for public debate) in which Spanish opinions and will regarding matters of foreign policy were clarified and made explicit.

Though in Franco's later times the public's disposition followed suit, moving to economic liberalization and the transformations of civil society, the foreign policy implications of those changes could not be articulated in an explicit and coherent way. Public debate was distorted and constrained by censorship and political repression (somehow mitigated during the 1960s and 1970s), and even oppositional parties lacked the informational base, the perspective, and the sense of responsibility that can be developed only in an atmosphere of freedom and open deliberation as correlates to political accountability. By contrast, the transition to democracy created the incentives and the opportunities necessary for the public and the (new) political parties to articulate their arguments and to state their commitments. These commitments became "credible" not because the new political class made them but because they were made in a framework of formal institutions and basic dispositions that seemed well established by this time.

Thus the combination of continuity and discontinuity in Spanish foreign policy over the thirty-odd years that stretch from the early 1950s to the mid-1980s corresponds to a sequence of growing Spanish involvement (as much economic and defensive as political) in the Western system that begins with the reluctant choices of Franco in the 1950s, continues throughout the changes in civil society and public dispositions in the late 1950s, the 1960s, and early 1970s, and leads on to the explicit and credible commitments of democratic Spain. Spain started as a peripheral member of the Western European community and ended as one of its fully paid-up members.

Four considerations of a more general character may be inferred from the discussion of the Spanish experience.

First, this experience shows how in the long run an authoritarian state's foreign policy can be influenced by a policy of economic liberalization (the effects of which far exceed those of a defense policy of alignment with the West) as it carries the economy toward a growing and seemingly irreversible interdependence with the economies of the capitalist democracies.

Second, this experience suggests that the long-term effects of such a policy of economic liberalization come about mostly indirectly, through the development of a civil society and changes in public dispositions, which prepare the way for changes in the basic premises of any foreign policy—namely, in the definition of a national interest and of a national identity. This change in the public disposition may be considered one of the basic preconditions for credible commitments being made in the matter.

Third, it may likewise be inferred from this experience that another (second) decisive factor in the formulation of credible commitments regarding foreign policy on the part of both the state and the public lies not so much in the mere change in character of the national polity from authoritarianism to democracy as it does more specifically in the development of a public sphere.

Fourth, the discussion of the Spanish experience may qualify the current debate about the interplay between internal and external factors in the determination of foreign policy.[3] Though that debate may have been enriched by the two-level games approach put forward by Putnam (1988) and others in an attempt to apply game theory to foreign policy by considering that the principal actor (the statesman) is performing on two stages (the international and the domestic) at the same time (so that the results of his actions on one stage constrain or broaden his margin for maneuver on the other), still that approach considers state actors who have stable preferences and act strategically.[4] Our argument directs attention to actors other than mere state actors, to the formation process of the actors' preferences, and to a range of actions wider than the one confined to the strategic ones. This argument refers to a theory of civil society (Pérez-Díaz 1993 and 1995) and makes some use of Oakeshott's conception of social and political dispositions (Oakeshott 1991).

FRANCO'S POLICIES IN THE 1940S: CULTURAL AND SOCIOPOLITICAL PREMISES AND INTERNATIONAL ENVIRONMENT

Franco's initial foreign policy was in keeping with his mentality and sociopolitical basis and his international environment. It was the policy responding to the goals of an ardent nationalist and to the sober understanding of a resolute and consistent "realist" thinker.[5] On the one hand, the Spanish state was to look carefully after its own interests: at the very least, its survival; at best, its chances for increasing its power and its wealth (possibly through colonial expansion). On the other hand, it tried to achieve these ends by behaving as a calculating, rational actor in a world where moral or legal considerations had little more than merely rhetorical or symbolic relevance, a world that was plunged into a war of immense proportions over which it could exercise no control and little influence. Therefore, Franco's alliances, including those with the nations that had helped him to win the war, were purely instrumental. Gratitude did not extend beyond the limits of self-interest, and Franco made it quite clear to Hitler that it was not in Spain's interest to become involved in a world war of uncertain outcome (especially given the condition in which the country found itself after the civil war), unless Hitler was willing to press the French into accepting the colonial demands that Franco put forward (Preston 1994:469 ff.), probably knowing only too well that Hitler would not agree to them.

Though Franco's views were broadly shared by a coalition of social and political forces (most of the army, the church, and the business community, part of the middle classes, and the peasants, and a political class comprising several "political families," such as Falangists, traditionalists, Catholics, and others, and civil servants), Franco's nationalist vision of the world was colored by a particular mentality that was a consequence of some crucial formative experiences. It was the experience of an "Africanist" military officer engaged from the very beginning of his career in a colonial war in Morocco in which he played a significant part from 1912 to 1926.[6] Franco shared with many of his fellow officers in the army a sentiment of national humiliation for the long decline suffered by Spain since the mid-seventeenth century. In their view, Spain had been reduced from the rank of a world power first to a regional power, then to a peripheral player, and finally to a battleground on which other nations could fight each other *par personne interposée*. Spain had lost her wealth, power, and status at the hands of other nations, and she had been pushed out to the margins of what was assumed to be the civilized world. Historical grievances against rival nations and dreams of renewal and renaissance in terms of the national glory to be attained at the expense of those rivals: this was the stuff that most of the patriotic ruminations of those Spanish military men were made of. In this melancholic and somewhat bitter drama, other nations could be but occasional friends or dangerous rivals to watch out for. The Moroccan adventure, coming almost immediately after the humiliation inflicted upon Spanish pride by defeat at the hands of the United States in 1898, offered an opportunity both to compensate for and to reinforce these sentiments.[7] In this respect the Moroccan experience was something akin to a dress rehearsal for the full spectacle of the civil war, when a large part of the nationalist side was seized by a quasi-mystical exaltation of the Spanish nation and considered the war as a first stage toward, and a precondition for, national rebirth.

This "nationalist" outlook was combined with an anti-liberal stand of a particular kind, the legacy of a particular historical development. In fact, the Spanish army's traditions of the nineteenth century and the first part of the twentieth were not anti-liberal; on the contrary, the most distinguished Spanish officers of the nineteenth century were both liberal and nationalist (Payne 1977). They became gradually more detached from the liberal-constitutional order after the disaster of 1898, when they had to face the unpopularity of the Moroccan wars and what they regarded as the increasing ungovernability of the country. Nevertheless, the army supported the constitutional monarchy of 1876 (with the interlude of a "soft" dictatorship between 1923 and 1929, which the army was instrumental first in imposing and later in deposing) and accepted the second republic in 1931. Still more to the point, even many of the military officers (including Franco himself) who rebelled against the established government in 1936 did so while proclaiming their allegiance to the republic (Payne 1967).

The military officers' understanding of the political situation in Spain in the thirties, however, was decisively influenced by their uneasiness with the social conflict and the public unrest, for which they held political party rivalries responsible, and by those parties' apparent inability to handle regional centrifugal forces and to provide some modicum of economic prosperity. The officers also resented the lack of sympathy toward the army and the absence of ideological affinities with it on the part of the leftist parties that had governed between 1931 and 1933[8] and that returned to power in the spring of 1936. Furthermore, they were alarmed by the explosion of political, social, regional, and anticlerical passions that same spring (which they interpreted in the light of the revolutionary events in Asturias in 1934), and they distrusted the government's apparent leniency in dealing with the situation. Thus the basic authoritarian features built into the army's routines and military ethos, combined with this interpretation of the situation, in the end led these officers to sympathize with some of the authoritarian traditions present in the Spanish political culture of the time. These traditions ranged from the propertied classes' pragmatic distaste for social conflict to the outright opposition to the liberal order shared by clerics and intellectuals (both those of a Catholic conservative bent, always reluctant to make a lasting peace with political liberalism, and those belonging to the new cohorts of Spanish fascism).[9]

The army's (political) "anti-liberalism," shared by the sociopolitical coalition of propertied classes, clerics, conservative politicians, and fascists, had three important features: it was compatible with a capitalist economy; it refrained from totalitarianism and allowed a limited political pluralism; and it gave the political leadership a wide margin for maneuver in order to adapt its policies to the circumstances.

In the first place, the coalition's anti-liberal stance was more political than economic as the anti-capitalist inclinations (and rhetoric) of the church and the Falangists fit in well with a long tradition of state interventionism in the economy that was fully compatible with the interests of the propertied classes (industrial, financial, and agricultural). The latter were interested in an open-market economy only up to a point: they had been barricaded behind one of the highest tariffs in the world since the beginning of this century (reinforced by the Cambó tariff of 1922) (Serrano Sanz 1987), and they were apparently happy to see the state regulate the labor market, repress strikes, and persecute the unions. Neither did they have any fundamental objections to the rhetoric and (within certain limits) the institutions of "corporatism," which seemed to form part of the "spirit of the times" for some decades (having been tried out in one form or another by all sorts of proponents of both right and left in the twenties and thirties).[10]

Second, the attacks of this coalition on political liberalism were qualified by the refusal of the majority of its components to see a truly totalitarian order emerge. Totalitarianism ran against deeply ingrained traditions in the church, the army, the business community, the professions, the middle classes, and the peasants (of the northern half of the country). All these groups took for granted that the denial of civic freedoms on the part of the authoritarian regime was meant not for them but for those defeated in the war (including the "liberals" themselves as well as the socialists, communists, and anarchists). As a result, although the new state began by imposing strict censorship and the forced unification of political organizations (first into "the party" and later into "the National Movement," as the single party came to be officially called), it was open enough to accommodate several "political families" (the Falangists, the Carlists, and the

Opus Dei, among others) (Linz 1964) and to initiate a (slow but near continuous) process of institutionalization of its political regime.

Third, under these conditions Franco enjoyed a wide margin for maneuver, which enabled him to define his role and the policies that he considered most appropriate to each situation. In fact, being a man of some basic ideas but no precise ideology, he defined himself as the arbiter between the political families, his function centering not so much on achieving (a mechanical) equilibrium among them as on redirecting and manipulating the pressure they exerted, with his aim being to maintain the political regime and his own personal power. From this perspective, Franco followed the evolution of the arguments of and the social support for these political families, occasionally deciding at each critical moment for one or other of the opposing tendencies but taking extreme care to confer the different parts of government on different families as a means of ensuring that the debate would follow its course, thus reducing the likelihood of challenges to his own authority. His commitment to political principles and institutions may have been genuine enough, but it was always subordinated to his disposition to move cautiously and focus on his main long-term goals.

Given these institutional and cultural premises, as well as the limited resources available to Franco for the task of reconstructing the economy and watching over the general upheaval created by World War II, there should be no doubt about where his tactical priorities lay. He applied his acute sense of reality to the tasks of controlling the domestic situation and surviving within the international context. His foreign policy may be interpreted as a (rather brilliant) exercise in survival techniques in an environment little short of chaotic, where he took advantage of his margin for maneuver (opened up to him by the diffuse "anti-liberalism" of the sociopolitical coalition that supported him) to experiment with opportunist adaptation to the circumstances. Franco's initial moves, with Spain as a nonbelligerent power sympathetic to the Axis, cannot be explained by a firm commitment to the Fascist cause but rather by a pragmatic opportunism in which Franco would continue to take pride when he approached the Allies once Hitler's fortunes started to wane. Thus, along with this change of fortune in World War II in favor of the Allies came the corresponding softening of gestures and rhetoric from the Francoist state, as well as a new equilibrium in the distribution of influence among its different political families.[11] Although these changes appeared to have a limited effect in the mid-forties, as they were not sufficient to allow Spain entry into the United Nations and to prevent the majority of foreign ambassadors from leaving Madrid, they were to give fruit later on. Within a few years, the ambassadors were back, in the wake of the new international climate of the Cold War, when in the West—in particular the United States—the political and socio-economic elites had reached the conclusion that the realism and staunch nationalism of General Franco deserved some kind of recognition and appreciation, on condition that his pro-capitalist stance should increase (and for some observers in the hope that his limited pluralism would eventually give way to a liberal regime).

THE CRUCIAL STRATEGIC CHOICES OF THE 1950S: ECONOMIC LIBERALIZATION AND LINKING SPAIN TO THE WEST

Franco's diplomatic isolation, which was already on the wane by the late 1940s, came to a definitive end in 1953 with the United States–Spain agreement for the use of military bases on Spanish territory and the Concordat between the Vatican and Spain. In fact, both pieces of diplomacy were clearly connected to each other and, although the importance of other factors and other agents must not be overlooked, we should remember the role played by prominent Catholic leaders in this respect, both inside and outside Spain. Catholics within Spain had achieved a certain preeminence in Spanish politics after the ministerial reshuffle in 1945 (to the detriment of the Falangist wing and as part of a process by which it was intended to present a less "Fascist" image to the outside world) and had focused their energies on foreign relations, searching for a reinforcement of Spain's geopolitical position and the legitimacy of her political regime abroad. Their efforts ran parallel to those of other Catholics outside Spain, particularly in the United States, who were instrumental in persuading the North American establishment and public opinion of the convenience of bringing nationalist conservative Spain back into the Western fold (Pollack 1987:14)—not a difficult task in view of the climate of the Cold War and the Korean War in the fifties.

But the signing of agreements was not only a matter of geopolitics and diplomacy, since economic considerations also formed part of the argument. From the U.S. point of view, it made sense to include Spain in the "grand strategy" of communist containment as well as the international economic policy that has been labeled "embedded liberalism" (Keohane 1984). According to this plan, American hegemony was used in the promotion of the long-term interests of an expansionary capitalist system that required the diffusion of a number of international economic regimes, which, in turn, required financial stability and the opening up of markets on the part of as many as possible of the nations located within the sphere of U.S. influence. In the case of Spain, her incorporation into this sphere could not be achieved through the Marshall Plan or other forms of European integration (all of which were linked to the outcome of World War II, in which Spain had not taken part), but it was worth achieving by other means. That was the intention of the agreements of 1953, which, although centered on the geopolitical dimension of that strategy, also contained recommendations relative to economic matters.[12]

From the Spanish viewpoint, however, outside pressure to liberalize the economy was to be taken *cum grano salis*. After the war a kind of modus vivendi or connivance had been established between business and politics. While foreign trade was controlled by the state through quotas and specific import-export licenses, the highly detailed governmental regulation of the economy seemed to guarantee stable economic returns (and political influence) for important sectors of the business community. The country, as a whole, achieved some industrial development and a steady rise in agricultural production, although given that Spain was building on a poor industrial base and considering the destruction caused by the civil war and her exclusion from the benefits of the Marshall Plan, it took her until the early fifties to regain the same level of economic activity as in the twenties.

After a short-lived euphoria around 1953–1955, the economic climate took a turn for the worse to the point of making a change in economic policies toward a more liberal position look almost inevitable. The economy had been growing at an annual rate of about 4% between 1953 and 1955 (Carreras et al. 1989:561–562), but given the state's lack of control over its own spending and its lax monetary policies, economic growth fueled inflation, which was further reinforced by across-the-board rises in nominal wages decreed by the Ministry of Labor in 1956 in response to labor unrest. The result was even more inflation, running at 10.8% by 1957 (Ros et al. 1978:442). This in turn aggravated the problems of the external sector. Import-substitution policies, which combined considerations of principle with sheer necessity, had been in place since the end of the civil war, and a cumbersome system of quota assignments and the concession of special import-export licenses had been introduced. To the banking community, which was becoming increasingly powerful and had growing interests in Spanish industry,[13] and to the majority of economists (Anderson 1974:99–107), industrial development now seemed to require a more uniform and general system to regulate foreign trade, a reduction in tariffs, and, above all, a simpler and more flexible exchange rate mechanism to substitute the kind of multiple exchange rates then in force.

Although the adoption of liberalizing measures was favored by foreign influence and stimulated by internal economic interests, the actual implementation of such measures cannot be fully appreciated without taking into account the effects of a change in mentality on the part of the economic profession. For some years, economic experts had been gaining in importance in the civil administration and on the staff of banks (and perhaps the larger corporations). A new generation educated at the Faculty of Economic Sciences (established in 1944) at the University of Madrid graduated in the early fifties. They had been trained in the virtues of the various brands of neo-Keynesianism that were becoming mainstream, orthodox economic thinking in the international agencies of the time, such as the World Bank and the International Monetary Fund.[14] They began to take up posts in the universities, the chambers of commerce, private banks, the Ministry of Commerce, and other public agencies, and as academics and civil servants, they soon led the public debate on Spanish political economy, engaging in discussions with foreign colleagues and experts. Within a few years, the majority of these experts (particularly those working in the Ministry of Commerce) found themselves arguing in favor of financial stability, expanding trade, and the opening up of the Spanish economy to the rest of the world, and supporting policies that would replace price controls with monetary and fiscal policies that were considered a more sophisticated and efficient means of state intervention in the economy. Some of them combined these arguments with others in favor of the abolition of monopolistic practices or the restriction of competition, and of reducing the concentration of economic power in Spain (Velarde

1954).[15] The professional authority of these arguments was substantially reinforced by their apparent confirmation in reality, by the rates of economic growth apparent in Western European countries in the fifties and after the Treaty of Rome was signed in 1957, and by the general convertibility of the main European currencies in 1958.

This background of difficulties in the external sector of the economy, of changes in the professional debate, and of the evolution of the European economy explains the genesis and content of the "new economic policy" of Francoism, summed up in the stabilization plan of 1959. The crucial move in that direction came in 1957 when Franco appointed his eighth government. The reasons for his decision were probably relatively simple, although at the time they were shrouded in mystery, and later they were to be overvalued in view of the consequences. Franco was dissatisfied with the state of the economy and wanted a new team made up of people who, as well as being politically loyal, appeared to be sensible and pragmatic when they discussed economic matters and who were able to work together (which had not been the case in his previous government). Such were Alberto Ullastres and Mariano Navarro Rubio, ministers of commerce and finance, respectively, who were followed somewhat later by Laureano López Rodó as planning commissioner and Gregorio López Bravo as minister of industry, all of whom were members of the Opus Dei, an order of lay Catholics.[16]

The new economic ministers took tentative steps in the fields of fiscal and monetary policies in 1957 and 1958, and, above all, they embarked upon two operations that were to give them a considerable degree of "legitimacy" for the policies that they hoped to implement at a later date. First, they placed Spain within a network of international economic organizations and then proceeded on a round of consultations with leaders and experts at the World Bank, the International Monetary Fund, and the Organization for European Economic Cooperation, from which they then undertook to accept the general recommendations and the corresponding rules of the game (Varela 1990:47–49; Viñas et al. 1979:1019). Second, they introduced a system of information and consultation to a strategic sample of Spanish public opinion made up of civil servants, professionals, entrepreneurs, and those responsible for a variety of public and private organizations, to whom they sent questionnaires and from whom they requested advice regarding the outlines of a new economic policy. This new policy was characterized by fiscal austerity, reform of the system of exchange rates, and liberalization of the Spanish economy, with the elimination of most price controls and, to a large extent, the liberalization of foreign trade, thus making Spain more attractive to foreign investors. It is noteworthy that the Spanish response was practically unanimous in favor of the plan, including that of the economists closest to the Falange and the civil servants in the Ministries of Labor, Agriculture, and Industry—ministries habitually concerned with detailed intervention in the economy (Anderson 1974:120–125). With the ground prepared, the crucial opportunity for the formulation and application of this policy came shortly afterward, when two years of high inflation and mediocre economic growth (1957–1959) ended in an acute crisis in the balance of payments.[17] Faced with the specter of a return to the "ration book"—that is, to the penury and isolation of the immediate postwar period,[18] Franco dutifully complied with his ministers' advice and made the critical decision on the stabilization plan of 1959.[19]

It is all too easy in retrospect to magnify what really happened in 1959 and to impute to the main actors in the drama an understanding of the situation and a foreknowledge of the consequences that they actually lacked. We must distinguish between the significance derived from events in view of their consequences and the significance of events in the eyes of the people who caused them (or allowed them to happen) at the time. The Spanish stabilization plan of 1959 (which was only partially modeled on the French plan of the preceding year) consisted of three kinds of measures. First—and this was the key—the system of multiple exchange rates was replaced by a single rate of sixty pesetas to the dollar, resulting in a substantial de facto devaluation of the Spanish currency. Second, a program of foreign and domestic trade liberalization was introduced, aiming at a substantial reduction in the levels of protectionism and state intervention, replacing most of the system of quotas and licenses by a new tariff law, and increasing the flexibility of the internal markets. Third, a ceiling was placed on public spending and on credit to the private sector, by means of which an attempt was made to curb inflation and reduce internal demand (Anderson 1974:141–147; Varela 1990:50–51; Sardá 1970).

From Franco's point of view, this move was consistent with a conservative, statist, and nationalist strategy. The plan was an ad hoc solution to a momentary crisis, a means of avoiding the worst consequences of an unexpected downturn in events, an opportunity to increase state control of the economic situation (control of inflation and, perhaps, of public spending), and a means of strengthening the prestige of the peseta as a stable currency and, therefore, of the political regime itself insofar as it would bring to an end the embarrassment and source of corruption created by a flourishing black market in foreign currencies. It was therefore a statist and conservative move, which attempted to reassert state control over socioeconomic life, not a move toward intentionally relaxing that control.[20]

Moreover, behind General Franco's decision lay his preoccupation with defining Spain and the Francoist state's place within the new European order. In this respect, Franco and his ministers took a long-term view. They felt that the liberal, capitalist order in Western Europe had a sufficient number of conservative and authoritarian components so as to permit a modus vivendi between Europe and Spain. The European economies were engrossed in experiments with mixed economies that the Francoists saw as similar to their own (with its mixture of markets and indicative planning, state control of the economy and tax policies),[21] notwithstanding the anomaly of the repression of free labor unions on the part of the Francoist state.[22] This anomaly was important, however, and it was linked to the ostensible difference between political regimes. In spite of this, for a long time the Francoist political class indulged in the belief that the difference was not that great "in reality" and that the Francoist regime was not that different from the fifth French Republic, which embodied authoritarian, personalistic, traditional, and even conservative values that were not that far removed from its own mentality.[23] In the last instance, the Francoists imagined that their anticommunism would prove a sufficiently solid base for envisioning some sort of long-term convergence between the Spanish regime and the more conservative elements of European politics. In the event that this did not occur, however, there was always the possibility of falling back to a defensive revindication of the "Spanish difference" in the name of some mysterious and deeply felt national idiosyncrasy—in which case they would hope to come to a commercial agreement with Western Europe and be left to their own devices with regard to political matters.[24] Such would appear to have been the mental scenario of Franco and his ministers when they committed themselves to their new economic policies. The actual consequences, however, were to differ considerably from their expectations. In order to explain this divergence we must place these policies within the context of the actual behavior of the economy and the political circumstances at the time.

The economic consequences of the plan were quite impressive, although to talk of consequences and suggest a strong causal link between the policies (*outputs*) and the effective results (*outcomes*) may be to engage in a *post hoc, propter hoc* fallacy. What is clear is that the initial response of Spaniards to the new policy (accustomed as they were to fearing and distrusting state authority, at least on economic matters) was to overreact to its recessionary components, and the economy came to an abrupt halt. But it took less than a year to recuperate: GDP, which dropped 0.5% in 1960, grew at a rate of 3.7% in 1961 and 7% in 1962 (Sardá 1970). What happened was that, thanks to the plan, Spain was able to benefit from the wave of sustained growth in the Western economy. Foreign capital poured into the country, and (most unexpectedly) two massive flows of people commenced between Spain and the rest of Europe that were to play a crucial role in the Spanish economy in the years to come: hundreds of thousands of Spaniards emigrated to Europe in search of work, and millions of European tourists came to spend their holidays in Spain. Emigrants' remittances and tourism receipts provided a stable solution to the Spanish balance-of-payments problem and not (as was expected) the upsurge in Spanish exports, which were never to match the increase in imports.[25]

Impelled by the winds of European prosperity, the Spanish economy grew at a rate of about 7.5% a year between 1961 and 1973 (Carreras et al. 1989:561–562), without the state ever managing to control either public spending or inflation, the central objectives of the stabilization plan (the same goals sought later with the development plans of the 1960s). The Francoist state tried to ensure that this growth had political effects and became part of the solution to its problems of legitimacy. We know that the legitimacy of any state is built up on the basis of motivations in which collective interests and sentiments weigh equally or more heavily than (and are at times confused with) ideological arguments or constitutional arrangements. Perhaps for that reason, the Francoist politicians thought that economic growth would contribute to legitimating the Spanish state, both because it satisfied wide interests and because a prolonged period of peace and prosperity could wipe out, or at least soften, the feelings associated with the memories of "suffering and penury" of the civil war and the postwar period, even on the part of the social groups who were defeated. Furthermore, as economic growth went on, the Francoist state embarked upon a (cautious and hesitant) strategy of political semi-reform (by which it was hoped that perhaps and in due course the Francoist political regime would be brought closer to the Western model).

The government embarked upon this semi-reformist strategy in a spirit of gradualism and experimentation and with profound ambivalence, always ready to withdraw into its old habits of authoritarian domination and political repression as soon as the costs or risks of its semi-liberal strategy became too high for its taste. In this respect, Franco's taste was very demanding, as was his aversion to overlooking the slightest challenge to his personal authority; this attitude (and a similar propensity toward defensiveness and inflexibility) became more marked in the late 1960s and early 1970s in reaction to the terrorist activities of ETA (Euskadi Ta Askatasuna, Basque Country and Freedom). Thus the semi-liberal strategy failed because, although it opened up the field for social pluralism and public debate (thanks to the laws that regulated collective bargaining and works councils, the new Press Law of 1966, and the de facto semi-toleration of political and union associations, strikes, and propaganda), it fell short of any basic reform of the political institutions. The state therefore failed to gain, at least to the extent that it wanted or needed to, in legitimacy in the eyes of the Spanish public or in prevailing public opinion in Europe. As a result, the implicit ad hoc compromise reached between Spain and the European Communities in 1962 led to a stalemate that lasted until the death of Franco in 1975. In 1962, Spain applied for negotiations that could ultimately have led to membership in the EC at almost the same time as the EC accepted the basic conclusions of the Birkelbach report to the effect that it committed itself not to take into consideration any applications for membership from countries whose political regime was not of the same liberal-democratic kind as those of the countries that were then members of the EC (Pereira Castañares 1991:94). So when in 1970 Spain came to a preferential economic agreement that was quite satisfactory to her interests, her prospects of becoming a member of the EC without changing her political regime continued to be nil. The combination of this exclusion from the EC and her exclusion from the Atlantic Alliance (for more complex motives) relegated Spain to a peripheral position within the Western geopolitical bloc, to which she still remained tied, however, as much by the preferential agreement of 1970 as by her pacts with the United States.

CHANGES IN CIVIL SOCIETY AND THE PUBLIC DISPOSITION IN THE 1960S AND EARLY 1970S

In general terms, an environment conducive to credible commitments entails the creation of a complex institutional framework of formal rules, informal constraints, and enforcement mechanisms (North 1990:58). Now, since third-party enforcement is difficult and unlikely in international transactions, formal institutions and informal constraints have to make up for it. A two-level games approach helps us to look for these institutions and constraints both in the international environment (the external game played among states) and in the interplay between the political class and the public (the domestic game). From the viewpoint of this "domestic game," credible commitments are the result of a fairly complex development that involves both the political elites and the public, and in the course of which the contents of those involvements become articulated and are made fully explicit. In the Spanish case, such development went through three stages: first, that of the elite's choices of economic liberalization and Spain's entry in formal international institutions; second, that of institutional and cultural transformations implying changes in civil society and public dispositions; and third, that of a democracy and of a public debate.

The most important consequences of the new policy of economic liberalization occurred in an indirect way and only to the extent that this policy, both in its inception and in its implementation, was connected to a set of social, cultural, and institutional changes (acquiring its full significance thanks to and as a result of this connection). The changes consisted of the development of some fundamental components of Spanish civil society, including her markets, her voluntary associations, and the scope for public debate (Pérez-Díaz 1993). This development, resulting in the activation of certain public dispositions, transformed the basic premises of the definition of Spanish national interest and identity, paving the way for significant changes in the definition of her foreign policy at a later date (even though, given the limited development of the public sphere, some of these changes were to occur only in a semiarticulated and implicit way).

In spite of the protectionist caution reflected in the tariffs of 1960 and the preferential agreement of 1970, the new economic policy led to the opening up of the Spanish economy to foreign markets to an ever-increasing degree. Between 1961 and 1975 exports rose from 5% to 8.3% of GDP, and imports rose from 7.5% to 13.4% (Viñas et al. 1979:1291, 1320); between 1959 and 1973 net inflows of private long-term foreign capital rose from $43.6 million to $1,133.1 million (Gámir 1975:141–143); between 1959 and 1975 the annual number of tourists entering Spain rose from 4.1 million to 30.1 million; and throughout the 1960s and early 1970s more than one million Spaniards emigrated temporarily or permanently to other countries of Western Europe (Carreras et al. 1989:76). These movements, in turn, brought about a massive exodus from the countryside to the cities, leading to all kinds of socioeconomic (and cultural) transformations in rural and urban environments, which caused the proliferation of innumerable problems of adjustment to change and conflicts of interest as well as to the emergence of associations of all kinds. The latter were formed as channels through which some sectors of the population might have a voice and some form of representation in public affairs and might be able to put pressure on the relevant authorities. In industry, works councils were set up to further negotiations on collective bargaining, which was becoming increasingly frequent in the sixties, accompanied by the use of debate and pressure tactics of all kinds, including strikes. Business, in turn, increased its organizational capacity, driven to do so not only by the experience of collective bargaining but also by the ongoing debate with the economic authorities (which received additional stimulus from the debates among the commissions for the development plan). The legal professions and the ecclesiastical establishment became active in connection with business and labor issues, setting up new organizations and instilling new life into the old ones (Pérez-Díaz 1993). All of this contributed to the creation of industrial associations and to others of a neighborhood or urban nature, which likewise pressurized the local authorities and became alternative institutions for the representation of interests in public affairs. The (cautious) overtures of the government on the question of an information policy were welcomed by these associations with impatience, on the one hand, and by a new generation of journalists and media editors, on the other, who made it a point of honor to continually test the limits of official toleration. These changes combined with dispositions on the part of Spaniards to produce changes in their perception of the interests and identity of the nation, which were to have important political implications.

Oakeshott has drawn attention to the importance of people's political dispositions, or inclinations, as distinct from their articulated attitudes and opinions, "to think and to behave in certain manners, to prefer certain kinds of conduct and certain conditions of human circumstances to others, to be disposed to make certain choices" (Oakeshott 1991:497). Oakeshott refers in that text to the "conservative disposition," but we can generalize from his comments and assume that such dispositions, conservative or otherwise, are the outcome of processes of habituation that have taken place, and have been furthered, by relatively stable institutional contexts. But we can also assume that such processes can be affected by certain crucial events. Applying this to the period under consideration, we observe that the most generalized disposition among Spaniards was anything but conservative, and this applies equally to the Spaniards with attitudes and opinions of an explicitly "conservative" nature. The fascists and military men rebelled in 1936 not in order to conserve most of the traditions that had accumulated in Spain in the previous century or century and a half but to eradicate them. They rebelled in the name of a "platonic idea" of Spain that in some way seemed to have been lost in her "dialectic descent" into historical reality. They proclaimed that they loved Spain and were ready to die for her. Their declaration of love, however, referred not to the real Spain but to an ideal Spain. Thus young Spanish fascists expressed their patriotism by saying that they loved Spain precisely because they did not like her:[26] a baroque statement much in the same vein as Tertulian's declaration of faith *credo quia absurdum*: "I believe because it is absurd to believe." That expression of love had a disquieting masochistic twist to it. Those who proffered it took for granted that a love of Spain was based on a feeling of scant appreciation or esteem and even less respect for the real Spain. Their love was based on the fact that the real Spain did not deserve it, and it was this lack of merit that urged them to give it to her.

All of this (emotionally a little strange, though perhaps attractive under certain conditions) is, in any case, just the opposite of the "conservative disposition," since, as Oakeshott suggests, the latter asserts itself when there is much to be enjoyed and, therefore, much that deserves to be loved (Oakeshott 1991:408). The stuff of the conservative disposition is made up of pleasure and contentment with what really exists and distrust of any change that could destroy the source of contentment. "Spanish conservatives" were, on the contrary, a dissatisfied and discontented lot, and much the same could be said of their political adversaries, moderate or extreme. The Liberals such as Ortega (a liberal *maître à penser* who had, however, a profound influence on Spanish fascist mentality) and members of the 1898 generation (or in a different way, the Catalan generation of 1901) were extremely critical of the real Spain that they knew and dreamed of changing—not to mention the socialists, the anarchists, and the communists, whose dreams were even more intense. The civil war arose out of this confused confluence of dreams, out of this generalized discontent of people who did not feel at home or at ease in the world in which they were obliged to live. This is why the language of socialist or national-syndicalist revolution came so easily to their lips and why it stayed around for so long (and provided common ground that eased the transition of quite a number of fascist and ultramontane Catholics into the radical progressivism of the sixties).

It was natural for people of such an unconservative disposition to feel attracted to the kind of "rationalist politics" to which Oakeshott refers (Oakeshott 1991:55 ff.), based upon ideas, principles, and plans for the reconstruction and reform of existing institutions. Contemporary Spanish politics, from the beginning of the nineteenth century right up to the civil war, had been of that kind: political regimes following one another in an endless succession of constitutions, governments, manifestos, and *pronunciamientos*, punctuated by guerrilla warfare, urban violence, revolutionary rhetoric, and intense partisanship—all in the name of political principle. The civil war of 1936–1939 was the culmination of the tradition of "rationalist politics," and the politics of the conservatives who won the war was a sui generis version of the same. They wanted to begin the construction of a new Spain from the foundations up, once they had eradicated the Spain contaminated by hostile principles. They were full of ideas and plans for the transformation of Spanish life—just as the Catholics tried to reconvert Spain to the Catholic faith (according to the canons of what would later be known as national catholicism [Pérez-Díaz 1993]), so Francoist politicians, together with their followers and allies, tried to reconstruct Spanish politics, society, and (to some extent) economy. To do this, public discourse under Francoism maintained the call to "principles" (first of the Falange and later of the National Movement) and apparently rhetorical references to the "coming revolution" for a very long time. It is clear that this talk was not persuasive for many, to whom the grandiloquent phrases rang hollow, but it resonated with the disposition of a country unhappy with its recent past and the present and probably haunted by the bitter memories of the civil war.

The modifications to economic policy and the resulting socioeconomic developments of the late fifties and sixties can be understood as an opportunity for Spaniards at that time to express their disposition for change rather than for preserving what they had. Thanks to this, the desire (or dream) of a different life, escaping out of the present, was given a new direction. Economic development and the opening up of Spanish economic and social life to Europe made it possible for many people to give free rein to their desire for change and to believe in its imminent realization.

It was not only, or even mainly, people of (declared) unconservative attitudes and opinions who took advantage of this opportunity. Those whose explicit beliefs and ideas were of a conservative nature showed equal or even greater enthusiasm, and they availed themselves of the opportunity in many ways, particularly through a profound transformation of their daily lives. "Conservative" housewives "invented" the "consumer" culture and radically modified the contents of their homes. The offspring of well-to-do middle-class families, dutiful sons and demure daughters, "invented" sexual permissiveness and changed their social mores and patterns of courtship in a very few years. "Conservative" farmers discarded their traditional agricultural techniques and implements, leaving their Roman plows and mechanical sowers and harvesters to rust in caves or out in the open air (if they were not forgotten or sold off as scrap iron). In a similar spirit ("conservative") priests gave themselves up to a frenzy of liturgical renewal and modernization, banishing their old images of golden-haired little angels, stolid saints, and sweet, sentimental virgins, many of which ended up in the flea markets to be sold off to antiquaries throughout the country.

Following the same logic, municipal architects, urban planners, and town councillors conspired to alter urban spaces in an equally radical way. They filled them with new buildings that imitated the international style of working-class cottages, so "admired" by Tom Wolfe, with their "imaginative" straight lines, low and "intimate" roofs, and "authentic" cement or brick facings, while ("conservative") mayors, spurred on by urban speculation and the comprehensible desire for grandeur, applied themselves to the task of modernizing their cities. And so they did—demolishing the old mansions and widening old streets for cars to get in and out of the old centers more easily, cutting through narrow lanes, secluded plazas, and little corners to fulfill a collective dream, so that where silence had once reigned supreme there should now be noise, speed, and progress.

All these modern and mundane rearrangements of everyday life and the human and physical landscape are of some relevance to our subject because they demonstrate the unconservative disposition of the population as a whole and because, linked to the changes in markets, the variety of associations that sprang up, and the public sphere of the sixties, they brought a profound change in the definition of the Spanish situation (affecting the masses as much as civil servants, businessmen, academics, clerics, or other elites), including the definition of national interests and identity, all of which was to affect the debate on, and to some extent the content of, public policies in general and foreign policy in particular, in the sense of making them fit in with a definition of Spain that had to become increasingly close to the standards set by the rest of the countries in Western Europe.

It so happened that the debates on public policy issues (mostly limited to economic and social policy matters: the stabilization plan, the development plans, income policies, concerted action, town and country planning, welfare provisions, and so on) were held with increasing reference to (and comparison with) European experience of the matter, in search of European solutions to Spanish problems. At the same time, the interdependence between problems in Spain and in Europe became increasingly obvious, to the point that people of all political shades eventually recognized the fact that economic growth and sociopolitical stability in Europe were preconditions for the prosperity of all. In time this led to the conviction that the very identity of Spain included being linked to and forming part of Europe. It was not a question of being in Europe or having Europe as a reference point but rather that Spain was an inseparable part of Europe.

All of these factors shaped foreign policy preferences in public opinion and eventually found an application in specific diplomatic issues during the last phase of Francoism (under Fernando Castiella, the minister of foreign affairs 1957–1969). Spain, protected from a hypothetical Soviet invasion by the military might of NATO, could afford to play along as a free rider (similar, in fact, though not identical, to what France was able to do) so that the strategic worries of the Spanish state were concerned with the fate of disputes on the southern flank of the peninsula. All of them were gradually influenced by

the general "Europeanization" of the understandings and preferences of the public and elites. It seemed that the issue of Gibraltar
(occupied by the British since the eighteenth century, the return of
which was a question of principle for the Spanish) would be dealt
with only within a European framework—as the object of a dispute to
be discussed by the Spanish and the British as fellow members of the
same European community of nations.[27] The issues of Moroccan
independence (in the fifties) and Equatorial Guinea (1968) and the
Spanish Sahara (later on) were to follow the same pattern of the general European decolonization process, with almost no attempt to
diverge from it.[28] Only the problem of the enclaves of Ceuta and
Melilla, claimed by Morocco, could still be treated as an issue of a different nature. Even so, most people thought that even if a review of
the standing of the two cities could be postponed, it would have to be
carried out in due course in a more general context, possibly linked
to the issue of Gibraltar. Likewise, in the case of the Canary Islands
(Spanish since the late fifteenth century), it seemed that the more
Spain was perceived as being an integral part of the Western community, the greater the chance that the Canaries' Spanish character
could be successfully defended in the long term against the claims of
the pro-independence parties.

In economic and political, though not strictly strategic, terms, the
attention of Spanish foreign policy in its widest sense concentrated
on relations with Western Europe; it was becoming increasingly obvious that the satisfaction of specific sectorial interests of the Spanish
economy (fisheries, industry, and agriculture) all depended on the
accommodation of these interests to the corresponding European
interests. This only corroborated the diffuse message of the changes
in institutions, culture, and everyday life to which we have already
referred. In sum, Spaniards came to the conclusion that the general
orientation of their foreign policy could be none other than to
increase involvement not only in the Western community but, more
specifically, in the group of countries of Western Europe, and this
conclusion came to seem the most natural thing in the world. In view
of this, the ritual references of Spanish diplomacy to the "special relationship" with Latin America and the Arab countries (which, by the
way, provided most of the oil on which the Spanish economy
depended),[29] although emphatic, could not disguise the fact that
those regions of the world were not the principal targets of Spanish
foreign policy, nor were such references the best indicator of what
was in reality its main focus.[30]

Democracy and the Public Sphere from the Mid-1970s to the Mid-1980s

The democratic politicians who came to power in the mid-1970s were able to build their foreign policy on two complementary foundations: they made use of the institutional network in which they found themselves as a result of the foreign policy traditions of the Franco years, and they were able to move beyond that tradition by appealing to the general dispositions of the public, which resulted from the transformations of the 1960s and 1970s. The transition to democracy gave rise to a new structure of opportunities for Spanish foreign policy, making possible the integration of the country as a full member of the Western community. This occurred as the consequence of both internal and external factors. The United States and Western Europe had supported the transition (that of Spain and, in general, those of the countries of Southern Europe) (Whitehead 1986), and this support had a persuasive effect on the sociopolitical coalition that had formed the basis of the previous regime. It convinced the doubters (in the army, the business world, and the bureaucracy) of the absence of any alternative to the course taken by new prime minister Adolfo Suárez and King Juan Carlos in the spring of 1976, reducing their fear of change and stimulating their interest in the advantages of full integration with the West.

This external pressure was consistent with the processes of change in Spanish life and the evolution of both the pro-Western disposition of public opinion (and the development of the public sphere) and the strategies of the political class. The different parties were in agreement on the fundamental direction of foreign policy toward full integration with Europe (in contrast to what happened in other democracies in transition in the south of Europe, like Portugal and Greece),[31] but moving in that direction did not require any alteration to the objectives of what had been Franco's foreign policy for the past twenty years.

The government of Suárez expended most of its energy on the task of ensuring the success of the democratic transition, and foreign policy was sidelined for most of his tenure. Initially Suárez was content to formalize the application to join the European Community in 1977— a unanimous application from all the Spanish parties—to which the EC, embroiled in an institutional and financial crisis from which it extricated itself only in about 1985, gave a polite answer and recommendations of patience. Suárez had inherited the renewed bilateral treaties with the United States (negotiated in 1976 by the minister José María Areilza [Areilza 1977:59–66]), which he believed were compatible with minor and rhetorical diplomacy (such as the gestures of embracing Castro and Arafat and sending a Spanish delegation to the Conference of Non-Aligned Countries in 1979). These symbolic counterpoints to the basically pro-Western orientation of his foreign policy reflected immaturity to some extent and also some degree of inertia in the maintenance of a tradition of "calculated ambiguity" (or naive Machiavellianism) of our diplomacy from the times of General Franco, although it may be that Suárez's strategic thinking had already changed by 1980, when, possibly influenced by the geopolitical implications of the second petroleum crisis, he authorized the minister Marcelino Oreja to negotiate Spain's entry into NATO.

For their part, the left-wing parties appeared on the political scene as bearers of a perhaps superficial, vaguely anti-American feeling that sprang from a combination of resentment toward the United States (partly because of the support Franco had received for more than twenty years), anti-capitalism, and sympathy for so-called Third World causes, as well as from a confused and unarticulated vision that rejected "the politics of the blocs." The Spanish socialists, however, depended too much on their European counterparts not to have to modify their position sooner or later. Thus they gradually toned down their rhetoric and moved closer to mainstream thinking within the European socialist family, under the influence of the German socialists, particularly Willy Brandt and Helmut Schmidt. As for the communists, eager as they were to gain credibility as a democratic party (and become, as they were called at the time, Eurocommunists), they moderated their expressions of solidarity with the Soviet Union, but they were, in any case, of only secondary importance.

Under these circumstances, it was remarkably easy to achieve an all-party consensus on the application for entry into the European Community, which was backed by public opinion. Such a move could never have been made under the Francoist state; it became possible only upon the arrival of democracy at the end of the process just described. Yet that move brought strategic and geopolitical consequences in its train that both the political class and public opinion were relatively slow to recognize, since they did not realize that being a full member of the EC implied a change of perspective and altered the nature of the relationship with Europe. As a peripheral element in Europe, Spain could take refuge behind a rhetoric of distance or neutrality between the blocs. But as a full member of the European Community, Spain could enjoy the political and economic benefits inherent in that position only if she also accepted the corresponding obligations on matters of foreign policy and defense. Thus, even if the general European orientation of Spanish foreign policy was unquestionable, the capacity and willingness of Spaniards to understand and assume the consequences seemed hesitant and reluctant. In fact, understanding and living with these consequences has been (and is) difficult; overcoming this difficulty may be seen as a test of the political maturity of the Spanish political class and public opinion and as a telling illustration of the importance of developing the public sphere in order to achieve the articulation of a consistent (and credible) foreign policy.

This difficulty was reinforced by the fact that Spain's application coincided with French reticence (based on the fear of competition from Spanish agriculture) and the climate of "Europessimism" that resulted from unsolved institutional and financial problems and prevailed until the summit of Fontainebleau in 1985 (Moravcsik 1991:57–61). It was reinforced also by the fact that the consensual nature of Spanish foreign policy was called into question when, shortly after the attempted military coup in February 1981, the minister of foreign affairs, José Pedro Pérez Llorca, in the government of Leopoldo Calvo Sotelo, engineered the almost backdoor entry of Spain into NATO in the fall of 1981. The socialists denounced the move on procedural grounds, arguing that it should have been previously agreed on between the government and the socialists. The government suggested that had the socialists been consulted, they would have blocked the move purely for electoral reasons. The government tried to justify its decision as part of a general strategy to provide credibility for the Spanish candidacy to the European Community and, later, as an attempt to create an apparently irreversible situation that the socialists (who were soon expected to come to power) would be unable to change (Calvo Sotelo 1990:204). Up to what point this tactic of the creation of a fait accompli is an ex post facto "rationalization" is a difficult question. The fact is that the PSOE (Partido Socialista Obrero Español, Spanish Socialist Workers Party) took electoral advantage of the issue of Spain's entry into NATO to attract leftist-minded sectors of the public to vote for them in the elections of the fall of 1982, suggesting insistently and emphatically that, once in power, they would take Spain out again.[32]

As we have suggested earlier, it is probable that around 1981–1982 the socialists were well on the way to being converted to "Atlanticism," as other European socialists had been. It may be, however, that the opportunity for an electoral advantage offered by the liberal use of radical rhetoric was just too much of a temptation to resist. Or perhaps their own views were still in the making and, under such circumstances, they allowed themselves to stray temporarily back toward their original and (possibly) more genuine sentiments, given that the majority of the socialist leaders had had their original formative experiences during the time of their opposition to Francoism in the 1960s and 1970s and had drunk from the (conceptually somewhat cloudy) waters of a socialism understood to be revolutionary.[33]

The socialists' electoral propaganda was successful, and they assumed power. In so doing, they modified the state of public opinion with regard to NATO. In earlier years the results of public opinion surveys on NATO had been ambiguous, with many "don't knows/not sures" and the rest divided up almost equally (but with more in favor until 1981). After the socialist campaign and victory, the number of "don't knows" dropped, and those who held an opinion were firmly against NATO.[34] Thus the socialists had been successful in crystallizing (confused or latent) public opinion in a direction that favored their electoral interests but, as was later demonstrated, that was contrary to their interests as the government of the country. In this way their success turned against them. Overcoming this contradiction took several years, and during that time the maturation process of public opinion on the issue was delayed.

The socialists had decided upon their strategy in view of domestic political considerations. But for this they had chosen an especially delicate moment on the international scene (dominated, to some extent, by the Soviet invasion of Afghanistan), which one of their mentors, the German social democrat Helmut Schmidt, had described as a change of phase and a return to the Cold War and the arms race (Schmidt 1985:15). Therefore, excessive tolerance toward the strategic frivolities of the new government on the part of the Western community was not to be expected. What followed was a fascinating mixture of a comedy of errors and a strange educational experience. Felipe González had named Fernando Morán as minister of foreign affairs, a man who was determined that Spain should not be part of NATO (Morán 1980:119–125). At the same time, González himself took the initiative on foreign policy and began to adopt a broader, more comprehensive view of Western defense requirements. He approved the deployment of the Pershing 1-A and Cruise missiles in 1983 and encouraged conversations between the Ministry of Defense and its European counterparts. All of this prepared the way for his later claim that his experience in power had gradually led him to understand the link between the entry of Spain into the European Community and her duty to contribute to Western defense, including her duty to remain within the Atlantic Alliance (PSOE 1986:297). In the end, González replaced Morán with Francisco Fernández Ordóñez and persuaded his own party to support him in his policy to keep Spain within NATO, with the addition of the proviso not to integrate Spain into the military command and to reduce the United States presence in Spanish territory.[35] After a debate during the second half of 1984 and throughout 1985, the party allowed itself to be persuaded, inasmuch as it lacked an alternative leader with any chance of success in an electoral battle. Then a referendum on the issue was called in January 1986, to be held in March. The government framed the question so as to include the provisos as a token to the left-wing sentiments of a large part of the public and as a way of making the evolution of its own position more plausible.[36] Public opinion fluctuated, moving from a majority against NATO in 1983–1984 and the first half of 1985 to a slight majority in favor during the first months of 1986 (CIS n.d.: 22–23). In the end the vote was 31% in favor, 24% against, with a high abstention rate of 40%, plus 4% blank votes and 0.7% invalid ones.

The referendum and the debate about it were rather confusing experiences for the public. The issue of remaining within NATO was clouded with that of the acceptance of González's leadership and the PSOE government. The link between the European Community and NATO was posited rather than explained, and the debate was conducted more in terms of ill-defined fears and anxieties (about war if the referendum passed or about the political instability resulting from González's defeat if it failed) than in terms of a commitment to a coherent and consistent political course of action. In spite of these limitations, the referendum gave additional stimulus to the discussion on foreign policy in a variety of public and private forums. Parliament had ratified the treaty of Spain's integration into the EC almost without debate, but the more controversial NATO affair was hotly debated and caused a flood of public declarations; these were somewhat unconvincing, since the PSOE had to retract earlier affirmations and the conservative party (Alianza Popular), having redefined the issue as domestic, in which case the subject of debate was the acceptance or rejection of González (Fraga 1986:40), surprised many of its followers by campaigning in favor of abstention.

To interpret the upsurge of political passion, punctuated by occasional argument, as a useful learning experience may be seen perhaps as an overly optimistic appreciation.[37] As a matter of fact, the immediate conclusion reached by the majority of professional politicians (including many of the political commentators) was decidedly pessimistic. They "learned" that the public was swayed by inconstant passions and lightly held opinions, which had to be feared and manipulated, and as a result, they had no desire to repeat this scenario on the following occasion. Thus they agreed almost unanimously to rule out the possibility of a referendum on the Treaty of Maastricht in 1992 (similar to the one held in France in September of the same year), despite the fact that the polls showed a majority opinion in favor of doing so.[38]

Nevertheless, good reasons also exist for qualifying and revising that melancholy reflection on public opinion. To begin with, the referendum obliged politicians to think carefully about public sentiment and to work hard at refining and explaining their own positions. The campaign gave rise to a series of opinion polls that had to be analyzed by the parties and a response given. Thus the public debate that took place can be construed as a two-level conversation: one, of explicit arguments and public statements among political contenders; the other, of the careful reading that they make of the polls, trying to ascertain the changes in public attitudes and to accommodate them.

Furthermore, the referendum is to be seen in the context of a sequential process for establishing institutional forums and mechanisms for public debate at many levels, which was to take place in the following years. Without going into the detail of these later years, suffice it to say that foreign policy, especially that relating to Europe, has acquired a growing importance on the agenda of the public administration; advisory and policy-making bodies have proliferated in this respect, together with a corresponding number of personnel—in the Office of the President, in the Ministry of Foreign Affairs and other ministries, and in the embassies abroad. Increasing attention has been paid to foreign affairs by regional governments, in particular those (like the Catalan and Basque governments) that desire to play a role on the European stage.[39] All of this has meant that, in the eyes of the public, government activities appear to be increasingly intertwined with the course of European events, and this is a dimension that has been emphasized by the mass media. We can also point to the growing interest in international affairs on the part of business and the unions, which have formed pressure groups to act on a level with European institutions, in an attempt to alert their members to the European dimension of their domestic problems.

As a result, by the early 1990s, Spain was enmeshed in a network of diplomatic, defensive, political, and economic interdependence with other West European countries, her economy had become just one more component of the European economy, and her foreign policy was dependent on her broader commitment to the process of European construction. At the same time, the country had gradually been required to learn the defense implications of that commitment. Her participation in the Gulf War of 1990–1992 (as an important logistic base for the U.S. war effort) and her role in the peacekeeping operations in different parts of the world (especially in the former Yugoslavia) bear witness to this learning process. In sum, by the early to mid-1990s Spain saw the main thrust of her diplomacy to be that of serving the basic tenets of a "liberal" foreign policy that tries to ensure the expansion of free trade together with worldwide financial stability, the promotion of democracy, the protection of civil rights, and the maintenance of world peace.

By the late 1940s, Spain was a country with a nationalist and protectionist foreign policy, known for her sympathies toward the Fascist powers, contaminated by the "original sin" of having received Fascist help in the establishment of her authoritarian regime. She was, therefore, treated almost as an outcast by the Western community. Half a century later, Spain has become a full citizen of the Western world and an active participant in the European Community. The irony of contemporary Spanish history lies in the fact that the fundamental transformation of foreign policy came about as the result of a number of factors, one of which was the basic continuity of certain objectives central to foreign policy between the authoritarian and liberal regimes during the period from the early 1950s to the mid-1980s (the period under consideration herein) and up to the present day.

Although Franco's economic liberalization policies were based upon particular institutional and cultural premises of his own, they were also the result of critical political choices made to locate Spain within a network of interdependence with the rest of the Western community. The consequential development of a civil society proved decisive in shaping the public dispositions that gradually changed the institutional and cultural premises of foreign policy. These developments in turn led to a redefinition of both Spain's national interests and her national identity, now far more clearly and emphatically tied to Europe. By the mid-1970s, this process was sufficiently advanced to make the democratic transition possible, bringing with it a fully consistent liberal foreign policy.

We can summarize our argument with four conclusions: (1) economic liberalization implied a significant change of Franco's policy in a pro-Western direction and also made the development of civil society possible; (2) the functioning and development of this civil society over a period of time brought about the shaping of the public's dispositions in such a way that it gradually changed the basic premises of foreign policy and implied a limited development of the public sphere, and hence political liberalization could be based not only on the "liberal antecedents" of economic liberalization but also—and above all—on the growth of civil society; (3) precisely because it was built upon these two bases, political liberalization was able to give birth to a pro-Western, liberal foreign policy, oriented toward Spain's full incorporation into the Western community; and (4) for that incorporation to be pursued, however, political liberalization had to include the development of the public sphere well beyond the limits imposed upon it by the previous authoritarian regime, so that both political and other elites and the public were required to debate and to take up explicit positions on matters of foreign policy.

From this discussion the suggestion of some generally applicable hypotheses may follow. First, we make a significant development of civil society a critical variable and a prior and necessary condition if economic liberalization is to be followed by political liberalization and by a fully consistent liberal foreign policy. In our interpretation "civil society" refers not merely to any kind of social organization that can be shown to function autonomously in relation to state power but to a specific type of sociopolitical organization, including the rule of law, and limited and accountable state, as well as markets, voluntary associations, and social pluralism, and a public sphere (Pérez-Díaz 1993 and 1995). Second, we suggest that the existence of a "Western-type" community of liberal polities, which the country in question can identify with (or have strong cultural and institutional affinities with and aim to belong to), is a strong facilitating condition for the successful completion of the sequence that goes from economic liberalization to political liberalization and a consistent liberal foreign policy. In turn, these two orienting statements imply the generally applicable conclusion that the weaker the civil society, and/or the weaker the perceived links with the community of liberal polities with which the country may identify (or aspire to be a member of), the less likely a successful completion of the transition from economic liberalism to political liberalism with a liberal foreign policy will be.

There is room for exploring the application of these hypotheses to countries with differing degrees of development of their civil societies and differing degrees of connection with the community of liberal-democratic (and advanced capitalist) societies, such as the countries of Latin America, the Arab world, and East Europe. They all have different degrees of development of civil societies of the Western mold and different degrees of cultural and institutional distance from them. The fact is, unlike the case of Spain and her relationship with Europe, it has been, and still is, very difficult for most Latin American societies either to want to identify themselves with a country like the United States (Mexico is a good illustration of this; see Cornelius 1994) or Europe (despite the obvious historical and cultural links with it) or to be able to do so. Also, Arab countries have always felt close not so much to a community of liberal polities of the Western kind as to a community characterized either by bureaucratic-authoritarian political regimes (some of them fairly similar to the Francoist regime) or by (more recently) Muslim fundamentalism (Carré 1991; Salamé 1994; Azmah 1993).

By contrast, the experiences of East European countries (particularly Poland, the Czech Republic, and Hungary) seem much closer to that of Spain. They have experimented (intermittently) with cultural and economic liberalization, and their civil societies have been able to develop (within limits) for a period of some years previous to the collapse of their totalitarian states; at the same time, they gradually strengthened their economic and sociocultural ties with Western Europe. This may indicate that some of these countries may have fulfilled most of the conditions for following the "Spanish model," and the evidence suggests that they are aware of this and are making use of that rationale in their dealings with the European Community (De la Serre, Lequesne, and Rupnik 1994).

Finally, and on another issue, we would like to add a note of caution regarding the "learning process" of Spanish opinion and the development of Spanish public debate. It has been the thrust of our argument so far that Spain has gone from "reluctant choices" to "credible commitments." Still, questions remain with regard to the degree of credibility of these commitments and of public support to them in difficult and confusing times. In this respect, it may give us pause to consider some of the ambivalences shown by Spanish public opinion. Let us remember that the results of the referendum of 1986 were 32% in favor and 24% against Spanish participation in NATO, with a 40% abstention rate; and that the government's question in that referendum was worded in such a way that the continuity of Spain within NATO was accompanied and counterbalanced by reservations that the government had an interest in emphasizing (which led some observers to conclude that the Spanish position was that of a semi-aligned country [Snyder 1988:145]). Later, during the Gulf War (1991) there was such a strong show of public sentiment against sending Spanish soldiers to the theater of operations that the government gave most of its logistical support to the United States Army in a covert manner, so that the public learned of it only after the event and mainly through the foreign press. In 1992 opinion polls indicated that people were still of two minds about the Spanish presence in NATO (INCIPE 1992:114), and there were telling signs of anti-American attitudes (fueled from both the right and the left), which sprang up again at the time of the renegotiation of the United States–Spanish treaty in 1992 (Alonso Zaldívar and Castells 1992: 210). Another question is whether Spain's identification with the European Union, which is apparently so obvious, may not in fact be based upon relatively fragile foundations; at least the political class saw it in this light when it refused to hold a referendum on the Maastricht Treaty (as France did, for instance) in 1992.

All these things considered, we should reflect upon the fact that the foreign policy of a democratic state is "credible" only when it can count upon the stable and reasoned support of public opinion, and gaining that support requires development of the public sphere, which, in the Spanish case, we must consider to be an ongoing process. And thus we are brought back to the general discussion of the two-level games approach. In the literature on the factors and conditions that affect the position of a government when it comes to negotiating foreign policy, there is usually an insistence on the domestic resources and restraints affecting it and, therefore, on the support of public opinion, but there is hardly any reference to the importance of the "intensity" of that support: in other words, the "extension" of the "win-set" (that is to say, the range of all the policy alternatives "ratifiable" by domestic actors) (Moravcsik 1993:24–30) may be considered, but the "intensity" of the different positions included in the win-set usually goes unnoticed. This is, however, a most critical problem, since intensity of the public support indicates the lengths to which the public may be disposed, and the costs and risks it may be disposed to endure, in backing such a position. By contrast, the ambivalence of the public detracts from the intensity of its support and results in "weakness of the will" (or "akrasia" or "lack of leadership") on the part of the political elites, as has been shown to be the case with the process of construction of the European Union.[40]

Notes

1. For a different view, see Alonso Zaldívar and Castells (1992:205–253) and Arenal (1992).

2. On the theory of civil society and its application to the Spanish case, see Pérez-Díaz (1993).

3. On the evolution of this debate, see Moravcsik (1993:5–17); an interesting critical review of the dominant theories on international relations in the post–World War II period is to be found in Gaddis (1992/93).

4. One of the major attempts to apply empirically and refine theoretically Putnam's schema can be found in Evans, Jacobson, and Putnam (1993).

5. "Realist" in the usual sense given to the term in the literature of international political science since Hans Morgenthau.

6. See Payne (1967); see also Preston (1994:35), where he includes Franco's comment to Manuel Aznar: "Without Africa, I could scarcely explain myself to myself"; for a more nuanced judgment on Franco's "Africanism," see Alonso Baquer (1993: 24–29).

7. Some of Franco's sentiments and beliefs can be traced through his cousin Franco Salgado-Araujo's collection of private conversations with him. See Franco Salgado-Araujo (1976).

8. In fact, not having agreed to a reform of the army in the 1930s, a large number of army officials retired from active service.

9. On social and clerical conservatism, see Tusell (1984), Pérez-Díaz (1993), and Payne (1984).

10. On business traditions since the beginning of the century, see Linz (1981), Cabrera (1983), Pérez-Díaz (1993), and López-Novo (1992). Corporatism clearly influenced the institutional design of the transitory regime of Primo de Rivera (Velarde 1969:68–69).

11. Accounts of this period of Franco's foreign policy can be found in Viñas (1984) and Portero (1989).

12. Articles 2.1.(b) and 2.1.(e) of the Agreement on Economic Assistance. The U.S. Congress had decided in 1951 to grant economic help to Spain for an amount of $1 million. To this was added another $25 million. However, the United Nations' opposition to these measures led the U.S. administration to abandon them, allowing the Import-Export Bank to grant a $62.5 million credit to Spain. See Ros et al. (1978:249).

13. Particularly active in arguing the case was the Servicio de Estudios of the Banco Urquijo. Also, in 1951, the four largest private banks funded a study group on the likely effects on Spain of an economic integration with other European countries. The study group was coordinated by José Larraz, a former minister of finance. Larraz later resigned as coordinator of these studies (1960), precisely because his lack of enthusiasm about association or integration into the Common Market was not shared by the banks. See J. Larraz (1961).

14. Many Spanish authors have coincided in the decisive role played by these experts in the negotiation and drafting of the stabilization plan of 1959 (in particular by those working at the Ministry of Commerce and the Bank of Spain). Interesting insiders' accounts can be read in Varela (1990), Sardá (1970), and Fuentes Quintana (1986).

15. See also Juan Velarde's account of those times in the preface to his book *Sobre la decadencia económica de España* (Velarde 1969:26–41).

16. A year earlier, in February 1956, Franco had dismissed two ministers (Ruiz-Giménez from the Ministry of Education and Raimundo Fernández-Cuesta as secretary general of the National Movement) who had proved unable to contain political unrest in the universities. By preventing political liberalization from going farther, this move seemed to contradict the main thrust of Franco's policy devices on the economic front.

17. At the beginning of July 1959 the balance of the Spanish Institute for Foreign Reserves was minus $76.3 million, and import licenses already granted amounted to $208 million, according to the calculation made by one of the main authors of the drafting of the stabilization plan (Sardá 1970:469–470).

18. Navarro Rubio, minister of finance, used this argument in order to persuade Franco of the necessity of the plan (Navarro Rubio 1991:125–126).

19. All of this is a curious example of the interrelations between foreign and domestic policies, giving an idea of the limits to the two-level games approach in its present form.

20. Part of the introduction to the text of the plan is indicative in this respect: "A greater economic flexibility . . . does not, under any circumstances, suppose that the state abdicates the right and the duty to watch over and control the economic development of the country. On the contrary, this function can be exercised with greater agility, by eliminating unnecessary interventions" (Comisaría del Plan 1965:44).

21. See, for example, López Rodó (1971:302–303).

22. Repression that went considerably further than the "policy of exclusion" of the worker movement introduced in France and Italy during the 1950s.

23. López Rodó valued the constitution of the Fifth French Republic highly for not subordinating the government to the deliberative assemblies, which he considered "a form of defective organization" (López Rodó 1971:87).

24. See, for instance, the words of Alberto Ullastres (minister of commerce at the time of the stabilization plan, and later Spanish ambassador to the European Communities), in December 1966, in answer to a question posed by *L'Européen* on Spain's lack of democracy: "In the meantime, please leave us alone, because Spain, which Europe has needed and will need, is the eternal Spain, with her [own] virtues and defects, her greatness and her servitude" (quoted in Ynfante [1970:343]). Or the words of Franco himself in 1962: "Given that on socio-economic issues we are working towards the same goals, our profound difference with Europe is not material but spiritual. We understand that what characterizes and breathes life into our Western civilization are the values of the spirit, since society would collapse if it were not illuminated by those values, and it is precisely in defense of this that we find ourselves most apart" (Del Río Cisneros 1975:791, 631, 792).

25. Exports grew at an annual cumulative rate of 11.2 percent for the period 1961–1975; imports grew at a rate of 15.1 percent (Viñas et al. 1979:1291, 1390).

26. In the words of José Antonio Primo de Rivera, the founder of Falange, himself, in his speech at the Cinema Madrid in 1935 (Primo de Rivera 1945:70).

27. In 1967, Franco himself began to speak in these terms: "Friendship and understanding with Spain is of far more value and transcendence to Great Britain than maintaining in their possession a few archeological redoubts. . . . I would like to banish from this negotiation the erroneous concept of a struggle between nations in which there can be winners and losers, replacing it with that of an unavoidable fact of our time, the resolution of which will be to the benefit of both nations and in the service of Western Europe" (Del Río Cisneros 1975:811). In spite of this perspective, a couple of years later Franco ordered the closure of the gates that separate La Línea from Gibraltar.

28. Although it would appear that Carrero Blanco intended to do so (against the wishes of Castiella), in that he pushed hard for a Statute of Autonomy, resisting the concession of independence demanded by the United Nations (García Domínguez 1977:67–73).

29. Franco in 1973: "In the present hydro-carbon crisis our traditional friendship with the Arab nations acquires a special relevance, and these people have known how to respond to this sentiment by placing our homeland among their friends" (Del Río Cisneros 1975:831).

30. These references were not purely ritualistic. Franco's "colonial" or "imperial" worldview was colored by beliefs about the role Spain had to play in the shaping of a community of Hispanic nations. Moreover, in the view of Spanish diplomats the courting of these Third World countries was seen as the only means for getting support for Spain's long-held vindication over Gibraltar, in view of the opposition or indifference displayed by the Western powers. This pattern of support from some and indifference or opposition from others can be confirmed by the votes cast in the General Assembly of the UN on the fight for Gibraltar (Morris and Haigh [1992:36–37, 44–45, 159–160]).

31. In contrast to what happened in other democracies in transition in the south of Europe, like Portugal and Greece, where the political class was divided on this issue (Alvarez-Miranda 1994).

32. On the debate about Spain's integration into NATO, see Gil and Tulchin (1988). On the linkages between Spain's integration into NATO and the process of modernization of the army, see Rodrigo (1989).

33. At the beginning of the transition period, in 1976 Felipe González (already secretary general of the PSOE and later, in 1982, to become prime minister) said: "NATO is nothing more than a military superstructure built by the Americans to guarantee the survival of capitalism. It is not only directed against the communist countries, as officially stated, but against all possible revolutionary transformations in capitalist countries themselves" (Share 1989:79). In 1982, another leading Socialist, Javier Solana (who became minister of foreign affairs in 1992), explained: "The international policy of a Socialist government has its backbone in the cause of peace, making of Spain a catalyst of concord and detente. For this reason, our country must not belong to NATO" (Santesmases 1985:74). The basic changes in the assumptions implied by these statements made them increasingly irrelevant in the following years, and the very people that pronounced them bore the responsibility of the full participation of Spain in NATO. In any case, these kinds of declarations remind us that those changes took place in a very short time and that they are still relatively recent.

34. Percentages in favor, against, and undecided about entry into NATO from 1978 up to the beginning of 1983: October 1978 (27, 15, 58); July 1979 (28, 26, 46); March 1980 (28, 18, 54); July 1981 (20, 35, 45); September 1981 (13, 43, 44); March 1983 (13, 57, 30). See CIS (n.d.):22–23.

35. Conditions that had been consistently and repeatedly tested by opinion polls carried out by the governmental CIS (Centro de Investigaciones Sociológicos, Center for Sociological Research).

36. The text of the question follows (Share 1989:83):

The government considers it appropriate for the national interest that Spain stay in the Atlantic Alliance according to the following terms:

1. Spain's participation in the Atlantic Alliance shall not include its incorporation into the military command.
2. The installation, storage or introduction of new nuclear arms in Spain will continue to be forbidden.
3. There will be a progressive reduction of U.S. military presence in Spain. Do you think it appropriate for Spain to remain in Nato under these conditions?

37. For a different view, see Pérez Royo (1988) and Tusell (1988).

38. According to a Demoscopia survey carried out between June 10 and June 13, 1992, 74% of Spaniards eligible to vote were in favor of holding a referendum. If it were held, 29% said they would vote for the treaty, with 9% against and a high percentage of "don't know" (62%). In any case, what was known about it was very limited: 24% had never even heard of the Treaty of Maastricht, and 35%, although they had heard of it, knew nothing about it. See El País, June 18, 1992, p. 6.

39. On the attitude of some of the Catalan circles on the subject, see the book Catalunya a l'horitzó 2010. Prospectiva mediterrània (De Jouvenel and Roque 1993: 255–348).

40. On this ambivalence and the subsequent problems for the development of a European public sphere, see Pérez-Díaz (1994).

REFERENCES

Alonso Baquer, Miguel. 1993. "Características militares de Franco." In Luis Suárez, ed., *Franco y su época*, pp. 17–38. Madrid: Actas.

Alonso Zaldívar, Carlos, and Manuel Castells. 1992. *España, fin de siglo*. Madrid: Alianza.

Alvarez-Miranda Navarro, Berta. 1994. "Integración europea y sistemas de partidos del Sur de Europa: Despolarización y convergencia." *Revista de Estudios Políticos* 85 (July–September): 147–167.

Anderson, Charles W. 1974. *The Political Economy of Modern Spain*. Madison: University of Wisconsin Press.

Areilza, José María de. 1977. *Diario de un ministro de la Monarquía*. Barcelona: Planeta.

Arenal, Celestino del. 1992. "La posición exterior de España." In Ramón Cotarelo, comp., *Transición política y consolidación democrática: España, 1975–1986*, pp. 389–428. Madrid: CIS.

Azmah, Aziz. 1993. *Islams and Modernities*. London: Verso.

Cabrera, Mercedes. 1983. *La patronal en la II República: Organizaciones y estrategia, 1932–1936*. Madrid: Siglo XXI.

Calvo Sotelo, Leopoldo. 1990. *Memoria viva de la transición*. Esplugues de Llobregat: Plaza y Janés/Cambio 16.

Carré, Olivier. 1991. *L'Utopie Islamique*. Paris: Presses de la Fondation Nationale des Sciences Politiques.

Carreras, Albert, et al. 1989. *Estadísticas históricas de España: Siglos XIX–XX*. Madrid: Fundación Banco Exterior.

CIS. n.d. *Actitudes de los españoles ante la OTAN*. Madrid: CIS.

Comisaría del Plan de Desarrollo. 1965. *Legislación económica. I. Estabilización*. Madrid: Imprenta Nacional del BOE.

Cornelius, Wayne A. 1994. "Mexico's Delayed Democratization." *Foreign Policy* 95 (Summer): 53–71.

De Jouvenel, Hugues, and Maria-Angels Roque, eds. 1993. *Catalunya a l'horitzó 2010: Prospectiva mediterrània*. Barcelona: Institut Català d'Estudis Mediterranis.

De la Serre, Françoise, Christian Lequesne, and Jacques Rupnik. 1994. *L'Union européenne: Ouverture à l'Est*. Paris: PUF.

Del Río Cisneros, Agustín, ed. 1975. *Pensamiento político de Franco*. Book 2. Madrid: Ediciones del Movimiento.

Evans, Peter B., Harold K. Jacobson, and Robert D. Putnam, eds. 1993. *Double-Edged Diplomacy: International Bargaining and Domestic Politics*. Berkeley: University of California Press.

Fraga Iribarne, Manuel. 1986. *Debate sobre política de paz y seguridad: Congreso de los Diputados 4 de Febrero de 1986*. Madrid: Publicaciones de Alianza Popular.

Franco Salgado-Araujo, Francisco. 1976. *Mis conversaciones privadas con Franco*. Barcelona: Planeta.

Fuentes Quintana, Enrique. 1986. "La economía española desde el plan de estabilización de 1959: El papel del sector exterior." In Tomás Martínez Vara, ed., *Mercado y desarrollo económico en la España contemporánea*, pp. 131–157. Madrid: Siglo XXI.

Gaddis, John Lewis. 1992/93. "International Relations Theory and the End of the Cold War." *International Security* 17, no. 3 (Winter): 5–58.

Gámir, Luis. 1975. "Política de comericio exterior." In Luis Gámir, ed., *Política econó-mica de España*, pp. 140–158. Madrid: Guadiana.

García Domínguez, Ramón. 1977. *Guinea: Macías, la ley del silencio*. Barcelona: Plaza y Janés.

Gil, Federico S., and Joseph S. Tulchin, eds. 1988. *Spain's Entry Into NATO. Conflicting Political and Strategic Perspectives*. Boulder: Lynne Rienner.

INCIPE. 1992. *Informe INCIPE 1992: La opinión pública española y la política exterior*. Madrid: Tecnos/INCIPE.

Keohane, Robert O. 1984. "The World Political Economy and the Crisis of Embedded Liberalism." In John H. Goldthorpe, ed., *Order and Conflict in Contemporary Capitalism*, pp. 15–38. Oxford: Oxford University Press.

Larraz, José. 1961. *La Integración Europea y España*. Madrid: Espasa-Calpe.

Linz, Juan J. 1964. "An Authoritarian Regime: Spain." In E. Allardt and Y. Littunen, eds., *Cleavages, Ideologies, and Party Systems*, pp. 291–341. Helsinki: Westermark Society.

——. 1981. "A Century of Politics and Interests in Spain." In Suzanne Berger, ed., *Organizing Interests in Western Europe*, pp. 365–415. Cambridge: Cambridge University Press.

López Novo, Joaquín. 1991. "Empresarios y relaciones laborales: Una perspectiva histórica." In F. Miguélez and C. Prieto, eds., *Las relaciones laborales en España*, pp. 131–146. Madrid: Siglo XXI.

López Rodó, Laureano. 1971. *Política y desarrollo*. Madrid: Aguilar.

Morán, Fernando. 1980. *Una política exterior para España: Una alternativa socialista*. Barcelona: Planeta.

Moravcsik, Andrew. 1991. "Negotiating the Single European Act." In Robert O. Keohane and Stanley Hoffmann, eds., *The New European Community*, pp. 41–84. Boulder: Westview Press.

——. 1993. "Introduction: Integrating International and Domestic Theories of International Bargaining." In Evans, Jacobson, and Putnam 1993, pp. 3–42.

Morris, D. S., and R. H. Haigh. 1992. *Britain, Spain, and Gibraltar, 1945–1990: The Eternal Triangle*. London and New York: Routledge.

Navarro Rubio, Mariano. 1991. *Mis memorias*. Barcelona: Plaza y Janés/Cambio 16.

North, Douglass. 1990. *Institutions, Institutional Change, and Economic Performance*. Cambridge: Cambridge University Press.

Oakeshott, Michael J. 1991. *Rationalism in Politics and Other Essays*. Indianapolis: Liberty Press.

Payne, Stanley J. 1967. *Politics and the Military in Modern Spain*. Stanford: Stanford University Press.

——. 1977. *Ejército y sociedad en la España liberal, 1808–1936*. Madrid: Akal.

——. 1984. *Spanish Catholicism: A Historical Overview*. Madison: University of Wisconsin Press.

Pereira Castañares, Juan Carlos. 1991. "Las dictaduras Ibéricas ante la Europa de la unidad: España." In Hipólito de la Torre Gómez, ed., *Portugal, España y Europa: Cien años de desafío, 1890–1990*, pp. 75–100. Mérida: UNED.

Pérez-Díaz, Víctor M. 1993. *The Return of Civil Society*. Cambridge: Harvard University Press. (Spanish version, *La primacía de la sociedad civil*. Madrid: Alianza, 1993.)

——. 1994. "Le défi de l'espace public européen." *Transeuropéennes* 3 (Spring): 39–48.

——. 1995. "The Possibility of Civil Society: Traditions, Character, and Challenges."

In John Hall, ed., *Civil Society: Theory, History, Comparison*, pp. 80–109. Cambridge, UK: Polity Press.

Pérez Royo, Javier. 1988. "Repercussions on the Democratic Process of Spain's Entry Into NATO." In Gil and Tulchin 1988.

Pollack, Benny (with Graham Hunter). 1987. *The Paradox of Spanish Foreign Policy: Spain's International Relations from Franco to Democracy*. London: Pinter.

Portero, Florentino. 1989. *Franco aislado: La cuestión española, 1945–1950*. Madrid: Aguilar.

Preston, Paul. 1994. *Franco "caudillo de España."* Barcelona: Grijalbo.

Primo de Rivera, José Antonio. 1945. *Obras completas*. Madrid: Ediciones de la Vicesecretaría de Educación Popular de FET y de las JONS.

PSOE. 1986. "Paz y seguridad en España [approved by the directive bodies of PSOE in December 1985]." *Revista de Estudios Internacionales* 7, no. 1 (January–March): 269–315.

Putnam, Robert. 1988. "Diplomacy and Domestic Politics: The Logic of Two-Level Games." *International Organization* 42 (Summer): 427–460.

Rodrigo Rodríguez, Fernando. 1989. "El camino hacia la democracia: Militares y política en la transición española." Ph.D. diss., Universidad Complutense, Madrid.

Ros, J., Joan Clavera, Joan M. Esteban, M. Antonia Monés, and Antoni Montserrat. 1978. *Capitalismo español: De la autarquía a la estabilización (1939–1959)*. Madrid: Edicusa.

Salamé, Ghassan, ed. 1994. *Démocraties sans democrates*. Paris: Fayard.

Santesmases, Antonio G. 1985. "Evolución ideológica del Socialismo en la España actual." *Sistema* 68/69:61–78.

Sardá, Juan. 1970. "El Banco de España, 1931–1962." In Alfonso Moreno, ed., *El Banco de España. Una historia económica*, pp. 421–479. Madrid: Banco de España.

Schmidt, Helmut. 1985. *A Grand Strategy for the West*. New Haven: Yale University Press.

Serrano Sanz, José María. 1987. *El viraje proteccionista en la Restauración: La política comercial española, 1875–1895*. Madrid: Siglo XXI.

Share, Donald. 1989. *Dilemmas of Social Democracy: The Spanish Socialist Workers Party in the 1980s*. New York: Greenwood Press.

Snyder, Glenn H. 1988. "Spain in NATO: The Reluctant Partner." In Gil and Tulchin 1988, pp. 140–158.

Tusell, Javier. 1984. *Franco y los católicos: La política interior española entre 1945 y 1957*. Madrid: Alianza.

———. 1988. "The Transition to Democracy and Spain's Membership in NATO." In Gil and Tulchin 1988, pp. 11–19.

Varela Parache, Manuel. 1990. "El plan de estabilización como yo lo recuerdo." *Información Comercial Española* (December–January): 41–55.

Velarde, Juan, ed. 1954. *Notas sobre política económica española*. Madrid: Publicaciones de la Delegación Nacional de FET y de las JONS.

Velarde Fuertes, Juan. 1969. *Sobre la decadencia económica de España*. Madrid: Tecnos.

Viñas, Angel. 1984. *Guerra, dinero, dictadura: Ayuda fascista y autarquía en la España de Franco*. Barcelona: Crítica.

Viñas, Angel, Julio Viñuela, Fernando Eguidazu, Carlos Fernández, and Senén Florensa. 1979. *Política comercial exterior en España, 1931–1975*. Madrid: Banco Exterior de España.

Whitehead, Lawrence. 1986. "International Aspects of Democratization." In

G. O'Donnell, Ph. C. Schmitter, and L. Whitehead, *Transitions from Authoritarian Rule. Prospects for Democracy*. Part 3. *Comparative Perspectives*, pp. 3–46. Baltimore: Johns Hopkins University Press.

Ynfante, Jesús. 1970. *La prodigiosa aventura del Opus Dei: Génesis y desarrollo de la Santa Mafia*. Paris: Ruedo Ibérico.

III

Economic Liberalization, International Institutions, and Foreign Policy

EIGHT

Economic Liberalization and the Politics of European Monetary Integration

Jeffry A. Frieden

The European Union (EU) has gradually liberalized economic activity among its member states.[1] From the inception of the EU, trade liberalization has been a central goal. In more recent years, there have been initiatives to reduce or eliminate restrictions on the free movement of capital, people, and services, culminating in the completion of the single European market in the early 1990s.

Perhaps the most ambitious attempt to unite the European economies is monetary integration (MI), understood to include measures ranging from fixing exchange rates to adopting a common currency. The EU's current policy agenda, indeed, projects the full adoption of a single currency by 2002, although there is some doubt about whether this goal will be accomplished.

Monetary integration, and especially full currency union, is difficult and controversial. While many developed countries have liberalized cross-border economic flows among themselves, very few have actually given up their monetary independence, and even fewer have merged their currencies. In Europe, MI has a checkered history. It failed quite miserably in the 1970s and early 1980s. In the mid-1980s, however, the plan for monetary union associated with the European Monetary System (EMS) and its exchange rate mechanism (ERM) seemed to achieve a great deal of success. Yet in 1992–1993 the EMS was hit by a major currency crisis, and it has survived only in modified form. Today, the future of MI is uncertain. On the one hand, several members of the EU appear thoroughly committed to currency union.

On the other hand, confidence in the ability of several other EU members to maintain their fixed exchange rate commitment has eroded substantially, and some EU members remain entirely outside the EMS.

This essay argues that the liberalization of European trade and investment had a profound impact on subsequent policies toward monetary integration. This is a special case of the broader argument that prior experiences of economic liberalization affect subsequent economic policy making, including policies to further reduce barriers to international economic activity. The essay argues for the importance of economic liberalization as a force pushing toward monetary integration, both in general and in the case of the EU.[2]

First I develop an analytical framework to understand how previous levels of economic liberalization affect European monetary politics. There follows a description of the relatively unsuccessful attempts at European monetary integration before 1979 and a summary of the more positive experience of the EMS since then. Next I present several factors important in explaining European monetary politics, emphasizing how levels of intra-EU flows of goods, finance, and direct investment over time and across countries are correlated with variation in the course of European monetary integration. I conclude with some observations about the implications of this analysis for the future of monetary plans in the EU.

ECONOMIC LIBERALIZATION AND MONETARY INTEGRATION

The current goal of European monetary integration is the creation of a single EU currency and central bank. The starting point was a series of attempts, serious discussion of which began in the late 1960s, to tie the currencies of EU members together in a relatively fixed exchange rate system. These attempts had limited success until the late 1970s, with the founding of the European Monetary System (EMS) and its exchange rate mechanism (ERM). By the late 1980s there was pressure for additional movement toward full economic and monetary union (EMU).

There are both theoretical and empirical reasons to believe that previous progress in liberalizing European economic exchange, especially trade and investment, had a substantial impact on the course of monetary integration. It hardly seems controversial that countries whose trade, financial markets, and investments are more closely tied to each other are more likely to fix their exchange rates and, at most, move toward currency union. This vague observation can, however, be given more logical rigor and analytical specificity on the basis of several interrelated theoretical perspectives.

A large literature in economics analyzes the circumstances under which national welfare is improved by a fixed exchange rate and at the limit by a monetary union.[3] As regards the choice of fixed or floating exchange rates, the crucial observation is that as an economy becomes more financially integrated with the rest of the world, the government is faced with a choice between monetary independence and exchange rate stability. In a financially open economy, interest rates are constrained to world levels.[4] In such an economy, monetary policy operates as much or more by way of the exchange rate than the interest rate: monetary expansion leads people to sell the currency, drives the exchange rate down, makes local goods cheaper in comparison to imports, and stimulates demand for domestically produced tradable goods. Fixing the exchange rate forgoes this instrument, foreclosing the possibility of independent monetary policy.

Higher levels of financial integration, then, lead to a trade-off between national monetary policy independence and exchange rate stability: either a financially integrated country allows its currency to fluctuate or it accepts the loss of monetary policy as an instrument. Put differently, as countries become more financially integrated, the effectiveness of national monetary policy declines. The efficiency of a fixed exchange rate—the social welfare gains to be had from a fixed rate—tends to rise along with financial integration.[5]

Monetary union can be regarded as a particularly binding form of fixed exchange rate regime. The literature on optimal currency areas argues that currency union makes economic sense for regions among which factors are mobile and economic shocks are correlated.[6] If two regions are so economically integrated that market conditions are closely linked between them, having a common monetary policy is efficient (and having separate monetary policies may be impossible). Labor and capital move relatively freely within the United States, which is why it makes sense for there to be one currency—given the mobility of factors and the integration of state economies, it would be difficult or impossible for Nevada, for example, to have a separate monetary policy from Arizona's even if the two states *did* have different currencies.[7]

Here, too, economic integration plays a crucial role. The more integrated economies are among themselves, the better off a monetary union will make them. This is true of short-term financial flows, longer-term investment and migration, and trade: greater integration raises the desirability of currency union. The economic analysis is therefore quite clear: the more economically integrated two countries are, the greater the attractiveness of fixed exchange rates and of currency union.

Such social welfare criteria are probably insufficient to explain European monetary politics, however, for two reasons. First, there is substantial evidence that Europe in the 1970s and early 1980s did not meet the criteria by which fixed exchange rates would improve social welfare and that today there is no unambiguous social welfare argument for EMU.[8] Before the late 1980s, the EU was not very integrated financially—capital controls were common.[9] Factors are not very mobile among the members of the EU, and EU economies are not so integrated that they share common macroeconomic conditions.

Economically, then, neither fixed exchange rates nor currency union is clearly welfare-improving at this stage within the EU. Put differently, even if one believes that governments are driven toward efficient economic policies, that could not explain the movement toward monetary integration in the EU, for neither fixed rates nor currency union is the most efficient set of monetary policies available to EU members. Certainly, as the EU has become more integrated over time, the economic desirability of fixed rates, and eventually of a single currency, has risen. But this simply means that the EMS and the EMU are somewhat more economically defensible than they once were, not that some set of welfare or efficiency-based economic principles can be evinced to explain the EMS or the EMU.

Second, even if such policies were unambiguously welfare-improving, we would have little understanding of the mechanism by which governments might be driven to pursue policies favorable to monetary integration: plenty of efficient policies are never adopted. This leads me to explore the implications of the trends discussed here at the domestic political level.

Just as higher levels of economic integration raise the social benefits of exchange rate stability, so do they increase the size and strength of domestic socioeconomic groups interested in predictable exchange rates. Currency arrangements have a differential effect on firms and individuals, which can be expected to translate into cross-cutting political pressures on national policy makers. Such arrangements are controversial on two dimensions—the exchange rate regime, especially whether the currency should be fixed in value, and its level, especially whether it should be strong (appreciated) or weak (depreciated).

The crucial political issue typically has to do with how important currency predictability is, relative to the ability of national monetary authorities to depreciate the exchange rate to increase the competitiveness of national producers. It is also important to keep in mind that eliminating the ability to devalue for high-inflation countries typically leads to a transitional (inertial) real appreciation of the exchange rate. This is especially troublesome for producers of tradable goods that compete primarily on price, as fixing the exchange rate in conditions of inflation above the EU average makes tradables producers less able to compete with other EU producers.

On the other hand, firms with strong international ties support MI's reduction in the vagaries of currency fluctuations. These effects are especially important to banks and corporations with investments throughout the EU. In addition, tradable producers with EU-wide markets, and for whom price competition is relatively less important—those whose appeal is based primarily on quality or technological prowess—may be less concerned about ability to devalue than about currency stability.

As countries liberalize their trade, finance, and investment, more of their citizens develop cross-border economic interests. Those involved in cross-border investment, traders, and exporters of specialized manufactured products tend to favor exchange rate stability to reduce the risk associated with their business interests in other countries. In this way, whatever the effects of economic integration on efficiency considerations associated with monetary union, it is likely to increase domestic political pressures for MI.[10]

My conclusion is straightforward: economic liberalization should increase the likelihood of initiatives to stabilize exchange rates. Financial integration heightens the trade-off between exchange rate stability and monetary independence. Integration of trade and investment makes the region in question more likely to meet the criteria for an optimal currency area. Whatever the social welfare implications of these trends, at a more concrete domestic political level, economic integration swells and strengthens the ranks of those who favor currency stability, thus MI.

This positive relationship between economic integration and the economic and political desirability of monetary integration should hold over time and across countries. That is, as countries in the EU become progressively more integrated on current and capital account, I expect interest in MI to grow. By the same token, I expect support for MI to be stronger in those countries with higher levels of intra-EU trade and investment. In the following discussion I first present a synoptic analysis of the course of European MI from the late 1960s to the present; then I present evidence about the relationship between this course and the level of economic integration within the EU.

THE WERNER REPORT, THE SNAKE, AND THE EMS: FROM QUALIFIED FAILURE THROUGH SKEPTICISM TO QUALIFIED SUCCESS

Discussions within the EU over the possibility of stabilizing exchange rates began only a few months after the signing of the Treaty of Rome.[11] As fissures appeared in the Bretton Woods system, these talks accelerated, culminating in the 1969 Werner Report, which recommended the beginning of a process of monetary union among EU members. Within a few weeks of its adoption, however, the Werner Report's recommendations were overtaken by the collapse of Bretton Woods.

In the confused months after the August 1971 American decision to go off gold, EU member states resolved to hold their currencies within a 2.25 percent band against each other and to allow this band to move within a 4.5 percent band against the U.S. dollar. This arrangement was known as the "snake in the tunnel," as EU currencies would wriggle within a circumscribed range vis-à-vis the dollar. In addition to the Six, Great Britain, Ireland, and Denmark joined the snake on May 1, 1972, to prepare for their entry into the union eight months later. Britain and Ireland, however, left the snake in June 1972; the Danes left shortly thereafter but rejoined in October.

The collapse of attempts to salvage an international fixed rate monetary regime in 1973 ended the "tunnel" aspects of the snake. From then on, the EU's goal was to achieve a joint float of member currencies against the dollar, without targeting how they would move relative to it. In other words, the only consideration from 1973 on was intra-EU exchange rates.

Even this more limited goal was difficult to achieve.[12] As already indicated, Britain and Ireland left the snake within weeks of joining, and in February 1973 Italy followed suit. In addition, throughout 1973 only a series of parity changes allowed the system to hold together, and even then France chose to exit in January 1974. The French returned in July 1975, only to leave for good eight months later.

Within three years of its founding, then, the only EU members still in the snake were Germany, the Benelux countries, and Denmark. Even within this narrowed arrangement, realignments were frequent, typically to devalue the Danish krone and/or revalue the deutsche mark. Although by 1978 the EU began moving toward the EMS, nothing in the previous snake experience gave much cause for hope that the nine EU members could fix their exchange rates in any meaningful way.

It is not hard to explain in a discursive way why four EU members (Germany and Benelux) were able to maintain fixed exchange rates among themselves, while five others (Denmark, Britain, Ireland, France, and Italy) were not, in varying degrees (I attempt a more systematic explanation below). The ease with which the Germany-Benelux link held is largely attributable to the fact that monetary and financial conditions in the Benelux countries were so tied to those in Germany. As for Denmark, despite the formal link to the snake, the krone was so frequently devalued against the unit of account that the ties were hardly binding. In addition, Danish membership in the snake was facilitated by the fact that two Scandinavian countries with which Denmark is closely tied economically and politically were also members: Norway from May 1972 to December 1978, Sweden from March 1973 to August 1977.

As for those incapable of staying in the snake, Britain and Ireland were new members of the EU, Britain's Labour government was in a state of economic policy turmoil, and North Sea oil complicated matters still further. Ireland's close economic links to Britain made it difficult to break from the pound, and, indeed, the Irish had tied their currency to sterling at a one-to-one no-margins parity since independence.

As for France and Italy, since the late 1960s they had had consistently higher inflation than Germany, and during the 1970s they showed little real interest in monetary union, preoccupied as they were with domestic macroeconomic difficulties. Their attempt to commit to MI was consistently blocked by domestic political opposition to the measures necessary to make this commitment possible. The importance of these two countries makes it useful to discuss their problems in more detail.

Italy went through a series of payments crises in the middle 1970s, all related to chronic inflation.[13] In 1974, consumer price inflation approached 25 percent, with a public sector borrowing requirement (PSBR) of 7.9 percent of GDP. In that year the government signed a standby agreement with the International Monetary Fund (IMF), which met with only moderate success. Although inflation declined to 11 percent in 1975, Italy plunged into its most serious postwar recession (GDP declined 3.6 percent), and the PSBR rose to 11.4 percent of GDP. Under union pressure, the employers' association agreed to a wage indexation scheme (the *scala mobile*, or escalator) that embedded past inflation in wages and thus production costs. In this context, the exchange rate was allowed to depreciate continually to maintain competitiveness.

A new IMF program in 1977 again attempted to restrain demand. The government tried in vain to get the trade unions and businessmen to renegotiate the *scala mobile* and reduce indexation, finally decreeing a loosening of the mechanism. Inflation bottomed out at 11.6 percent in 1978, but the PSBR was 14.3 percent of GDP in that year and stayed above 10 percent of GDP through 1980, by which time consumer price inflation (CPI) was again rising at 21 percent a year. The country appeared to be in a vicious circle of massive budget deficits, inflation, indexed wage increases, and continual lira depreciation. It was hardly surprising that Italy showed no particular interest, other than verbal, in monetary union through the 1970s; no informed observer regarded a commitment to a stable lira as remotely credible.

France was doing only slightly better.[14] When Valéry Giscard d'Estaing became president in 1974, consumer price inflation was running at nearly 14 percent. With the franc out of the snake, the government of Jacques Chirac first tried monetary stringency, which reduced inflation a couple of percentage points but brought growth to a halt. In 1975, Chirac attempted to stimulate the economy with a fiscal policy that was relatively lax by French standards (a PSBR of about 3 percent of GDP, compared to the traditional near-balance). France rejoined the snake in July 1975, but by early 1976 unemployment was still high and the current account deficit was growing. In March 1976, after the left did very well in regional elections, Chirac took the franc out of the snake; a few months later, Giscard dismissed Chirac and appointed Raymond Barre to the premiership.

For almost five years after his appointment, Prime Minister Barre implemented austerity programs. Yet inflation was stubbornly high, nearly 11 percent for the period; unemployment rose continually even as real wages stagnated; and the current account remained in deficit. The government apparently attempted to shadow other European currencies,[15] but domestic conditions drove it to continual franc depreciation to maintain competitiveness. By 1980 inflation was still 13.5 percent, unemployment was 6.3 percent (triple 1973 levels), and five years of austerity seemed to have accomplished little except pave the way for a Socialist Party electoral victory of March 1981. In this context, French assurances about the desirability of monetary union were no more plausible than those of Italy.

The experience of the 1970s held out few hopes for success in the 1980s. The EU's two major high-inflation countries, France and Italy, had been unable to fix their exchange rates with other EU members. Resistance to austerity measures, and pressures from tradables producers to maintain international price competitiveness, led to continual rounds of franc and lira depreciations against the deutsche mark. Therefore, for the first several years of the ERM's existence, almost no informed observer believed that it would hold. Nonetheless, by the mid-1980s, the EMS had achieved quite substantial success.

Renewed discussions of EU monetary union began to gather momentum in October 1977, when Roy Jenkins, president of the European Commission, made a prominent public appeal for MI. In April 1978, French president Giscard d'Estaing and German chancellor Helmut Schmidt proposed a new European monetary system, and in December 1978 the EMS was approved by the European Council. Its implementation was delayed by wrangling over implications for the EU's Common Agricultural Policy (CAP), but in March 1979 the EMS and its exchange rate mechanism went into effect. All EU members except the United Kingdom affiliated with the ERM, which allowed a 2.25 percent band among currencies (6 percent for the lira).[16]

The prevailing opinion at the time was that French and Italian inflation rates were too high and intractable to allow the EMS to operate as planned. Indeed, in the first four years of its operation there were seven realignments of EMS currency values. During this period, deutsche mark revaluations and lira and franc devaluations reduced the DM value of the two problem currencies by 27 and 25 percent, respectively—hardly a sign of commitment to fixed rates.

Over the following four years, however, between April 1983 and January 1987, there were only four more realignments, generally smaller than the previous changes. Over the second four years, the lira and the franc were brought down 13 and 9 percent against the mark, respectively. Indeed, after 1983 exchange rate variability within the EMS declined substantially, while monetary policies converged on virtually every dimension.[17] From January 1987 until September 1992 there were no realignments within the ERM, while Spain, the United Kingdom, and Portugal joined the mechanism and Finland, Sweden, and Norway explicitly linked their currencies to the European Currency Unit (ECU).

Perhaps most important in this process was the unexpected turnaround in French policy in the early 1980s. In this case, a newly elected Socialist government, torn between its expansionary macroeconomic policies and its commitment to the EMS, chose the latter. Analyses of these events abound, and I will not go into them in detail.[18]

In the aftermath of the French shift and less dramatic changes in Ireland, Denmark, and Italy, European integration more generally picked up speed. Over the course of 1985 and 1986, EU members discussed and adopted the Single European Act, which called for the full mobility of goods, capital, and people within the EU by January 1, 1993.[19] From then on, national barriers began falling. Most capital controls were gone by 1991, and the prospect of a unified market for goods defined much of the economic and political activity of the Union in the run-up to 1993. Indeed, as economic integration advanced and the EMS appeared to be stable, EU members devised plans for full monetary union and incorporated them into the 1991 Maastricht Treaty. Afterward, of course, these plans were derailed by German unification and the 1992–1993 currency crisis, a point to which I return below.

For present purposes, I focus on the period between 1973 and 1990. The principal developments that need to be explained are twofold. At the EU level, it is puzzling that MI was relatively unsuccessful in the 1970s but relatively successful in the middle and late 1980s. Within the EU, the variation in national willingness and ability to abide by the strictures of MI demands explanation. In the next section I turn to an evaluation of some of the factors that contributed to the unanticipated success of the EMS and that have affected national attitudes toward MI.

EXPLAINING THE COURSE OF EUROPEAN MONETARY INTEGRATION

European monetary integration is a complex phenomenon involving developments at the international, regional, and national levels, in both political and economic spheres. I do not pretend to present a full explanation of the process, only to outline some factors I regard as crucial and to highlight the importance of economic integration for MI. This is not, in other words, a rigorous test of the hypothesized relationship between economic integration and pressure for MI, nor is it an argument that this variable is the only one that matters. It is simply a demonstration of the posited correlation.

First, however, it is important to mention several factors that were undoubtedly also crucial in spurring MI within the European Union. One such factor was the CAP.[20] In the context of major agricultural subsidies, the EU sets union-wide food prices. When a currency is devalued, the EU reference price would normally be raised in the devaluing country to counterbalance the devaluation—thus "passing through" the exchange rate change to food prices. The inflationary impact of this pass-through would mitigate the devaluation's attempt to restore price competitiveness in the nonagricultural sectors. For this reason, the EU devised a series of compensatory arrangements and accounting exchange rates. For our purposes, what is important is that exchange rate fluctuations complicate union agricultural policy by changing compensatory farm payments in ways that could disrupt the delicate balance within the EU on farm policy. This was indeed one of the original reasons for early moves toward MI, and it remained important through the adoption of the EMS. However, the CAP is a constant, and while it explains the persistence of EU attempts at MI, it cannot explain variation in their success. The importance of the CAP might vary by country, thus explaining variation in commitment to MI, but there is no evidence that national support for MI is related to reliance on the CAP.

One reason why the EMS was more successful than the snake is the major increase in the amount of money available to EMS members for short- and long-term financing of payments deficits. Very short-term financing arrangements were extended from thirty to forty-five days. The capacity for short-term financing was expanded from 6 billion to 14 billion ECU. Medium-term financing commitment ceilings were raised from 5.45 billion to 14.1 billion ECU. Finally, 5 billion ECU in concessionary development loans over a five-year period were made available, essentially to Ireland and Italy, as a side payment to the two countries with the largest adjustment burden.[21] All told, the resources committed to the EMS were about three times those committed to the snake, which made affiliation with the system that much more attractive to potential members. There is little evidence, however, that the funds involved were particularly important to the process—Italy did not even use its concessionary finance, and the other funds were rarely central to EMS developments. And again, with the exception of the concessionary funds to Ireland, this factor cannot explain variation among EU members.

A third, somewhat less tangible but nonetheless crucial, change between the snake and the EMS was the relationship between them and broader EU participation. There was never any sense that the snake was an essential component of the EU; neither national politicians nor union leaders had staked much political capital on the arrangement. The EMS was different. The French and German heads of state launched the attempt with great publicity, and the European Commission regarded the EMS as of paramount importance. EMS success was publicly related to other aspects of European integration in ways that implied that a country unable to stay in the ERM would become a second-tier member of the European Union.

This linkage of the EMS with the broader program of EU integration was indeed decisive. In the early 1980s, with the European economies beset by stagnation and unemployment, many segments of society began to look upon an intensification of European economic integration as the last best hope for the region.[22] The process culminated in the Single European Act, and as the pace of European integration quickened, MI came to be viewed as a near-essential component of a broader process.

Linking MI with EU integration affected the domestic political lineup in many member nations. Previously, it had been possible to oppose national policies necessary to sustain a fixed exchange rate, while evincing great enthusiasm for the EU generally. With the 1992 program tied to the success of MI, such a division of the question was less feasible. To take one example, many national labor movements had resisted the austerity measures necessary to reduce national inflation to German levels, while supporting European integration; commitment to the EMS was separable from commitment to the EU. With the two no longer divisible, labor movements had to decide whether their opposition to austerity outweighed their support for the EU, or vice versa. This linking of the two agenda items was crucial to the eventual success of the EMS commitment in France, Italy, and Ireland; to British, Spanish, and Portuguese accession to the ERM; and to the Nordic countries' link to the ECU in preparation for their application for full EU membership. So this was clearly an important factor, one that has been dealt with in detail elsewhere.[23]

All these factors are important for explaining the course of European monetary union. I focus, however, on the influence of economic integration. I believe that liberalization of intra-European trade and capital flows played a major role in leading EU members toward MI. I also believe that those EU members whose economies were more integrated with that of Germany, the monetary leader of the union, were more likely to pursue MI.

To analyze the relationship between economic integration and exchange rate policy, it is useful first to present some summary measures of the currency movements observed in the period in question. Two measures of exchange rate variations are presented in table 8.1. Panel A indicates the degree to which each currency in the EU depreciated in nominal terms against the deutsche mark (DM) during the snake (1973–1978), the EMS (1979–1990), and over the two periods combined (1973–1990). Panel B presents the coefficient of variation (a measure of variability) of each EU currency against the DM during the snake, the EMS, and the two periods combined. For ease of exposition, and in line with common distinctions drawn by observers, the countries are divided into three groups. Hard-currency countries are those that stayed in both the snake and the EMS. Soft-currency countries are those that left or never joined the snake and whose participation in the EMS has been limited or troubled. The two intermediate countries, France and Ireland, left the snake but have been relatively stable members of the EMS.

The division between hard, soft, and intermediate currencies is largely borne out by the statistical measures used. In addition, a general trend toward reduced exchange rate variability can be noted between the snake and the EMS, as is to be expected. It should be

TABLE 8.1

EU Currencies During the Snake and the EMS

A. Cumulative percentage depreciation of nominal exchange rates against the deutsche mark, select periods

Country	1973–1978	1979–1990	1973–1990
Hard currencies			
Netherlands	7.0	4.5	11.9
Belgium/Lux	4.4	30.8	48.5
Denmark	28.3	38.97	7.0
Intermediate currencies			
France	43.7	46.4	110.6
Ireland	95.6	42.0	172.7
Soft currencies			
UK	95.6	28.0	149.5
Italy	92.4	66.1	291.6
Spain	86.4	64.7	212.7
Portugal	161.5	245.4	920.2
Greece	74.1	420.3	927.7

B. Coefficients of variation of nominal exchange rates against the deutsche mark, select periods

Country	1973–1978	1979–1990	1973–1990
Hard currencies			
Netherlands	2.05	1.51	3.24
Belgium/Lux	2.93	10.00	14.0
Denmark	7.34	9.25	18.43
Intermediate currencies			
France	11.43	13.86	23.0
Ireland	20.66	12.94	24.68
Soft currencies			
UK	20.66	15.80	21.86
Italy	24.24	17.86	33.59
Spain	23.35	20.20	34.93
Portugal	32.92	42.34	66.6
Greece	18.52	52.11	71.7

Source: International Monetary Fund, International Financial Statistics Data Base (Year 1992). Periods run from first quarter in the first year to fourth quarter in the last year of the periods.

Note: Only figures for pre-1995 EU members are shown.

noted that the absolute depreciation figures are not comparable, as the EMS period is more than twice as long as the snake. The only slightly anomalous case is that of sterling, which appears more stable against the DM than most accounts would have it. This is largely because North Sea oil and the Thatcher administration led to a significant appreciation of the pound in the early 1980s, which was reversed with a vengeance in the middle and late 1980s (and with even more of a vengeance after September 1992). In any event, the evidence in table 8.1 is meant simply to indicate that statistical data reinforce the more discursive story told above. This is particularly worth doing because in the statistical evaluations that follow, the coefficient of variation figures are used as the dependent variable. The reader should easily be satisfied that this figure both makes sense economically and accurately reflects real trends in the variability of currencies.

The first step is to try to explain increased interest in MI within the EU. Here again I argue that higher levels of commercial, financial, and investment flows within the union should strengthen the position of those most interested in stabilizing currency values. And the statistical record does indeed indicate a significant increase in the importance of intra-EU trade and payments over the 1970s and 1980s.

By far the most reliable intra-EU economic figures are those having to do with trade. Table 8.2 shows the relationship between manufactured exports within subgroups of EU members, on the one hand, and their combined GDP, on the other. Manufactured exports are the relevant consideration for my purposes: agricultural trade is mostly controlled by the Common Agricultural Policy (CAP), and other nonmanufactured trade is relatively unimportant. More generally, as explained above, it is exporters of relatively specialized manufactured products (rather than standardized commodities) whom I expect to care about currency stability.

As table 8.2 indicates, intra-EU manufactured exports have become increasingly important since the early 1970s. This is true whether one looks at the founding members of the union or at its expanded size. The increase is continuous, and although the several percentage points in question might seem to be a small increment, they are in fact quite significant by most standards, and as trends. For example, if the rate of change in intra–EU 12 trade as a share of total GDP were to be sustained, by the year 2000 the EU 12 would be exporting manufactured goods equal to about 22 percent of their total GDP among themselves. This can be compared to *total* American manufactured exports, which are typically below 7 percent of American GDP.

Unfortunately, data on financial and investment flows within the EU are far less readily available than those on trade. The best avail-

TABLE 8.2

Intragroup Manufactured Exports of EEC6, EC9, and EU12 (Percent of GDP)

Group	1972	1978	1985
The EEC 6	8.18	9.35	10.05
The EC 9	9.95	12.1	14.01
The EU 12	9.95	11.98	14.25

Source: OECD Compatible Trade and Production Data Base (COMTAP) 1971—1986. Manufacturing is as defined by the International Standard Industrial Classification (code 3) and *Basic Statistics of the Community* (Office for Official Publications for the European Communities), vols. 15, 22, 25.

Note: The EEC 6 are the Union's founding members: Belgium, France, Germany, Italy, Luxembourg, and the Netherlands. The EC 9 are these plus Denmark, Ireland, and the United Kingdom, which joined in 1973. The EU 12 are these plus Greece, which joined in 1981, and Spain and Portugal, which joined in 1986.

able analysis is that by Jeffrey Frankel and his colleagues.[24] In an attempt to measure the level of financial integration within the union, they looked at levels and trends of covered interest rate differentials with Germany. This approach incorporates both interest rate differences and market expectations of exchange rate movements; the remaining differential is presumably the result of country risk, capital controls, and other forms of incomplete market integration. Data are available only after about 1980 (the relevant forward currency markets largely did not exist before then) and are thus not satisfactory for my purposes. They nonetheless help to indicate characteristics of intra-EU financial integration.

The analysis by Frankel and his colleagues shows that financial markets in Benelux, the United Kingdom, and Ireland were very closely tied to those of Germany. This is probably as expected, for Benelux finances have long gravitated toward Germany, while the UK and Ireland have very open financial systems. Financial conditions in France, Denmark, Italy, Spain, Portugal, and Greece were much less strongly tied to those of Germany, as most of these countries had relatively closed financial systems and capital controls. Denmark is a bit of a puzzle but is probably best explained by the link between financial conditions there and in neighboring Scandinavian countries. In all these last cases, however, financial conditions in the EU were converging rapidly, particularly in the countries least tied to Germany. By the late 1980s and early 1990s, indeed, most observers believed that financial markets within the EU were very closely linked.

A third dimension of economic integration has to do with foreign direct investment (FDI). Analysts have long believed that multinational corporations with pan-European investments are a major force supporting European integration, including monetary integration. It is regrettable that reliable data on intra-EU FDI are available only from about 1980 on. Table 8.3 presents a synopsis of these data, which indicate the importance of stocks of intra-EU FDI as a share of GDP in the early and later 1980s. The data are for a scattered set of years, and quite a few observations are missing. There are far better data available on both stocks and flows of FDI after the late 1980s, but this is too late to play any part in *explaining* monetary integration. Despite their shortcomings, the data in table 8.3 are both indicative and the best available.

As far as change over time goes, table 8.3 demonstrates the dramatic increase in intra-EU direct investment over the course of the 1980s (I evaluate intercountry differences below). It is in fact striking how rapidly FDI stocks grew in some countries. For example, Danish direct investment in the EU, and in the DM zone (defined as Germany and Benelux combined), as a share of GDP grew by a factor of more than four times in just eight years; EU investment in Spain and Portugal as a share of their GDPs grew more than threefold in just six and eight years, respectively. It can also be noted that in virtually every case, EU and DM zone direct investments grew as a share of each country's *total* direct investments as well. In other words, over the course of the 1980s all EU members experienced significant increases in the importance of intra-EU direct investment, and their direct investments became more concentrated in the EU.

With some exceptions, however, these data are of little assistance in evaluating the impact of changing levels of intra-EU FDI over time on incentives for EU monetary integration, for the simple reason that to a great extent the FDI in question was *responding* to existing currency arrangements. The potential exceptions are for those countries that were members of the EU but not the EMS during the 1980s. In these cases—the soft-currency countries in table 8.3—increased levels of FDI presumably responded to considerations not directly related to currency variability. Undoubtedly the most important factor here was the gathering pace of European integration more generally. British firms invested very heavily in the EU as the United Kingdom was drawn more fully into the European market, and EU firms invested at unprecedented levels in Spain and Portugal as these two countries joined the union. It might well be the case that the important increases in intra-EU direct investments to and from these countries raised the costs of currency fluctuations for them and con-

TABLE 8.3

Stock of Intra-EU Foreign Direct Investment by 12 EU Member States, Early and Late 1980s (Percent of GDP)

	Inward DM Zone EU 12		Outward DM Zone EU 12		Total DM Zone EU 12	
Hard-currency countries						
Netherlands						
1984	2.29	5.35	5.34	10.73	7.63	16.08
1989	3.80	8.58	6.13	13.57	12.38	22.15
Belgium/Lux						
1980	3.6	5.39	0.62	2.02	4.22	7.41
1988	4.47	10.04	1.6	4.83	6.07	14.87
Denmark						
1982	0.31	0.40	0.14	0.34	0.45	0.74
1990	0.54	0.95	1.48	3.81	2.02	4.76
Intermediate countries						
France						
1982	0.99	1.49	0.41	1.01	1.40	2.50
1989	1.26	2.89	1.66	3.45	2.92	6.34
Ireland						
1981	—	4.71	—	—	—	—
1986	—	5.01	—	—	—	—
Soft-currency countries						
UK						
1981	0.67	1.03	0.78	2.33	1.45	3.36
1989	3.32	4.72	3.02	5.85	6.34	10.57
Italy						
1980	—	0.99	—	0.82	—	1.81
1989	—	2.79	—	2.44	—	5.23
Spain						
1983	0.79	1.84	0.02	0.07	0.81	1.86
1989	2.64	7.07	0.03	0.88	2.67	7.95
Portugal						
1980	0.37	0.90	0.06	0.42	0.43	1.32
1988	0.87	2.95	0.01	0.27	0.88	3.22
Greece						
1978	—	1.23	—	—	—	—

Source: Table 9, Country Tables in *The World Investment Directory*, vol. 3, Developed Countries (New York: United Nations Publications, 1993), and *Basic Statistics of the Community* (Eurostat: Brussels), vols. 27, 25, 22.

Note: — indicates data not available.

tributed to a strengthening of pro-MI sentiment in them. It is, however, impossible to assess this possibility with the data currently available.

Because the statistical record concerning FDI is somewhat spotty, it can be supplemented with more general figures. The increased level of international capital movements between the early 1970s and the early 1980s is well known. This was a global phenomenon, but capital flows increased significantly to and from the European Union. Between 1975 and 1979, long-term investment flows into and out of major EU countries (both among themselves and elsewhere) averaged $35.1 billion a year; in the 1980–1984 period, despite a major recession, they averaged $64.2 billion a year. Short-term net bank flows rose from $9.3 to $19.4 billion a year between the two periods.[25]

The higher levels of international goods and capital market integration within the EU had two effects. First, increased financial integration raised the probability that divergent macroeconomic policies would lead to countervailing trends on capital and currency markets. This is simply another illustration of what was discussed above: higher levels of capital mobility made independent monetary policy inconsistent with a fixed exchange rate. Greater financial-market integration within Europe tended to quicken the rate at which divergent national monetary policies led to substantial capital flows and eventually currency crises. Financial integration made the resolution of the conflict between national monetary autonomy and exchange rate stability pressing.

The second impact of higher levels of economic integration within Europe, again as discussed above, was on the interests of domestic economic actors. As trade and capital flows within the EU grew, ever larger segments of EU business communities developed more important markets and investments in other EU nations. The growth of intra-EU trade and investment, therefore, increased the real or potential support base for economic policies that would facilitate and defend such economic activities. Stabilizing exchange rates within the EU was a prominent example of a policy that benefited the growing ranks of economic actors with cross-border intra-EU economic interests, whether these were export markets or investment sites.

The expectation that the level of interest in MI in the EU as a whole be correlated with the level of intra-EU trade and investment appears to be supported by the data. The next question is whether differing degrees of national support for MI are correlated with different levels of integration in EU goods and capital movements. To evaluate this, I present data on cross-national variation in trade and investment within the EU.

Table 8.4 shows the importance of intra-EU trade for members of the union. Manufactured exports as a share of national GDP are used, for the reasons discussed above. Two figures are shown, one indicating the importance of trade with the EU as a whole (i.e., the current twelve members), one the importance of trade with the deutsche mark zone, defined as Germany and Benelux. This latter figure should be the principal focus for an analysis of interest in MI, as such policies have since the start implied tying the national currency to that of Germany (and thus of the DM zone). In other words, this segment of my argument is that domestic political support for linking the national currency to the DM will be a function of the importance of a country's trade with the DM zone. Data are presented for two time periods, the early 1970s before the advent of the snake, and 1979–1982, during the early years of the EMS.

Several features of the trade data are striking. First is the extremely high level of Benelux trade with the DM zone: the three countries' manufactured exports to the area are a major share of their GDP. Second, the importance of intra-EU, and DM zone, trade has risen in every country (with the minor exception of Belgium/Luxembourg DM zone trade, which was already at extraordinarily high levels). The increase has been quite remarkable in some cases, notably that of Ireland. Third, the importance of DM zone trade appears to be strongly related to willingness to tie national currencies to the DM. The only ambiguous cases are those of Denmark and Italy. Danish manufactured trade with the EU and the DM zone is important, but not sufficiently important to explain fully its strong commitment to MI. Italy's *inability* to commit to MI is a bit out of line with its relatively important DM zone trade ties. But both cases are borderline, and there are indeed special circumstances that help explain each.[26]

A similar cross-national comparison can be carried out for foreign direct investment, using the data in table 8.3. These data, despite all their shortcomings, do show that, very generally, intra-EU and DM zone foreign direct investment was more important for those countries that went on to tie their currencies to the DM than for other EU

TABLE 8.4

Manufactured Exports of 12 EU Members to the EU and the Deutsche Mark Zone (Germany plus Benelux) (Percent of GDP)

Country	Manufactured Exports to EU/GDP, %		Manufactured Exports to D Mark Zone/GDP, %	
	1970–1973	1979–1982	1970–1973	1979–1982
Hard-currency countries				
Netherlands	21.46	25.74	13.52	15.30
Belgium/Lux	30.77	35.51	17.81	17.62
Denmark	7.86	10.59	2.37	4.42
Intermediate countries				
France	6.70	8.27	4.20	4.52
Ireland	15.78	29.94	1.74	7.97
Soft-currency countries				
UK	4.85	7.08	2.08	3.37
Italy	7.32	9.46	4.05	4.43
Spain	2.62	4.33	0.99	1.30
Portugal	6.45	10.20	1.58	3.63
Greece	2.48	4.27	1.36	2.23

Source: OECD Compatible Trade and Production Data Base (COMTAP) 1971–1986.

Notes: "Intra-EU" trade includes trade to the 12 pre-1995 members of the EU.

Manufacturing is as defined by the International Standard Industrial Classification (code 3) and *Basic Statistics of the Community* (Office for Official Publications for the European Communities), vols. 15, 22, 25.

members. To reiterate, one cannot read too much into these data, both because there are too many gaps (especially for FDI in the DM zone) and because the time period is in the middle rather than at the beginning of attempts at monetary integration. For example, it is quite plausible that the very high levels of Benelux investment in and from Germany are attributable at least in part to the fact that their currencies were stable against the DM during the snake, before a large part of the stocks measured in the table were accumulated. Nonetheless, there is a general trend in the expected direction. Anomalies persist, however: most prominently, Denmark has far "less" FDI than might be expected.

At this point it is worthwhile to raise the problem of simultaneity in these data. It is well known that stabilizing exchange rates among countries tends to increase trade and payments among them. In this case, it might be argued that the correlation between levels of trade,

TABLE 8.5

*Exchange Rate Variability Against the Deutsche Mark During the Snake
and the EMS: The Role of Trade*

Independent variables	1973–1978	1979–1990
Constant	22.80512	29.67497
DM bloc trade, 1970–1973	-1.28674[**]	
	(3.13)	
DM bloc trade, 1979–1982		-1.55702[*]
		(-1.89)
		Degrees of freedom 8 8
R squared 0.551		0.308

Notes : [**] = significant at the 5% level. [*] = significant at the 10% level. t-statistics in parentheses.

Dependent variable: Coefficient of variation of the nominal exchange rate against the deutsche mark during the period.

financial, and investment flows and currency stability is picking up the reverse causal mechanism: it is not that economic integration is increasing the political support for monetary integration but that policies for currency stability adopted for other reasons are speeding economic integration.

There is no doubt that economic integration is indeed encouraged by currency stability. Two points should be made. First, I have tried here (and will do so below) to use levels of economic integration *before* the monetary agreements to explain policy and performance *during* them. At the limit, if the pattern of economic integration in the early 1970s, before any serious monetary initiatives, can explain currency policy between 1973 and 1990, I am on relatively solid ground. Unfortunately, data for the early 1970s are available only for trade and not for FDI and financial flows.

Second, there is in fact no necessary contradiction between my argument and its reverse. In fact, the reason EU-oriented economic agents, in my analysis, support monetary integration is precisely that they expect it to increase the level of intra-EU trade and payments. Put somewhat differently, my framework leads me to expect that high levels of trade and payments will be correlated with currency stability *both* because economic integration increases political support for monetary integration, and vice versa. Of course, I would like to be able to disentangle cause and effect, especially chronologically, but

TABLE 8.6

Exchange Rate Variability Against the Deutsche Mark During the Snake and the EMS, 1973–1990: The Role of Trade

Independent variables	(1)	(2)	(3)	(4)
Constant	41.87484	44.57226	46.16819	46.69254
DM bloc trade, 1970–1973	-2.14725*			
	(1.96)			
DM bloc trade, average of 1970–1973 and 1979–1982		-2.33544*		
		(2.11)		
EU trade, 1970–1973			-1.40795*	
			(2.07)	
EU trade, average of 1970–1973 and 1979–1982				-1.23089*
				(1.96)
Degrees of freedom	8	8	8	8
R squared	0.324	0.357	0.349	0.325

Source: The data are from the previous tables, specifically tables 8.1 and 8.4.

Notes: * = significant at the 10% level.

t-statistics in parentheses.

Dependent variable: Coefficient of variation of the nominal exchange rate against the deutsche mark, 1973–1990

The independent variables are the country's manufactured exports to the EU (defined as the 12 current members of the EU), and to the deutsche mark zone (Germany, Belgium, Luxembourg, the Netherlands), as a share of GDP for the years in question.

data limitations make this difficult. In any case, it should be kept in mind that monetary, financial, and investment integration probably feed back to increase each other, and that where early 1970s data are not available I have trouble breaking into this feedback process.

Nonetheless, I can present some more evidence to bolster my argument. Rather than simply relying on casual inspection of the data, I try more systematic methods to show correlation between the importance of a country's trade and investment with the DM zone and its willingness to stabilize its currency against the DM. The easiest way to accomplish this is to run a series of regressions in which the dependent variable is the variability of the national exchange rate against the DM (as discussed above), and the independent variables measure the importance of DM zone trade and investment for the country. I present the results in tables 8.5, 8.6, and 8.7.

In table 8.5, I measure the impact of the importance of a country's manufactured exports to the DM zone to its economy at the outset of the snake and the EMS, on the variability of the country's currency against the DM during the snake and EMS periods.[27] The results indi-

TABLE 8.7

Exchange Rate Variability Against the Deutsche Mark
During the EMS: The Role of FDI

Independent variables	(1)	(2)
Constant	27.15187	23.24115
Intra-EU FDI, early 1980s	-1.84203*	
	(1.86)	
DM bloc FDI, early 1980s		-3.03405
		(1.79)
Degrees of freedom	8	5
R squared	0.302	0.391

Source: Tables 8.1 and 8.3.

Notes: * = significant at the 10% level.

Dependent variable: Coefficient of variation of the nominal exchange rate against the deutsche mark during the period.

Independent variables are, as indicated, intra-EU and intra-deutsche mark zone (DM bloc) direct investment (FDI) as a share of each country's GDP in the early 1980s. Intra-EU data are for all pre-1995 EU members; total FDI for Greece and Ireland is assumed equal to outward FDI. DM bloc data are for the Netherlands, Belgium and Luxembourg, Denmark, France, the United Kingdom, Portugal, and Spain. Specific dates are as indicated in table 8.4.

cate quite clearly that the higher the country's DM zone trade as a share of its GDP before the currency agreement, the less likely its currency was to fluctuate against the DM. The results are statistically significant, and the coefficients are quite large.[28]

Perhaps the most striking result is that contained in table 8.6. The regression results in columns 1 and 3 look at the impact of trade with the DM zone and the EU in the early 1970s on national currency variability from 1973 until 1990. Although obviously a great deal went on over the two decades, it is quite remarkable (especially in light of the preceding discussion of simultaneity) that the results remain quite robust: trade patterns before 1973 had a strong and systematic impact on the likelihood that countries would tie their currencies to the DM after 1973.[29]

The data on financial integration do not allow for a similar test, for the simple reason that the measures of financial market integration available are for the core period of the EMS rather than at its start. Here the simultaneity problems are insurmountable. Nonetheless, as the discussion above indicates, there does seem to be some relationship between financial integration and interest in monetary integration. The Benelux countries and Ireland are strongly linked to

German financial markets, and they have been enthusiastic about MI. Countries less closely linked have been less enthusiastic, but the relationship is not so strong.

Given the somewhat better—but still unsatisfactory—data available on intra-EU direct investment, regression results on this dimension are presented in table 8.7. It can be seen that levels of intra-EU direct investment in the early 1980s are strongly correlated with currency stability between 1979 and 1990. Results are similar for direct investment to and from the DM zone, although they do not quite reach conventional levels of statistical significance (and there are very few observations).[30] With all the warnings already expressed about the data on FDI, and the unavailability of information on the independent variable before the currency arrangements (because of the absence of FDI data from before 1973), these results should be regarded with wariness. Nonetheless, they do tend to confirm my argument about the impact of intraregional investment on the incentives to fix regional currency values.

These data appear to support the contention that higher levels of economic integration have increased political pressures for exchange rate stability within the EU.[31] The growing ranks of integrated and export-oriented EU producers saw continued currency unpredictability as a major cost to them. As policy makers faced an ever starker choice between giving up monetary independence to maintain a fixed exchange rate, on the one hand, and floating away from the EMS, on the other, the rising importance of intra-EU trade, finance, and investment helped tip them toward the EMS.

The relative success of European monetary integration in the 1980s, then, was attributable to several factors. I have emphasized how increased economic integration increased the immediacy of resolving the conflict between national monetary policy autonomy and currency stability, even as it increased the support for a resolution that would stabilize exchange rates. It is also the case that member states invested far more money in the EMS than they had in the snake, and these funds were a significant incentive to governments for whom the EMS commitment implied difficult domestic economic-policy decisions. Finally, the linkage between MI and EU integration more generally increased the overall level of support for MI, by gaining the political support of groups that had been hostile or indifferent to MI until it became clear that monetary and broader economic union were practically indivisible.

IMPLICATIONS FOR THE FUTURE OF EUROPEAN MONETARY INTEGRATION

My assertion that the liberalization of international economic activities has systematic effects on pressures for monetary union, both over time and across countries, has clear implications for the future of MI in Europe. As is well known, even as plans for forward movement toward a full currency union gathered speed in 1992, a major currency crisis called even the less ambitious EMS into question.

Changes in the level of economic integration over time cannot explain the 1992–1993 crisis of the EMS. The members of the ERM were certainly more integrated in 1992 than they had been a decade earlier, yet the system did not hold together. Other factors, widely commented on in the literature, were undoubtedly central to the crisis.[32] Problems began with German unification, which led the Bundesbank to fear inflation and raise interest rates. The resultant European recession put EMS member governments under substantial political pressure to pursue more expansionary monetary policies. The only ways to do so were either to leave the ERM or to convince the Bundesbank to loosen its monetary policy. The Bundesbank would not budge, which left national governments with the difficult choice of either following Germany into even more recessionary policies or breaking the link to the ERM.

This development threw the crisis back into the realm of domestic politics. A rise in British interest rates to defend sterling, for example, would have been passed on by mortgage lenders, and many within the ruling Conservative Party worried about the objections of property owners. For its part, the Italian government might have enacted drastic fiscal measures to make its commitment to lower inflation more credible, but in the midst of a deep political crisis this was difficult to achieve over the objections of public employees and others who feared that their positions would be threatened. The German authorities might have loosened monetary policy but for the Bundesbank's traditional concern about inflation, which was reinforced by strong anti-inflationary constituencies in the German body politic.

The problems were exacerbated by growing political conflict over European integration as a whole. In the aftermath of the June 1992 failure of the first Danish referendum on the Maastricht Treaty, and with the results of the September 1992 French referendum in doubt, serious questions were raised about the future of the Maastricht process. The prospect of "de-linking" MI from European integration more generally—which was eventually realized—served to weaken the credibility of EMS members' commitments to the system.

In any event, in September 1992 the British and Italian governments took their currencies out of the ERM and allowed them to float. In subsequent months, the currencies of Spain, Portugal, and Ireland were devalued, although they remained in the mechanism. In summer 1993, with the system again under attack on currency markets, remaining ERM members agreed to widen fluctuation bands to 15 percent (the Dutch guilder remained in a 2.25 percent band). While the reduced ERM has been stable, questions persist about the future of monetary integration.

Although the causes of the 1992–1993 crisis were only partly related to the theme of this essay, three observations can be made. The first is that the economic objections to MI in Europe were amply borne out by the crisis. German unification subjected Europe to an economic shock, and this shock was asymmetric—it affected Germany but almost no other country. Germany's subsequent attempt to counteract expansionary fiscal measures with tight money only proved that a monetary policy appropriate for Germany could be inappropriate for its EMS partners. This indicates the truth of the assertions, reported above, that the EU is far from being an optimal currency area.

Second, the higher levels of financial integration obtaining in the Europe of 1992 clearly did, as anticipated above, heighten the conflict between monetary independence and exchange rate stability. Germany's EMS partners found themselves with the starkest of choices: either follow Germany's very restrictive monetary policy into recession or leave the ERM and allow their currencies to depreciate.

Third, given this stark choice, the responses to the crisis were roughly in line with the cross-national expectations indicated above. The EMS members most fully integrated into EU trade and payments—France, Belgium, the Netherlands, and Luxembourg—held fast. Those at the lower end of trade and investment integration—the United Kingdom and Italy—dropped out. Spain, Portugal, and Ireland, with relatively high levels of integration, were forced to devalue (under tremendous economic pressure) but made major efforts to stay in the ERM at their new parities. Denmark is something of an anomaly, as it is relatively less integrated than the other northern European EMS members but was able to avoid a devaluation; Danish ambivalence about the EU presumably expressed itself in other ways. In any case, and in a rough manner, the crisis appears to bear out most of my expectations: the level of sacrifice undertaken to sustain the fixed exchange rate was roughly proportional to the level of economic integration with the rest of the EU, and especially the deutsche mark zone.

In any event, given my analytical framework and the experience of twenty-five years of European MI, we can ask what the future of European monetary politics is likely to bring. EMU is unlikely to be implemented as originally designed at Maastricht. My analysis leads, however, to a series of predictions that imply that some form of monetary integration is likely to proceed.

The general level of intra-European trade and investment is very high and growing. Indeed, the completion of the single market will only spur economic integration within the EU. I thus believe that the general pressures for MI within the EU will continue to increase over time. If the link I posit between economic integration on the one hand and broad economic and domestic political pressure for MI on the other is present, we should see a continuation—in fact, an increase—in interest in MI.

There is no doubt, however, that interest in monetary integration varies across countries. Those most tied to the EU—and especially to its economic and financial anchor, Germany—should be most enthusiastic about moving forward with plans for monetary union. As indicated above, if interest in MI varies with level of general economic integration with the EU, France, Germany, and Benelux should be its strongest supporters; Denmark, Ireland, Spain, and Portugal should be less enthusiastic but still favorable; and Italy, Greece, and the United Kingdom should be least favorable of all. It is interesting to note that new EU member Austria is undoubtedly in the first group, while new members Sweden and Finland are closer to the second. Thus any future MI is almost certain to include Austria, and likely to include Sweden and Finland.

This implies that a "two-tier" EMU process is likely to ensue. Those countries that are most closely integrated on current and capital account are likely to proceed toward monetary union. Those that are least integrated are likely to remain behind. This leaves, of course, great room for variation and discretion. The southern European countries may decide to undertake the massive sacrifices necessary to ensure that they are not left out of MI efforts; Germany itself may shy away from further monetary union. What I expect is a tendency in this direction; specifics will be determined by a combination of domestic political developments within EU members and strategic interaction among them.

Previous liberalization of intra-European trade, finance, and investment has been crucial to the course of European monetary integration. I expect this effect to persist, and to be important for the future in two ways. First, the high and growing level of goods and capital movements within the union will increase the likelihood of *some* sort of monetary union. Second, variations in national reliance on EU markets and investments will affect national political debates over monetary union. In these ways, past decisions on economic liberalization will have a strong impact on policy toward monetary union in the European Union.

Notes

The author acknowledges support for this research from the Social Science Research Council's Program in Foreign Policy Studies, the German Marshall Fund, the UCLA Institute for Industrial Relations, and the UCLA Center for International Business Education and Research. He also acknowledges research assistance from Roland Stephen and comments from Barry Eichengreen, John Goodman, Miles Kahler, Peter Lange, and other participants in the Social Science Research Council Liberalization and Foreign Policy project. A substantially different version of this essay appeared in *Comparative Political Studies*.

1. Throughout this essay, I refer to the organization that has variously been known as the European Economic Community, the European Communities, and the European Union with this last (currently preferred) name. This designation may be somewhat misleading at times, especially in reference to historical developments, but it has the attraction of consistency.

2. There are, of course, other potential explanations for the course of monetary integration. For a general survey, see Barry Eichengreen and Jeffry Frieden, "The Political Economy of European Monetary Integration: An Analytical Introduction," *Economics and Politics* 5, no. 2 (July 1993), as well as the other articles in this special issue of *Economics and Politics* dedicated to the topic.

3. For a more detailed discussion of these issues, see Jeffry A. Frieden, "Invested Interests: The Politics of National Economic Policies in a World of Global Finance," *International Organization* 45, no. 4 (Autumn 1991).

4. To be precise, it is covered (exchange rate–adjusted) interest rates that are constrained to be equal. The insight is that of the famous Mundell-Fleming approach, which originated with Robert A. Mundell, "The Appropriate Use of Monetary and Fiscal Policy Under Fixed Exchange Rates," *IMF Staff Papers* 9 (March 1962): 70–77; see

also his "Capital Mobility and Stabilization Policy Under Fixed and Flexible Exchange Rates," *Canadian Journal of Economics and Political Science* 29, no. 4 (November 1963): 475–485. The basic model can be found in any good textbook discussion of open-economy macroeconomics; a useful survey is W. M. Corden, *Inflation, Exchange Rates, and the World Economy*, 3d ed. (Chicago: University of Chicago Press, 1986).

5. This is a bit oversimplified and assumes that exchange rate stability is desirable in and of itself. There is no question, however, that the trade-off between exchange rate stability and monetary autonomy, absent or weak in a financially closed economy, grows in importance as the economy becomes more financially open.

6. The approach is set forth in Robert Mundell, "A Theory of Optimum Currency Areas," *American Economic Review* 51 (1961): 657–665; and Ronald McKinnon, "Optimum Currency Areas," *American Economic Review* 53 (1963): 717–725.

7. Of course, economic integration and currency union can interact: having one currency makes it easier for factors to move within a region. On such interactive effects in international monetary relations, see Jeffry Frieden, "The Dynamics of International Monetary Systems: International and Domestic Factors in the Rise, Reign, and Demise of the Classical Gold Standard," in Robert Jervis and Jack Snyder, eds., *Coping with Complexity in the International System* (Boulder: Westview Press, 1993).

8. Barry Eichengreen, "One Money for Europe?" *Economic Policy* (April 1990): 118–87.

9. Since the middle 1980s capital controls have been removed, and the EC has become more integrated financially. This, however, does not explain the course of the EMS *before* financial integration.

10. Again, the nuances are important. Most developing countries are quite trade-open, but exporters typically do not favor a fixed exchange rate. This is normally because the exports in question are either commodities or standardized manufactured products, for which price competitiveness is paramount. The ability to maintain or restore competitiveness by way of devaluation, in these circumstances, tends to outweigh whatever advantage exchange rate predictability may hold. In the EC, however, almost all exports are of specialized manufactured products.

11. On early monetary plans and developments, see Loukas Tsoukalis, *The Politics and Economics of European Monetary Integration* (London: George Allen and Unwin, 1977), esp. pp. 51–111; and Jacques van Ypersele, *The European Monetary System: Origins, Operation, and Outlook* (Brussels: Commission of the European Communities, 1985), pp. 31–45.

12. Tsoukalis, *Politics and Economics*, pp. 112–168; Peter Ludlow, *The Making of the European Monetary System* (London: Butterworth, 1982), pp. 1–36; Peter Coffey, *The European Monetary System—Past, Present, and Future* (Amsterdam: Kluwer, 1987), pp. 6–16. A useful chronology of the "snake" is found on pp. 123–125 of Coffey's book.

13. On this period, see Antonio Fazio, "La political monetaria in Italia dal 1947 al 1978," *Moneta e Credito* (September 1979): 269–319; Cesare Caranza and Antonio Fazio, "L'evoluzione dei metodi di controllo monetario in Italia, 1974–1983," *Bancaria* (September 1983): 819–833. A summary in English is in *Why Economic Policies Change Course* (Paris: OECD, 1988), pp. 74–82; a more analytical survey is Paolo Guerrieri and Pier Carlo Padoan, "Two-Level Games and Structural Adjustment: The Italian Case," *International Spectator* 24, nos. 3–4 (July–December 1989): 128–140.

14. Two good surveys are Gilles Oudiz and Henri Sterdyniak, "Inflation, Employment, and External Constraints: An Overview of the French Economy During the Seventies," in Jacques Melitz and Charles Wyplosz, eds., *The French Economy: Theory and*

Policy (Boulder: Westview Press, 1985), pp. 9–50; and Volkmar Lauber, *The Political Economy of France: From Pompidou to Mitterrand* (New York: Praeger, 1983), pp. 81–158. See also D. Besnard and M. Redon, *La monnaie: Politique et institutions* (Paris: Dunod, 1985), pp. 178–198.

15. This is at least what Oudiz and Sterdyniak argue ("Inflation, Employment, and External Constraints," pp. 32–35).

16. Ludlow is especially detailed on the negotiations and early operation of the EMS; see also Ypersele, *The European Monetary System,* pp. 71–95; and Horst Ungerer, *The European Monetary System: The Experience, 1979–82,* IMF Occasional Paper 19 (Washington, D.C.: IMF, 1983). Excellent surveys of the EMS experience more generally are Francesco Giavazzi and Alberto Giovannini, *Limiting Exchange Rate Flexibility: The European Monetary System* (Cambridge: MIT Press, 1989); Michele Fratianni and Jurgen von Hagen, *The European Monetary System and European Monetary Union* (Boulder: Westview Press, 1991); and John Goodman, *Monetary Sovereignty: The Politics of Central Banking in Western Europe* (Ithaca: Cornell University Press, 1992).

17. Relative parity changes calculated from *Policy Coordination in the European Monetary System,* IMF Occasional Paper 61 (Washington, D.C.: IMF, 1988), p. 19; information on exchange rate variability is provided on pp. 20–34.

18. See especially Jeffrey Sachs and Charles Wyplosz, "The Economic Consequences of President Mitterrand," *Economic Policy* 2 (April 1986): 262–322; David Cameron, "The Franc, the EMS, *Rigueur,* and 'l'Autre Politique'": The Regime-Defining Choices of the Mitterrand Presidency," (mimeographed, New Haven, 1992); Pierre Favier and Michel Martin-Roland, *La décennie Mitterrand 1. Les ruptures, 1981–1984* (Paris: Seuil, 1990); Philippe Bauchard, *La guerre des deux roses: Du rêve à la réalité, 1981–1985* (Paris: Bernard Grasset, 1986); and Serge July, *Les années Mitterrand* (Paris: Bernard Grasset, 1986).

19. On which, two analyses are Wayne Sandholtz and John Zysman, "1992: Recasting the European Bargain," *World Politics* 42 (October 1989); and Andrew Moravcsik, "Negotiating the Single Act: National Interests and Conventional Statecraft in the European Community," *International Organization* 45 (Winter 1991).

20. On the connection, see Kathleen McNamara, "Common Markets, Uncommon Currencies: Systems Effects and the European Community," in Robert Jervis and Jack Snyder, eds., *Coping with Complexity in the International System* (Boulder: Westview Press, 1993).

21. Ypersele, *The European Monetary System,* pp. 61–64. The subsidy component of the concessional loans was a billion ECU.

22. For one among many possible interpretations of this trend, see Louka Katseli, "The Political Economy of European Integration: From Euro-Sclerosis to Euro-Pessimism," *International Spectator* 24, no. 3/4 (July–December 1989): 186–195.

23. See, for example, Geoffrey Garrett, "The Politics of the Maastricht Treaty," and Lisa Martin, "International and Domestic Institutions in the EMU Process," both in *Economics and Politics* 5, no. 2 (July 1993).

24. Jeffrey Frankel, Steven Phillips, and Menzie Chinn, "Financial and Currency Integration in the European Monetary System: The Statistical Record," in Francisco Torres and Francesco Giavazzi, eds., *Adjustment and Growth in the European Monetary Union* (Cambridge: Cambridge University Press, 1993), pp. 270–306.

25. Long-term flows include FDI, bonds, and equities. Calculated from Philip Turner, *Capital Flows in the 1980s: A Survey of Major Trends,* BIS Economic Papers, no. 30 (Basle: BIS, 1991), pp. 42–75.

26. Denmark, for example, has important nonmanufactured exports to the EC. And its willingness to link to the DM is related, as mentioned above, to its close ties to the other Nordic countries, all of which in one way or another have also indicated a desire to link their currencies to the DM. Italy, of course, has faced severe domestic difficulties in reducing inflation to German levels. Perhaps more important from the standpoint of this essay, its trade ties with the DM zone have grown more slowly than those of any EC member outside the zone, and its intra-EC FDI (as shown below) remains relatively small.

27. It might be objected that the 1979–1982 trade data are from the first years of the EMS and it is thus wrong to treat them as exogenously determined. This course was taken, however, because earlier trade data would have been during the snake and thus conceivably determined by *it*. It might also be pointed out that currencies varied a great deal during the first few years of the EMS. In any case, when the regression is recalculated using 1976–1978 trade data as the explanatory variable, the results are essentially identical to those reported. In this context it is especially important to point out how strong the impact of 1970–1973 trade patterns is on subsequent currency policies (see below). This is a powerful argument *against* the endogeneity of trade patterns.

28. The removal of Spain, Portugal, and Greece, which were not EC members in the 1970s and which are outliers on both dimensions in both periods, does not affect the results. If intra-EC (rather than DM zone) trade is used, the coefficients are predictably smaller and significance levels somewhat lower, but the results remain strong and statistically significant.

29. It might be argued that early 1970s trade patterns were themselves a result of pre-1970 differences in currency variations. This is empirically incorrect. There were few currency movements between 1960 and 1969—it was the heyday of the Bretton Woods system—and those that there were ran largely in the *opposite* direction of explaining early 1970s trade. For example, in the 1960s the currencies of Italy, Greece, and Portugal varied *less* against the DM than did those of all other EC currencies except the Dutch florin.

30. Omitting observations for Greece and Ireland, for which data are incomplete, does not affect the results. Attempts to use both intra-EC trade and FDI as explanatory variables in a multivariate regression are complicated by the fact that the two are very strongly collinear. For example, when 1979–1982 DM zone trade is regressed on early 1980s DM zone FDI for the countries for which data are available, the resulting coefficients are large, the r squared is 0.744, and the t-statistic is 3.82. In the absence of more detailed statistical sources, more complex multivariate regressions are impossible.

31. This conclusion is complementary to one finding of Russell Dalton and Richard Eichenberg in "Europeans and the European Community: The Dynamics of Public Support for European Integration," *International Organization* 47 (1993). They show that differences in national public support of European integration are very closely related to the country's level of intra-EC trade. Indeed, this is found to be the most important economic factor in their model: the inflation rate has a strong negative effect, but when the two are comparably scaled, intra-EC trade is far more powerful.

32. For an excellent survey, see Barry Eichengreen and Charles Wyplosz, "The Unstable EMS," *Brookings Papers on Economic Activity* 1 (1993).

NINE

Financial Liberalization and Regional Monetary Cooperation:

The Mexican Case

Sylvia Maxfield

Economic liberalization can be self-reinforcing and/or destabilizing. Few cases highlight this more clearly than the case of Mexican finance, where, in the space of a few years, problems related to Mexico's international capital account led to both populist backlash and rapid liberalization. In 1982 the country's banks were nationalized and foreign currency exchange was severely circumscribed. By 1985 the country was pursuing financial sector liberalization faster than the World Bank thought wise. By 1992 the commitment to financial liberalism had become linked to plans for "binding" institutional change: greater central bank independence and possibly formal bilateral or multilateral monetary policy coordination.

This essay looks at one instance of Mexican financial liberalization: commitment to a more market-guided foreign exchange policy in 1991. With the benefit of hindsight one can see that this shift from a fixed rate to a band did not prevent dramatic and sudden devaluation in 1994. But in the aftermath of that crisis, Mexico is once again moving away from a fixed government-set rate toward a market-driven band. The following discussion explores how and why the shift from a fixed to a more flexible exchange rate regime might be related to the likelihood of Mexican commitment to institutionalize North American monetary cooperation. It is a speculative exercise designed to complement this volume's overall focus on the connection between liberalization and foreign policy.

Plausible explanations of the causal logic behind stabilizing or destabilizing liberalization in this case could center on the impact of internationalization on sectoral interests and policy preferences, or on government concerns with enhancing credibility, independent of sectoral interests. The central analytical point of this essay is that the dichotomy frequently associated with these two types of explanations is false. The credibility imperative is cited to explain many recent Mexican economic policy initiatives ranging from the Economic Solidarity Pact to the North American Free Trade Agreement.[1] It is, however, difficult—if not impossible—to understand when and why credibility becomes a priority without understanding the actual and historical impact of the "structural power of capital."[2] In concrete terms, analysis of the structural power of capital leads us to observe the preferences and actions of groups of entrepreneurs or wealthy individuals. The larger the percentage of entrepreneurs or wealthy individuals with global investment options, the greater the likelihood that a poor policy environment will contribute to a lack of national credit and investment. The more global investment options, the greater entrepreneurial demand for credible national policies that preserve the ability to operate globally. The greater the international competition for capital among different national governments, the more important government credibility is. Purveyors of investment or credit will require especially strong credibility-enhancing efforts of any government with a history of broken policy promises.

Although many strictly political factors, such as the nature of the rules of electoral competition, shape the weight and extent of a government credibility deficit, the economically driven aspects of credibility constitute a necessary part of the explanation. In the Mexican case surveyed here, growing economic integration put the issue of credibility on the agenda. Integration increased the potential costs of a credibility deficit and the potential benefits of a credibility surplus. The more globally integrated the Mexican economy, the greater the loss of potential investment or credit correspondent to low credibility, and vice versa. In Mexico, a history of liberal policy regarding currency convertibility in combination with cycles of inflation and currency overvaluation had created distrust of government commitment to a fixed exchange rate. A desire to solve this credibility problem shaped the Mexicans' choice of a more flexible foreign exchange regime, which some hoped would eventually be backed by a bilateral or multilateral agreement on monetary and exchange rate policy.

Loosening the reins of government control over the level of the peso-dollar exchange rate has increased the credibility of the Mexican government's commitment to liberalization and monetary stability, as was explicitly intended. But proponents of this policy are keenly aware that both increased central bank independence and formal bilateral or multilateral monetary policy agreement would provide key signals of the likelihood of Mexican politicians' future behavior when confronted with conflict between short-term political interests and policy commitment.

This analysis of financial liberalization and foreign monetary policy in Mexico suggests that, to the extent that financial liberalization increases international integration, liberalization is likely to lead to monetary cooperation in the medium to long term. This is because of integration's impact on the size and preferences of the group of entrepreneurs/wealthy individuals with international investment options, and on this group's ability to shape the priority that government actors assign to credibility enhancement. Economic integration increases capital's exit options. To the extent that nations and their political leaders need credit and investment, integration increases politicians' vulnerability to the perceptions of credibility deficit held by purveyors of credit and investment. The greater capital's exit options, the more important the credibility of government commitment to policies intended to create a felicitous national environment for capital. Commitment to foreign monetary policy can be credibility-enhancing. Thus financial liberalization is likely to contribute to a stable cooperative pattern in foreign monetary policy by leading politicians to prioritize the credibility of government commitments to policies desired by internationally mobile capital.

Although this logic is motivated by the impact of changing international opportunities on the preferences of capitalists and on their power to influence politicians, institutional change, whether in domestic institutions or in a country's participation in international arrangements, is a component of stabilizing liberalization in several ways. It is a powerful signal of politicians' independent commitment to credibility-building as well as an indication of future constraints on possibly less-self-disciplined politicians. It is also clear that domestic institutional change and international commitment are mutually reinforcing; each lends force to the other, with causal influence running in both directions simultaneously.

ORIGINS OF A CREDIBILITY PROBLEM: FREE CONVERTIBILITY AND FIXED EXCHANGE RATES

Mexico has had a long-standing commitment to free exchange convertibility combined with a unilateral dollar peg of the exchange rate. This historical commitment to international financial liberalism in the sense of freedom to convert currency has not been matched, until recently, in other areas of international financial transaction.[3] The combination of free convertibility and a unilateral, but unsustainable, peg and other restrictions on capital mobility has created cycles of external shocks and domestic policy errors leading to creeping peso appreciation, speculative attack on the currency, recession-inducing devaluation, and occasionally a nationalistic policy backlash such as occurred at the end of the Cárdenas, Echeverría, and López Portillo administrations.[4] Commitment to a fixed exchange rate itself is a function of the nationalistic symbolism popularly imbued in the dollar-purchasing power of the peso.

This history of exchange instability contributed significantly to the credibility problem that is an important part of the context of further liberalization moves in the 1990s. Dollarization, use of the U.S. dollar rather than the peso for the major purposes usually served by money, and destabilizing capital flows have been a constant threat to the Mexican financial system at least since the beginning of the Mexican revolution in 1910. In the aftermath of political and economic upheaval, the exchange rate did not stabilize until the 1930s. After two years of floating peso exchange rates, in 1933 Mexican president Cárdenas fixed the peso's value at 3.6 to the dollar, where it remained until a speculative crisis in the wake of the Mexican government's 1938 nationalization of the oil industry forced a devaluation.[5] At that time Cárdenas considered and rejected the option of exchange controls, on the grounds that they would be impossible to implement, given the long U.S.-Mexican border, and that the governments' administrative capacity was too limited. After a short period of managed floating, the peso was returned to a fixed exchange regime, disrupted only by speculation-forced devaluations in 1949 and 1953.

In 1955 Mexico entered an exceptional period of exchange rate stability; the peso remained at the same fixed rate, 12.5 to the dollar, until 1976. Some observers believe the peso had become unsustainably overvalued by as early as the late 1960s. In any case, inflation accelerated extremely rapidly in Mexico during the early and mid-

1970s, with rates far above those in the United States. Although Mexican president Echeverría had sworn he would "defend the peso like a dog," the accumulated overvaluation led to speculation and capital flight, finally forcing devaluation in 1976.

After this adjustment, the Mexican government returned again to a fixed exchange rate regime.[6] Discovery and pumping of vast oil reserves in Mexico, combined with excess liquidity in the international banking system, led to a huge inflow of foreign exchange. This foreign exchange bonanza put upward pressure on the peso again, leading to an even more severe speculative attack and massive capital flight in 1982. Speculation intensified after the central bank withdrew from the exchange markets and allowed the peso to float freely in February 1982. In August 1982 the government announced a dual exchange rate system composed of a free market rate and a preferential, central bank–managed rate for specified priority imports.

This cycle of overvaluation fueled by inflows of foreign exchange from borrowing and oil exports, speculation against the peso, capital flight, and devaluation culminated in September 1982 in the sudden nationalization of domestic banks and imposition of exchange controls for the first time in postrevolutionary Mexican history. The free market exchange rate was eliminated as part of the implementation of comprehensive exchange controls. The government restricted transfer of funds outside of Mexico, even tightly limiting the amount of foreign exchange that could be acquired for international travel. Proceeds from exports had to be repatriated and sold immediately to the banks, while dollars for imports were rationed.[7]

The September 1 financial policy backlash reflected the temporary hegemony of heterodox economists in government and their constituency of labor and small-to-medium-size industrialists over neoliberal economists and their constituency of large-scale capitalists. The conflict between these two coalitions was termed "the fight for the nation" (*la disputa por la nacion*) by Carlos Tello, architect of the bank nationalization.[8] This long-standing dispute in Mexican politics had been heightened by the boom in international financial markets and its differential impact within Mexico in the late 1970s. Benefits of the boom flowed disproportionately to large-scale Mexican entrepreneurs. The international integration of Mexican financial markets created new opportunities for large-scale capitalists and fueled financial speculation. This in turn provided a material basis for popular-sector resentment of the bankers' windfall and for the belief of "left-wing" government economists that liberal capital regulation was undermining the state's capacity to induce and guide capital formation in the name of equitable growth. These economists argued that bank nationalization would allow the government to regain lost control over the national financial system and harness the financial sector to the goal of economic restructuring. Furthermore, easy access to foreign loans during the debt boom of the 1970s and early 1980s undermined the leverage of the Mexican finance ministry and central bank to oppose proponents of bank nationalization.

International funds dried up with Mexico's dramatic policy shift, and in a new atmosphere of international capital scarcity, purveyors of foreign exchange found themselves once again able to guide financial policy generally. Exchange controls began to be removed in December 1982, and plans for bank reprivatization were made. A new three-tier exchange rate system was introduced, composed of a preferential rate, a less preferential "controlled" rate, and a free rate. In the following years the preferential rate and the controlled rate were collapsed into a single rate. In 1986 the Mexican government began to try to bring the controlled and free rates into closer alignment by minimizing official support for the controlled rate. In 1987 the government moved back to a fixed rate system; after a large devaluation, the peso-dollar exchange rate was fixed for almost a year. Between 1989 and 1991 there was a single exchange rate subject to a minimal, pre-announced, and constant daily devaluation vis-à-vis the dollar.

In the context of a fixed rate system with free convertibility it is not surprising that an externally vulnerable economy and a political mythology that made devaluation virtually taboo left Mexico vulnerable to speculative attacks on the peso. Speculation about devaluation was also entirely reasonable given long-run trends in the real value of the peso. McLeod and Welch show that when the real peso value appreciated, it tended historically to return to the mean level within three to four years.[9] The message that peso appreciation sent to investors was to expect partial reversal within several years. Despite Mexico's comparatively liberal policy on exchange convertibility, exchange rate instability and the nationalistic policy backlashes that it sometimes engendered limited the hope for economic liberalization and, with it, long-term fixed investment in Mexico both by nationals and foreigners.

The Mexican central bank, the Banco de Mexico, finally broke with the directly government-controlled exchange rate regime in late

1991. Although it was denied publicly, in 1991 U.S. and Mexican central bank officials began probing the possibility of a monetary agreement involving a bilaterally negotiated currency band, or target zone, within which the peso's value would be set by exchange market conditions. At its outer limits the band would be backed by currency swap or reserve-sharing agreements and occasional summits like those among the G-7 countries between the nation's central banks.[10] When support for this idea seemed to wane within the U.S. Federal Reserve system, discussion took place within the Mexican central bank over the idea of linking Mexican concessions on opening the financial sector in free trade negotiations to achievement of a multilateral exchange rate agreement including emergency credits for maintaining parity.[11] But in November 1991, the Banco de Mexico unilaterally liberalized control of exchange rate movements, allowing the market to price the peso within a target zone. The change in policy was discussed publicly only beginning in April 1992, when the band was further widened.

This liberalization of exchange rate policy has provided for the growth of a futures exchange market, a development that has reduced the destabilizing impact of capital flows on the exchange rate and thereby reduced the likelihood of nationalistic backlashes against international liberalization and integration.[12] Mexican central bank officials remain interested in the idea of a formal international monetary agreement to back the target zone.

The history of exchange instability and its detrimental impact on investment and growth, related to Mexico's historical commitment to one aspect of international financial openness—free exchange convertibility—is an important part of the general context in which this further exchange policy liberalization and monetary cooperation initiative occurred. Yet many questions remain. What explains the particular timing of this decision? Why was instability addressed with a unilateral commitment to a target zone rather than with controls on convertibility?

ECONOMIC INTEGRATION AND THE TIMING OF POLICY CHANGE

Negotiation of the North American Free Trade Agreement led naturally to some comparison with the Single Europe Act and the

Maastricht Treaty.[13] At a fall 1991 meeting, "Policy Implications of Trade and Currency Zones," sponsored by the Federal Reserve Bank of Kansas City, Mexican central bank director Miguel Mancera was forceful in denying any similarity between North American and European integration and in negating the possibility of a move toward monetary coordination between the United States and Mexico. "I would say [the same]," responded former U.S. Federal Reserve Bank board chairman Paul Volcker, another participant in the meeting. "It may be politically suicidal and economically premature to say anything else. But I also have a feeling," continued Volcker unabashed, "that they doth protest too much."[14]

Those arguing against the parallels between the European and North American situations and against the likelihood of U.S.-Mexican monetary coordination stressed the political motive behind European monetary coordination, arguing that no such political rationale exists in the North American case.[15] Nevertheless, there is an economic argument for European monetary coordination that is potentially valid in the U.S.-Mexican case also. Support for monetary coordination within the context of European integration did not develop until the late 1960s, after the initial stage of the trade union was under way. By the end of 1969, however, two years of monetary crises and the consequent exchange rate instability had made it clear to leading European officials that lack of monetary coordination and the resulting potential for exchange rate instability posed a threat to the customs union.[16]

The overarching purpose behind the North American Free Trade Agreement was to increase capital inflows into Mexico.[17] Exchange instability could threaten both the agreement and the capital inflows that it was meant to induce.[18] During NAFTA negotiations, despite the threat to exchange rate stability, the Mexican government kept the peso slide slow in order to help stabilize inflation and raise foreign purchasing power to facilitate import of inputs necessary for expansion of nontraditional exports. There were several dangers in this situation. The current account deficit resulting from exchange rate–facilitated foreign purchasing threatened to become unsustainable. The peso's real appreciation also posed a menace to Mexican export competitiveness. The administration of President Salinas hoped that the growth and productivity boost expected from the U.S.-Mexican trade agreement would allow the Mexican economy to catch up with its overvalued exchange rate before the threat of speculation against the peso rose. Another danger stemmed from the potential animus to the Free Trade Agreement that a sudden devaluation, making Mexican exports more competitive, could create in the United States.

The U.S. Federal Reserve was sufficiently convinced of the importance of monetary aspects of North American economic integration that it increased the dedication of its research personnel to Mexico-watching, and in particular to consideration of Mexican exchange rate policy. Federal Reserve economists advocated change in the Mexican exchange rate regime to protect the promise of U.S.-Mexican trade and Mexican growth in general. Congressional representatives in the United States also began to call for a fourth supplemental agreement to the North American Free Trade Agreement, one that provided for exchange rate stability.[19]

The Mexican central bank sent a study mission to Europe to gather information on European exchange policies and monetary integration. The goal was to formulate a report, based on European experiences, about the likely impact on Mexico of possible regional monetary integration. After carefully studying the Spanish case in particular, Mexican central bankers came to believe that a bilateral target zone might create conditions for another long period of monetary and exchange rate stability like that of the "stabilizing development" years from 1955 to 1970.

As a first step, the Banco de Mexico, with presidential approval, decided to go ahead with a unilateral target zone beginning in November 1991. The Banco de Mexico decreased the rate of pre-announced crawling devaluation for the purchase price of pesos and stipulated a freeze in the sale price. This widened the "bid-ask" spread in the interbank peso market. The strong positive market reaction to this move, evident in a nominal appreciation within the target zone, encouraged the Banco de Mexico to widen the band even further in March 1992. As part of the renegotiation of the tripartite wage and price agreement in November 1992 the band was further widened.[20]

CREDIBILITY, INSTITUTIONS, AND POLICY CHOICE

Destabilizing pressures on the exchange rate can be dealt with in a variety of ways. In fact, just as Federal Reserve and Banco de Mexico economists argued the merits of a target zone, other noted international economists argued against it.[21] The palatability of a multilaterally backed target zone had to do with Mexican government politicians' concerns about increasing the credibility of their commitment to policies designed to create a profitable investment environment. History had created a credibility problem, but its growing importance corresponded to rising competition for national credit and investment stemming from economic integration. The multilaterally backed target zone was attractive to policy makers both because it was desirable to purveyors of foreign exchange and capital in the short run and because of its longer-run credibility-enhancing effects.

Frieden argues that capitalists in developing (capital-scarce) countries will oppose policies that involve increased capital mobility because it will increase domestically available capital and lower the return to capital. Why, then, would Mexican bankers and large-scale industrialists historically have opposed exchange controls and currently support a multilaterally backed target zone?[22] Why also would bankers and large-scale industrialists support a policy that will generate a futures market, dampen the impact of actual or threatened capital flight, and thereby weaken their ability to influence policy?

The answer lies in the incentives created by growing integration. The ability to profit from relatively long-term business investments designed to exploit regional integration is limited by the need to preserve the capital flight option. For those contemplating investment in sectors that are positively affected by the rise in regional integration, such as auto parts, chemical products, petrochemicals, and glass, regional integration is raising the opportunity costs associated with keeping capital liquid. The greater these opportunity costs, the greater the extent to which threatened capital flight becomes a second-best strategy for dealing with an uncertain policy environment.

The target zone makes exchange-rate-related medium-to-long-term investment risks more directly a function of market conditions rather than capricious government action. It facilitates development of a peso futures market through which regionally operating businesses can cover their exchange risk. There is further incentive for business to support not only a more market-guided exchange rate policy but also a bilateral or multilateral agreement to back it. Such an agreement would presumably reduce the need for the disciplining use of capital flight. The target zone solution to exchange instability is attractive to government politicians for the potential impact it could have on the credibility of government policy commitments in the eyes of creditors and investors with international operations and options.

In the Mexican case, exchange rate history had created a credibility problem that constrained Mexican growth. International commitment and change in the central bank charter are part of an effort to make institutional changes in response to the constraint represented by low credibility.[23] The hope is that these institutions will then themselves become part of a new constraint that would increase credibility by signaling the government's willingness to make political sacrifices in the name of policy commitment. There is a further desire to facilitate a mutually reinforcing dynamic between international monetary and exchange rate commitment and increased central bank independence.[24]

Under a floating exchange rate regime, a central bank theoretically has complete freedom in the monetary policy area; for example, there is no balance of payments or exchange rate constraint on central bank financing of government deficits. Under a fixed exchange rate regime with capital controls, a central bank also has considerable freedom in the conduct of monetary policy. But in a fixed or close to fixed system with no exchange controls, inflationary policies result in capital outflows and threaten the exchange rate. Depending on the flexibility in international exchange rate commitments, capital account convertibility can impose greater discipline on both monetary and fiscal policy.[25] In other words, if internationally committed on exchange rates, capital mobility reduces government freedom in the conduct of monetary and, to some extent, fiscal policy.[26] Government policies of raising revenue through seignorage or other forms of inflation tax lose viability, and this increases pressure to limit government spending.[27]

A bilaterally or multilaterally negotiated exchange rate system would tie the hands of the central bank in the conduct of monetary policy and also impose constraints on government fiscal policy. It could increase the credibility of a government's commitment to stability-oriented macroeconomic policy. In more technical terms, it could help solve the classic time-inconsistency problem involved in discretionary conduct of monetary policy.[28]

Mexican central bankers are interested in moving beyond the unilateral target zone to a bilateral or multilateral target zone agreement precisely because a unilaterally decided-upon target zone or peg does not have the full credibility-enhancing effects of a bilateral or multi-lateral agreement. In the case of a unilateral peg, adjustment to eco-nomic shocks would have to be borne by the pegging country alone. As an analyst of East European monetary problems points out, some asymmetry is necessary in order to achieve the disciplining effect of fixed or near-fixed exchange rate regimes, but multilateral schemes usually provide for some burden sharing in the case of short-term shocks.[29] One-sided exchange rate commitments are more likely to provoke speculative attacks. Second, multilateral agreements require the consent of all parties for exchange rate adjustment, making the target more credible than in the case of unilateral pegging.

The credibility-enhancing motive for international financial liber-alization and cooperation is especially strong in low-income coun-tries, which can least afford the expected output losses associated with stabilization. The more credible the government's anti-inflation policy, the less resistance from potential private-sector investors, both domestic and international. In other words, the more credible the government's macroeconomic policy, the shorter the time those con-templating new investments in Mexico wait before committing them-selves. This is another way of saying that macroeconomic policy cred-ibility reduces the inflation-output trade-off. Credibility can cut the output losses associated with anti-inflation campaigns.

Given the potential for reducing this inflation-output trade-off, it is not surprising that government macroeconomic policy credibility has also been cited as an important source of motivation for interna-tional monetary cooperation in South and East European cases.[30] In writing about the Spanish commitment to the EMS, a Banco de España official writes that joining the EMS increased public confi-dence in the government's anti-inflationary stance by altering the incentives for policy makers to pursue inflationary policies.[31] Similarly, in the Portuguese case there is the hope that external finan-cial and monetary liberalization will enhance the credibility of gov-ernment adjustment efforts. By joining a monetary union, writes a former Portuguese central bank economist, "the authorities 'tie their hands.' . . . Such an explicit external commitment to an exchange rate rule works domestically as a reputational constraint."[32]

Related to a desire to use a multilaterally negotiated exchange rate regime to enhance the credibility of government commitment to macro-stability is the desire also to strengthen the credibility of the central bank, the main gatekeeper between the domestic and international economies. The 1991 annual report of the Federal Reserve Bank of Dallas highlights the role that exchange rate pegs could play in enhancing the credibility of Latin American central banks. Central bank independence, cautions the report, "may not be sufficient to restore credibility to monetary policy. If central banks can sustain low money growth . . . ," the report continues,

> fixed exchange rates may become unnecessary shackles. Until that time, however, Latin American governments may temper the power to print money with a strong constraint, such as some form of exchange rate regime whereby their currencies are linked to a low-inflation currency, like the U.S. dollar.[33]

Similarly, changes in the legal independence of East European central banks are an important first step toward enhancing the credibility of those governments' stabilization and liberalization goals, but most economists agree that currency convertibility and multilateral exchange rate agreements will have to supplement domestic efforts. After analyzing the expected credibility impact of the various exchange rate regime options: a unilateral peg, EMS membership, or full currency union, a West German central banker concludes that, for many of the reasons outlined above, a multilaterally agreed-upon peg would provide the biggest boost to stabilization efforts in East Europe.[34] In these instances the idea is that multilateral agreements provide credibility to national central banks. The hope is that with an external rule binding monetary policy, and to some extent fiscal policy also, executive branch agencies and legislators involved in fiscal policy will become increasingly accustomed to respecting central bank authority on macroeconomic policy issues. The self-reinforcing recursive dynamic between the domestic and the international levels is evident: a more authoritative central bank is presumably a central bank better able to pursue future international financial liberalization and international monetary cooperation. In the West European situation, for example, the Bundesbank is expected to lend credibility to the multilateral monetary agreement.

This essay has examined the decision to increase the scope for market definition of Mexican exchange rates as part of an effort to illuminate the circumstances under which financial liberalization can be self-reinforcing. What are the conditions that might lead from a liberal policy regarding exchange convertibility to a higher probability for cooperative foreign monetary policy?

Regional and global integration put the issue of exchange stability on the agenda. The choice of a more market-guided exchange rate policy responded to the way integration increases government sensitivity to the need for credibility in the eyes of creditors and investors. By lessening the potential for arbitrary government decisions to affect investment and credit risk, the government hoped to increase the attractiveness of Mexico as an investment and credit site and signal its commitment to credibility-enhancing actions. The importance of credibility in the context of economic integration and the concomitant rise in international competition for capital drives a search for institutional changes that enhance credibility. A logical credibility-enhancing corollary to the target zone is multilateral cooperation on monetary and exchange rate policy. The decision to follow a more market-guided exchange rate policy in Mexico is likely to be accompanied by a sustained commitment to cooperative foreign monetary policy because both respond to the logic of growing economic integration. Economic integration increases the potential international investment options open to wealth holders. It also increases international competition for capital; this makes governments more sensitive to the need for credibility in the eyes of wealth holders. To an increasing extent, policies will be chosen for their anticipated impact on credibility and, through it, on capital flows. The importance of credibility, which drives stabilizing liberalization, is shaped by the extent to which international integration increases international competition for capital.

Notes

I thank Albert Fishlow, Jeffry Frieden, Judith Goldstein, Stephan Haggard, Ron Linden, several anonymous reviewers, and especially Miles Kahler for comments on earlier versions.

1. See Katrina Burgess, "Fencing in the State: International Trade Agreements and Economic Reform in Mexico" (Princeton University, no date, mimeographed).

2. For an overview, see Adam Przeworski and Michael Wallerstein, "Structural Dependence of the State on Capital," *American Political Science Review* 82, no. 1 (1988).

3. Since the mid-1970s a number of developing countries have begun to reduce controls on private capital inflows and outflows, on the entry of foreign financial firms, and on the international operation of domestic financial enterprises. Restrictions on the international movement of capital can be categorized in several ways: most broadly, they can refer to capital inflows or capital outflows and/or to

short-term or long-term capital flows. The actual methods of control can range from requirements for authorization of individual transactions involving cross-border capital movement to generalized controls on foreign currency exchange. Capital account liberalization is defined as the gradual elimination of national restrictions on foreign currency exchanges and other restrictions on international capital transfers. Foreign exchange controls are relatively easy to detect, and requirements for liberalization are clear. It is often harder to get a comprehensive picture of other national restrictions on capital flows. The OECD Capital Movements Code directs attention to operations that restrict the following: direct investment or disinvestment, buying and selling or "admission" of securities, operations in real estate, buying and selling of short-term securities normally dealt with in the money market, credits directly linked to international trade in goods or services, cross-border financial credits and loans, operation of accounts with credit institutions, personal capital transfers, physical movement of capital assets, and disposal of nonresident-owned funds.

4. On Mexican capital account controls, see Stephen Haggard and Sylvia Maxfield, "The Political Economy of Internationalization in the Developing Countries," *International Organization* 50, no. 1 (1996): 35–68.

5. Ricardo Torres Gaytan, *Un siglo de devaluaciones del peso mexicano* (Mexico City: Siglo Veintiuno Editores, 1982), p. 199.

6. Despite the end of the Bretton Woods fixed exchange rate regime in 1973, most developing countries kept their currencies fixed vis-à-vis the dominant currency in their region and/or in their trade relations.

7. For a review of this policy, see Stephen Zamora, "Exchange Control in Mexico: A Case Study in the Application of IMF Rules," *Houston Journal of International Law* 7, no. 1 (Autumn 1984): 103–106; Ignacio Gomez Palacio, "Mexico's Foreign Exchange Controls: Two Administrations, Two Solutions—Thorough and Benign," *Inter-American Law Review* 16, no. 2 (1984): 267–299.

8. Rolando Cordera and Carlos Tello, *La disputa por la nacion* (Mexico City: Siglo XXI, 1979).

9. Darryl McLeod and John H. Welch, "Free Trade and the Peso" (paper prepared for the 66th annual Western Economic Association International Conference, Seattle, July 1, 1991), fig. 2.

10. Mexican government officials *are* publicly committed to peso-dollar linkage of some kind. See "Mexican Trade Gap 'No Bar to Fixing Peso,'" *Financial Times*, November 5, 1991, p. 8.

11. Patricia Armendáriz, "Zonas de paridad cambiaria: El caso Europeo y una propuesta para Mexico" (October 1991, mimeographed).

12. For example, in April 1992 Nomura Securities moved $6 billion out of Mexico in one day with only a slight short-term change in the exchange rate. For more on this point, see McLeod and Welch, "Free Trade and the Peso."

13. See Tamin Bayoumi and Barry Eichengreen, "Monetary and Exchange Rate Arrangements for NAFTA" (paper prepared for the Interamerican Seminar on Macroeconomics, Buenos Aires, May 7–9, 1992).

14. Federal Reserve Bank of Kansas City, *Policy Implications of Trade and Currency Zones: A Symposium Sponsored by the Federal Reserve Bank of Kansas City* (Kansas City: Federal Reserve Bank of Kansas City, 1992).

15. One of the reasons the French supported monetary coordination was to raise

the barrier to British entry into the common market. German support also had to do with the political goals of counterbalancing Eastern Europe and preparing for a less reliable U.S. role in Western European defense.

16. Loukas Tsoukalis, *The Politics and Economics of European Monetary Integration* (London: Allen and Unwin, 1977), p. 82.

17. See, for example, Jaime Ros, "Free Trade Area or Common Capital Market?" *Journal of Interamerican Studies and World Affairs* 34, no. 2 (Summer 1992): 53–92.

18. Of course, the sources of exchange rate instability in Mexico, a relatively small open economy, are at least partially different from the sources of exchange rate instability in Western Europe in the late 1960s. Exchange rate uncertainty has had a particularly negative impact on Mexican investment. For data on this, see McLeod and Welch, "Free Trade and the Peso."

19. Statement of Representative John J. la Falce, House Committee on Small Business hearings, "NAFTA and Peso Devaluation: A Problem for U.S. Exporters?" May 20, 1993; Richard Lawrence, "Exchange-Rate Policy Urged as One of NAFTA Side Deals," *Journal of Commerce*, May 21, 1993, p. 5. The other three supplemental agreements discussed by the United States, Canada, and Mexico covered environmental impact, labor standards, and "import surge" protection.

20. See Raul A. Feliz and John H. Welch, "The Credibility and Performance of Unilateral Target Zones: A Comparison of the Mexican and Chilean Cases" (paper prepared for the Western Economic Association International 68th Annual Conference, Lake Tahoe, June 20–24, 1993).

21. Rudiger Dornbusch, testimony to House Committee on Small Business hearings, "NAFTA and Peso Devaluation: A Problem for U.S. Exporters?" May 21, 1993.

22. "Bankers viewed an arrangement which decreased the Banco de Mexico's role in the foreign exchange markets as very positive," report Feliz and Welch ("The Credibility and Performance of Unilateral Target Zones," p. 3).

23. Sylvia Maxfield, *Gatekeepers of Growth: The International Political Economy of Central Banking in Developing Countries* (Princeton: Princeton University Press, 1997), ch. 6.

24. Mexicans hope both to get credibility from the U.S. Fed and to increase Mexico's ability to commit to cooperative monetary policy by increasing the independence of the Banco de Mexico. This reflects an implicit recognition of Woolley's argument that the EMS cannot hope to get credibility from the Bundesbank without demonstration by all participating governments of willingness to bear the political costs of monetary cooperation. As Bayoumi and Eichengreen note, the Bundesbank is probably a sounder anchor than the U.S. Fed. In the Mexican case, however, the value of *any* anchor is better than none (Bayoumi and Eichengreen, "Monetary and Exchange Rate Arrangements for NAFTA," p. 9).

25. Helmut Reisen, "Macroeconomic Policies Towards Capital Account Convertibility," in H. Reiser and B. Fischer, eds., *Financial Opening: Policy Issues and Experiences in Developing Countries* (Paris: OECD, 1993).

26. Tsoukalis, *The Politics and Economics of European Monetary Integration*, p. 38.

27. William H. Buiter and Kenneth M. Kletzer, "Reflections on the Fiscal Implications of a Common Currency," in A. Giovannini and C. Mayer, eds., *European Financial Integration* (New York: Cambridge University Press, 1991), p. 233. The economic logic behind this is that with an exchange rate peg, inflation-inducing macroeconomic policy would raise the foreign exchange price of domestically produced goods faster (depending on the extent of foreign inputs) than that of foreign goods. The nation's

export ability would shrink, depending on price elasticity in foreign markets, while imports surged. This might lead to a decline in output and a rising trade deficit. To support the exchange rate at its pegged rate, the central bank would have to spend international currency reserves to purchase national currency and keep the currency's price up. Fears of devaluation and rising inflation would grow.

28. See Susanne Lohmann, "Optimal Commitment in Monetary Policy: Credibility Versus Flexibility," *American Economic Review* 82, no. 1 (March 1992): 273–286.

29. Peter Bofinger, "The Transition to Convertibility in Eastern Europe: A Monetary View," in J. Williamson, ed., *Currency Convertibility in Eastern Europe* (Washington, D.C.: Institute for International Economics, 1991), pp. 129–130.

30. For a rigorous presentation of the logic behind this argument, see Francesco Giavazzi and Marco Pagano, "The Advantage of Tying One's Hands: EMS Discipline and Central Bank Credibility," *European Economic Review* 32, no. 5 (1988): 1055–1082.

31. Jose Vinals, "The EMS, Spain, and Macroeconomic Policy," in P. de Grauwe and L. Papademos, eds., *The European Monetary System in the 1990s* (New York: Longman, 1990), p. 205. Also see Banco de España, "La incorporacion de la peseta al mecanismo de cambios del Sistema Monetario Europea," *Boletin Economico* (July–August 1989): 71–89; Juan Ayuso, "The Effects of the Peseta Joining the ERM on the Volatility of Spanish Financial Variables" (Banco de España, Servicio de Estudios, Documento de Trabajo no. 9106).

32. Francisco Torres, "Portugal, the EMS, and 1992: Stabilization and Liberalization," in de Grauwe and Papademos, *The European Monetary System in the 1990s*, p. 228.

33. Federal Reserve Bank of Dallas, *Federal Reserve Bank of Dallas 1991 Annual Report: Economic Liberalization in the Americas* (Dallas: Federal Reserve Bank of Dallas, 1992), p. 13.

34. Bofinger, "The Transition to Convertibility in Eastern Europe," p. 138.

CONCLUSION

Liberalization as Foreign Policy Determinant and Goal

Miles Kahler

Democratic triumphalism, encouraged by the end of the Cold War, the collapse of apartheid in South Africa, and challenges to authoritarianism in the developing world, has faded. For pessimists, the rise of authoritarian movements in Russia, China's resistance to political reform, the faltering of political opening in Africa, and the shift of Central Asia toward one-man despotisms all suggest that the latest wave of democratization may have begun to recede. Those convinced that the latest democratic gains will not be reversed see the current pause as merely a stage on the winding road to democratic consolidation. Economic liberalization has also suffered its own, less severe setbacks, as former communists in East Europe have returned to power promising to soften, but not reverse, market-oriented policies. Despite severe shocks, such as the Mexican financial crisis of late 1994, most governments have maintained their attachment to economic liberalization, even in the face of high economic and political risks.

Established liberal democracies have reduced their expectations for democratization and their commitment to the spread of democratic governance. The mood among policy makers and analysts was recently described as "less sanguine about democracy's prospects, more sober about the difficulty of promoting it and more skeptical about whether its triumph in several strategic countries would enhance American interests."[1] The new and more cautious attitude toward political and economic liberalization reflects doubts about the inevitability of democratic extension and consolidation (accepting the "wave" pattern of past democratization), the necessarily benign consequences of democratization and economic liberalization for foreign policy, and the ability of established market-oriented and liberal democratic societies to foster their institutional choices in other societies. This volume shares this reflective stance toward liberalization and foreign policy and extends understanding of both the international consequences of liberalization and those strategies most likely to consolidate economic reforms and liberal democracy.

FOREIGN POLICY AND LIBERAL DEMOCRACY: THE DISTINCTIVENESS OF DEMOCRATIC DYADS

The foreign policies of democratic dyads have received rigorous scrutiny in recent international relations scholarship. Because of its potential importance if confirmed, that scrutiny is deserved. Nevertheless, investigation of democratic dyads has produced ambiguous findings, findings that are both extended and questioned in this volume. First, the scope of the distinctiveness of democracies in their foreign policies toward one another widens. Although most attention has been directed toward 3D findings on the absence of war and incidence of militarized disputes, Kurt Taylor Gaubatz argues in this volume for an additional range of international behavior—alliance commitments—in which democratic dyads display significant differences from other regime combinations. As Gaubatz suggests, a powerful tradition in international relations theorizing holds that democracies should be less capable of maintaining international commitments, given the volatility of public opinion (reflected in foreign policy choices) and the rotation of elites. Despite the methodological difficulties in testing propositions regarding alliance duration, Gaubatz offers strong evidence that democracies undertake international commitments toward other democracies that are more durable than those made between states with other types of regimes (including democracies and nondemocratic states).[2]

As described in the introduction, many conventional theories of foreign policy fail to explain the distinctiveness of democratic dyads, since the foreign policies of democracies toward other regime types are not distinctive. This reflective quality has produced persistent undertheorizing of the 3D findings. One explanation—that democ-

ratic institutions impose constraints on executives—
carefully by Lisa Martin and Joanne Gowa. In her detaile
of legislative influence over foreign policy in two liberi
cies—the United States and Britain—Martin appears to (
support for the importance of these quintessentially liberal political
institutions for foreign policy outcomes. Even in liberal democracies
that are conventionally believed to display executive dominance,
such as Britain, she discovers legislative influence exercised through
carefully calibrated delegation regimes that do not display overt day-
to-day oversight of policy. Broadly put, political liberalization, if it
implies the introduction of elected legislatures, is likely to have more
impact on foreign policy than is often recognized.

A second set of conclusions may also be drawn from Martin's arguments, however, conclusions that parallel Gowa's criticisms of simple
checks-and-balances assumptions regarding liberal democracies.
Martin's examination of the United States Congress and the British
Parliament underlines the considerable variation that exists *within*
the set of liberal democratic regimes. Different delegation models
produce different policy outcomes: the gatekeeping power that the
British executive exercises over the legislative agenda is key in this
regard. But even that power is highly dependent on particular procedural rules that may be issue-specific. "Checks and balances" and
the grosser measurements of liberal democracy may not capture the
level of institutional detail that is required to explain variation in foreign policy outcomes. Although she does not address institutional
equilibria in nondemocratic regimes, Martin's account raises
another issue that Gowa emphasizes: whether authoritarian regimes,
which may appear to have very simplified institutional outlines, contain institutional checks and balances that only closer analysis will
reveal.

Gowa argues against democratic exceptionalism, not only on the
grounds that the "selectorates" of authoritarian regimes can supply
checks and balances but also because political-market failures may
render democracies more "authoritarian" (responsive to narrowly
based interests) than simplified images allow.[3] In the second case,
"concentrated benefits and diffuse costs and variable barriers to collective action impede the effective operation of checks and balances."[4] Liberal democratic regimes may also be less "liberal" in the
issue area of foreign policy than in other spheres of public policy. The
electoral connection may not be stringent, and informational asym-

metries may be highly significant, despite the greater transparency of democratic processes in general.

Gowa presents a strong case that many significant institutional constraints on foreign policy are not captured by the liberal-authoritarian distinction. Institutions characteristic of liberal democracies may parallel authoritarian regimes and produce similar effects in both types of regime. Even the competition of political parties in electoral settings may have analogues in the political tests that are periodically confronted by authoritarian regimes or in intra-elite rivalry. The arguments of Martin and Gowa suggest greater disaggregation in dealing with the consequences of regimes and their institutional design for foreign policy. Martin's institutional analysis offers one avenue for undertaking that disaggregation: undermining conventional views of legislative abdication and then exploring the subtle institutional distinctions that produce quite different foreign policy outcomes.

Calling into question one institutional commonplace associated with democracies—checks and balances—opens the way to considering other institutional attributes that are more characteristic of liberal democratic regimes (and less often authoritarian regimes) and that may have more direct attachments to the policy realms in which democratic dyads appear to be distinctive. Gaubatz draws attention to one crucial linkage: transparency in domestic politics and the ability to make commitments to domestic audiences. Although increased transparency is part of the definition of liberalization presented in the introduction, most explanations of liberal democratic foreign policies have not emphasized it. As Gaubatz points out, however, "in the international arena, the ability to link external commitments transparently with internal commitments will allow democratic states to draw on domestic audiences to aid their international credibility."[5] Peter Cowhey has suggested the avenues by which institutional differences *among* democracies can make it "harder or easier to make or reverse promises."[6] Several of these dimensions also divide most democratic from most authoritarian regimes, particularly the ability to monitor and influence political decisions, which is directly related to political transparency.

The link between commitments and transparency can in turn be linked to the distinctive conflict behavior of liberal democracies through James Fearon's explanatory model of rational state decisions for war over negotiated agreements.[7] The two crucial parts of

Fearon's model are private information and commitment problems, each of which, arguably, will be diminished between two democratic states. Whatever the incentives of a state's elites to retain private information regarding resolve or capabilities, in a democracy their ability to do so will be eroded. At the same time, following Gaubatz and Cowhey, the commitment capabilities of liberal democracies toward each other may also be higher, because of the transparency of decision making and the importance of relatively wide domestic audiences. Although wars of misperception are not covered by Fearon's model, on his logic, several categories of military conflict are likely to be rare between democracies.

In addition to extending the scope of 3D results and disaggregating the explanations offered, the contributors to this volume have also enlarged understanding of the foreign policy of democratic dyads across time. Some claim that the "democracies rarely, if ever, make war on one another" finding extends to the nineteenth century (assuming a satisfactory definition of democracy can be agreed upon) but that it strengthens in the twentieth century, particularly after 1945.[8] Even skeptics who challenge this finding for earlier periods (pre-1914) concede that the rarity of war between democratic dyads does hold in the post-1945, Cold War era.[9]

Whether the distinctiveness of democratic dyads holds across time is important: longer time spans and larger numbers of polities increase confidence in the findings and lend support to the importance of democracy as an explanation for this behavior. At the same time, the Cold War years suggest important alternative explanations, particularly those based on the international system. Structural realists, who argue for such external determinants of foreign policy, have dominated the ranks of critics of the 3D findings, even as their scope has expanded. Joanne Gowa suggests security interests (defined by alliances) as a more plausible explanation for the apparent behavior of democracies toward one another in this later period.

Claims that democracy is a less plausible explanation than alliance membership are, however, called into question by empirical results and alternative explanations. Russett and Maoz find that democracy has a significant and independent effect on the behavior of democratic dyads even when alliance relations are controlled.[10] Also, defining the interests reflected in alliances as solely those derived from external threats (rather than the character of regimes) is a neorealist assumption. A far more refined analysis of the content of alliances (and the threats that they were formed to meet) would be required to clarify which interests are dominant.

Two additional explanations for the strengthening of distinctive foreign policy behavior between democratic dyads in more recent decades are presented here. The first is democratic consolidation over time, in Lisa Martin's terms, the establishment of a stable institutional equilibrium. (Alternatively, one could argue that democratic norms become more embedded in both domestic political practices and foreign policy.) Stable democracies may behave differently from recently established or contested ones. The issue of transitional regimes and their foreign policies is discussed in the next section. A second explanation relies on the density of democratic regimes and the effects that their clustering has on reinforcing norms and creating expectations about "normal" democratic foreign policy. The regional differences that are apparent in the preceding case studies lend support to the importance of this effect.

Transitional Regimes or New Democracies?

The four cases of political liberalization examined here—Spain, East Europe, the Middle East, and sub-Saharan Africa—offer mixed support for a coherent category of transitional regimes with its own foreign policy characteristics. For cases on the periphery of liberal democratic Europe, there is little evidence of a distinctly transitional phase in democratization that is the source of foreign policies more militarized or conflictual than either the preceding authoritarian or succeeding "consolidated" phase of democracy. Using the criterion of widespread support for the democratic rules of the game, Spain certainly and several East European countries probably have achieved consolidated democracy. Foreign policies between these regimes and other democracies resembled those of other democratic dyads, although Spain witnessed a vigorous national debate over alignment with other democracies in NATO.

The reasons for these relatively untroubled transitions and benign foreign policies are given in essays by Ronald Linden and by Victor Pérez-Díaz and Juan Carlos Rodríguez. A negotiated transition to democracy in Spain was imitated by other nascent democracies in Latin America and East Europe. When they were installed, democratic institutions were accepted by most sectors of society. The institutions were seldom challenged, and they did not figure in conflict over foreign policy. Economic liberalization in Spain and, to a degree, in East Europe had produced a civil society whose foreign policy interests and orientations could be confirmed and clarified by democratic institutions. The underlying pattern of interests in Spanish society favored the European orientation of the Franco regime, begun as a necessary corollary of its program of economic liberalization. Continuity in economic policies, including external economic policies, eased the political transition and confirmed the broad foreign policy orientation of the new regime.

As Linden describes, foreign policy institutions in East Europe have demonstrated both rupture and continuity.[11] From a political system that was characteristically illiberal on all dimensions—opaque, monopolized by the Communist Party, penetrated by a key external constituent, the Soviet Union—the foreign policy process was rapidly opened to much wider participation and transparency. The end of Communist Party monopoly and the proliferation of new parties across East Europe was, in Linden's view, the most significant institutional change. In other respects *formal* institutions changed relatively little, but "existing structures began to be infused with genuine political power." Foreign policy bureaucracies, at least initially, displayed considerable continuity from the old regime to the new.

Electoral incentives in a newly competitive political setting also had significant effects on post-liberalization foreign policies. Change has been greatest when the old regime and its dominant ideology were closely linked to a particular set of external policies or an external orientation. In Spain, therefore, the introduction of liberal institutions produced less change in external orientation. The further integration of Spain into European institutions, permitted by democratization, produced change only at the margins of Spanish foreign policy by eliminating a nationalist and "Third World" strand employed by the previous regime to demonstrate its autonomy.[12] In East Europe, on the other hand, political liberalization was more likely to imply a wholesale change in foreign policy. Long-standing attachments to the Warsaw Pact and the Council for Mutual Economic Assistance were rapidly discarded after democratization and alignment with Western institutions, such as the European Community and NATO, were eagerly sought. As Linden describes, activism directed toward new Western alignments has been undertaken to extract resources, but it has also served to gain domestic popularity on the cheap for the new regimes.[13] The new dynamics of electoral competition reinforced foreign policy change that was already encouraged by the international environment.

In other regions as well, the introduction of liberal democracy demonstrated fewer international consequences when the preceding regime had not been closely identified with a particular external stance. Authoritarian regimes that had been Cold War allies of the United States were most likely to reflect significant shifts in public opinion after political liberalization. In South Korea, expressed anti-Americanism increased; in other cases, such as Greece and the Philippines, a similar reaction against the senior ally, widely voiced across the political spectrum, was intensified by a perceived dependent or colonial relationship with the United States and other industrialized countries. An "explicit connection between the political regime and its external links" had long been taken for granted in Greece. After democratization in the mid-1970s, the socialist opposition party, PASOK, had opposed membership in the European Community, which it regarded as confirmation of Greece's dependent status in the international system. As the possibility of attaining power grew closer, PASOK's line shifted. After becoming the governing party in 1981, PASOK dropped its opposition but demonstrated little ideological affinity for European institutions and took an "openly pecuniary approach" to retaining membership in the EC.[14]

Despite a shift in the international strategic environment (the end of the Cold War) political liberalization in these cases produced foreign policy outcomes that were similar to those predicted by the literature on democratic dyads. There was little evidence of de-alignment of democracies or disruption of alliance ties between democracies. As Linden points out, there has been little increase in the use or threat of military force in East Europe since democratization, and none between states with firmly implanted democratic institutions. (As he points out, the wars in the former Yugoslavia are difficult to classify as either interstate or wars between consolidated democracies.) In general, the new regimes have demonstrated a tendency to align themselves with existing democracies, represented by the European Community and NATO. These negotiated transitions to liberal democracy suggest that the category of transition as a particular and uniformly conflict-prone category requires disaggregation. As the cases of the Middle East and sub-Saharan Africa demonstrate, however, the contested and tentative character of certain democratic transitions may produce foreign policies that diverge substantially from the paradigm of democratic dyads.

Lisa Anderson's account of liberalizing Middle Eastern states calls into question predictions based on states with long-standing democratic institutions.[15] As she describes, the alignments of liberalizing regimes in the region following the invasion of Kuwait in 1990 ran counter to both neorealist and liberal theorizing. Instead of bandwagoning toward the strongest coalition, Jordan, Yemen, and Algeria gravitated, for domestic political reasons, toward Iraq, which was clearly the weaker party to the conflict. Instead of aligning themselves with a coalition led by the Western democracies, these liberalizing regimes sided with a repressive, one-party dictatorship. Although these governments did not engage in military conflict with the United Nations forces, their newly installed liberal institutions and the absence of a history of liberal governance permitted political forces hostile to the West—nationalist, anti-imperialist, Islamic—to overwhelm either institutional or normative pressure for democratic alignment. Even transnational ties, which are often portrayed as reinforcing liberal foreign policy among societies with "multiple channels of contact," did not prevent distancing from the democratic coalition: knowledge of Kuwaiti society in Jordan produced hostility, not sympathy; Saudi and Persian Gulf subsidies of the Islamic Front (FIS) in Algeria were overwhelmed by domestic political imperatives.

Jeffrey Herbst's predictions of an end to the stable boundary regime in sub-Saharan Africa indicate that the internal dynamics of political liberalization may sometimes overwhelm normative or institutional predispositions to maintaining a cooperative regime.[16] The norm of respect for existing boundaries in Africa was itself the creation of a cartel of largely authoritarian rulers. In part for self-protective reasons (sketched by Joanne Gowa), they rarely threatened one another's territorial integrity. That cartel could be eroded by an opening of the political process. As Herbst describes, radical reversals of group status are possible as political participation widens; the need to mobilize the rural peasantry using ethnic symbols promises heightened conflict along cleavages that will put enormous pressure on the boundary regime. Instead of continued international cooperation among similar states, political liberalization in Africa threatens to overturn a long-standing cooperative arrangement.

The foreign policies of liberalizing regimes in the Middle East and sub-Saharan Africa stand in contrast to the foreign policies of transitional states in Europe. Several working hypotheses may link the politics of transition to illiberal foreign policies in these cases and others. As Lisa Martin argues in her account of the first liberalizing states—England and the Netherlands—the most important distinction among liberalizing regimes is success or failure to exclude foreign policy from transitional politics. This failure may take at least three forms. Lisa Anderson's account of Jordanian and Algerian foreign policy in the face of rising Islamist opposition illustrates one pattern. Liberalization in these two states was hardly consensual: elements of the opposition aimed at the destruction of the existing regime, not a brokered transition. Conflict had not reached a revolutionary stage, however. Both regimes and their oppositions could, therefore, use foreign policy as a convenient vehicle for their competition and conflict in a permissive international environment.[17] Herbst's predictions about the African boundary regime are based on a similar pattern of transition in that region: "winner take all" transitions that include little notion of pacts or power sharing between old political coalitions and new.[18]

A negotiated transition may explicitly or implicitly exclude foreign policy from contests over future institutional design. It can also reduce the incentives to react against the previous foreign policy orientation (which might have included alignment with democratic states or a suppression of nationalist claims). As Huntington notes, this constellation is most likely when the liberalizing regime is a one-party state. In such transitions, the representatives of the old regime may search for a new ideological support for their position. Typically that ideology is nationalist or religious. In certain recent cases, such as the former Yugoslav republics, such an ideological shift on the part of members of the old regime had dire consequences for external aggressiveness and conflict. In the former Soviet republics, where a similar transformation has taken place, conflict has increased but has not in most cases resulted in military confrontation.[17]

A transitional pact may also affect foreign policy by explicitly or implicitly *including* foreign policy in bargaining. The roles of particular institutions, such as the military or the existing national security bureaucracies, may be protected or these institutions may be offered new roles: each choice may have external implications. One of the reasons that the Spanish socialists embraced NATO, after years of opposition to membership, was its appeal as an alternative role for an interventionist military. Huntington notes that the nationalism of both Karamanlis and Papandreou during Greece's transition was designed to win favor with the military. The new political leadership was torn between its desire to resolve old quarrels with its neighbors and the need for a "traditional enemy" to occupy its military planners.[18] He goes so far as to suggest in his "guidelines for democratizers" the need to "balance gains from the removal of foreign threats against the potential costs in instability at home."[19]

Both the former Yugoslavia and the tentatively democratizing states in Africa described by Herbst suggest a final source of transitional foreign policy uncertainties. Democratization in ethnically divided societies may mobilize conflicts over the shape of the political community itself. As Robert Dahl and others have noted, nothing in democratic theory or practice provides a sure guide to the boundaries of a democratic polity. Such conflict can easily blur the boundary between interstate and intrastate conflict as well, particularly if ethnic loyalties spill across national frontiers. In East Europe, as Linden notes, a democratic (or democratizing) peace has held against such ethnic politics; about Africa, Herbst is more pessimistic that the authoritarian cartel sustaining the current boundary regime will persist.

The recent experience of South and East Europe, as well as Latin America, belies any generalized and alarmist claims that transitional states are particularly prone to interstate conflict. Throughout a wave of political transitions that surpassed any of the previous periods of democratization there was little evidence of a persistent increase in interstate conflict linked to these political changes. In Europe the end of the Cold War brought some increase in violence (none strictly interstate), but by 1994 the violence had subsided to levels lower than those during most of the Cold War years.[20] Although the transition was hardly complete (according to the definition employed here) in all regions of democratization, the case for discriminating among transitional regimes and their foreign policy behavior is very strong.

The South and East European cases considered in this volume seem to differ from transitional regimes in other regions by the political dynamics of their transitions, the speed of their institutional consolidation, and their acceptance of liberal international norms. In short, they demonstrated most of the characteristics of established democratic dyads more rapidly than many would have predicted. The contrasts among the transitional regimes discussed here were also regional, however, pointing to another set of hypotheses that may explain the foreign policies of transitional regimes: their historical relationship to preceding waves of democratization and their spatial relationship to other, established liberal democracies.

DEMOCRATIC CONSOLIDATION OR THE EBBING OF THE THIRD WAVE?

Although this volume has not dealt systematically with the historical and spatial distribution of political and economic liberalization, the clustering of these developments across time and space is important in explaining foreign policy outcomes. As Huntington has described, democratization (and, by extension, political liberalization) has occurred in waves over time, often followed by reverse waves that return some democratic regimes to authoritarianism. Participation in previous waves of democratization, however transient, seems to have significant effects on the consequences of contemporary democratization. The foreign policy behavior of liberalizing regimes in the Middle East and Africa, excluded from earlier waves of democratization, differed substantially from that in the states of South and East Europe.

Political liberalization has also occurred in spatial waves that overlap with these historical cycles and that have had even more significant foreign policy consequences. Spatial proximity, which reduces the costs of recognition, has been demonstrated as highly important in the emergence of cooperation in nature.[21] Kurt Taylor Gaubatz has suggested that democracies have tended to form clusters historically (apart from a brief period in the interwar years), even though he could find no resulting advantages in capabilities vis-à-vis nondemocracies. The latest wave of democratization seems to demonstrate the significance of geographical contiguity or proximity. Political liberalization has been most apparent in the European periphery (first Southern, then Eastern Europe) and in Latin America, two regions adjacent to the liberal heartland of Western Europe and North America. The third wave of democratization described by Huntington is limited to those regions with the addition of Pakistan and part of the East Asian periphery (South Korea, Taiwan, and the Philippines).

Two of the cases examined here (Spain and East Europe) are contiguous with the established liberal democratic "core." Their foreign policies were shaped by their aspirations to join the all-important

European clubs, which shaped their external behavior, as described by Pérez-Díaz and Rodríguez and by Linden. The influence of Western Europe can be seen as anticipatory socialization, given electoral demands for an orientation toward Europe. The existing European democracies "defined" democratic behavior for these aspirants on their periphery. A more rationalist, state-centered account would include the implicit sanctions and rewards that European democracies wielded toward economies heavily dependent on their trade, investment, and foreign aid. European clubs were unique in having an explicitly democratic entry criterion; one, the Council of Europe, is the strongest regional human rights regime. Latin American democracies, despite their proximity to the largest democracy, could not aspire to the club benefits offered to democratizing Europeans. The norm of nonintervention and suspicions of American meddling have also made it difficult to construct an explicit democratic club. Even in the absence of formal institutionalization, however, democratic norms of foreign policy behavior became more widespread as the density of democracies in the Western Hemisphere approached that of Europe.

Only in the 1990s has political liberalization appeared in a less than tentative way in regions more distant from the liberal democratic core: in the Middle East (Jordan, Yemen, Tunisia, Algeria) and in sub-Saharan Africa (including South Africa). In these late-liberalizing regions political change has often been limited to tentative and formal steps toward democratization.[22] Lisa Anderson and Jeffrey Herbst suggest that the foreign policy consequences of liberalization are likely to be less predictable and more prone to conflict in these regions than in those states whose foreign policies are constrained by and identified with more powerful democratic neighbors in the liberal heartland. The same judgment may apply to the former Soviet Union, where democratic institutions remain contested, and neoauthoritarian solutions have found recent favor. Apart from the Baltic states, none of the countries in the former Soviet Union had more than ephemeral participation in preceding waves of democratization. Their distance from the liberal heartland of Europe and the rival core of Russia (which defines its "club" by ethnicity or history, not political regime) suggests a different liberalizing trajectory and possibly different foreign policy outcomes.

Asia provides a third and intermediate regional case. Democratic governments, growing in number, are found on the periphery of the region; at the core are large and resolute (if challenged) authoritarians. Although subregional groups for the peaceful management of conflict exist (Association of Southeast Asian Nations, or ASEAN) and a regionwide club devoted to economic liberalization has emerged (Asia-Pacific Economic Cooperation, or APEC), no regional grouping is specifically dedicated to human rights or the promotion of democracy. Many governments in the region argue forcefully that those issues should not find their way onto the international agenda.

ECONOMIC LIBERALIZATION, INTERNATIONAL INSTITUTIONS, AND FOREIGN POLICY

Globally, the latest wave of economic liberalization preceded the third wave of democratization. After gaining a foothold in the academic and policy worlds in the late 1960s, neoliberalism produced the orthodox experiments of the southern cone of South America (under political authoritarianism) in the 1970s.[23] The success of the East Asian newly industrializing countries—which, apart from Hong Kong, were only partly liberalized political economies—was an important spur to other liberalizing experiments, particularly in China and Vietnam. International economic conditions, especially the end of easy bank credit for many developing countries and successive oil shocks (both the price inflation of the 1970s and the price deflation of the mid-1980s), also contributed to the growing pressure on elites in the developing countries to adopt market-oriented policies and to open their economies to foreign trade and investment.[24]

By the mid-1990s, economic liberalization had spread widely, and few developing countries remained untouched. With the end of the Cold War, the collapse of the Soviet market, and a sharp decline in Russian economic assistance, even the last holdouts—Cuba, North Korea, and India—were forced to reconsider their statist orthodoxy. One unprecedented feature of the latest wave of liberalization is clear: although several distinct variants of market economies may exist, no coherent alternative program exists after the near demise of unreformed (nonmarket) communism and the decline of statist options.

One feature of this latest wave of economic liberalization has been important in shaping the adoption of market-oriented policies and their foreign policy effects. Like political liberalization, economic liberalization has deepened unevenly across regions. As outward-oriented policies have taken hold and government commitment to more liberal policies has grown in importance for economic actors, regional groupings to sustain economic opening have proliferated. Regional free trade agreements have been the most prominent new "clubs" sustaining economically liberal policies. Their agendas have broadened beyond the lowering of impediments to exchange at the borders to include investment, standards, and other behind-the-border issues. They have also linked industrialized and developing countries for the first time. The consequences of this clustering of liberalizing countries have been similar to the regional clubs that sustained democratization. One of the most important has been the formation of new multilateral institutions and sharply increased interest in joining existing institutions.

Four national cases in which economic liberalization is prominent—China, Mexico, Spain, and the European Union—demonstrate the dependence of programs of economic liberalization on international institutions and the importance of those institutions in shaping the foreign policy consequences of such liberalization. These cases span the spectrum of political regimes from an unreformed authoritarianism (China) to established liberal democracies (the European Community). This range of political liberalization (from effectively zero to established liberal democracy) permits a quasi-experimental control for the effects of political regime. In each of these cases, economic liberalization appears to have had independent and significant effects in encouraging cooperative strategies in national foreign policies, independent of the effects of political liberalization.

China, which combined a program of economic liberalization that emphasized external opening with a resolutely authoritarian regime, illustrates the consequences of economic liberalization in the absence of any marked change in political regime. Dramatic growth in China's economic interdependence with the capitalist world during the 1980s (exports were close to 20% of GNP in 1990) has created new domestic institutions and interests that influence foreign policy. The new sphere of external activity is dominated by the Ministry of Foreign Economic Relations and Trade, founded in 1982, soon after the initiation of the economic reforms. MOFERT has become an "immense bureaucratic empire many times larger than the Foreign Ministry."[25] The highly centralized system of the Maoist era became much more decentralized, with much greater debate on foreign policy issues. Most significantly, provincial actors outside Beijing, empowered by rapid economic growth and attached to expanded international economic ties, have attempted to construct their own foreign economic policies when possible and have intervened in policy debates at the center when those ties were endangered by international conflict.[26]

Although the Chinese government initiated external cooperative strategies and sought membership and participation in international economic institutions, its authoritarian political system served as a largely successful gatekeeper between domestic interests and international regimes.[27] Such institutions provided an increment of credibility to domestic reformers, but China, like other successful Asian economies, found it less necessary to purchase credibility through cooperation with international economic institutions. Although institutional membership provided a more efficient means of managing its proliferating international economic ties, China resisted any cross-issue linkage that could be exploited by its international economic partners.

Mexico, another single-party state that initiated a dramatic break in the 1980s with its statist past, also experienced a transformation of its foreign policy under President Carlos Salinas de Gortari. Persistent anti-Americanism disappeared as the logic of economic liberalization reinforced Mexico's economic dependence on its northern neighbor. As one of Salinas's critics has argued:

> Whatever the other implications this strategy had, its consequences for foreign affairs were perfectly clear. It made no sense, on one hand, to put all of Mexico's eggs in one basket (namely the one that held foreign financing, business confidence and U.S. support) and then proceed to kick and quarrel with the owners of the basket. The inconsistency of the former policy was eliminated: Mexico would no longer try to maintain its activist, assertive and frequently anti-American policy in Central America, the United Nations and elsewhere.[28]

The decline of nationalist ideology also complemented Mexico's new strategy of engagement with international economic institutions: Mexico joined the General Agreement on Tariffs and Trade (GATT), whose liberal trading principles had previously been anathema, and relations with the International Monetary Fund and the World Bank became increasingly cordial. In another striking break with the past, the Salinas government enthusiastically completed negotiations for the North American Free Trade Agreement (NAFTA).

External liberalization has not always been a self-reinforcing and dominant strategy for Mexico's political elites. In an earlier discussion of capital account liberalization and closure, Sylvia Maxfield highlights a backlash effect in which the distributional effects of liberalization create an opposition that uses its political and institutional bases to counterattack. During the bank nationalization of 1982, the liberalizing coalition tied to international financial markets and opposition to external financial controls, suffered a temporary defeat at the hands of its national populist opponents.[29]

Under Salinas, a strategy of international collaboration was employed to enhance the credibility of exchange rate policy in the eyes of both international creditors and investors and the domestic electorate. By aligning Mexican policy with that of the United States, the Mexican president (and presumably future presidents who endorsed the liberalization program) could raise the costs of another backlash by the opponents of liberalization. In addition, NAFTA, another key international reinforcement of the Salinas economic program, could be threatened by volatile Mexican exchange rates. Preserving valued cooperation in one sphere required movement toward greater exchange rate stability.

Liberal international economic policies do not always point toward greater institutional collaboration in managing exchange rates, however. In her contribution to this volume, Maxfield endorses an interest-based explanation for the gradual acceptance by Mexican policy makers of a bilateral or multilateral framework for exchange rate management. Internationally connected banks in Mexico have a strong interest in collaborative firebreaks to nationalist policy reversals. Nevertheless, the broad support of domestic and international investors for an exchange rate corollary to NAFTA contains a paradox, as Maxfield makes clear. By such solutions to Mexico's debilitating cycles of devaluation and overvaluation, mobile financial interests in Mexico seemed willing to forgo their oldest instrument of influence with the government: capital flight. In answer to the question of which strategy was most effective and least costly for domestic capital, a target zone for exchange rates (backed multilaterally) and a futures market to hedge against unforeseen shocks seemed the favored choices. Growing economic integration in North America, symbolized by NAFTA, produced a redefinition of interests by key sectors of Mexican business.[30]

The Spanish transition to democracy, described by Pérez-Díaz and

Rodríguez, was deeply influenced by the program of economic liberalization that had been pursued by the Franco government. Decisions
that followed from the 1959 stabilization program committed the
Franco government to an external economic path that was not initially intended by either Franco or portions of the dominant political
coalition. International institutions, such as the International Monetary Fund and the World Bank, provided crucial external credibility
for the original stabilization program, which was a sharp break with
Spain's nationalist and isolationist past. Economic liberalization then
created a powerful set of economic interests that argued for continuity in pursuing integration with Western Europe during a time of
political transition. Overall, the consequences of economic liberalization—unforeseen when the program began in 1959—resulted in
external and internal constraints on Spanish policy that virtually
guaranteed foreign policy continuity across the democratic transition. Chief among those constraints was the deepening cooperative
relationship with the European Community.[31]

Like Maxfield, Jeffry Frieden explains growing collaboration in
exchange rate management, but he does so in a different economic
and political setting: the industrialized and stable democracies of the
European Community. Frieden offers a final example of the power of
economic liberalization and regional integration in advancing an
agenda of deepening European monetary cooperation and building
regional monetary institutions. Policy makers in Europe, like those in
Mexico, sought a credible anchor for their turn toward anti-inflationary policies in the late 1970s and early 1980s: the EMS (with its
clear link to the deutsche mark) was clearly the best available counterweight to the inflationary expectations of their own populations.[32]
Both anti-inflationary turn and initiation of economic and monetary
cooperation enhanced the role of the central banks in member countries: central bank predominance guaranteed that monetary cooperation would take a particular form, centered on foreign exchange
management by a network of central bankers. In addition, instability
in exchange rates could have called into question other more politically sensitive parts of the European Community, in particular the
Common Agricultural Policy.

As Frieden notes, however, these motivations for intensified monetary cooperation can explain the persistence of plans for collaboration but cannot explain the variation in such interest among EC
members over time. Frieden's model of European monetary integra-

tion is one in which the interests produced by economic liberalization ratchet up support for monetary cooperation in Europe. Swelling support for monetary cooperation in Europe is a consequence of increasing levels of intra-European trade and investment. Sectors most dependent on intra-European transactions supported closer monetary collaboration as a way of lowering the exchange rate risks implied by their exposure to other European economies. Monetary institutions and the cooperation that they embodied in turn made an outcome of expanded trade and investment more likely in the eyes of private investors. Although the process appeared to be self-reinforcing, Frieden notes that the EMS suffered a grave crisis in 1992–1993, one that called into question a Europe-wide Economic and Monetary Union. Nevertheless, the cause of that exogenous shock was the German response to reunification, not economic nationalism. On the basis of a close, demonstrated link between economic liberalization, economic interests, and monetary collaboration, Frieden predicts that monetary union will proceed, whatever its temporary setbacks.

LIBERAL DEMOCRACY AS A FOREIGN POLICY GOAL

Interest in the foreign policy consequences of democracy and other political regimes has been stimulated by the third wave of democratization, which reached its apogee after the end of the Cold War. Arguments that democracies rarely if ever make war on one another were useful for those who urged a positive policy of promoting democratization. As Tony Smith has shown, democracy promotion has been a central and bipartisan theme in American foreign policy throughout the twentieth century.[33] Although the pacific consequences of democratization have been part of its appeal, it seems likely that other goals, such as political stability, would have sustained its prominent place in the foreign policy of the United States.

Policy makers and publics must define the priority assigned to support for liberalization, in light of its international effects. Those who accept that democratic dyads have peaceful and otherwise beneficial foreign policies toward one another more often endorse democratization as a central foreign policy goal. For some enthusiasts of democratization, extending the third wave is sometimes portrayed as a virtual panacea for all international threats confronted by the industrialized democracies.[34]

Despite the panoply of programs and actors promoting democracy, however, there is surprising lack of agreement on two crucial points: how effective outside actors can be in furthering democratization and which instruments are most effective in promoting the beneficial consequences of democratic governance. In part because he includes the latest cases of democratization in East Europe, Samuel P. Huntington assigns a greater weight to external influence, although conceding that previous waves of regime change were more deeply influenced from the outside.[35] With the exception of Huntington's work, the voluminous literature on democratic transitions offers conflicting estimates of the influence that external actors have had on recent episodes of liberalization. Most analysts have argued that the initiation, pace, and outcome of political transitions have been determined largely by internal political factors and that external actors have at best limited influence over the process.[36] Assessments of the positive effects of external influence on democratization also divide those examining the Latin American experience with democratic transitions and those who have concentrated on the European balance sheet. Abraham F. Lowenthal's evaluation is typical in its skepticism about American promotion of democracy in Latin America: efforts by the United States government "have rarely been successful, and then only in a narrow range of circumstances"; in the twentieth century the overall effect of American policy was "usually negligible, often counterproductive, and only occasionally positive."[37] At best, bilateral American efforts have had a discernible influence in those "highly unusual, very finely balanced circumstances when foreign influence can tip the scale—or else in the small nearby nations most penetrated by and vulnerable to the United States."[38] In general, however, external efforts to promote democracy often stimulate a nationalist backlash, create relations of dependence that thwart a democratic equlibrium, and shift with domestic political trends in the promoting (rather than target) country. Most American programs have simply been too small: the "magnitudes of the task and of the solution are vastly out of proportion with one another."[39]

European democracy promotion is regarded in a far more positive and influential light. In both Mediterranean and East Europe, existing liberal democracies played a significant role in encouraging and consolidating democratic transitions.[40] In the case of Turkey, for example, European pressure produced important steps to align Turkish political and social practices with those of Europe.[41] As the case studies in this volume confirm, two crucial features distinguished the European record from that of Latin America: influence was exerted multilaterally (through the European Community or other European institutions) rather than bilaterally, and democracy was encouraged through the incentive of membership in a highly regarded club rather than through political conditionality, the wielding of carrots and sticks to induce compliance.

This contrast between Latin America and Europe illustrates an initial policy conclusion that can be drawn from these studies of the foreign policy consequences of liberalization. The use of clublike arrangements to encourage democratic politics and liberal foreign policy was effective in the European cases. The aspiration to join such clubs, particularly the European Community, was an important incentive to maintain and deepen democratic consolidation in Spain and more recently in East Europe. The apparent influence of such membership incentives was dependent on several features of the European setting that were not replicated in other regions. First, the key clubs had credible membership criteria that included democratic governance. The EC's criteria were credible since they were embedded in Article 237 of the Treaty of Rome and further specified in the 1962 Birkelbach Report. Despite assiduous efforts, the Franco regime was signaled firmly that it would not become a full member of the European Community while it remained under authoritarian rule. Greece's status as an associate of the EC was frozen after the colonels' coup in 1967; Turkey faced similar sanctions in the early 1980s.[42]

The term "sanctions" is not entirely accurate, however: failure to progress toward full membership (or more desirable associate status) was not viewed in the same light as the inducements and sanctions that accompany political conditionality. Not only is membership in a club by its nature multilateral (the criteria are not set by a single country), it cannot be viewed as intrusive or as violating "sovereignty" in the same way as conditionality. Few nations question whether another group of nations can establish their own criteria for an association to which they belong; many nations question whether democratization and other "internal" political issues can be linked legitimately to economic concessions.

If a credible set of democratic admission requirements is one element in the success of such clubs in Europe, the desirability of membership—on economic grounds—is the second. The European Community has been far more influential than the Council of Europe in sustaining democratization because of the clearly defined economic benefits of membership. Even elites that are not imbued with democratic norms may choose to follow democratic rules of the game in order to win the economic benefits of membership. In contrast to the exercise of conditionality, however, linkage between democratic behavior and economic inducements is implicit in membership: the careful modulation and monitoring of compliance that absorbs conditionality is less necessary.

Clubs also serve as reference points for democratic norms in both domestic politics and foreign policy. Despite these advantages, however, few have been established during the third wave of democratization. Latin America might appear to be a candidate for such a club, but the region's strong norm of non-intervention (and suspicion of the United States) has hindered its creation. Although it has pursued a more active role in the 1990s, the OAS has not been very effective in promoting democracy.[43] Other groups have begun to multilateralize political conditionality and external pressure for democratization, but few have set stringent conditions for participation, and even fewer have membership benefits that would strengthen attachment to democratic norms.[44]

If clubs have played a valuable role in confirming democratic consolidation and the characteristic foreign policies of democratic dyads, they have been equally important in economic liberalization. Economic liberalization and its positive effects (on economic growth and the development of civil society in particular) pose another dilemma for those managing institutional membership. Widening of membership must constantly be weighed against bending the rules of adherence (which are often less sharp by definition than democratic criteria are) in order to reward progress in economic liberalization. This dilemma has appeared in the case of China's admission to the World Trade Organization (WTO): "engagement" and the benefits of further liberalization are set against maintaining the existing rules (and credibility) of international economic institutions. A different sort of risk is illustrated by Mexico's financial crisis in December 1994. International economic institutions may provide a valuable increment of credibility to national governments that are pursuing economic liberalization. Those governments may, however, rely too heavily on that borrowed credibility (as Mexico did in the case of

NAFTA). The "joining" impulse that seems to accompany economic liberalization, as described in this volume, can exaggerate the benefits of institutional membership for elites under pressure.

A further set of conclusions with policy implications concerns transitional democracies. Latin America and Europe appear to engineer an acceleration of democratic consolidation. Liberal democracies must become "established" as quickly as possible (as they have in southern and central Europe) in order to avoid the often perverse foreign policy consequences of political liberalization (illustrated in the Middle East and possibly in sub-Saharan Africa). In regions without a critical density of existing established democracies, external support for consolidation is particularly important. Given the absence of one barrier to backsliding (the ratchet effect of a club), a crucial feature of support for democratization should be its *long-term* character: too often, a competitive election is held, democracy is declared, and then international interest and support decline rapidly. These conclusions support most other assessments of successful pro-democracy programming. Rapid consolidation is important to avoid a lag between new democratic institutions and the recognition and acceptance of those new institutions by democratic neighbors; such a lag can be curtailed by support and oversight from the outside.

The end of the Cold War and the absence of an overwhelming nondemocratic strategic threat have led some to argue that "sustained international support for the consolidation of democratic regimes would demand hitherto untapped sources of Western maturity and tenacity in such a context."[45] Paradoxically, the most recent wave of democratization may demonstrate the shortcomings of democracies in their failure to support democratic consolidation over the long haul. To win the rewards of a world of established liberal democracies, existing democratic powers must sustain fledgling regimes beyond their often troubled (and internationally disturbing) early years. Any devices that can remove such programs from the vagaries of short-term perceptions and politics are likely to yield foreign policy benefits.

Another familiar nostrum of the literature of democratization—support for civil society—is called into question in its simplest form by contributors to this volume. Many endorsements of strengthening civil society are based on unexamined beliefs that civil society is a unique reservoir of democratic norms. Unfortunately, as the Middle

Eastern and African cases illustrate, civil society can also be a source of ethnically charged or politically illiberal movements, whose influence on foreign policy will not confirm democratic norms. A narrower definition of support—framed as constructing transnational links between nongovernmental groups in established democracies and those in liberalizing societies—may produce more predictable benefits. For their counterparts in transitional societies, groups in established democracies could provide benchmarks for democratic action and modest incentives to observe those parameters.

Finally, transitional regimes are less likely to enjoy a smooth consolidation of democracy if foreign policy itself becomes part of the conflict over new institutions. That risk argues for two additional measures by existing democracies. Established liberal democracies can shape the immediate international environment by reducing insecurity: international threats will complicate democratic consolidation and provide an additional instrument of self-protection for the governors of the old regime (particularly the military). At the same time, external efforts to influence the process of democratization, particularly bilateral measures, should be undertaken with an eye to reducing nationalist reactions in the target state.

Overall, these prescriptions resemble those propounded by skeptical observers of international intervention in democratic transitions. Policy to promote democracy should be "both steadily funded and implemented over many years . . . overt, but quiet, carried out in a low-profile manner."[46] Even if established democracies can implement such policies, perpetual peace will not be guaranteed. New or established democracies may backslide into authoritarian rule. Democracies will also behave in a belligerent fashion toward nondemocracies. Nevertheless, given the positive foreign policy benefits that have flowed from the latest wave of democratization in at least some regions and the modest resources that are devoted to democracy promotion, the costs and risks of supporting the consolidation of democracy are certainly justified.

Notes

1. Judith Miller, "At Hour of Triumph, Democracy Recedes as the Global Ideal," *New York Times*, 18 February 1996.

2. Kurt Taylor Gaubatz, "Democratic States and Commitment in International Relations," ch. 1 in this volume.

3. Joanne Gowa, "Democratic States and International Disputes," ch. 3 in this volume.

4. Ibid., p. 111.

5. Gaubatz, "Democratic States and Commitment in International Relations," p. 41–42.

6. Peter F. Cowhey, "Domestic Institutions and the Credibility of International Commitments: Japan and the United States," *International Organization* 47, 2 (Spring 1993): 299–326.

7. James D. Fearon, "Rationalist Explanations for War," *International Organization* 49, 3 (Summer 1995): 379–414.

8. Bruce M. Russett, *Grasping the Democratic Peace: Principles for a Post–Cold War World* (Princeton: Princeton University Press, 1993), p. 20, pp. 73–74 (for reasons that the 3D findings may have strengthened). Gaubatz notes that democratic and nondemocratic involvement in alliances tracked each other closely until the 1920s, when defense pacts (the most "committed" of alliances) between democracies demonstrated a significant increase ("Democratic States and Commitment in International Relations").

9. Henry S. Farber and Joanne Gowa, "Polities and Peace," *International Security* 20, 2 (Fall 1995): 123–146.

10. Russett, *Grasping the Democratic Peace*, pp. 84–86.

11. Ronald H. Linden, "Liberalization and Foreign Policy in East Europe," ch. 6 in this volume.

12. Victor Pérez-Díaz and Juan Carlos Rodríguez, "From Reluctant Choices to Credible Commitments: Foreign Policy and Economic and Political Liberalization—Spain, 1953–1986," ch. 7 in this volume.

13. Linden, "Liberalization and Foreign Policy."

14. Susannah Verney, "To Be or Not to Be Within the European Community," in Geoffrey Pridham, ed., *Securing Democracy* (London: Routledge, 1990), pp. 205, 215.

15. Lisa Anderson, "Democratization and Foreign Policy in the Arab World: The Domestic Origins of the Jordanian and Algerian Alliances in the 1991 Gulf War," ch. 4 in this volume.

16. Jeffrey Herbst, "Political Liberalization and the African State System," ch. 5 in this volume.

17. For two contrasting instrumental uses of nationalism, see V. P. Gagnon Jr., "Ethnic Nationalism and International Conflict: The Case of Serbia," *International Security* 19, 3 (Winter 1994/95): 130–166; and Charles F. Furtado, "Nationalism and Foreign Policy: The Case of Ukraine" (paper prepared for the 1992 annual meeting of the American Political Science Association, Chicago, 3–6 September 1992).

18. Samuel P. Huntington, *The Third Wave: Democratization in the Late Twentieth Century* (Norman: University of Oklahoma Press, 1991), pp. 247–248.

19. Ibid., p. 252.

20. Nils Petter Gleditsch, "Democracy and the Future of European Peace," *European Journal of International Relations* 1, 4 (December 1995): 555.

21. Martin A. Nowak, Robert M. May, and Karl Sigmund, "The Arithmetics of Mutual Help," *Scientific American* 272, 6 (June 1995): 80–81.

22. Although parliamentary elections had been held in thirty-five of forty-eight sub-Saharan African countries by 1996, in thirteen of these cases the elections were "seriously flawed" or "marginally free and fair," and in another four the electoral

results were later reversed by nondemocratic means (Michael Holman, "Fitful Africa Deepens Donors' Dilemma," *Financial Times*, 8 February 1996, p. 4).

23. For an account of the rise of the new orthodoxy, see Miles Kahler, "Orthodoxy and Its Alternatives," in Joan Nelson, ed., *Economic Crisis and Policy Choice* (Princeton: Princeton University Press, 1990), pp. 33–61.

24. On the contribution of the international economic environment to the trend toward economic liberalization, see Barbara Stallings, "International Influence on Economic Policy," in Stephan Haggard and Robert Kaufman, eds., *The Politics of Economic Adjustment* (Princeton: Princeton University Press, 1992), pp. 49–52.

25. A. Doak Barnett, *The Making of Foreign Policy in China: Structure and Process* (Boulder: Westview Press, 1985), pp. 93, 96.

26. See Lin Zhimin, " 'Walking on Two Legs': The Domestic Content of China's Policy Toward the Asia-Pacific Region," *China Report* 3, 2 (April 1992); and He Di, "China's Foreign Policy in Deng's Era" (paper prepared for the SSRC Conference on Foreign Policy Consequences of Economic and Political Liberalization, 9–11 July 1992).

27. Harold K. Jacobson and Michel Oksenberg, *China's Participation in the IMF, the World Bank, and GATT* (Ann Arbor: University of Michigan Press, 1990).

28. Jorge G. Castaneda, "Salinas's International Relations Gamble," *Journal of International Affairs* 43, 2 (Winter 1990): 410.

29. Sylvia Maxfield, *Governing Capital: International Finance and Mexican Politics* (Ithaca: Cornell University Press, 1990).

30. Sylvia Maxfield, "Financial Liberalization and Regional Monetary Cooperation: The Mexican Case," ch. 9 in this volume.

31. Pérez-Díaz and Rodríguez, "From Reluctant Choices to Credible Commitments."

32. Wayne Sandholtz, "Choosing Union: Monetary Politics and Maastricht," *International Organization* 47, 1 (Winter 1993): 1–39.

33. Tony Smith, *America's Mission* (Princeton: Princeton University Press, 1994).

34. For example, Larry Diamond, *Promoting Democracy in the 1990s: Actors and Instruments, Issues and Imperatives* (New York: Carnegie Corporation of New York, 1995), pp. 1–7.

35. Huntington, *The Third Wave*, pp. 85–100.

36. See, for example, Guillermo O'Donnell and Philippe C. Schmitter, *Transitions from Authoritarian Rule: Tentative Conclusions About Uncertain Democracies* (Baltimore: Johns Hopkins University Press, 1986), p. 19; Giuseppe Di Palma, *To Craft Democracies* (Berkeley: University of California Press, 1990), pp. 188–189; Thomas Carothers, *In the Name of Democracy* (Berkeley: University of California Press, 1991), p. 249.

37. Abraham F. Lowenthal, ed., *Exporting Democracy: The United States and Latin America, Themes and Issues* (Baltimore: Johns Hopkins University Press, 1991), p. 243.

38. Abraham F. Lowenthal, ed., *Exporting Democracy: The United States and Latin America, Case Studies.* (Baltimore: Johns Hopkins University Press, 1991), p. 278.

39. Thomas Carothers, *In the Name of Democracy* (Berkeley: University of California Press, 1991), p. 218.

40. See, in particular, Geoffrey Pridham, ed., *Encouraging Democracy: The International Context of Regime Transition in Southern Europe* (Leicester, UK: Leicester University Press, 1991); and Geoffrey Pridham, Eric Herring, and George Sanford,

eds., *Building Democracy? The International Dimension of Democratization in Eastern Europe* (New York: St Martin's Press, 1994).

41. Ali L. Karaosmanoglu, "The International Context of Democratic Transition in Turkey," in Pridham, *Encouraging Democracy*, p. 171.

42. Pridham, *Encouraging Democracy*, p. 215.

43. On the OAS, see Laurence Whitehead, "Fragile Democracies, International Support, and the Practice of Foreign Policy-Making" (paper prepared for the SSRC Conference on Foreign Policy Consequences of Economic and Political Liberalization, 9–11 July 1992), p. 5; and Diamond, *Promoting Democracy in the 1990s*, pp. 36–37.

44. For example, the OAU (Diamond, *Promoting Democracy*, pp. 37–38) and several groups in Central America (Joan M. Nelson with Stephanie J. Eglinton, *Encouraging Democracy: What Role for Conditioned Aid?* [Washington, D.C.: Overseas Development Council, 1992], pp. 55–58).

45. Laurence Whitehead, "East-Central Europe in Comparative Perspective," in Pridham, Herring, and Sanford, *Building Democracy?*, p. 53.

46. Carothers, *In the Name of Democracy*, pp. 258–259.

Index